african
ecomedia

african ecomedia

network forms, planetary politics

cajetan iheka

DUKE UNIVERSITY PRESS
Durham and London 2021

Library of Congress Cataloging-in-Publication Data
Names: Iheka, Cajetan Nwabueze, author.
Title: African ecomedia: network forms, planetary politics / Cajetan Iheka.
Description: Durham: Duke University Press, 2021. |
Includes bibliographical references and index.
Identifiers: LCCN 2021000888 (print)
LCCN 2021000889 (ebook)
ISBN 9781478013815 (hardcover)
ISBN 9781478014744 (paperback)
ISBN 9781478022046 (ebook)
Subjects: LCSH: Afrofuturism. | Arts, African. | Figurative art—Africa. |
Mass media and art—Africa. | Environmental sciences—Philosophy. |
Human ecology—Africa. | Ecology in art. | BISAC: SOCIAL SCIENCE / Media Studies |
HISTORY / Africa / General
Classification: LCC NX587. I34 2021 (print) | LCC NX587 (ebook) | DDC 700.96—dc23
LC record available at https://lccn.loc.gov/2021000888
LC ebook record available at https://lccn.loc.gov/2021000889

Cover art: Fabrice Monteiro, "Female figure, trees, and fire,"
from *The Prophecy.* © 2015 Artist Rights Society (ARS),
New York / ADAGP, Paris.

Duke University Press gratefully acknowledges The Frederick W.
Hilles Publication Fund of Yale University, which provided
funds toward the publication of this book.

for Clara Famutimi
who will not hold this

contents

illustrations

acknowledgments

Kenneth Harrow inspired this project with his invaluable advice that I consider the ecologies of African film as I worked on my first book. I am grateful to Ken for the advice, for feedback on early drafts, and for his dedication to my scholarship. While the seed of this book was sown in Michigan, it was in Tuscaloosa, Alabama, that I conceptualized its earliest version. I thank the College of Arts and Sciences and the Department of English at the University of Alabama for the gift of time and funding. Colleagues at UA offered feedback and other forms of assistance: thanks to Cassie Smith, Joel Brouwer, Lauren Cardon, Trudier Harris, James McNaughton, Albert Pionke, Utz McKnight, Lamar Wilson, David Deutsch, Heather White, Steve Tedeschi, Nicholas Kerr, and Tricia McElroy. My gratitude also goes to Jocelyn Hawley for being a terrific research assistant. Mark and Paige McCormick welcomed my family into theirs; I am grateful for their friendship.

Stephanie Newell helped me to visualize teaching at Yale and facilitated a smooth transition. I am grateful for the opportunity to work with her. I must acknowledge Lanny Hammer, David Kastan, and John Durham Peters for convincing me that a move to New Haven would be good for this book—it has been! I am lucky to call them colleagues and to be able to depend on their wise counsel. The imprint of John's groundbreaking work on media is all over this book. For welcoming me to Yale and for being dependable colleagues, I thank Jill Campbell, Jill Richards, Alanna Hickey, Joe Cleary, Tasha Eccles, Cathy Nicholson, Priyasha Mukhopadhyay, Joe North, Caryl (Caz) Phillips, R. John Williams, Sunny Xiang, Emily Thornbury, Michael Warner, Caleb Smith, Marta Figlerowicz, Ardis Butterfield, Ben Glaser, Jackie Goldsby, Margaret Homans, Jonathan Kramnick, Naomi Levine, and Ruth Yeazell. As department chair, Jessica Brantley has been a consistent supporter of my endeavors. She organized a manuscript workshop and approved funding for reproducing this book's images. Sarah Harford and Jamie Morris offered superb administrative support for the workshop.

The Faculty of Arts and Sciences funded the manuscript workshop through the Scholars as Learners initiative. I am grateful that I can continue to count on Tamar Gendler and Katie Lofton for support. The Whitney and Betty MacMillan Center for International and Area Studies, and the Frederick W. Hilles Publication Fund of Yale University offset the book's production costs. Outside my home department, Roderick Ferguson, Tavia Nyong'o, Lisa Lowe, Jill Jarvis, Laura Nasrallah, Paul North, Dan Magaziner, Ayesha Ramachandran, Jill Jarvis, and Paul Sabin have been remarkable interlocutors. I am indebted to them for their encouragement.

The manuscript workshop brought Byron Santangelo and Brian Larkin to New Haven, where they joined Michael Warner and Cecile Fromont for an afternoon of intense, productive conversation. I appreciate the quartet for reading the manuscript and for their incisive, constructive criticism. Jill Richards convened a writing support group that included Sunny Xiang, Jill Jarvis, and Marta Figlerowicz; I am grateful for their perceptive feedback on the introduction and epilogue. I am also indebted to Moradewun Adejunmobi, Connor Ryan, Nathan Suhr-Sytsma, Jeanne-Marie Jackson, Carlos Alonso Nugent, Evan Mwangi, and Stephen Rust for providing useful feedback. The manuscript also benefited from two anonymous reviewers appointed by Duke University Press; I am in awe of their ambition for this book, and the inability to rise to their challenge is my fault alone. Elizabeth Ault believed in this project from the initial pitch and maintained her positive energy throughout the process. I am grateful for her editorial care and stewardship of the African studies list at Duke University Press. I thank Benjamin Kossak and the production team for transforming the manuscript into a book.

For valuable feedback that enriched the manuscript, I thank the organizers and participants at invited lectures and symposia at Johns Hopkins University, Pennsylvania State University, the University of Wisconsin–Madison, Emory University, Rice University, New York University, the

University of Oklahoma, the University at Buffalo, and the Chicago Architecture Biennial. I commend Yesomi Umolu for curating a terrific Chicago Biennial and inviting me to participate. Fabrice Monteiro, Pieter Hugo, Ed Kashi, Guy Tillim, and Olalekan Jeyifous gave me permission to reproduce their amazing images. I am thankful for the gift of their art. Federica Angelucci and Sinazo Chiya of the Stevenson Gallery in Cape Town facilitated the inclusion of Hugo's and Tillim's photographs. An excerpt from chapter 3 appeared in the *Cambridge Journal of Postcolonial Literary Inquiry*. I thank the editor and the press for the opportunity to use the work here.

I have been blessed with a remarkable network of mentors, friends, and co-travelers in the fields of African studies, postcolonial studies, and the environmental humanities. I am indebted to Jeanne-Marie Jackson, Connor Ryan, Jack Taylor, Anna Feuerstein, Paul Ugor, Bala Saho, Chima Korieh, Madhu Krishnan, Maureen Eke, Isidore Diala, Leonald Mbah, Bhakti Shringarpure, Chris Onyema, Joeken Nzerem, Jude Akudinobi, Niyi Afolabi, Evan Mwangi, Nathan Suhr-Sytsma, Yesomi Umolu, Chielozona Eze, Amatoritsero Ede, Abdulhamit Arvas, Byron Santangelo, and Duncan Yoon. Ato Quayson's scholarship and mentorship mean so much to me; I am grateful for his generosity and for the model he embodies.

Finally, I deeply appreciate my family, including my parents and brothers. Knowing how proud they are of my academic career keeps me going on difficult days. Nothing makes sense without my brilliant and beautiful wife Eve and our sons Kamsiyonna and Kenenna. I hope we can take pride in this book together. Kamsi, thank you for watching *Black Panther* with Dada. I thank the Famutimis for their love, and regret that Clara Famutimi did not live to see the outcome. I dedicate this book to her beautiful memory in appreciation of her selfless love and sacrifice.

introduction

Ryan Coogler's Afrofuturist film *Black Panther* was released to global acclaim in February 2018.[1] The film, inspired by the Marvel comic-strip series, casts Chadwick Boseman as T'Challa, the king of Wakanda, a fictional resource-rich African country that escaped colonial subjugation. Masquerading as another poor African nation, Wakanda maintains an isolationist policy to ensure that its technological prowess is enjoyed solely by its citizens, until, that is, the appearance of the antagonists, Ulysses Klaue (Andy Serkis), vibranium thief, and T'Challa's cousin, the American-born Eric Killmonger (Michael B. Jordan), who battles the king for the throne. While T'Challa prefers to maintain the status quo as he ascends the throne following his father's death, Killmonger plans to utilize Wakanda's resources to extend its influence across the world when he becomes the ruler of Wakanda temporarily.

The widespread enthusiastic reception of *Black Panther* was unique for a film depicting black people and centered on Africa. Usually, the most commercially successful of such films are critiqued for objectifying black bodies, for branding the continent as a site of disaster, and for distorting the history of black people. *Black Panther* was instead hailed from America to Zimbabwe. People of African descent commended the pan-African sensibilities of the film, including its use of isiXhosa, one of the national languages of South Africa. They also applauded the spectacular costumes, drawn from across the continent, as well as the centering of black characters and cultural rituals. The movie's portrayal of strong black women was also celebrated, as was the configuration of the fictional Wakanda as a space endowed with stupendous wealth and unparalleled technological capabilities.

And yet, despite the film's achievements, including its positive representation of the continent's cultures and people, its futuristic vision relies on the illusion of infinite resources and reinstates the continent as a site of conflict fueled by resource control. Wakanda's wealth and its energy are derived from vibranium, to which it has exclusive access, and the film's conflict revolves around the struggle for control of this powerful resource. The struggle for vibranium endangers humans and environments, be it the explosion triggered by Klaue as he steals vibranium in Wakanda or the death of N'Jobu (Killmonger's father) in America for betraying Wakanda. The violence of the scenes set in the British Museum and South Korea, and even the fight between T'Challa and Killmonger, index this endangerment of environments. Spread across space and time, these scenes are linked by violence to human and nonhuman worlds due to the quest for vibranium. The violence in *Black Panther* resonates because the extraction of resources such as oil and uranium, echoed in the film's vibranium, has engendered similar social conflict and ecological degradation from the Niger Delta in Nigeria to Arlit in Niger. As I elaborate in the epilogue, the conflict in *Black Panther* reverberates with current problems on the continent, where disaster follows resource control. Coogler's futuristic Wakanda resembles Africa now.

The future promised by the film is not only implicated in the Africa-in-crisis trope; it also relies on an infinite supply of vibranium, which is not in keeping with the realities of our finite planet. Both T'Challa's isolationism and Killmonger's interventionism are undergirded by the same ethos: the limitlessness of resources. T'Challa's inward orientation is supported by the belief in Wakanda's sufficiency in the present and the future, while Killmonger sees no reason to hold back given the same infinite availability of resources. *Black Panther* must repress the stark realities of finitude and ignore the environmental cost of obtaining vibranium in order to present a nation of unmatched resources and advanced technological capabilities. We need to turn to African media to understand the socioecological implications of resource extraction on the continent and in order to begin the work of imagining eco-conscious futures that sidestep the repetition of the problematic present in *Black Panther*. This book takes a step in that direction.

African Ecomedia examines the ecological footprint of media technologies in Africa as well as the representation, in media, of ecological issues affecting the continent, including degradation from oil and uranium extraction, dumping waste, and the politics of animal conservation. In focusing on the ecology of images and images of ecology pertaining to Africa, I address the limited attention given to African cultural artifacts in ecomedia studies.[2] In particular, I pay attention to the materiality of infrastructure, which has recently become a major focus of media studies. Brian Larkin, Lisa Parks and Nicole Starosielski, Jussi Parikka, and John Durham Peters are only some of the scholars who have called for an infrastructural disposition toward media.[3] Africa remains marginal to discussions of materiality in media studies and in the subfield of ecomedia studies, yet the fossil fuels and ore crucial to media's workings, like oil and coltan, are mined on the continent, and castoff electronic devices often end up there. I demonstrate Africa's centrality to the making, use, and disposal of media devices while highlighting important insights on the planetary crisis inscribed in African cultural artifacts—representational media in their own right—including film and photography.

These African cultural inscriptions provide the appropriate site for understanding the ecological footprint of media, and they offer inspiring examples of the infinite resourcefulness crucial for ethical living and media production in a time of finite resources. Cultural inscriptions here encompass film, photography, sculpture, and video art. In addition to demonstrating that the "promise of [media] infrastructure" is undermined in Africa by the ecological consequences of its ruins, I examine the ethics of representing those ruins and highlight alternative media practices suitable for an era of ecological precarity.[4] I analyze African media arts as employing network forms: in their entanglement of time past, present, and future; in their interconnection of spaces across boundaries; and in their depictions of the interrelationship between humans and animals.

Media, as Peters evocatively describes them, "are vessels and environments, containers of possibility that anchor our existence and make what we are doing possible."[5] One of the things that media make possible is communication. Devices such as cell phones and computers have made keeping in touch with family members in Nigeria easy and instantaneous from my base in the United States. They also allow me to project African environments so that my students can at least glimpse a virtual reality of the continent's spaces. We rely on media devices to be informed of the ecological problems plaguing the world, especially in faraway spaces.[6] But as important as these affordances of media are, the devices at stake, from cell phones to computers, are implicated in ecological degradation.

These devices are made up of components that engender ecological degradation, including oil and coltan mined in Africa. As Stephanie LeMenager reminds us, "oil itself is a medium that fundamentally supports all media forms . . . from film to recorded music, novels, magazines, photographs, sports and the wikis, blogs, and videography of the Internet."[7] As will become clearer in the pages of this book, the extraction of oil, among other carbon-based resources, entails serious ecological disturbance imperiling human and nonhuman lives across the continent. Unfortunately, the adverse ecological consequences of media do not cease with their production. In *Geology of Media*, Jussi Parikka asks, "what composes technology in its materiality and media after it becomes disused, dysfunctional media that refuse to die?"[8] If some of the compositional elements of media technologies are sourced from Africa, then the continent is also where some of these "dysfunctional media that refuse to die" go after their planned obsolescence. As we see in chapter 2, the recycling of these devices to obtain metals is a toxic enterprise that releases carcinogenic chemicals into the ecosphere. Burning the discarded devices to retrieve valuable metals involves chemical processes that expose human and nonhuman bodies to toxicity at such sites in Africa.[9] Media devices may be valuable facilitators of real-time communication and critical purveyors of modern life, but their toxic legacies also qualify them as "material participant[s] in the apparatus of destruction."[10]

In addition to media arts and media devices, Africa's extractive objects and agricultural products—media in the expanded sense—such as oil, uranium, coltan, and bananas are also complicit in ecological degradation. I embrace Peters's expanded sense of media, which for him include "water, fire, sky, earth, and ether . . . that sustain existence."[11] I illuminate other media that facilitate existence for Africans, and for people in other climes to which the continent's oil, uranium, bananas, and coffee are exported. To be sure, these resources provide Africans with employment opportunities and generate foreign exchange earnings for their countries. These objects also position Africa in the world, linking the continent's sites of extraction to other parts of the world where they are consumed. However, the benefits of these exchanges do not comprise the whole picture. Consumers in Africa often must pay more for goods they have directly produced or for those sourced from their environments.[12]

As chapter 3 shows, these objects come at a huge cost to their communities of extraction, where they leave behind devastated environments. Sean Cubitt's work on uranium mining in Niger, for instance, reports that the "mines leach water from pastoral land and gardens; radioactive dust from the open-pit mines settles over the parched landscape; and the air itself is with it."[13] The situation is similar in the Niger Delta, which has recorded ᵥ devastating consequences of petro-capitalism, and the dissonance between the promise of modernity and the harsh realities of putrescence.[14] The scenario is worsened, from Niger to Nigeria, by the ineptitude and profligacy of governments that have relinquished their responsibilities as guarantors of people's well-being and regulators of corporations. My point is this: media, broadly conceived, make possible communication and sustenance, but they are equally tethered to social and ecological degradation in Africa from their production, distribution, consumption, and disposal.

Ecomedia studies is primely positioned to scrutinize this contradiction—of the possibilities and problematics of media—by "balancing a consideration of media representations, media infrastructures, and media materiality."[15] From its initial ecocritical investigation of representation, in nonprint media such as television and film, of the relationship between the human and non-human world, the scope of ecomedia studies has broadened to accommodate a broader array of materials—textual and visual—as well as to examine the infrastructures underpinning media technologies and to provide a heuristic for considering "the imbrication of media forms . . . within systems and environments."[16] I favor an encompassing definition of ecomedia including textual materials such as literary texts and periodicals, film and photography, as well as mass media and new media technologies. Peters's conceptualization of media as "not only devices of information" but "also agencies of order," "civilizational ordering devices," and as things "always in the middle" is particularly inspirational for the broad sense of ecomedia here.[17] Agricultural products such as bananas and mineral resources including oil and uranium are equally entangled in the complex web of ecomedia in this book.

Like the conventional media devices, resource media constitute the middle of a relationship between the site of extraction and the point of consumption, between Africa and Euro-America in this context. As civilizational ordering devices, they determine a nation's position and disposition in geopolitics. Nigeria's standing in the world is influenced by its oil deposits, making the country a strategic international stakeholder in the region. In this sense, talk of Nigeria's diminished importance in the context of the United States' growing oil independence and turn to renewable energy sources evidences the important value of oil as a medium of world-building. Similarly, developmental projects within the country are made possible by oil earnings, making oil significant for the country's claims to modernity. Oil revenues not only provide the basis for Nigeria's worldliness and its civilizational claims; they also enable the government to maintain fragile peace among competing interests within this geographic construction. Exported to foreign climes, resource media connect the continent to consumers across the world who derive sustenance from them. These users consume African media as food, as energy resources for powering their devices, and as (un)-seen components of their media technologies.

As the quintessential media predating mass and new media technologies, elemental media are indigenous inhabitants of the ecomedia sphere. Elemental media precede the arrival of media devices, media arts, resource media, and other recent immigrant arrivals threatening the survival of native ecomedia and the rest of the planet. These latter arrivals belong to the ecomedia corpus because their making, use, and disuse implicate them in ecological degradation and/or environmental transformation. In this book, media enter the orbit of ecomedia if they meet at least one of the following conditions: their infrastructural logic produces fire and/or other toxins that contaminate elemental media (including air, water, earth); they critique human exploitative relationships with the environment, and where possible propose strategies for eco-restoration. Ecomedia processes catalyze ecological consequences in the form of environmental degradation and/or advocacy for environmental awareness, renewal, and sustainability, making this media genre an assemblage of natural elements and cultural attributes with apparent superstructures and implicit infrastructures.

Media infrastructures work by invisibilities and forgetting.[18] Although they "have mediating capacities" and they "shape the nature of economic and cultural flows," as Brian Larkin reminds us,[19] it is also true that they often repress the violence involved in their production, distribution, consumption, and disposal. This book turns to visual materials in order to counteract the invisibility and forgetting that infrastructures relish. Africa is the other repressed and invisible factor in the operations of media infrastructure as the continent remains at the margins of intellectual discussions and geopolitics despite its major contribution to global modernity and the supply chain. In foregrounding the continent and a visual archive, I intend to account for the socioecological costs of media processes and unearth what happens behind the scene of a global supply chain. There is a significant visual archive produced in and/or about Africa that needs critical attention for its engagement with critical issues concerning media, labor, toxicity, and ecology. This book begins the work of unpacking the complexities of the archive and hopes to precipitate additional work on other aspects of a growing corpus.

More specifically, the treatment of waste aesthetics and waste's toxic im-

Introduction

print on human and nonhuman bodies in the following pages shows one affordance of visual culture. Zooming in on visual materials enables me to conceptualize toxicity as a network form that spreads across bodies and spaces in African communities. I understand toxicity as the aftermath of the logics of capitalist accumulation and excessive consumption that has generated the Anthropocene, characterized by the alterations that humans have made for centuries and continue to make to the climate.[20] As Bill McKibben puts it, "we are no longer able to think of ourselves as a species tossed about by larger forces—now we are those larger forces."[21] The Anthropocene has been subjected to critiques, the most prominent being that the term elides differences among humans, or as Joni Adamson puts it, the concept authorizes "the essentialized categories of the human."[22] Some of these critiques indict the "rich, especially the rich in the wealthy industrialized countries, mainly in the West," for being responsible for anthropogenic climate change that disproportionately impacts poor communities in Africa and elsewhere.[23] In one influential critique, Kathryn Yusoff demonstrates how the field of geology is yet to account for the expenditure of black and brown bodies in the Anthropocene, a mistake that necessitates her concept of "Black Anthropocenes." Like Yusoff's, this project is attentive to "inhuman proximity organized by historical geographies of extraction, grammars of geology, imperial global geographies, and contemporary environmental racism."[24] Attending to the particularities of Africa in this book allows me to "provincialize" and to "pluralize" the Anthropocene.[25] Reframing Yusoff's question—"Who then is objectified by geology's grammar of materiality?"—this project of particularities, provincialization, and pluralization asks: Who then is objectified or rendered invisible by media studies' grammar of materiality?[26] Answering this crucial question finds me attending to the social and ecological costs of global media production and consumption in Africa.

African Ecomedia uniquely brings together and intervenes in the fields of media studies, the environmental humanities, African studies, and the energy humanities. Recent interventions in media studies have turned to the waste emerging from the production and planned obsolescence of media devices including cell phones and computers. These studies have foregrounded the "gigantic rubbish heap" that media generate in their production, distribution, and consumption, as well as the off-loading of waste to out-of-sight locations in the Global South.[27] Interestingly, China has taken center stage in this discourse on the production of media devices and sites for the dumping of electronic waste. Less attended to is the fact that fossil fuel and mineral resources necessary for media production are mined in conditions that imperil human and nonhuman inhabitants of African ecosystems. Furthermore, when electronic devices reach the end of their short life cycle, thanks to their planned obsolescence, some are exported to African locations such as Agbogbloshie in Ghana. Studies of these topics have either ignored or paid little attention to Africa, or have not engaged the rich representational media devoted to these issues.

Focusing on media arts including film and photography as well as resource media such as oil and uranium alongside their impacts on and implications for elemental media (fire, air, water, earth), this book offers a model for an ecological media studies for the twenty-first century. The accent on a supply chain network that begins with extraction and ends with disposal offers a comprehensive, encompassing account of media and positions the continent at the heart of the materiality discourse in media studies and related fields. In the process, my approach also yields a new interpretation of digital labor and the notion of free labor that broadens our understanding of these concepts (chapter 2). For digital labor, I make a case for apprehending the term outside the confines of the internet, in the sweaty, smelly dumps of Agbogbloshie. An infrastructural logic requires a broadening of the digital labor category to produce a decolonial conceptualization that keeps together hardware and software as well as intellectual and manual labor.

Although the notion of free labor implies unwaged work that is willingly given, I demonstrate that the African context puts pressure on the concept of "wages" and the voluntary nature of such work. Are the metal recyclers wage earners when their paltry earnings are determined by what they find rather than a predetermined payment for defined working hours or a particular task? How should we understand these earnings that are incommensurate with the toxic risk of electronic recycling? Can we still describe free labor as "willingly" or uncoerced, given that the contemporary worker, especially in Africa, has limited choices or no choice in a precarious economy characterized by high unemployment, "short term contract and employment at will"?[28] My conclusion from Agbogbloshie is that the toxic risks of metal picking and recycling qualify these efforts as free labor coerced from the worker by a global capitalist system. With its attunement to labor, materiality, and toxicity from an African standpoint, this book responds to the call for a greater interaction of African media studies and the mainstream media field for the transformation of both areas of inquiry.[29] I relocate Africa at the origin and conclusion, at the beginning and end, of media matter, so to speak.

The concentration on ecological issues in this book expands the purview of African media studies. Many exciting projects have emerged in African cinema and the study of the Nollywood scene in Nigeria.[30] Photography in Africa has also received a good amount of attention, just as the broader visual art world on the continent has been the subject of recent studies.[31] A few of these studies also focus on media infrastructure in Africa.[32] Despite the prominent place accorded the environment in the materials studied in these books and the continent's disproportionate share of environmental risks, questions of ecology remain mute in these projects. This gap necessitates a comprehensive study of ecological dynamics in media culture beyond literature. *African Ecomedia* addresses this gap.

African Ecomedia also contributes to the visual turn in the environmental humanities. It expands on texts such as Sean Cubitt's *Ecomedia* and two collections on the subject, edited by Stephen Rust, Salma Monani, and Sean Cubitt.[33] Additionally, it builds on recent monographs, including John Parham's work on the intersections of green media and popular culture, LeMenager's study of the pervasion and perversion of petroleum culture, and Ursula Heise's demonstration of how cultural perceptions of endangered species and the environment shape conservation discourses and praxis.[34] *African Ecomedia* buttresses a central tenet of Elizabeth DeLoughrey, namely that "Anthropocene scholarship cannot afford to overlook narratives from the global south."[35] To use Scott Slovic's littoral imagery, these studies belong to "the vast sea of 'environmental studies'" in the humanities designed with the intention of helping us "understand our place on this planet."[36] Although we all share the goal of critiquing "slow violence" and accelerated forms of ecological violence, the margin of these projects—Africa—constitutes the center of my intervention.[37] In turning to the form and affective power of images, including the safari photograph that circulated following Cecil the Lion's death at the hands of an American dentist in Hwange Park, Zimbabwe, in 2015, I enrich and expand the purview of African and postcolonial environmental humanities beyond their literary predilections.[38]

African studies share with the environmental humanities the envisioning of solutions to intellectual and social problems, and my project continues that tradition. With the planetary crisis and the worsening rate of global inequality, prognostications of the future have increased. The prediction and imagination of future possibilities have been largely technocratic and economistic, with the attendant risk of reifying the problems connected to global capitalism. The imaginative breadth and flexibility of media arts make them appropriate tools to think with for alternatives to the current scenario.

Negative assumptions about Africa, and blackness more broadly, have meant that the continent and its people hardly feature in forecasts of the future. My study positions Africa at the center of imaginative musings on possible futures unencumbered by climate change, among other aberrations of modern life.

Africa ought to be seen not only as a site of ecological degradation but also as a generative site for apprehending the ecologies of media alongside alternative media practices and modes of ethical living. Jean Comaroff and John L. Comaroff anticipate my move here when they suggest that we look to Africa for inspiring epistemological models.[39] Africa provides examples of what I call *imperfect media* in the epilogue—that is, low-carbon media practices and the infrastructures of finitude that are critical for ameliorating ecological precarity in the future. This book offers a decolonial vision of the future that takes Africa seriously in tackling the planetary crisis. In this vein, I offer a fresh perspective on the Africa-China relationship. The current discourse predominantly focuses on whether China is a colonial power or if the relationship is premised on a win-win paradigm for all sides (chapter 5). Existing scholarship, which I review in the final chapter, has yet to seriously consider the ecological impact of China's footprint in Africa, a step that I propose is necessary for complicating the binary framing of the Africa-China discourse. Another binary that I move away from is the tendency to understand the continent's urban spaces as sites of precarity or possibility. Moving from the representations of Johannesburg in South Africa to Lagos, Nigeria, I also show how artists appropriate the challenges and possibilities in African urban spaces for envisioning the sustainable city of the future.

In sum, this book positions Africa as the ground zero of the energy humanities. This emerging subfield probes the social, cultural, political, and environmental assemblages of the fossil infrastructures underpinning the global economy.[40] As Dipesh Chakrabarty puts it, the "mansion of modern freedoms stands on an ever-expanding base of fossil-fuel use."[41] The touchstones of human civilization—freedom, modernity, democracy—are indissociable from the ascendancy of the oil regime.[42] Despite the saturation of fossil fuels in multiple facets of human lives, or what Bob Johnson describes as the "mineral rites" underpinning even the most quotidian of human activities, there exists an energy unconscious.[43] *African Ecomedia* joins the growing corpus interested in unraveling human entanglements with fossil fuels, cataloguing the social and ecological costs of that entanglement, and interpreting speculations of alternative futures. The media arts assembled in this study counteract the energy unconscious by making visible, legible, and apprehensible the flow of energy in our lives, including our media cultures. They are also invested in bridging the distance between the sites of energy production in Africa and scenes of consumption in the West.

Africa deserves special attention in the energy humanities not only because the continent discloses the most visceral social and ecological costs of current energy regimes but also because its artistic expressions energetically model world-making scenarios oriented toward sustainable futures. As the energy humanities simulate a post-carbon future, the African examples here challenge the field to consider more seriously the afterlives of nonrenewable infrastructures dotting the continent's environment. Media studies, the environmental humanities and the energy humanities are attuned to the realities of our finite planet, even if the philosophical orientation of the modern world is the idea of infinite resources. The environmental degradation resulting from resource depletion also animates these interdisciplines. Africa's gift to these fields is the location of a comprehensive comprehension of environmental devastation resulting from resource extraction alongside existing and speculative infrastructures of finitude suitable for a diminished planet.

Insightful Reading: In Praise of Indiscipline

The interdisciplinary orientation of this book is indebted to the fields of visual culture studies, postcolonial studies, African studies, media studies, and the environmental humanities. Visual culture lends itself to an interdisciplinary approach that locates cultural objects in their historical and environmental contexts.[44] I consider the constructedness of the images under investigation, the artists' choices, as well as the social contexts that render them as texts, bearing in mind that "the meanings of the image . . . cannot be completed within the text as a self-sufficient entity."[45] My method also involves attentiveness to what is outside the frame of these images, alongside the apparatuses of production, distribution, and consumption. This book is guided by conceptions of mixed media that have circulated in visual culture studies, including in the work of W. J. T. Mitchell, and of Marita Sturken and Lisa Cartwright. For Mitchell, "all media are mixed media, and all representations are heterogeneous; there are no 'purely' visual or verbal arts."[46] I also take seriously the idea that "image, text, sound, and objects also converge in the social production of meaning, and can no longer be studied in isolation."[47] By using African visual culture to challenge and redefine media concepts and theories, I resist the urge to ghettoize African media studies, and I join in "de-westernizing media theory to make room for African experience."[48] My plumbing of the visual economy of African ecomedia in order to produce an interdisciplinary study necessitates a unique approach that I call *insightful reading*.[49]

Insightful reading is particularly important for some of the materials analyzed in this book. In the foregoing discussion of *Black Panther*, I mentioned that the film avoids the usual critique of black representations as objectifying the black body or working toward the exoticization of blackness or of perpetuating black suffering for the white gaze. From literary studies to the study of visual culture, it has become commonplace to argue that a work exemplifies the "postcolonial exotic" or poverty porn.[50] Some of the images in this book can be easily dismissed as poverty porn or iterations of the postcolonial exotic. In fact, some interlocutors at invited lectures have expressed discomfort at the exposure of black bodies in some of the photographs and questioned the rationale for including them. I take the objection to the depiction of black suffering seriously, but these images can be read for productive insights into the conditions that they present. As will become clearer in the pages of this book, exposure is a crucial strategy for tackling ecological violence.

Insightful reading makes a demand like that of Ariella Azoulay, who theorizes the civic duty that viewers owe to the photographed subject.[51] Azoulay's civic duty is neither to look away nor derive pleasure from the suffering of the Other. The demand is much more for the cultivation of the civic skill to stay with and address the horrors of the photographed. Denying the audience of a photograph the role of mere spectator, Azoulay repurposes the disturbing image as "a tool of a struggle or an obligation to others to struggle against injuries inflicted on those others."[52] Images offer aesthetic or perverse pleasures, but they do more than that. The lesson of Azoulay's work, which is also my philosophy of reading, is that the image of suffering makes a claim on the viewer to act responsibly. For my purposes, the borderless citizenship animating Azoulay's civil contract translates into a planetary citizenship with membership across spaces and species. Insightful reading presupposes a civil contract among the photographer, the photographed, and the viewer regardless of national, racial, ethnic, sexual, gender, and class affiliations. Viewers can be mere spectators, refuse to look, or responsibly engage with the claims being made by the photograph. Insightful reading serves the purpose of responsible engagement.

An investigation into the etymological root of "insight" is germane here: the word refers to inner sight, wisdom. Insightful reading demands that we not look away from the disturbing photograph or text but rather keep it in sight, probe its provenance as well as its pedagogical function. It is possible to ask the following question of such a work: What can we learn from it that could undermine the degradation of the photographed subject? It is too easy to dismiss such representations because the issues they address do not necessarily disappear when we avoid them. We should instead keep them in sight, watch them, and even listen to them for the possibility of redress, a process that involves an eclectic mix of methodological approaches. This would involve descriptive/surface readings as well as deep/close readings. Proponents of surface reading insist that textual surfaces hold gems that we lose when we look too deeply or closely.[53] For Stephen Best and Sharon Marcus, for instance, the "surface is what insists on being looked at rather than what we must train ourselves to see through."[54] While the surface can yield productive material, insightful reading also entails seeing through the surface to plumb depths. It entails surface inquiry, but it does not invalidate the deployment of deeper exploration in order to generate wisdom about the material.

Insightful reading also employs rich contextualization and enjoys the benefits of theory. While probing both surface and depth, insightful reading also involves looking sideways at the context of production—that is, to the history and politics of the situation offered in the cultural artifact. It is not anti-theory; if it is "a partisan of anything, it is of 'theoretical cubism': the deployment of multiple perspectives and grids" to produce a robust interpretation of the object under scrutiny.[55] This form of reading is all-encompassing and eclectic as it searches for the wisdom in a text. It invites us to stay with the disturbing image in order to generate insights not in service of exploiting the Other but in order to understand exploitation in a critical fashion and possibly begin the work of repair. Images of subjection in media culture do not offer a foreclosed meaning. Their surfaces and depths as well as their context and theoretical models can be deployed to generate sympathetic and ameliorative insights about them.

My approach allows the problematic image to serve the ends of a black radical tradition, a tradition that has strategically exposed violent images to problematize antiblack violence. Take for instance the 1955 decision of Emmet Till's mother to hold an open-casket funeral for her son, lynched in Mississippi for flirting with a white woman. Mamie Till-Bradley had the option of protecting her son's dignity by refusing to show his swollen and mutilated body. In choosing, instead, for the world to see the disfigured fourteen-year-old body, Till's mother was not objectifying her son or making a spectacle of black suffering. She wanted Americans and the world to stay with the image of the dead teenager in order to appreciate the racial ecology of black suffering in the United States. Till-Bradley's decision was an invitation to keep the younger Till's body in sight, to not look away out of discomfort or disgust. The insights on racism decipherable from Till's death motivated the exposure of his body, which catalyzed a wave of civil rights activism in the United States.

The antiblack violence against Till is located on a continuum with the forms of violence against African bodies in this book, culminating in my discussion of the intersectional resonances of the Black Lives Matter movement and the 2015 killing of Cecil the Lion in Zimbabwe (chapter 4). Like Till's image, the images of ecological degradation displayed in these pages are better appreciated as evidence for problematizing and seeking an end to antiblack violence rather than as instruments of perpetuating the status quo. Besides being instantiations of antiblack violence, there is a sense in which Till's image joins the media forms analyzed in this book as exemplars of ecological violence. Till's death and the dumping of his mutilated body in the water continued the desecration of the American ecosystem inaugurated with the displacement of its indigenous population and the transplantation of people, plants, and animals to the New World. The shedding of Till's blood degraded his body and land just as his temporary burial in water tarnished not only his image but the image of water as well. In short, human and nonhuman bodies constitute the site of violence against ecology in Till's tragic death.

Embarking on a critical program of exposure, I refuse to look away from disturbing images because such action would not abolish the objectification of black lives in Africa and beyond. To be sure, the artists producing these media generate revenue from making art about the suffering of black people and some of the representations verge on the erotic and the exotic. But they are also tools for grappling with social exploitation and ecological degradation. Take the example of photographs of Agbogbloshie metal pickers in chapter 2. While they depict the degradation of black bodies, I draw insights from within and beyond the images to understand their disclosures about the exploitation of labor and toxicity in that space. My investment in Ed Kashi's images of the Niger Delta in chapter 3 can be read in a similar light. Some of Kashi's images are erotic but, in my reading, this trope leads to a sophisticated engagement with labor and toxicity that reveals a trajectory of exploitative extraction that dates to slavery. These insights are made possible with the interrogation of these images with theoretical enunciations and deep contextualization. The commonplace temptation to avoid these images notwithstanding, they contain wisdom regarding the environmental crisis and require that we keep them in sight and make use of our inner sight to decipher their import.

The eclecticism characterizing insightful reading also guides my choice of primary materials. I analyze documentary and fictional films, photographs, sculpture, and video art for their formal and thematic value for ecological politics. Although I am careful to note distinctions among media forms and genres, the binary between popular and artistic media that often favors the latter does not hold here. For instance, I do not consider conventional African cinema to be superior to Nollywood films. Popular forms can be the site of social critique and the articulation of agency, and are avenues "for multiplicitous constructions of citizenship, identity and democratic participation."[56] The "episteme of the African street," to use Stephanie Newell and Onookome Okome's phrasing for the knowledge embedded in popular cultural works, is better seen as "creative . . . documentation of ordinary people's vitality and responsiveness to political and social transformations."[57] In place of the high art/popular culture dichotomy, I adopt a "pluralistic eco-aesthetic" that locates eco-value in a variety of media.[58] Artistic photographs such as Fabrice Monteiro's collection about Dakar find space in this book alongside the safari photograph that circulated in the wake of Cecil the Lion's death in 2015, just as documentary films, including Idrissou Mora-Kpai's *Arlit* and Femi Odugbemi's *Makoko: A City Afloat*, cohabit with Wu Jing's popular film set in Africa, *Wolf Warrior 2*.[59] I read these texts for their potential for archiving ecological problems, mobilizing ecological affect, and imagining alternative world-making scenarios.

While I discuss a range of media, photography and film occupy the center stage of this project. Photography and film have been at the center of meaning-making in Africa since the colonial era. Photography, for instance, was mobilized in Africa soon after its invention in the nineteenth century. Whereas it served the indigenous elite as a technology for demonstrating their subjectivity, status, and power, it also served the colonial mission's goal of objectifying Africa and its people.[60] Photographs of Africans were used to justify their inferiority and the colonial mission across Europe.[61] Africa's environments—its flora and fauna—were also recorded and classified with the aid of the camera. These records formed an integral part of Western epistemology on the continent.

In the twentieth century, however, the democratic potential of photographs was realized at the height of nationalist agitations for independence. Africans in Bamako, Lagos, and Dakar, to cite just a few examples, visited photography studios to produce portraits of themselves, their friends, and their families.[62] As Kobena Mercer describes these portraits, "what we see on display are some of the most powerful and creative transformations of photography's role as a mirror to the making of our modern selves."[63] The self-making character of these images enables Adéléké Adéèkó to establish an interesting connection between the adulatory function of praise poetry and of photographs in his study of Yoruba arts: "the progression from praise poetry to the studio portrait is undeniable."[64] Not all of these pictures were taken in studios, as the archive of the eminent Malian photographer Malick Sidibe demonstrates. Sidibe and other photographers made images of Africans at parties, at clubs, and even outdoors.[65] Although the photographic subjects may not have always intended it, their images provided a counternarrative to the derogatory, unflattering images of Africans in the colonial photographic imaginary.

Film had a later start date on the continent, where it was mobilized as an example of the "colonial sublime" to mesmerize people and control their subjectivity.[66] The British Colonial Film Unit promoted colonial values such as hygiene and respect for colonial authority with the camera. The inferiority of Africans assumed in colonial photography was also prevalent in the cinema, which elided Africans altogether or portrayed them in negative terms.[67] As Manthia Diawara puts it, European filmmakers "considered the African mind too primitive to follow the sophisticated narrative techniques of mainstream cinema. Thus, they thought it necessary to return to the beginning of film history—to use uncut scenes, slow down the story's pace, and make the narrative simpler by using fewer actors and adhering to just one dominant theme."[68] It was not until the mid-twentieth century that Africans made films that put Africans at the center of the conversation. These early films, including the work of Ousmane Sembène and Med Hondo, attempted to "facilitate the freedom of the oppressed with social justice and equality in every area of life."[69] The project of decolonization at the heart of these visual representational practices involved grappling with the dialectics of modernity and tradition, and of the city and the countryside.

Although critics have hardly paid attention to them, the environment and environmental concerns have always been at the heart of photographs and films in Africa. Photographs and films usually positioned Africans in relation to their environment, which either inhibited their mobility or facilitated their freedom. In Safi Faye's *Kaddu Beykat*, the first film by an African woman to gain critical acclaim, women are positioned in relation to the large expanse of land that they have to cultivate, and the idyllic, rural space of the countryside is contrasted with the hostile, exploitative city.[70] As the film depicts the drought that has rendered farming difficult in this area of Senegal, the environment moves beyond mere setting to become an important theme. We see an analogous foregrounding of the environment in the media arts I analyze in this book, most of which were produced in the first two decades of the twenty-first century.

Africa may be struggling in other sectors, but its cultural economy has continued to yield a bountiful harvest, from literature to film to fashion. The growing number of cultural artifacts—textual, pictorial, aural, and others—devoted to African environments is, furthermore, a recognition of the climate crisis and the increasing risks to our "animate planet."[71] My point is that these texts are of the world and are in the world. However, the worldliness of these texts should not be read as signs of their correspondence to reality. With Pooja Rangan, I ask, "how does documentary [and other media] render suffering . . . immediate" while also being mindful of the constructedness of this immediacy?[72] I am interested in the poetics of mediation and the techniques of revelation and concealment that they allow.[73]

Network Forms, Planetary Politics

A planetary ethos, based on a nonexploitative mode of being-in-the-world, remains a project of futurity, but before its realization we must grapple with the exploitative thrust of current modes of global interconnection. The network society can be traced to developments in information and media technologies in the 1970s.[74] These technological advancements gave rise to accelerated information flows and to what David Harvey terms "space-time compression."[75] To acknowledge the ascendancy of transnational networks in the 1970s, however, is not to dispute the transnational character of earlier movements and networks. Among these are the institution of slavery from the sixteenth till the nineteenth century, and the colonial encounter that yoked Europe to the rest of the world, albeit unjustly and unequally. As Frederick Cooper does well to remind us in an essay lamenting the capaciousness of the term *globalization*, even before the Atlantic slave era there were movements of people and goods across transnational spaces in, for instance, the Mongol empire.[76] Yet that earlier internationalism was different from the new global form that debuted in the 1970s. One distinction is that the earlier form of international engagements was predestined to secure, rather than erode, national/territorial integrity and power.[77] Further, without the benefit of modern communication technologies and their sophisticated infrastructure, the earlier epochs lacked the speed and efficiency of the later era.

The 1970s gave rise, then, to an accelerated pace of connection. If people, goods, and information had taken some time to arrive at their destinations across the world in the days of yore, the technological revolution of the 1970s dramatically sped up transmission. As Manuel Castells notes, the "information technology revolution was instrumental in allowing the implementation of a fundamental process of restructuring of the capitalist system from the 1980s onwards."[78] This restructuring meant that goods and services could move across the world at an unprecedented speed. We can say the same for the movement of human beings as well. Globalization's ease of movement, however, left many out of its success story. While proponents of globalization celebrate its contributions to the advancement of human civilization, others have been quick to highlight the barbaric obverse of the civilizational script. Simon Gikandi refers to this tension when he observes that "the discourse of globalization seems to be perpetually caught between two competing narratives, one of celebration, the other of crisis."[79]

The socioeconomic fallout of globalization coupled with the nation-state's coercion in Africa have inspired migration and exile outside the continent. Many of these émigrés are writers, artists, and other media producers who bring their condition of expatriation to bear in their work. The Nigerian writer Tanure Ojaide has written of how migration became a prominent theme for African writers who left the continent in the 1990s and 2000s.[80] This is also true for African filmmakers and other media artists who left for favorable climes in which to practice their craft. Even for those who stayed behind, the declining local support for artistic production meant that many turned to external sources for funding, which often shape the resulting work. Put differently, a subset of African media is shaped by transnational and cross-cultural contacts transcending the nation. Such works belong in the class of network forms because of the imbrications and connections between the global and the local at their core.[81]

Networks are about the multiplicities and complexities that structure life in the contemporary moment. When it works well, a network can serve as an antidote to totalitarianism and ethnocentrism. By embracing interconnection instead of isolation, networks shun parochialism. Considering this positive valuation of networks, it is no wonder that Patrick Jagoda describes them as "an evocative metaphor of relationality or a nonhierarchical model of interconnection."[82] Networks undergird the cosmopolitan obligation to welcome strangers, but when summoned by ecocritics, they also capture humans and nonhumans in what Serpil Oppermann and Serenella Iovino term a "disanthropocentric alliance."[83] The ecocritic at the forefront of this conversation is Ursula Heise, whose notion of eco-cosmopolitanism insists that it is practically impossible to identify any locality without some global embeddedness. Heise expands upon a non-anthropocentric consideration of the network when she places the human and nonhuman in an entangled, interspecies relationship, complicating conceptualizations of an absolutely distinct human.[84] Taken together, liberatory understandings of networks as multiplicitous and as interconnective technologies accord with the ecological vision of this book.

What do these have to do with form? Jagoda leads in the direction of an answer when he writes that the "problem of global connectedness cannot be understood, in our historical present, independently of the formal features of a network imaginary."[85] As Caroline Levine reminds us, network forms are "defined patterns of interconnection and exchange that organize social and aesthetic experience" and their primary affordance is "connectedness."[86] In a moment of cross-cultural encounters, transnational affiliations, and dissensus, it makes sense that the ensuing representational media will be marked by the displacement and interconnections characterizing networks. In the current context, the emigration of African artists and the outward turn to the West and elsewhere for funding, circulation, and an audience has meant that a significant corpus of media produced since the 1990s is especially marked by network sensibilities in formal and thematic terms.

The artists studied in this book mix genres and influences to produce works abandoning the idea of a contained Africa for a portrait of the continent in the world. While strategically taking advantage of the affordance of networks, these artists are also mindful of the inequality of network connections when it comes to Africa. From placing a spotlight on the digital divide unduly disadvantaging most people on the continent, to critiquing unequal access to a comfortable life, to foregrounding the extreme exposure of human and nonhuman bodies to toxic matter due to global interconnection, these ecomedia producers avoid romanticizing networks. While adapting networks' useful characteristics to produce and distribute their works, the media creators in this book recognize that they also carry hierarchical and exploitative impulses.[87]

Networks are responsible for many of the ecological problems represented in African ecomedia as they facilitate the transmission of toxicity across bodies and spaces. But they also constitute the condition of possibility for these works. Yochai Benkler celebrates the affordances of the digital networked economy including both the increased individual autonomy and nonmarket social cooperation they engender.[88] Benkler spotlights achievements in the cultural sphere: the democratization of the means of production, expanded and accelerated means of distribution, and elevated opportunities for cultural critique that the digital age facilitates.[89] Benkler may not have subjected networks to the kind of critique that illuminates their exploitative crevices, but his thesis survives scrutiny in the following pages. Networks—some capitalist, others in the nonmarket mode—allow the training of artists and funding of their work, as well as the circulation of their projects and those of their predecessors that may have influenced them.

Overview of Chapters

In the works I examine throughout this book, we see not only the interrelationship of times (chapter 1) and spaces (chapters 2 and 3). We are also invited to acknowledge the human-nonhuman ecological network that gets elided when the focus is unduly placed on the human or when we fail to acknowledge that "the very idea of nature" is "a cultural formation" (chapter 4).[90] As chapter 5 shows, urban spaces in Africa intermingle times and spaces, and they serve as sites of interconnection between humans and nonhumans. In other words, the African city is a site of entanglements and is the place where people and things function as network infrastructures. *African Ecomedia* is composed of five chapters, which are linked by the dimensions of network forms (time, space, human-nonhuman entanglements), and closes with a concluding epilogue.

Scholars have tempered the celebration of new media's novelty by pointing to the residue of the old or the past in such projects.[91] I bring the sense of "media as historical subjects" to bear in my first chapter.[92] In a reading of Wanuri Kahiu's short film *Pumzi* and Fabrice Monteiro's collection of photographs *The Prophecy* undertaken in this chapter, I pinpoint fragments from Africa's past and echoes of earlier cultural forms in the imaginative futures that these cultural projects showcase.[93] Also, I bring a critical take to Afrofuturistic projects. While acknowledging their emancipatory possibilities, I draw attention to their pitfalls, including the fact that they often repeat the problems of the past and present. I identify one such pitfall in the disappearance of Asha, Kahiu's protagonist, in the closing shots of *Pumzi*. The film's localization of the science-fiction genre and its excellent portrayal of a black female protagonist are laudable, but its envisioning of a transformative future hinges on the disappearance of Asha, which, I argue, echoes the silencing and obliteration of black women in the present. Asha's disappearance to make way for a tree also recalls the displacement of human communities for wildlife conservation in Africa and other postcolonial locales.

If temporal entanglement frames chapter 1, chapter 2 takes on spatial interconnection in Pieter Hugo's *Permanent Error*, a collection of photographs devoted to the recycling of electronic goods in Agbogbloshie, Ghana, and Frank Bieleu's *The Big Banana*, a film on the workings of a transnational banana plantation in Cameroon.[94] My analysis demonstrates the social and ecological violence associated with Africa's connection to the world. My reading of Hugo's work also reframes the conceptualization of digital labor and free labor. I argue specifically that infrastructural work in Agbogbloshie must be considered an aspect of digital labor, and that the unwaged nature of metal recycling alongside its risks qualify this activity as free labor. My approach expands the consideration of digital labor beyond the work that occurs on the internet and reconfigures the concept of free labor to account for other forms of unwaged labor that produce value, some of which is indirectly coerced.

Chapter 3 takes up the question of ecological trauma, which has already emerged in the first two chapters. I examine here the traumas affiliated with resource extraction in the Niger Delta region of Nigeria (oil) and Arlit, a town in Niger (uranium). As "radiant infrastructures," oil and uranium radiate, producing energy.[95] Each of these resources "connotes the luster of hope," but in reality they also emit "harmful radiations with carcinogenic effects."[96] In reading Michael Watts and Ed Kashi's *Curse of the Black Gold* alongside Idrissou Mora-Kpai's film *Arlit*, I consider how extractive minerals leave African communities contaminated and traumatized.[97] While trauma studies usually foreground the past and the present, I show that the ecology of the Niger Delta demands serious consideration of the trauma of the future, of the yet-to-come, in apprehending the problematic of suffering. Focusing on the trauma of the future enables me here to examine the link among ecological trauma, displacement, and migration.

Human-animal entanglement is the focus of chapter 4, which makes the case for putting African studies and African diaspora studies in closer dialogue. The circulation of a safari image following the killing of Cecil the Lion in 2015, during the Black Lives Matter activism in the United States, provides a jumping off point for this chapter. I argue that the "problematic of race" undergirds Cecil's death and the circulation of the image under investigation, and that race remains the underexplored fundament of wildlife media, including the CNN film, *Trophy*, co-directed by Shaul Schwarz and

Christina Clusiau.[98] I posit in the concluding section of the chapter that Orlando von Einsiedel's film *Virunga* activates a borderland for intertwining human-nonhuman interests and cultivating positive interspecies relationships.[99] This chapter allows for apprehending vulnerabilities across species and opens the space for much-needed dialogue between African studies and African diaspora studies.

The African city provides a space for considering the multiplicities of networks—temporal, spatial, and interspecies—already discussed in this book. I read urban space in Africa as a relational ecology as I turn in the final chapter to media representations of the environments of African cities. Focusing on Guy Tillim's collection of photographs *Jo'burg*, Wu Jing's film *Wolf Warrior 2*, Femi Odugbemi's film *Makoko: Futures Afloat*, and Olalekan Jeyifous's Afrofuturist 3D architectural renderings in *Shanty Megastructures*, I argue that ecomedia focusing on urban space in Africa constitute it as the site of everyday precarity, the space for geopolitical-cum-ideological contestation that endangers the biosphere, and as a site for articulating sustainable futures.[100]

In the concluding epilogue, I bring together the logical implications of the major arguments of the book—namely that Africa is a paradigmatic site for understanding the ecology of media infrastructure and that the continent's media arts contain examples of the infinite resourcefulness crucial for making media in a time of finite resources. Drawing on examples from African cinema and Nollywood, and from the everyday recycling of objects through repair and reuse, I argue that the continent has much to offer in terms of the much-needed low-carbon media that can be marshaled as alternatives to the excessive consumption undergirding mainstream media and our era more broadly. Here, I make a case for a kind of media of the future that I call *imperfect media*. Considering what we know about the value of media for communication, entertainment, and sustenance, we cannot jettison them due to their ecological complicity. Our responsibility as media producers and consumers therefore is to consider how to recalibrate their production, distribution, consumption, and recycling to mitigate those adverse ecological implications already outlined. How can we reorient media approaches toward "low wattage culture," which attends to the "practicality of ecological awareness"?[101] Imperfect media, undergirded by finitude or the recognition of the dissipation of energy sources, is a major step in the direction of ecologically conscious media practices.

While analyzing a range of media, *African Ecomedia* is not exhaustive. There remains a rich body of work awaiting critical consideration and it is my hope that this book inspires further attention in this area. Such scholarship might examine Nyaba Leon Ouedraogo's photographic project on Agbogbloshie, *The Hell of Copper*, as well as George Osodi's *De Money*, an exploration of gold mining in Ghana, and his *Oil Rich Niger Delta*.[102] There are other Niger Delta projects such as Victor Ehikhamenor's oil-drum art installation *Wealth of Nations* and the film *Black Gold* by Jeta Amata.[103] Timaya's "Dem Mama" provides an example of the depiction of the Niger Delta oil crisis in popular music.[104] I briefly discuss Zina Saro-Wiwa's video short *Sarogua Mourning* in chapter 3, but her broader oeuvre is worth considering for its eco-inflections.[105] The Nigerian photographer Andrew Esiebo's projects on urban life in Africa are worth considering, as are films such as Neill Blomkamp's South African science-fiction film, *District 9*, and *Crumbs*, the postapocalyptic science-fiction romance set in Ethiopia by director Miguel Llansó.[106] There is a plethora of wildlife films that would round off this list, including *Blood Lions*, *The Last Animals*, focusing on the killing of elephants for ivory, and *Stroop*, on the intricacies of the rhino horn business.[107]

The bourgeoning archive has invited us to look responsibly. Let the work of unpacking African ecomedia begin!

waste reconsidered

afrofuturism, technologies of the past, and the history of the future

Henri Bergson teaches us how to read philosophers: we must begin by taking a step back from their thought in order to return to its sources, weigh the influences that nurtured it and pinpoint the ideas of which the doctrine is a synthesis.—SOULEYMANE BACHIR DIAGNE, *African Art as Philosophy*

I appreciate the attraction of sun-dappled days past, but only as a means to conjure something new and as a path to new possibilities.—MATT HERN, *What a City Is For*

Two questions drive this chapter. First: What can an analysis of Africa's waste aesthetics contribute to understanding and transforming the culture of excess? And second: In an era of environmental crisis and climate change, what is the role of the African past in articulating alternative futures? From the introduction, it is obvious that the planet faces an existential threat from climate change. It is also certain that market-based Eurocentric models of social and economic development have led to increasing levels of inequality, exacerbated environmental pollution, and put the planet at extreme risk. Africa has always been at the heart of developmental modernity.[1] The slave trade, which inaugurated the modern moment, centered on the racialization of black bodies, and what Aimé Césaire would call their "thingification."[2] Successive eras of human development have also affected Africa, be it the colonial era or the neoliberal turn marking the era of globalization. What is clear from these historical moments is uneven development or the forced insertion of Africa into the global world order. James Ferguson has gone on to examine the global movements of finance and capital that skips certain parts of the world, especially Africa. When capital does touch down in certain parts of the continent, it is to enclaves of capitalist production like the Angola oil compound that Ferguson discusses, or in service of the accumulation by dispossession that is the signature of the postcolonial African elite.[3]

In this state of things, Africa has been relegated to the sideline, to "the hopeless continent," as the cover image of the *Economist* described it in 2000.[4] This dystopian vision of Africa is the product of what Kodwo Eshun describes as the "futures industry." In his words: "Within an economy that runs on SF capital and market futurism, Africa is always the zone of the absolute dystopia. There is always a reliable trade in market projections for Africa's socioeconomic crises. Market dystopias aim to warn against predatory futures, but always do so in a discourse that aspires to unchallengeable certainty."[5] This negative image of the continent runs deep in time, in its naturalization in colonial renditions of Africa, in Hegel's sense of its ahistoricism, and in more contemporary manifestations of the continent as a site of conflict, disease, and degeneration. This persistent negative portrayal has also justified interventions in the continent, including the colonial encounter, the structural adjustment programs imposed on it in the 1980s and 1990s, and the continuous pressure on African governments to further embrace the privatization and deregulation of essential industries such as the petroleum industry. In this scheme of things, Africa becomes the laboratory and disposal zone of modernity rather than its condition of possibility.

These dystopian perceptions of Africa raise a pertinent question. How then can we rewrite the continent's story into the narrative of a common future? Or how do we create a future, "forcing an African presence into systems designed, by virtue of their strategies of access, to exclude it"?[6] Mark Dery proposes a possible answer with *Afrofuturism*, a term he coins to name "speculative fiction that treats African-American themes and addresses African-American concerns in the context of twentieth-century technoculture—and, more generally, African-American signification that appropriates images of technology and a prosthetically enhanced future."[7] Although Dery is not preoccupied with the continent per se, the estrangement experienced by African Americans in the Americas, to which they were forcefully brought and where they were only reluctantly granted citizenship, in some ways connects to the experiences of their counterparts in Africa. When Dery speaks of Afrofuturism, he is interested in the possibility of utopian spaces that black bodies, formerly enslaved people, could forge a home in. This state of possibility hearkens back to the utopian wanderings of Sun Ra and the imaginative worlds that Octavia Butler and Samuel Delany make available in their fiction. Afrofuturism has become handy for artists and critics producing and/or analyzing cultural productions depicting the continent. Afrofuturism has been used to describe the fiction of Nnedi Okorafor, including her novel *Lagoon*, set in Lagos, and the Marvel blockbuster film *Black Panther*, set in Wakanda, a fictional nation in Africa. These African projects join their African American counterparts in the search for alternative spaces for black bodies and other life forms, human and otherwise. Together, they recognize that the future promised by the capitalist present is antithetical to the promise of black life and warrants an alternative. The imaginative musing of the Afrofuturist project is determined to activate counter-futures ensuring black survival and thriving.

Temporal entanglement is at stake in this Afro-centered alternative. The making of the future in Afrofuturism is a layering of time and historical junctures. It is a rejection of linearity and the acceptance of time conjunctions. Afrofuturism marshals recognizable aspects of history and mythic dimensions, but it also deploys the generic characteristics of science fiction. To understand the turn to the mythic-cum-historical past in Afrofuturism, we would do well to heed Frantz Fanon's submission that, "When the colonized intellectual writing for his people uses the past he must do so with the intention of opening up of the future, of spurring them into action and fostering hope."[8] Invoking the past here does not mean a return to a source or a wholesale adoption of precolonial norms. Rather, as Fanon sees it, it is for the purpose of deriving inspiration that could drive innovation for the future. The past here provides imaginative resources for constructing "speculative histories," pointing to "possible alternatives, . . . histories and futures."[9]

In the reading of Wanuri Kahiu's short film, *Pumzi*, and Fabrice Monteiro's series of photographs, *The Prophecy*, undertaken in this chapter, I show the place of Africa's past in the imaginative futures that these cultural projects showcase.[10] To put this another way, this chapter traces the "discourse networks" that are the condition of possibility of Kahiu's and Monteiro's projects.[11] The chapter discloses the indebtedness of these recent cultural artifacts to older forms, therefore putting pressure on their newness. We see not only the evocation of older cultural forms and the redemption of the African past in these works but also their enlistment in the mapping of an alternative future. In disclosing the formal and thematic influences of these Afrofuturist projects, this chapter builds on recent work in media studies challenging the novelty of new media with an archaeological scrutiny of their links to prior cultural forms.

Why is the work of this chapter important? First, the turn to waste aesthetics enables a critique of consumerism and the catastrophes of war and commodification. Kahiu's and Monteiro's projects demonstrate that we have polluted the land, sea, and atmosphere—in short, that the rate of current consumption is unsustainable. Yet these artists insist on the possibility of rejuvenation and overturning. Put differently, the redemptive potential of waste suggests that the current culture of excess can be transformed into something beautiful and conducive to an ecological ethics.

Furthermore, we can visualize Africa's contribution to the project of futurity from the trashy objects analyzed in this chapter. Waste is an appropriate heuristic for examining Africa's contributions to the imagined future, considering the reduction of the continent to dirt or backward space in the colonial imaginary and the elision of its contributions to modernity. The redemption of waste mirrors the rehabilitation of Africa's maligned past, just as the possibilities inherent in discarded objects parallel the potential contributions of the "dark continent" to bringing about desired futures. Most importantly, waste aesthetics provides a template for understanding the temporal entanglement that is Africa. Just as waste art is a compendium of the past valuable object, its discarded excess, and the transformed aesthetic artifact, African time rejects linearity, insisting on the fusion of past, present, and future. The archaeological project undertaken in this chapter also problematizes the radical novelty of new media by showing that newness enters the world through the past. In the end, the works studied below confirm that the journey to the future must embrace the past and present and that Africa's temporality and resources—denigrated in the past—have much to contribute to averting ecological catastrophe. As much as it sets its sights on the future, the work of this chapter is also a postcolonial recuperation of marginalized and denigrated perspectives.

To be sure, there is no one African value or defined set of values. "African" here encompasses the various material, discursive, historical, and mythic resources that communities across the continent have marshaled to defend their humanity, to define their subjectivities, and to position themselves in the world. Like the components of Deleuze and Guattari's assemblage, these resources are rootless and draw from a range of sources, many of which come from contact with people outside the continent through trade, migration, and colonialism.[12] The complexities inherent in the conception of African value or identity speak to what Chika Okeke-Agulu calls the "incorporative, compound consciousness of African subjectivity."[13] By this he refers to the open-ended, encompassing range of possibilities of fashioning Africanness. The complex of African subjectivity is open to the world. This indefiniteness also captures the continent's overwhelming geographical and cultural reach and differences. In its positive sense, this open-endedness allows the mobilization of an array of resources and materials, from a range of places and times, in the configuration of sociality across the continent; it is also the condition of possibility for the work of this chapter, which uncovers the multiplicities of historical, discursive, and religious resources at work in Kahiu's and Monteiro's projects.

The rest of the chapter is divided into three sections. In the first, Kahiu's *Pumzi* is discussed in relation to the variegated pasts it marshals to counteract a future of extinction. My argument is that this postapocalyptic film mixes the conventions of science fiction with Kikuyu myths, allusions to earlier films by African women, and Wangari Maathai's ecological activism to illuminate a path toward ecological sustainability. While impressive and successful on many levels, the disappearance of Kahiu's female protagonist at the end of the film illuminates the limits of its liberatory potential and ecological politics, and it invites other projects of futurity. I examine one such project, Monteiro's photographs, in the second section, revealing how he deploys various pasts including the Négritude philosophy predominant in the 1930s and 1940s, the Set Setal movement of 1990s Dakar, as well as the belief in supernatural spirits in Africa and beyond, to create affective images.

Despite their differences, including the fact that Kahiu's work is a film while Monteiro's is a series of still images, waste grounds their artistic visions, and both artists promote recycling in their works, which necessitates a discussion of this artistic practice in the third section. Also in this section I highlight the work of other African artists involved in trash aesthetics or recuperation. The works I discuss in this penultimate section critique excessive consumption and pollution as well as emphasize recycling and reuse. I conclude the chapter with a brief reflection on the aesthetic and political implications of marshaling pasts as technologies in the making of a planetary future.

Pumzi: Science Fiction Meets Indigenous Technologies

We need a new method, Ian Baucom writes, for describing "a future marked by the threat of extinction"—that is, a future marked by a "collective, planetary, being-toward-death."[14] I begin with Baucom's work because it captures the postapocalyptic character of Kahiu's third film, *Pumzi*, shot in South Africa. Kahiu, who was born and lives in Kenya, trained at the University of California, Los Angeles School of Theater, Film, and Television. She directed two films before her sci-fi debut: her first feature film, *From a Whisper*, is a fictional rendering of the 1998 terrorist attack at the United States embassy in Nairobi, Kenya, while her second, *For Our Land*, is a documentary on the lifework of Wangari Maathai, the Kenyan environmentalist and Nobel Prize winner.[15] Most recently, she directed the acclaimed *Rafiki*, detailing lesbian love in a homophobic society.[16] The film was banned in her native Kenya for its homosexual theme.

While Kahiu's other films are set in the present or recent past, *Pumzi* is set thirty-five years after the end of World War III, otherwise known as the Water Wars. Like other films about the apocalypse, *Pumzi* demands an awareness of the ecological threat posed by nuclear weapons.[17] These films have become increasingly relevant in the context of global warming and the threats of climate change. In them, the viewer is invited to decipher possible futures awaiting humans absent the reversal of current anthropogenic emissions levels. However, despite the commitment of such film projects to overturning the destruction of the planet, there is the risk that their preponderance promotes "nuclear conditioning" and delivers a "nuclear anesthetic" making viewers inured to their dystopian vision.[18] The increasing number of such films runs the risk of preparing the audience for the ecological worst rather than moving them to curtail pollution. *Pumzi*, however, works to counteract the negative effect of saturation with a unique stamp: its Africanization of the science-fiction genre.

Kahiu's film stands out because of its immersion in the sci-fi genre, its adaptation of indigenous African resources, and because of its transformative female protagonist. Early in the film, the viewer is shown newspaper entries indicating the scarcity of water, as well as images of fossils and skulls signaling death. We are also shown bottles holding remains of formerly existing beings. The only survivors of this catastrophe are sheltered in a futuristic version of Noah's ark. This is not a multispecies ecosystem like Noah's ark where various species enter in pairs. This is an anthropocentric scene with cleaners and managers as well as technicians and scientists. The film's protagonist, Asha, is a technician at the Natural History Museum this post-modern edifice hosts.

Pumzi is indeed a welcome addition to the sci-fi corpus, which has been critiqued for its elision or inadequate treatment of race and the perpetuation of a digital divide. In her introduction to an influential special issue of *Social Text* on Afrofuturism, Alondra Nelson writes: "racial identity, and blackness in particular, is the anti-avatar of digital life. Blackness gets constructed as always oppositional to technologically driven chronicles of progress."[19] Nelson points to the fact that the future projections enabled by science fiction have yet to account for Africa's contemporaneity or its coevalness. The continent and black people more broadly are either absent or subsumed within the present racial typologies that confine them to a marginal status. Again they remain ahistorical, as they were in colonial discourses, or are the victims of the technological divide that marginalizes them in terms of access to digital infrastructure.

Scholars dealing with African science fiction have also foregrounded its ambivalence when it comes to the treatment of marginalized communities.[20] They point out that while its liberatory promise can be useful for imagining just worlds for Africans and African Americans, the tools of science fiction have also been instrumental to the exploitation of these populations. Other scholars have recognized the colonialist impulse of science fiction by connecting its rise to the decline of empire, arguing that science fiction provided virtual spaces of conquest at a time of diminished geographical availability for imperial expansion and control.[21] A turn to *Pumzi* shows the operation of this ambivalence, with the ark being a haven of safety and energy efficiency but also a site of control. Kahiu's film would fit into the apocalypse genre of science fiction, which has moved from a predominantly Western genre to a global one.[22]

Pumzi's excellent female director and strong female protagonist are attractive to viewers at this historical moment when representations of women, especially black women, in the media are under scrutiny; its positioning of women behind and before the camera also provides a fine starting point for discussing the film's mining of the past. To be sure, films such as *Pumzi* are a departure from the nationalist-inclined films of early African cinema emblematized in the work of Ousmane Sembène. Such films, inspired by the tenets of Third Cinema, offered a corrective to negative portrayals of Africa and its people in the colonial imaginary, served as ideological tools of anti-colonial resistance, and, following independence, decried the corruption and ineptitude of the emerging national bourgeoisie.[23] Kahiu's film, in contrast, can be categorized under more recent experimental film since the 1970s, when national commitment started to take the back seat and films emerged that drew attention to their artifice and sophistication.[24] *Pumzi* owes its condition of possibility to the shift in the 1970s that de-emphasized the grand narrative of the nation in African filmmaking and authorized alternative cinematic styles and perspectives.[25] Science-fiction film is one of those emergent cinematic modes in Africa, and so is the Nollywood phenomenon in Nigeria, which I turn to in the epilogue.

While *Pumzi* is indeed unique, we can find in it traces of the work of earlier female African filmmakers such as Safi Faye, whose *Kaddu Beykat* is recognized as the first acclaimed film by a female African director, but also Assia Djebar, whose film *La nouba* centers on the Algerian war of independence.[26] Besides the fact that all these films are directed by women, three additional aspects of the earlier films resonate in *Pumzi*: the positioning of women as undertakers of difficult manual labor; women's confinement; and the possibility of female resistance and agency. When *Kaddu Beykat* opens, we encounter women bearing various loads as they make their way home to continue domestic chores. Later in the film we see women working on the land as they cultivate their crops. Meanwhile, the significant presence of men at the end of the film shows them relaxing under a tree and reveling in leisure. This positioning of women's burdens is equally present in *La nouba*, where the physical and psychological impacts of war on the women portrayed are clearly visible in five film fragments. In the first one, for instance, a woman is seen confined to the home, where she is nursing a disabled husband who is apparently abusive. This confinement and the burdening of women with manual labor are decipherable in *Pumzi*, where Asha experiences physical and psychological confinement in her laboratory workplace. The first view of the walled-off edifice comes in the form of an aerial shot that establishes it as an ordered and hierarchical space. As the film unfolds, Asha cannot leave the grounds of the museum without permission, and when she applies for it to enable her to ascertain the source of the rich soil delivered to her, the request is denied. Asha's dream that portends a future of de-extinction is interrupted by the machinic command asking her to take a dream suppressant.

We need to take seriously Asha's dream—showing her submerged during a water crisis—as well as its suppression by her handlers. This dream is preceded by Asha examining the soil sample she receives and then laying her head on her desk. The film's quick cut to water is enhanced by visual effects illuminating the water and magnifying its ripples. In a film set against the background of water scarcity and radioactivity, abundant water brimming with plant life provides visual pleasure. Yet the spectacular character of the dream sequence is not mere entertainment, as it "produces a 'positive' form of ecological expression."[27] This dream sequence, magnified by light, sound, and the ripples as well as by the quick flash of the tree at the end, does carry symbolic power as it lays bare Asha's anxieties about the present and her hope for the future. With the imbrication of tree, water, and human, the film's ecological thematic is made manifest here so that it foreshadows the film's ending. The viewer too is interpellated by this scene, and asked to identify with Asha against her handlers and to desire the future she wants. More than Asha's anxieties are at stake here, however. Asha's dream concretizes her desire to overcome the devastation around her, a desire that maps well onto the viewer's desire to overcome the ecological crisis threatening planetary existence. If the protagonist's dream reflects the possibility of overturning the apocalyptic destruction following World War III, it inculcates in the viewer hope that humanity can avert the worst consequences of climate change. Seen this way, the dream sequence "serve[s] not only as a reminder, an eco-memory, but a road to hope."[28] Asha's dream is crucial to the film's ecological theme, useful for mapping a better life, and for offering a glimpse of futurity. The suppression of the dream is therefore tantamount to maintaining the status quo to the detriment of an alternative future.

When Asha eventually breaks out of confinement, the expansive, barren landscape she traverses recalls those that the women brave in Faye's and Djebar's films. As in the earlier films, extended shots are used to foreground the woman's labor, to demonstrate Asha's overwhelming task of finding an uncontaminated, fertile spot where she can plant and make possible a new future for humanity. The large-scale task undertaken by this female technician against the will of her handlers at the museum underscores the role of female manual labor, no less arduous than that embarked upon by the characters in the earlier films. Yet Kahiu's film is transformative for the female resistance and agency it foregrounds. An explanation for the film's reworking of earlier tropes and themes can be found in MaryEllen Higgins's writing: "African cinema winds shift directions, deterritorialize, remember ancestral breaths, transport them, gather new breaths, take new and unexpected aesthetic turns."[29] While illuminative of futures and filled with what Higgins would call "ancestral breaths" from the past, *Pumzi* is also a film of its time, one that arrived in an era of female empowerment and visibility. As such, Kahiu can imbue her female character not only with the strength afforded her predecessors in Faye's and Djebar's films but also with the option of breaking out of confinement to undertake her task. It is significant that the female cleaner in the museum facilitates this escape, whereas the men are the security offi-cials who forcefully take her to the gymnasium area of the isolated edifice.

Moreover, the scientific contraption sheltering Asha and her colleagues echoes the exclusionary neoliberal spaces of science fiction.[30] Asha cannot even revel in her dream, as she is quickly returned to the world of waking reality with the command to take her dream suppressant. When she receives the soil sample with an unusually high water content, suggesting that life exists outside, she is asked to destroy the material, and her request to leave is denied. Besides denying her autonomy and agency, this decision also denotes exclusion and reeks of the fear of contagion. The survivors of the nuclear war in *Pumzi* fear contamination from the outside and prefer the confines of their walled-off space.

But we must ask: How did Asha and other occupants of this space gain entrance? How were they selected? Are they those who could buy their way in? What about the excluded? Furthermore, why would the council insist on destroying the soil sample with its potential regenerative capabilities? Is this decision linked to the need to preserve the status quo instead of cultivating a more distributive commons? There are no definitive answers to these ques-tions in the film, but there is room to ask them as we consider the presentist character of the Natural History Museum and how its mediation of access, inclusion, and exclusion follow the neoliberal logic guiding the contempo-rary moment.[31]

While conceding the confining attribute of arks, *Pumzi* makes clear their subversive possibilities. Asha chooses to forgo her privilege, to pursue a nomadic form of resistance with the potential of creating a better future. To do this, she uses the rich soil sample to grow a nursery plant from the seed stored in the museum, and when the growth potential is established, she breaks out to find a new home for the root and for humanity. Matthew Omelsky links *Pumzi* to similar science-fiction works foregrounding planting seeds in an otherwise postapocalyptic environment, such as Octavia Butler's *Lilith's Brood*.[32] Omelsky's mapping of a sci-fi corpus that includes *Pumzi* is productive, but it is also possible to map an alternative genealogy that links this work to a more local tradition, one that recognizes the influences of Maathai and a broader Kikuyu cosmology.

In addition to its participation in the imagining of alternative futures and the portrayal of an admirable black woman technician as its protagonist and its strong allusion to Maathai, an African woman scientist and ecologi-cal visionary, *Pumzi*'s adaptation of Kikuyu myths is one of its remarkable achievements. In one of the film's early shots, we see the etymological root of Maitu, the name of the community within which the museum is located. The high-tech community derives its name from Kikuyu. The unpacking of the name showcases a rich ensemble of meaning. Maitu means mother, and interestingly, the word *seed* is placed beside *mother* in this film shot. Mother or seed, there is a nudge toward root or origin, bolstered by the film's insistence on translating the name and locating it in the Kikuyu linguistic tradition. The presence of seed early on also foreshadows the primary role it will later play in the film. Of course the film's name, "breath" in Swahili, also nods to roots or origin. Breath is the primary condition for life or living. The allusions to roots, origins, and tradition all suggest that the future cannot be contemplated without recourse to the past. We see here an insistence on grappling with the past in order to understand the present and be able to imagine the future. The film invites the viewer to take in a cultural milieu beyond the high-tech possibilities of the walled-off community in the articulation of a just future. If that space is, as discussed earlier, exclusionary and exploitative, the work of Kahiu's film is to imagine an alternative. The soil sample delivered to Asha in the film is crucial to this exercise in futurity.

Under the impression that the soil must have come from her boss, the voice issuing directives to her in the film, Asha proceeds to examine the sample. She then finds out she was wrong; the soil is from an unknown source. I find this moment in the film interesting because until this point everything seems mapped out, defined, and working according to an ordered society. Asha is asked to destroy the package but refuses. As she examines the sample, we learn it contains no radioactive material. The soil is fertile and has an unusually high water content, very significant in a time of drought. Where is the soil from? Since the film itself is highly speculative, it is proper to speculate as to the source of the soil. In the absence of malicious material, the soil probably comes from a benevolent hand. But if nothing grows or exists outside the community, is it possible that the soil comes from the gods, from the divine, the otherworldly, giving humans another chance to regenerate the earth? Or maybe the soil is from a water mermaid, the kind evoked in Monteiro's work in the next section. Why not? In Asha's dream soon after examining the soil, she is transported into the water, where we see her swimming. Or could Asha be the water goddess herself who swam to earth from the dream to save the world with the soil? Notice that Asha's lower body is invisible to the viewer in the water. We only have access to her upper body, the proper human part.

Kahiu's film extends its investment in local Kenyan cosmology by making strong allusion to the Kenyan environmentalist Wangari Maathai. Maathai is most known for her work with the Green Belt Movement, a nongovern-mental organization that invested in planting trees in Kenya and inspired similar movements across the world. The organization succeeded in planting millions of trees, even as it fought government and private interests against deforestation. Maathai found tree planting valuable because of its poten-tial for enriching both human and nonhuman lives.[33] Maathai's afforestation project is echoed in Asha's labor in Kahiu's film. Worthy of note as well is that Kahiu established her credential as an eco-filmmaker with a documen-tary on Maathai titled *For Our Land*.[34]

"If films are made on the body of other films," as Higgins claims, then *Pumzi* can be said to be a fictional reincarnation of *For Our Land*.[35] The docu-mentary genre and oral storytelling technique adopted in the earlier text allow for a more direct discussion of issues in ways that *Pumzi*'s style does not. Two such issues in the earlier film are the sacredness of land and its status as a commonwealth. Maathai references the Kikuyu tradition of rec-ognizing trees as sacred and the inculcation of these values by her mother. In the film's title and in the work proper, the pronoun "our" is repeated to emphasize common ownership of land and the importance of a distributive logic that pays obeisance to such a principle. The conflict in the film then, one to which Maathai devotes her life, is the tension between such a prin-ciple and the actual practice of the allocation of land to a few for political and economic gains. *For Our Land* links these exploitative practices to the colonialist destruction of forests and the replacement of indigenous trees with exotic ones that served British interests. The first image of Maathai in the film locates her in a decimated forest, the backdrop providing visual evi-dence of environmental devastation.

This interpretation of the documentary is useful for apprehending Asha's nomadic resistance in *Pumzi*, where she opts to plant the root outside the confined space of the museum. Asha could have followed the logic of indi-vidualism and planted the root within the museum's confines, or she could have ingratiated herself with the governing council members by heeding their instructions to destroy the soil sample. If the future is "the unclosed space for new development in front of us" and is "open by definition," Asha's escape is in recognition of the incompatibility of the closed space with the project of futurity.[36] In opting for a radical departure, Asha formalizes her desire to return the soil to the commons. The choice of open space where a broader spectrum of humans and nonhumans can derive sustenance from the tree signals a rebuke of privatization, of a "profit-obsessed colonial cos-mos," and an endorsement of the reappropriation of land for the common good.[37] Asha's deterritorialized choice, like Maathai's, comes at the cost of physical assault by the security men, which evokes the multiple arrests and detentions of the Nobel Laureate described in *For Our Land*.

The ecological filmmaking experience gained with *For Our Land* propels Kahiu to experiment with the science-fiction genre, to which she adds African indigenous resources.[38] When Asha leaves the museum, she begins the search for a possible fertile ground, armed with what Darko Suvin would call the "novum," the "strange newness" introduced into the film.[39] Appearing from an unknown source in a time of water scarcity, the soil fits Suvin's paradigm as it "entails a change of the whole universe of the tale, or at least of crucially important aspects thereof."[40] In *Pumzi*, the soil changes Asha's perspective about the outside world and motivates her resistance against her confinement.

The novum not only alters Kahiu's tale but also enables the possibility of a regenerated earth. Asha's walk through the desert takes over four minutes, which the camera devotes to the devastated landscape. This long take uses wide shots to foreground Asha's overwhelming task and her vulnerability in the face of a toxic landscape. With low, somber music that sets the mood but also allows the viewer to hear Asha's footsteps, her walk invites a meditative contemplation on the part of the viewer. Nothing is growing on this land. Even a place that has the mark of a river shows no sign of water. The nonhuman sounds of twittering birds and other beings are conspicuously missing from the film's acoustic ecology. This is a wasted landscape—empty, barren, and dry—and the camera's wide shots want the viewer to take these qualities in. As I elaborate in chapter 3, absconding from the museum and Asha's journey reflect the journey of those who flee the continent through the desert and by other unorthodox means. Like Asha, many of these people have been denied entry visas. If these would-be immigrants are seeking a better life for themselves, Asha, armed with a plant, is seeking opportunities for the commons.

To return to the film's ecological politics, Asha's walk is truncated when a blossoming tree appears on the horizon; upon getting closer to it, she finds tree stumps and branches bereft of leaves. The tree that Asha finds is reminiscent of Mugumo, the sacred tree in Kikuyu tradition. The tree, with which the film ends, returns us to the beginning where the film advocates for roots and points of origin. We are also reminded of the nod to motherhood early in the film and Maathai's acknowledgment of her mother's influence on her ecological consciousness. In Kikuyu ways of being-in-the-world that Maathai learned from her mother, the Mugumo tree is exempt from exploitation and so can be read as embodying the possibility of ecological preservation. In showing the perils of irresponsible uses of the environment, *Pumzi* invites us to consider another road less traveled, that of the Kikuyu worldview it presents to us very early in the film, and which returns in the image of the tree at the end. Of course, the Kikuyu, like the rest of us, are not exempt from environmentally destructive engagements. However, there may be something to learn from their cultural system or preservation of the Mugumo as humanity works to avert the ecological catastrophe that *Pumzi* warns against.

Where is Asha in all this? Lying down to rest after planting the tree, Asha disappears to make way for the tree in the exact spot she had occupied. The film ends immediately after this. Not surprisingly, this ending has generated critical analysis worth introducing and extending here. Omelsky focuses on interspecies entanglement in his reading of the ending: "The postrevolutionary new ontology at the end of *Pumzi* is one in which human and nonhuman merge to form mutant life. Plant life, human life, and toxic life blur into a beastly multispecies ontology."[41] Omelsky's analysis of ontological transformation is noteworthy as it displaces human exceptionalism and superiority to make room for entanglement. Highlighting the sacrificial bent of the film's protagonist, Pamela Phatsimo Sunstrum contends that Asha "makes the ultimate sacrifice in her pursuit of a radically new future."[42] Like Omelsky's, Sunstrum's reading is persuasive. After all, individual sacrifice for the communal and cosmological good anchors the epistemologies of various African communities. Asha's can fall within that ambit. Yet this ending raises certain problems. The film's portrayal of a strong black woman is commendable, but its ending undermines this feminist impulse and its project of futurity.

African feminists' critique of the silences and silencing of black women resonates with Asha's disappearance. Simply put, *Pumzi*, in the end, excludes its female protagonist from the future that it envisions, therefore falling short of Molara Ogundipe-Leslie's recommendation in her work on "Stiwanism," for "the inclusion of African women in the contemporary social and political transformation of Africa."[43] Like the biblical Moses, Asha is our guide to the promised land but she cannot enter it; like Christ, another biblical figure, she has to disappear for social transformation to occur at the end of the film, making this a case of what I call "Stowanism"—that is, social transformation obliterating woman. As progressive as Kahiu's film is in its portrayal of a strong female lead, the sacrifice or disappearance of this black woman negates the radical strategies called for in the imagination of a counter-future. The film confirms that "choosing an oppressed and omitted group for study does not necessarily alter the kinds of knowledge that are produced."[44] Kahiu did position a black woman at the center of her film—a rarity for the science-fiction genre—but this does not ensure Asha's survival and endurance in the film's future.

The film's problematic ending is somewhat anticipated by the originary framework of the film's opening mentioned earlier, with its injunction to return to root or mother. This originary position recalls the now trite trope of Mother Africa deemed essentialist, critiqued for conflating women with land and equating them with maternal laborers, "silent observers who simply fulfilled their destiny without questioning it."[45] Asha's disappearance constitutes the sacrifice of women that is all too frighteningly familiar in the current order marked by the exploitation of women's bodies, especially those of color. Does the film's ending mean that there is no place for complete female emancipation in the future to come? Why does the black female body remain a site of violence and erasure in this possible future? This critique applies to the cyborgian interpretation offered by Omelsky because at the end of the film, a tree, a recognizable nonhuman, takes the place of the woman. Decentering the human is a commendable project, but Asha's disappearance evokes limits of conservation efforts in Africa and across the Global South. The prominent objection, which I discuss further in chapter 4, involves the displacement of humans to make way for nonhuman animals and "pristine" wilderness. How can we posit a future where the entanglement of the human and nonhuman is respected but each species is also able to thrive on its own?

My appraisal does not detract from the achievements of Kahiu's important film, but it implies that the film's project of futurity is incomplete. While its emphasis on cultivating, on making rather than destroying, as well as its vision of recycling, are exemplary, the film's ending suggests "the torment of nonfulfillment and incompleteness."[46] My reading of the ending of Kahiu's film discloses the limit of its futuristic rendering, which should concern us because the problems of the past and the present cannot persist in the future. To be sure, the solution is not to discountenance or abandon Afrofuturistic projects. We must continue the imagining of futures because our survival depends on them, but we can mitigate their shortcomings so that the future they promise looks nothing like our present and past. Overall, the closing shots of Kahiu's film invite further projects of critiquing the present and imagining more complete futures. One such project, Monteiro's collection of fascinating photographs, is discussed next.

Monteiro's *The Prophecy* and Chiaroscuro:
Concealment, Revelation, Futurity

The age of digital media is an age of images, so much so that it is estimated that over 1.2 trillion photographs were taken in 2016 alone and that, over 400 hours of content get uploaded to YouTube every minute.[47] In this context of image saturation and of the risk of getting numbed by the proliferation of images, how do we produce affective photographs? In other words, how do we create images with affective meaning and ability to move the audience to address pressing environmental problems? To adapt Teju Cole's statement to my purposes, how do we create the unique image when "the flood of images has increased our access to wonders and at the same time lessened our sense of wonder"?[48] How can an artist produce images that can hold the viewer's attention given the "modern problem of attention" in the face of relentless distractions?[49] It seems that Fabrice Monteiro had these issues—the proliferation of images, the culture of mindless swiping and sharing, the problem of attention, as well as the numbing effect of the magnitude of available images—in mind when he produced his arresting collection of photographs.

Originally trained as an industrial engineer and based in Europe, Monteiro, the son of a Beninois father and Belgian mother, relocated to Senegal, where he completed *The Prophecy*. The project was inspired by the pollution that Monteiro observed as he tried to take up surfing on his return to West Africa. He came to photography from his work as a fashion model, inspired by the New York photographer Alfonse Pagano, his friend and mentor. Collaborating with Ecofund and the Senegalese designer Doulsy, who made the costumes for *The Prophecy*, Monteiro brought together his interests in fashion, digital photography, and an artistic sensibility attuned to his environment. He had previously worked on *Marrons*, a collection of photographs shot in Benin, depicting shackled enslaved subjects, and *The Way of the Baye Fall*, which documents the lives of a small Muslim sect in Senegal.[50] We can decipher a similar influence of Dakar's rich cultural scene in the digital photographs constituting *The Prophecy*. I suggest that these fascinating photographs owe a debt to technologies of the past, including the rich cultural tapestry of Dakar, found materials, as well as an African and diasporic resource: belief in supernatural entities. Delineating these resources can also enrich our understanding of the aesthetics and politics of the collection, which critiques a culture of waste and suggests transformative possibilities to the viewers.

Before examining these photographs, however, it is important to trace the history of photography in Dakar but also on the continent more broadly. The earliest manifestations of photography in Africa, as in the case of cinema seen earlier, served the colonial project. The camera was deployed to mesmerize the colonized and functioned as an aspect of the "colonial sublime."[51] As Brian Larkin explains, these technologies were meant to showcase the superiority of the Europeans, but also served to interpellate the colonial subject into empire's orbit. Photographs were also instrumental for shaping the perception of the colonized among the colonizers; they served "Europe's appetite for exotic, colonized peoples as specimens of curiosity inciting a lurid benevolence."[52] In other words, these pictures were deployed to frame Africans and the continent as primitive people to justify their subjugation.

Although Africans themselves did not make films until the mid-twentieth century, they learned and practiced photography especially around the coastline of West Africa by the late nineteenth century.[53] St Louis and later Dakar feature prominently in this cartography of photography by Africans. Some of these early photographers were returnees from Brazil and the United States, while others learned from Europeans and African Americans who visited these parts. Photography, while new, was relatable to existing imaging arts such as the *ako* and *gelede* of the Yoruba of southwestern Nigeria.[54] These early photographers mostly took pictures of kings and other elites who could afford their services and were interested in bolstering their image and authority.[55] It was not until the mid-twentieth century, in the era of decolonization, that photography's democratic potential was realized in Africa. Beginning in the 1940s, African photographers opened studios where they served the needs of clients who wanted portraits of themselves and their families. In Dakar, for example, Salla Casset and Meissa Gaye were among the earliest to set up studios.[56] From the photographs of Malick Sidibe and Seydou Keita, to mention just two of the most renowned, we see people posing to express their subjectivities.[57] The African subjects, especially the women with their fine clothes and poses, engaged in autopoiesis, in self-making, as they participated in the project of modernity. These photographs, taken in the studio, in the dance halls, on the beach, and even in rural areas, portray the modernity of their subjects. What was interesting about these images was the ability of the people to take control of the way they wanted to be seen. While the photographer's skill and style were crucial to the process, the agency of the photographed was certainly indispensable.[58]

Monteiro's photographs share some features with those of his predecessors, but they also depart significantly from those of the immediate post-independence era. In its unique composition of images, Monteiro's collec-

1.1 Landfill at Mbeubeuss, *The Prophecy* © Fabrice Monteiro, 2015

tion offers a slice of life and tells us of the way people live; it offers a sense of
material culture. Of course, it is also a product of digital technology, with
its sophisticated editing toolkit. Digital photography has been taken to task
for its manipulability, for complicating Roland Barthes's sense of the photograph as a "certificate of presence."[59] Critics of digital photography contend
that it undermines the indexical quality of photographs if images can now
be produced entirely on a computer or if a photograph can be easily adjusted
with cost-efficient software technologies such as Photoshop. Although its
reach may have expanded under the digital regime, editing has always been
at the heart of the photographic darkroom. In fact, it is at the level of editing that certain idiosyncratic artistic styles are developed. We should see
photography as "combining possibilities of fidelity . . . with those of manipulability."[60] Moreover, manipulation is not always a bad thing, as it has the
advantage of making the invisible come to life, an important attribute when
it comes to environmental issues. In fact, before we proceed any further, it is
crucial to disabuse our minds of the photograph's aura or its correspondence
to an extant reality; as mediated documents, photographs are constructed

1.2 Discomfited winged figure and animal waste, *The Prophecy*
© Fabrice Monteiro, 2015

and participate in a social process of meaning-making, a process implicated in power and ideology.[61]

If Monteiro's predecessors mostly present human bodies to look their best, the display of detritus in *The Prophecy* shows humanity at its worst. In one image taken at Mbeubeuss, we see a waste dump littered with all sorts of trash (figure 1.1). In another image, shot at an abattoir, we see cattle horns, the remains of animals slaughtered for food (figure 1.2). Used cables also join the list of detritus in Monteiro's work. Since at least the days of Eugène Atget, photography has been enlisted in crime detection and its resolution.[62] As Benjamin himself puts it: "Should not every photographer . . . expose guilt on his pictures and identify the guilty?"[63] It is a common practice to take pictures of crime scenes, including of victims and suspects. Even Susan Sontag maintains the crime-photograph connection: "Photographs furnish evidence. Something we hear about, but doubt, seems proven when we're shown a photograph of it. In one version of its utility, the camera record incriminates."[64] This crime history of photography applies to Monteiro's work, which depicts assemblages of crime scenes.

Consumption is the major crime on display in these photographs. Sieg-fried Kracauer may as well be describing Monteiro's photographs when he writes that "most people turn their backs on garbage cans, the dirt under-foot, the waste they leave behind. Films have no such inhibitions; on the contrary, what we ordinarily prefer to ignore proves attractive to them."[65] If the waste dump is often ignored, elided, or invisible in feel-good pictures, including selfies that we post on social media and archive on our electronic devices, themselves consumerist objects with planned accelerated obsoles-cence (see chapter 2), Monteiro's photographs make the remnants of con-sumption practices visible.

Asked about his artistic influence in an interview, Monteiro acknowl-edges the Italian painter Caravaggio (1571–1610), reputed for reviving inter-est in chiaroscuro in the sixteenth century. Monteiro, in the same inter-view, declares his preference for this artistic technique, entailing contrasting shadow with light in composition.[66] The contrast of darkness and light is especially useful for understanding *The Prophecy* and the disclosures at the heart of the collection's ecological significance. Many images in Monteiro's work make interesting use of dark shades illuminated by light. One example can be found in the heap of waste in the picture taken at Mbeubeuss (figure 1.1), a major dumping site outside Dakar since the late 1960s. In this image, the immediate background is cloudy, as if smoke from incinerating the waste blocks the line of vision. However, the darker background is contrasted by the foreground figure, whose form is accentuated by light. The light is most visible on the left arm, which points downward toward the heap of waste. The waste, which the composition orients the viewer toward, is ren-dered legibly. The directional hand combines with light to illuminate hu-man waste. More importantly, the darkness/light dichotomy, more broadly, speaks to the relationship between the hidden status of waste, often cast away, and the work of revelation that Monteiro undertakes in *The Prophecy*. Whereas waste is meant to be deposited out of sight (in the dark), Monteiro casts illuminating light on the dark to reveal the repressed. Monteiro's cam-era shines light to mark the return of the repressed.

The casual disposal of the horns in figure 1.2 brings to fore the question of the environmental standards of meat processing at this site. Are the animals being processed in safe conditions, and what happens to the waste, which includes animal blood and photographed horns? Meat processing and its af-fordability also raise the question of food security and access. Who can afford meat and who cannot? Who is most likely to be affected by improper and un-sanitary disposal of the waste elements? The blood and horns justify posing

Jeremy Bentham's famous question in relation to Monteiro's work: can the animal suffer? Successive scholars, including Jacques Derrida, Matthew Calarco, and Cary Wolfe, have taken up this question in their treatises on the othering and racializing of the animal for exploitative practices such as laboratory testing, sports, and human consumption of animal bodies and their produce.[67] While the critique of these scholars is crucial, we should exercise caution in categorizing the eating of animals in postcolonial contexts within the same exploitative logic, considering that the socioeconomic conditions in these societies preclude the affordability of alternative protein and vitamin sources for many people.[68] Nevertheless, the remnants invite a critical recognition of animal subjectivities lost to meat production—under what conditions were they raised and killed?—and the pollution resulting from indiscriminate disposal of animal waste.

One of the greatest achievements of Monteiro's photographs is the ability to make visible the rapacious destruction from "eating the ocean."[69] As the work of Elizabeth DeLoughrey, Nicholas Mirzoeff, and Nicole Starosielski, among others, has shown, the sea is a site of capitalist expansion and exploitation. Yet the myth of the romantic sea devoid of human troubles persists. The currency of this mythic thinking can be partly attributed to aquatic opacity. Unlike land, on which marks are easily inscribed, large bodies of water can absorb much transformation without appearing disturbed. In fact, for many, "as if nothing happened" is a popular refrain for describing dumping bodies or things in the water. A range of studies marking the oceanic turn in cultural studies has done well to problematize this ahistorical rendition of the ocean. Starosielski, for instance, suggests that "rather than see the world's oceans and underwater environments as beyond the social, we might ask how cultural understandings of inhabitation, ownership, and rights over undersea environments have been historically constructed, whose interests have been served by these constructions."[70] Mirzoeff endorses a materialist and historical reading, one that understands the sea "as a material force and presence; as a place where power is marked and contested; and as a mythical or spiritual form of life that threatens humans and yet is also their vital support."[71] This materialist-historic reading is at the core of Elizabeth DeLoughrey's notion of "sea ontologies," which entails depicting "maritime space as a multispecies and embodied place in which the oceanic contours of the planet, including its submarine creatures, are no longer outside of the history of the human."[72]

Monteiro's photographs portray violent inscriptions on water as a result of our consumption practices and the resulting waste. Data visualization en-

1.3 Figure clothed in nets, *The Prophecy* © Fabrice Monteiro, 2015

tails the accessibility of information; we can thus speak of Monteiro's effort as geared toward the production of an accessible and easy form that allows us to understand the data of excess, manifested here in the waste motif. Speaking of waste, "the disavowed other of the commodity," blood and water appear to be mixing in the image with the cattle horns (figure 1.2), providing an answer to my earlier observation that there are no proper waste disposal channels here.[73] The Atlantic Ocean, the receptacle of blood from the earlier slave trade, for which Senegal's island of Gorée is world famous, is now asked to absorb more blood from the abattoir. What else is the ocean asked to swallow? What other crime is it meant to hide?

Monteiro's camera exhumes discarded nets, which are repurposed into regal dress (figure 1.3). I will return to repurposing in the next section, but the presence of the nets is a trace of something else: the culture of waste and improper disposal that the repurposed clothing counters. These nets could also be those of the local fishermen who have been rendered jobless. Due to the activities of commercial trawlers, many of them big vessels from Europe and other parts of the world, fishing communities along the African coast have seen a massive decrease in fish stocks due to overfishing. Elspeth Probyn writes of the "historic and colonial trade routes that persist in the strip mining of African fisheries by the Global North."[74] The nets used by these vessels also often trap young, immature fish, which threatens generational continuity. Capitalist consumption and expansion remain insatiable, which is why these foreign vessels perpetuate the "hydro-colonial" as they prowl the earth in search of new territories to reconquer for consumers at home.[75] Monteiro's photographs remind us of the instrumentality and agency of water in colonial practices, including the slave trade and formal colonization of the African continent as well as the more contemporary issue of illegal fishing, mining/drilling projects, and the dumping of toxic waste across the continent.

Monteiro's nets have also caught other things that point to the ocean as a dumping ground. Considering that oceans are unbounded by arbitrary national boundaries despite the territorial inclination of their surveillance and exploitation, the debris caught by the net can stand in for the dumping of toxic waste in the region's waters.[76] Oil companies operating in Nigeria's Delta have also dumped toxic material in the water rather than adopt the more environmentally friendly methods mandated in their home countries. These events may be happening far away from Dakar, but water's fluidity and flow, its transgeographic form, make it reasonable to think of the interlinking of these sites with Dakar's maritime environment. What these practices validate is a notion of aquatic zones, especially ones located in Africa, as "sacrifice zones."[77] Monteiro, however, exhumes the bodies buried in an attempt to get away with crimes. By staging bodies of waste, remnants of animal bodies, and other materials exhumed from the sea, Monteiro reestablishes a crime scene, one that indicts humanity for unbridled consumption. The aquatic crimes include not only that ocean resources are depleted or that the ocean serves as a dumping ground. The ocean floor is now wired, which is why the cable wings from one of the images (figure 1.2) echoes the undersea network, the underwater cables that Starosielski writes about as facilitating communication and internet possibilities in this digital image.[78] As will be evident in the next chapter, oceans carry our electronic waste too. The trashy mundane objects and things around us often escape our notice and we can easily avoid meeting them with our gaze. Monteiro's camera succeeds in bringing these objects into focus and foregrounding their presence. Yet there is more to the visibility offered by Monteiro's collection, which brings me to a constant presence in all the pictures.

If Asha's disappearance in *Pumzi* marks her transcendence to the realm of the ancestors, Monteiro incorporates the "divine feminine principle" by introducing a supernatural female figure that recurs in various guises across the series of photographs.[79] To tease out the extra-human dimension of the photographs, it is instructive to turn to the question of appropriate protocols for making affective images in an age of digital media with which I started this section. One answer provided by Cole is relevant for understanding Monteiro's photographs: "another approach is to take photographs that exclude humans."[80] Monteiro's photographs focus primarily and enduringly on the nonhuman. Even the few photographs that feature humans relegate them to the side and make them easy to miss, as if their appearance is accidental. These images decenter the human, compelling the viewer to dwell on nonhuman assemblages and their implications for planetary life.

If various objects appear for different ends in the photographs, the constant presence of the supernatural produces "enlightenment and terror."[81] In a number of images, while the upper part of the figure's body is properly human, we cannot properly define the lower part, which spreads out like a fish tail. Monteiro's half-human, half-nonhuman being resonates with the Mami Wata figure, who is known to embody human attributes in the upper half and fish characteristics below. It is significant as well that this figure is emerging out of the water in many images, facing the land, with her back to the water. In one particular image, she is swimming in the water, with the lower part enveloped in colorful attire, hiding her lower physiognomy (figure 1.4). This positioning in relation to water substantiates her status as a water mermaid or Mami Wata. Mami Wata is known for taking various shapes and forms across cultures; in the various manifestations in Monteiro's images, the figure exudes the dual aura of beauty and terror, and of familiarity and strangeness, binaries that correlate with the blessing and punishment that Mami Wata bestows.[82] This binary of good/evil resonates with the spectacle/terror dichotomy operating in Monteiro's photographs. The extraterrestrial character is delightful but also evokes terror.

This liminal figure is not fully in the water and not fully on the land in some of Monteiro's photographs. Dressed regally in some of the images, Mami Wata seems ready for an important mission, one of warning humanity of their environmental excesses. She brings along in those moments trash from the sea, evidence of a crime committed against humanity and nonhumanity by humanity. We can also read her arrival in another way, as the displacement of an inhabitant of water by the devastating activities of humans. The image with the cow horns possibly conveys this message most strongly (figure 1.2). We see here a figure not standing tall and dignified as in the other images. Rather, she appears burdened with the cable. Kneeling, she is bent to her right, suggesting the exacting nature of the cables. Whether viewed as

I.4 Female underwater, *The Prophecy* © Fabrice Monteiro, 2015

communications technology as I suggested earlier, as a stand-in for pipelines that carry oil, or as a metaphor for other forms of pollution of the ocean, the flightless "wings" appear discomfiting.

In interviews, Monteiro has mentioned the Greek Gaia and the West African djinn as inspiration for *The Prophecy*.[83] The allusion to Gaia is particularly instructive as she is the personification of the Earth itself. Read in this sense, Monteiro's photographs produce the Earth clothed in detritus, overwhelmed with waste, and suffocated by smoke and the smell from human rubbish. When she is not bent, tangled, or choked by human waste, she is standing tall as if defiant in the face of excrescence. One can conclude that the semantic field of Monteiro's dense photographs is expandable to accommodate all these beings at once: Gaia, Mami Wata, and the djinn can be said to constitute a non-phallocentric, non-Christian trinity at work in Monteiro's art to illuminate and critique the destruction of the Earth.

The complexity of the haunting presence is meant to engage the viewer of *The Prophecy* and appears inspired by "the incessant urge *to show what we cannot see*."[84] The viewer of Monteiro's collection, distracted by the cell phone, iPad, and other electronic purveyors of images, is invited to sit with the majestic extra-human dressed in trash, regal in her appearance despite being clothed in waste. Images of Africa and Africans taken amid trash have often been critiqued for denying the dignity of Africans, but here in Monteiro's hands we can see a figure covered in trash and still revel in such an image. This sublime figure is attractive and also induces fear in the perceiver, who is "alternately repelled" and drawn to the photographs.[85]

The attractiveness of Monteiro's feminine figures invites a seeing and a seeing again, but we must ask if this seeing results in an exploitative gaze, linked to male viewing practices or a more redemptive "look," which is non-masculine and "de-phallicized."[86] The figure appearing in different guises invites a look (in place of the gaze). These images are not designed for mere consumption like the waste they are composed of; rather, they invite considerable labor from the interpellated subject, who is asked to consider their own contributions to the culture of waste. That the collection of photographs returns to a similar theme in photo after photo, albeit with variations, invites the audience to stay with the problem of environmental degradation they deal with and to reflect on it. Even if the viewer scrolls through the images quickly, they are returned in image after image to the same problem. This repetition encourages a de-phallicized look which is not headed toward mastery.

This non-phallocentric interpretation is bolstered by the position of the female figure in many of the images. It is significant that as imposing as the extra-human character is, her positioning makes it possible to confront the environmental degradation on display. In a discussion of the ontology of mediated vision, Tom Gunning asserts that "Spirit Photographs portray spirits alongside 'normal' figures in familiar spaces (posed subjects in a studio or room), but the two sorts of bodies appear oddly superimposed upon each other or illogically juxtaposed."[87] While it is true that Monteiro portrays spirits alongside earthly things, what Gunning calls "this collision of separate orientations" does not apply to *The Prophecy*.[88] There is nothing odd or illogical about the worldliness of spirits or the fact that their cultural logic is compatible with conventional rationality. Monteiro's images are an ode to the multiplicity of worlds in the African postcolony. In place of illogic, the ghostly and the everyday are carefully arranged so that they complement each other in the elucidation of the message of the photographic medium. In fact, mundane trashy materials are the constitutional fabric of the spirit in Monteiro's work.

The relationship between the mundane and supernatural is useful for understanding the composition of Monteiro's photographs. Take the image showing desertification, for instance (figure 1.5). The extra-human figure is not in the center but more to the left, making it possible to see and reflect on the bare trees standing in the distance. In the image where she appears as a tree (figure 1.6), she is positioned more to the side in a way that makes visible the burning of the bush in the background, both to her left and right.

Another picture positions this more-than-human figure directly in front of a car and beside a truck, where she is surrounded by smoke, which heightens her mystical quality (figure 1.7). To properly understand this photograph, we should turn to Cole's writing on cars: "they are our shadow on the earth, our prosthesis."[89] Cars act as our extensions: they make mobility and migratory behavior possible. In a sense, they are our "shadows," literally. However, automobility entails "conflicting, contradictory, and overlapping lived experiences."[90] In addition to the inequality and accidents associated with motor vehicles, there is another sense of contradiction worth considering in relation to Monteiro's image: cars as producers of waste and enablers of degradation. Seen this way, the smoke conferring a mystical quality in the photograph can also represent the carbon emissions from both vehicles. The emissions obscure part of the figure, and it seems as if she is blocking her mouth and nose to avoid inhaling toxic fumes. Moreover, the construction of roads, on which vehicles are driven, often results in the disturbance of ecosystems and displacement of various life forms. What is more, the fuel that currently powers them emerges from dirty extractive processes, and in oil's transportation, especially when it spills into the water, there is further evidence of pollution.

In one photograph where the extra-human figure comes out of the water (figure 1.8), we can see a ship—a symbol of maritime business, often the purveyor of toxic waste and oil, and part of the infrastructure of large-scale fishing. Her positioning to the side again makes it possible to see the incorporation of the sea as an instrument of market expansionism and resource accumulation. In this visual economy, there is a chance to see the water-spirit alongside other components mobilized in the piece as a "federation of actants," collaborators in the project of affecting humans to tackle environmental degradation.[91]

No contemporary thinker of the image and visuality has done more than Teju Cole to unpack the complexion of the sea. In *Blind Spot*, the novelist, essayist, and photographer uses the adjoining text to peel the calmness and beauty from apparently tranquil images of oceans and seas, especially the Atlantic and the Mediterranean. What Cole achieves with words is made possible by the roughness of the water surface in Monteiro's pictures. The water across the images appears rough, suggesting a storm in some cases and

1.5 Female and bare trees, *The Prophecy* © Fabrice Monteiro, 2015

even flooding that overwhelms the human and the land in others. In this image, where the extra-human figure is emerging from the water, it is as if the water itself has become plastic or some kind of shiny, man-made material near the figure's feet, and is climbing up, engulfing her.

Thus far I have shown that the contrast between light and shadow in chiaroscuro is apposite for understanding the illumination of waste in *The Prophecy*. Waste, unwanted matter cast away, attains foreground prominence because of Monteiro's use of light. Now I want to plumb the dark shades of Monteiro's art in order to shed light on prior cultural formations that it signifies. The efficacy of Monteiro's photographs relies on their mining of the past, including the animist sensibility of various African cultures.[92] Waste, for example, is a residue of the past. Even the idea of a traditional photograph is steeped in pastness. In Barthes's words, photographs mark "for certain what has been."[93] Monteiro's supernatural figure is the outstanding technology of the past in this series. As already mentioned, this striking figure, which can be Mami Wata or a spirit more broadly, draws on an indigenous perspective on the environment. This is the classical Fanonian mining of the past for the making of the future. For Fanon, a people emerging out of the

Chapter One

1.6 Female figure, trees, and fire, *The Prophecy* © Fabrice Monteiro, 2015

colonial doldrums should resort to the past not to dwell there but to recuperate valuable materials that can facilitate the fabrication of their future.[94] Although his Marxist sensibility would disallow his approval of mystical-religious elements, the plumbing of the religious-mythic imaginaries of the past here falls within the ambit of Fanon's remarks. For me and for others to whom I have shown these pictures, in the spirit figure is the striking element, the "punctum," Barthes's terminology for an "element which rises from the scene, shoots out of it like an arrow, and pierces me."[95] My bodily response to Monteiro's otherworldly character is inseparable from my cultural sensitivity toward admiring and fearing Mami Wata. In this bodily response the precognitive and the cultural become hardly separable. That initial apprehension of the superhuman figure happens preconsciously, but even that is hardly divorceable from the larger social script that is woven into my body: a belief in the supernatural at the nexus of Christianity and African indigenous religious practices.

The influence of African supernatural practices in Monteiro's work connects with another past with roots in Senegal: the Négritude philosophy propounded by Senegal's first president, Léopold Senghor, alongside Aimé

1.7 Female figure, car, and truck, *The Prophecy* © Fabrice Monteiro, 2015

Césaire and Léon Damas. Formulated in the 1930s against French racism when the three were studying in France, Négritude sought to rehabilitate blackness, to position it as a site of admirable humanistic values.[96] Négritude celebrated the spiritual values of Africa, its animist sensibility, and the attribution of significant agency to the nonhuman. These principles are discernible in the artworks produced under the influence of the movement. Much about this philosophy has been critiqued, and this needs no rehashing here, but what is important is the impact of that ideology on the artistic productions of Senegal.[97] Joanna Grabski provides an exemplary discussion of the significance of Négritude for the works of artists training at the École des Arts following Senegal's independence in 1960. Of one such artist, Papa Ibra Tall, Grabski writes:

> Tall's works are characterized by epic themes relating to Pan-African culture and formal qualities elaborated in Senghor's writings on Négritude. *Woï Benneel (First Song)* (1963), and *La semeuse d'*étoiles (Sower of Stars) (1960s), are exemplary of Tall's early work. For instance, *Woï Benneel* evokes the genesis of African civilization whereby a curvaceous, larger

1.8 Female coming onshore with ship behind her, *The Prophecy*
© Fabrice Monteiro, 2015

than life female figure appears to emerge from the earth in swirling currents of power. Tall's skilled draftsmanship is evidenced by the meticulously detailed patterns animating the composition. *La semeuse d'*étoiles depicts an energetic and fluid female figure scattering stars that fall around her.[98]

Grabski captures the impact of Négritude on Tall's representational strategy, but what interests me in this quotation is the affinity with Monteiro's work in terms of the "larger than life female figure." Both artists surely foreground female power and agency, which finds its parallels in Senghor's Négritude poetry, especially "Black Woman."[99] Where detailed patterns animate Tall's work, waste powers Monteiro's, and where Tall's female figure scatters stars, Monteiro's distributes smoke. Whereas Tall's figure appears from the ground, from land, Monteiro shifts the source, in most of the images, to water in the twenty-first century, which is fitting considering that oceans now join land as sites of exploitation and surveillance. Although separated by time, which has also seen the waning of Négritude, Tall's work and Monteiro's share an interest in cosmological powers as embodied in female figures. Both artists are drawing from a common ancestral repository of knowledge and working toward addressing challenges confronting their society.[100]

Another Senegalese social/artistic movement anticipated Monteiro's work: the Set Setal movement of the early 1990s.[101] "Set Setal," which translates from Wolof, a lingua franca in Senegal, as "clean" and "to clean up," enshrines a movement to combat social and urban decay in Dakar. As the Senegalese historian Mamadou Diouf explains: "the movement aims to improve the environment of the neighborhoods, to remove the garbage and dirt. But it also seeks to clean up or reform political and social practices."[102] Developments that resulted in Set Setal include the lost-school-year strikes in 1987/88, the presidential elections of 1988, and the structural adjustment programs that swept the continent in the 1980s.[103] Students participated in strikes in 1987 to demand educational and social reforms. In 1988, the opposition presidential candidate, Abdoulaye Wade, designated as the candidate for social change, failed in his bid to unseat the incumbent Abdou Diouf, who had once served as Senghor's prime minister and succeeded him as Senegal's second president. Senghor handed over a nation reeling from economic stagnation, unrest, and massive debt to his successor, who in turn implemented the structural adjustment program of the IMF and the World Bank. Subsequently, the government cut investment in the provision of social services, which further impoverished people. Unlike Senghor, who positioned art and culture at the heart of the national enterprise, and allocated a substantial portion of the annual budget to underwriting the arts, thereby setting the stage for Dakar's position as "an art world city," Diouf's administration represented a setback to the culture industry.[104] The retrenchment of such support was one more regrettable loss of the post-Senghor era in Senegal.

The Set Setal movement emerged in light of the aforementioned developments. Members of the movement cleaned up roads, made art (graffiti and murals were prominent) from recycled materials to promote cleanliness and good governance, as well as invoked indigenous and transnational figures/events such as Nelson Mandela in their work. Set Setal's investment in cleanliness and its use of art made from recycled materials to pursue this goal, as well as its indigenous and cosmopolitan energies, remain consistent with Monteiro's modus operandi in *The Prophecy*. Take this discussion of Set Setal's artistic process by Diouf for example: "The spectacular character of [the] statues, which have taken over the space of the neighborhood, issues out of a heterogeneous ensemble of signs that are 'cultural and historical

Chapter One

references.' The materials—salvaged objects from urban everyday life (metal, plastics . . .); carved trees trunks, twisted and erected on stilts, like monuments, bearing calabashes and canaries (the village)—are diverted from their usual, and often religious, functions."[105]

This description certainly coheres with the materials on display in Monteiro's photographs, which continue Set Setal's mission to promote environmental principles by highlighting waste but also repurposing it for artistic means. Like the Senegalese youth laying claim to their city despite their economic precarity, Monteiro's project remakes urban space with the same set of tools: imagination and creativity. Set Setal also set the stage for the indigenous and global sensibilities in Monteiro's work, with its synthesis of disparate sources. The name may have a Wolof origin, but the movement's icons extend beyond the confines of Senegal. The history of artistic productions on cleanliness and waste removal in Senegal would include Set Setal's work but must also account for its re-manifestation in *The Prophecy*. In the 1990s, young people mobilized the masses through their artistic works, including the well-known "Set," Youssou Ndour's hit song, which can be considered the movement's anthem. In the early twenty-first century, Monteiro continues this project of mobilization, calling for the transformation of space not only in Senegal but across the planet, this time armed with the affordances of digital photography.

Recuperative Art: Trashy Past, Golden Future

Kahiu's and Monteiro's projects foreground the past in their conceptualizations of alternative futures. One more past, dominant in the work of both artists, is their revaluation of trash, or in Robert Stam's evocative language, their "redemption of detritus."[106] The most obvious is Monteiro's recycling of trash as the subject of his photographic compositions, but then Kahiu is invested in a similar practice when she depicts the recycling of Asha's urine and sweat in a bid to generate water and when the outside scenes of her film reveal wasted space. In both cases, the artists are problematizing the boundaries between the inside and the outside of the body.[107] They are also troubling the public/private dimensions of waste-belonging.[108]

The conjunction of waste with Africa is at the heart of defining modernity. As an out of the way place, the place of primitivism that necessitates civilizational redemption, the continent has been categorized by Europeans in abject terms. The "indiscriminate" disposal of waste is considered a sign of backwardness and is one rationale for the colonial mission of developing a civil culture of cleanliness and orderliness, or as Stephanie Newell puts it in the case of colonial Africa, "a rhetoric of difference is mapped onto the body of others through a spectrum of dirt-related words."[109] In more recent times, however, with waste figuring as a corollary of modernity and consumerism, it becomes obvious that we have never actually been modern. This consumerist tendency has inspired artistic expressions that make use of found objects, fecal matter, and other forms of waste.

Monteiro's photographs can be seen in a similar light, but he is not the only African artist doing this and neither is this peculiar to the continent. Repurposing waste for art shows that it is as viable a means of artistic creation as more "traditional materials."[110] Grabski contends that artists involved with recuperation in Dakar are not motivated by "a shortage of conventional art supplies" as many assume. She claims that the "shifts in thinking about artistic practice, articulated in the art school's curriculum and pedagogy, were crucial to making the materials of the city into the materials for art."[111] Grabski locates the works of Senegalese artists in a global continuum, one that corresponds with "the postmodern turn to a detritus aesthetic."[112] But we can do away with the binary, as it is possible to accommodate global and local inflections in artistic choices. The turn to this form of art in the 1980s and 1990s in Senegal corresponds to the period of economic strangulation occasioned by privatization and other conditionalities of the IMF and World Bank. It thus makes sense that in addition to responding to a global movement, local artists in Senegal and across the continent were also making do with what they could find.

From the preceding section, we have seen Monteiro's deployment of trash to create the beautiful and the sublime. Yet Monteiro's pictures show that modernity itself is synonymous with waste. In the image taken at the waste dump in Mbeubeuss, for instance (figure 1.1), the towering figure clothed in trash may mesmerize us, but Monteiro is that occasional artist whom Laporte foretold: "Occasionally a poet will uncover the origin of the metamorphosis and send gold back to its 'damned earth.'"[113] Monteiro, the visual poet, surrounds the towering figure with heaps of trash, making sure that the viewer does not lose sight of the origin, the damned earth.[114] Monteiro's images indict humanity for its excesses, for its involvement in trashing the planet.

While Monteiro's photographs are perspicacious and orient us to see things we are wont to ignore, there is also room to supplement their blind spots. One such blind spot concerns the contestation over the future of Mbeubeuss as a waste dump. The pictures exclude the pickers and other laborers who ply their trade there and have made it home. Against the wishes of these people, the government prefers to shut down the place because it is a national embarrassment, also citing health and environmental hazards. But the workers there want to keep their jobs, even if they support certain changes to improve the environmental conditions. These workers have since formed a pickers' association to articulate their position in a formal and systematic fashion.[115] Pictures have their optical limits and Monteiro's are no exception. From the photograph of Mbeubeuss, for instance, one would not know that the waste site functions as a terrain of "governing by disposability" and political control.[116]

The second occlusion concerns toxins and other waste hazards. Karl Schoonover helps in clarifying the problem: "The problem of waste today is not only what we are conditioned not to notice in our field of vision, but also what is simply impossible for human perception and photographic images to register."[117] Toxins would fall under the category of the imperceptible that Monteiro's camera cannot quite capture. Studies in new materialisms have pointed us to the agency of matter, including the "vital materiality" of trash "generating lively streams of chemicals and volatile winds of methane."[118] In the case of Senegal, the "high organic content, stench, and propensity for quick putrefaction in the Senegalese heat makes household trash in Dakar visceral, lively matter."[119] This lively matter seeps into the human skin and soil, from where it can pollute food and water sources. The exposure of children to lead and other toxic materials in Mbeubeuss is equally dangerous.[120] The vitality of dirt requires that toxicity not be left out of our interrogation of Monteiro's work.

Trash aesthetics, in the works of Monteiro and Kahiu, critique consumerism and encourage reuse. Their reworking of trash into art demands a slowness antithetical to the supersonic speed characteristic of capitalist consumption. In their veneration of reuse rather than the fetish of the new, these artists foreground the ecological principle of recycling in their formal and/or their thematic preoccupations. In *Pumzi*'s version of recycling, for instance, bodily sweat and urine are not allowed go to waste in a period of water scarcity. These bodily excesses are literally savored in this film. Asha collects her urine, which is recycled back into water. There is also the recycling of sweat that humans can savor in the fruit of the root planted by Asha as the film ends. Even the root, the seed of the future at the film's close, is an offshoot of what has come before, therefore representing another form of recycling. In Kahiu's natal Kenya, an organization known as Ocean Sole employs artists to make art from flip-flops collected from Kenya's coastline. These shoes have been washed onto the shore by ocean currents. Reminiscent of Monteiro's images dealing with oceanic waste and its threat to the ocean's soul, Ocean Sole's recycling exercise, according to the organization's mission statement, transforms "flip-flop pollution into art and functional products to promote our oceans."[121]

All considered, the foregoing discussion of trash aesthetics has touched on manifestations of creativity and innovation, improvisation, the critique of consumerism, and environmentalism. These characteristics overlap and are not easily separable in the hands of sophisticated artists such as Ghana's El Anatsui, arguably the most influential African trash artist. El Anatsui's career spans a long period, and space prevents me from delving into his work in a substantial fashion.[122] His bottle-cap installation series speaks to the concerns of this chapter. El Anatsui, like many of the artists working in this area, believes that "artists are better off working with whatever their environment throws up."[123] Glass and plastic bottles with colorful caps are a common sight across the continent. While the bottles are easily recyclable in various ways, the caps are usually discarded. El Anatsui is treating his environment as a site of creativity and improvisation when he turns to these caps. El Anatsui's work also illustrates that waste in "aestheticized form" is "a figure for what remains possible in the aftermath of catastrophe."[124]

El Anatsui's art evokes traumatic memory, suggesting that at least in the African context, we can also locate a traumatic script in waste aesthetics. To probe the "specific genealogies and legacies" of the whiskey bottles providing El Anatsui's caps is to decipher a legacy of violence.[125] Whiskey is a Western imposition in Africa, considering the way it displaced indigenous gin as the authorized alcohol in colonial West Africa.[126] In this displacement can be found early traces of the current scenario wherein Africa serves as a market for imported finished goods. The more brazen traumatic memory evoked by whiskey and other such bottles is that of slavery and colonialism on the continent. Whiskey and rum facilitated the slave trade as attractive exchange commodities and gifts for African kings and elites. They were diplomatic tools that eased tensions and made sure that the train of slavery and empire ran efficiently. These bottle tops are thus reminders of painful pasts.

Wangechi Mutu's *Suspended Playtime*, an installation that uses discarded bags and twine to create soccer balls suspended from the ceiling, is relevant here.[127] The artist has been applauded for her "conceptualizations of our troubled earth ethics," and for "her inventive use of materials."[128] Mutu's resourceful reappropriation of the bags illuminates her outstanding talents but also the improvisational and creative character of the children who cannot afford actual balls across the continent.[129] She makes possible a micro-visualization of lack and trauma. Speaking of trauma, the head-like balls in Mutu's work also evoke states of emergency in parts of Africa, moments when children's playtime has been literally suspended by wars and other forms of violence depriving them of innocence.

Another form of loss can be seen in Cyrus Kabiru's sculptures, made from discarded metal. One of the fascinating dimensions of Kabiru's art is the outcome: glasses, which belong to overlapping spheres of art and utility.[130] Kabiru's project can be read as a nostalgic longing for a time when Africa made the things it uses. This was the time when Ajaokuta Steel in Nigeria made steel for local use and when textile factories boomed across the continent, before locally produced cloth and clothing were replaced by cheap clothes from China and secondhand ones from Europe and America. Kabiru's work fulfills one function of nostalgia—namely, "the past not as the seed of the present, but its rebuke."[131] Produced in the context of importation of many of the continent's material needs and ideas, Kabiru's project, like the other works discussed in this chapter, "rebukes" the present in its recollection of previous local products.

Nostalgia may rebuke the present, but it also inspires "future-directed movements for justice."[132] Glasses serve an aesthetic function when they are mere accessories, but they can also be a human prosthesis, the extension of (wo)man. If we take the latter configuration, Kabiru's glasses can be read as a camera of the future. By this I mean that glasses magnify and enhance our vision. In his emphasis on redirecting local energies into making rather than consuming, the artist produces a vision of the future just as Kahiu's and Monteiro's cameras do. In his art made from found objects, Kabiru contends that Africa's progressive future will have to come from revitalizing comatose industries and sourcing materials locally.

Traumas indicate loss, but they also provide an opportunity to work through the pain toward healing. As Patricia Yaeger puts it, "artists and architects have embraced the globe's junkyards as their own, often healing them in the process."[133] Who is being healed here? The artist or the junkyards? I would say both in the case of African artists. Kabiru draws on the past to offer a future of local economic productivity with implications for bettering the lives of the people left out of globalization's success stories. Unlike the current order, where economic prosperity is delinked from environmental consequences most of the time, Kabiru's vision locates recycling at the core of the future.[134] The artists at Ocean Sole also connect entrepreneurship with conservation. By reusing waste and found objects as well as critiquing consumerism, and offering alternative visions of being, the artists discussed in this chapter participate in imagining counter-futures. Critique is devoid of resignation in these works, carrying the promise of the healing of the world-turned-junkyard. The process of making art, of working through the debris of existence, also provides an opportunity of healing for the artists themselves, an opportunity for working through the traumas of postcoloniality and globalization.

Conclusion: African Past as Postcolonial Angel of Futurity

In a seminal article, Anne McClintock offers a robust critique of the teleology of progress assumed in the "postcolonial" moniker.[135] This linear teleology, which proceeds from the past to the present and onward to the future, underlines Western social theory. Yet when we look at the postcolony, we find theoretical and empirical evidence of a "time of entanglement."[136] My analysis of entanglement provides a humbling reminder that new media are never totally novel since they always contain fragments of the past. The cultural productions examined in this chapter have demonstrated their elasticity and flexibility as conveyors of multiple temporalities. In fact, the use of trash is apropos for this context because of its capacity to carry the trace of a before-life, manifest a present life, and imagine an afterlife.

Africa's marginality in the current global order is no longer news; what is novel and significant is the opportunity that the works scrutinized here provide for remapping the cartography of the future. Just as garbage aesthetics reconstitutes trash, fragments of the African past can illuminate a future untethered to the logic of accumulation by dispossession. A recourse to the African past has ecological significance in an era of climate change. In other words, we can learn from the environmental knowledge implicated in these cultural artifacts. We can learn that trees, the ocean, and other ecological beings are more than objects at our service, that they are deserving of respect in our relationships with them, and that it is this kind of relational disposition, premised on mutual belonging and respect, that will prevent the extreme scenarios painted in *Pumzi* and *The Prophecy*. The culture of recycling and reuse also shines through Kahiu's and Monteiro's projects as a strategy of ethical living in the contemporary era. If the racial cartography of the current world order makes it difficult to create spaces where black people can thrive, this chapter coalesces on futuristic visions with African resources at their core without romanticizing the artistic projects. My analysis of *Pumzi*, for instance, pays attention to its blind spots, including the fact that its imagined future repeats present problems, while nudging cultural producers and critics to ensure that that their futuristic projects do not replicate the challenges of our past and present. The next chapter extends the discussion of the temporal dimension of networks by taking up their spatial interconnections.

spatial networks, toxic ecoscapes, and (in)visible labor

South African photographer Pieter Hugo produced his series of photographs *Permanent Error* after reading a *National Geographic* article about Agbogbloshie, the electronic waste (e-waste) site located on the bank of Korle Lagoon, close to the center of Ghana's capital, Accra.[1] Originally designated as an industrial area, Agbogbloshie housed a market for foodstuffs from the northern part of Ghana from the 1980s before it became famous for electronics and metal recycling in the 2000s.[2] Hugo was so affected by the chilling images of e-waste burning that he decided to visit Agbogbloshie, where he made his award-winning collection of photographs. Approximately one year before Hugo's visit, the Burkina Faso-born photographer Nyaba Leon Ouedraogo had also accidentally encountered Agbogbloshie. On a visit to Ghana during the Africa Cup of Nations soccer competition there, he rode in a taxi in which the driver asked to show him a place—Agbogbloshie. That visit was the springboard for his series of photographs, *The Hell of Copper*, devoted to the site where monitors, compact disks, and other gadgets from within and outside Ghana are recycled with grave ecological consequences.[3]

Agbogbloshie exists partly for the retrieval of metals from digital gadgets including computers. Some of the objects burned at this site to retrieve valuable metals come from Euro-America, where they have been used and cast away, while others originate from local use. Before beginning their lives as cell phones, computers, and other forms, these gadgets require copper, coltan, and other resources mined in Africa. The conditions of mining these materials in places such as the Congo are devastating and dangerous, and the recompense is so little compared with the risks involved. Agbogbloshie is part of this ecology of risk, which stretches across the continent. Cell phones, laptops, computers, and television sets may help us gain access to environmental knowledge and distant environments, but their complicity in ecological degradation should remain in view as well.

Hugo's and Ouedraogo's projects belong to a body of representational media devoted to the socioecological problems in Agbogbloshie. These projects have been critiqued for their apocalyptic and dystopian renditions of this area of Ghana, where scrap from electronic items as well as other metals are recycled and reused in repairs.[4] These representations have also been censured for focusing on a restricted imagery of doom while leaving out the vibrant economy of "the computer refurbisher's shops, secondhand computer stores, homes, offices, schools and internet cafes where the computers are used."[5] In turning to images of Agbogbloshie supplied by Hugo, my intention is not to reiterate the aforementioned Afro-pessimistic vision. My disclaimer is particularly important given the choice of Hugo—a white South African—for this chapter. Hugo's identity as a white South African photographer already implicates him in a fraught racial economy. It does not help that Hugo concentrates on images of suffering and abjection of people of color. His Nollywood project, for instance, verges on the grotesque in its unflattering depictions, while his project La cucaracha, shot in Mexico, includes disturbing, exoticized images.[6] Hugo's approach opens his work to the kind of criticism leveled against Western voyeurs for producing dark images of Africa and Africans for the titillation of a Western audience.[7] Another objection is that these artists commodify the bodies they represent. I take this point on commodification, which resonates with the craft of Hugo and other artists in this book, very seriously. One art auction site records the sale of Hugo's image of Abdulai Yahaya (discussed below) for $15,000 while estimating that another (that of Naasra Yeti) will sell for between $20,000 and $30,000.[8] Details of the workings of the art market is beyond the purview of this treatise, but Hugo certainly did not pay his subjects a fee commensurate with the hefty amounts his images fetch. There is an example here of the monetization of the labor of those subjects who posed for the camera.

These objections notwithstanding, it is too easy to ignore or look away from Hugo's work and that of other artists whose representational practices we might be uncomfortable with. I propose here that Hugo's work, especially *Permanent Error*, deserves what I have described as *insightful reading* in the introduction: a looking and relooking that asks what we might learn about and from the scene of suffering. We can read such images strategically, not to repeat the trite complaint of poverty porn but in order to offer a sophisticated explanation of the logics of exploitation at work in them. In what follows, I model a reading of disturbing images that scrutinizes them for their ecological and sociopolitical value. More specifically, Hugo's work yields an analysis of the toxicity of recycling operations in Agbogbloshie and testifies to the exploitation of labor in this Ghanaian space. The field of Hugo's artistic work extends the site of exploitation of labor beyond the recycling and gathering work being undertaken by the laborers in Agbogbloshie. They are expending labor when they pose for photographers and filmmakers, labors that are monetized as films and photographs can sell at outrageous prices. While extracting work out of his photographic subjects, Hugo's art makes visible the exploitation of toxified laborers whose rewards are incommensurate with their output and the risks of engagement.

My reading broadens our understanding of waste and toxicity and intervenes in the scholarly discourses on digital and free labor. I argue that infrastructural work at Agbogbloshie be considered an aspect of digital labor, and that the economic exploitation and toxic risks associated with recycling metals qualify these activities as free labor. This chapter extends the scope of digital labor and redraws the boundaries of free labor to include the kind of work performed in Agbogbloshie. I also interrogate the extent to which the kind of work we categorize as free labor is willingly given. In addition to Hugo's *Permanent Error*, I also analyze Franck Bieleu's film *The Big Banana*, on the ecological footprint of banana plantations in Cameroon, before briefly considering, in the conclusion, Julia Dahr's *Thank You for the Rain*, a climate change film that offers a corrective to the androcentricity of Hugo's and Bieleu's works.[9]

The network form is a product of the network society that Manuel Castells and other theorists have traced to the 1970s.[10] This form has been praised for its affordances, including the possibilities of connection that it allows.[11] People across spaces have been empowered by digital network forms to communicate and circulate, to trade and travel. These are positive developments but a view of networks from an African standpoint is crucial for deciphering their exploitative dimension. Alexander R. Galloway and Eugene Thacker capture this exploitative tendency when they write that "networks also carry with them the most nonhuman and misanthropic tendencies."[12] Africa's forced insertion into the global economy, with slavery and colonialism, has always placed it in a disadvantaged position, one that the continent has yet to escape decades after most of its countries gained independence. One way that the disadvantage materializes in the contemporary era is in the allocation of ecological damage.[13] Africa's connection to the world yields waste in return.

We can also say that in Africa, toxicity manifests one example of network form as it spreads across nations and oceans and across humans and other bodies occupying local environments on the continent. Toxicity is a trope of the works under consideration, be it in Hugo's elaboration of a toxic ecoscape due to e-waste, or Bieleu's visualization of toxicity transported to human and nonhuman bodies from agrochemicals in Cameroon. Toxicity is a network form considering its movement and transformation of human and nonhuman bodies as well as the environment. Ultimately the cultural texts problematize the concept of globalization/networks by zooming in on the experience of Africans often left out of the gains of modernity even as they are left with its lethal debris. The achievements of these media artifacts include their rejection of despondency by embedding pathways toward alternative models of planetary imbrications, the kinds that would qualify as "metaphors for nonsovereign ways of being in the world."[14] I read these pathways as means of planetary world-making in the latter section of the chapter.[15]

In what follows, network will take many forms, beginning with Hugo's photographs circulating in a book published by a German press. The book creates a network of text and image to press its argument, while the condition of possibility for the photographs is the article on the dump site that the photographer encountered on the internet. Even the waste site is made possible by the often asymmetrical relationship between Ghana and the western world that enables the local use of mobile technologies and permits ships carrying used electronics to berth and offload their containers in Ghana. *The Big Banana*, the second artifact analyzed in the chapter, brings us the workings of a transnational corporation in Cameroon, the impact of its practices on local communities, and the possibility of alternative transnational solidarities forged between the Cameroonians and their fair trade collaborators in the United States. The filmmaker had originally planned to do a film on the mayor of this region but then discovered a sprawling web of malfeasance that redirected the film's focus. In Bieleu's film, bananas serve as the medium linking a rural community in Cameroon, where the fruit is produced and the film is banned, to sites of consumption in Europe and America.

Toxicity, Digitality, and Free Labor in Pieter Hugo's *Permanent Error*

Hugo's collection of photographs demonstrates that Africa and its people remain repressively yoked to the global order even in the twenty-first century. The structural adjustment programs of the 1980s succeeded in pressuring African governments to deregulate their economies and open them up to private investment. Meanwhile, across Europe and America, awareness was growing of environmental toxicity at home, especially around communities of color. The environmental justice movement, beginning in the 1980s, drew attention to the alarming environmental racism that disproportionately endangered African American and Latinx communities. This awareness was followed by the tightening of environmental laws and regulations, the aftermath of which was a shift of the burden to communities of color in Africa and Asia. To be sure, poor and minority communities remain disproportionally affected, especially in the United States, but a great deal of waste was subsequently shipped to the poor countries of the world for disposal. Lawrence Summers, serving then as World Bank chief economist, justified this transfer of risks in a leaked internal memo in which he argued that the mortality rate of people in developing countries is high anyway and as such they would be hardly affected by additional toxins in the atmosphere. For Summers, an added advantage was the idea that those poor countries were bereft of environmentalists who would raise the alarm as they did in the United States and Europe.[16]

The dumping of e-waste in Ghana follows a trajectory of an understanding of the continent as a dumping site. The continent's territorial waters have been subject to the dumping of toxic waste, including in Koko, Nigeria. But arguably the most famous case is the Trafigura incident, which involved the dumping of oil waste in Ivory Coast in 2006. The waste emanated from the operation of the multinational corporation Trafigura in Mexico, and was moved to Europe where the cost of proper disposal was considered prohibitive, after which the decision was made to move it to Ivory Coast. The case attracted international attention and condemnation because of the environmental risks it posed to the affected communities. In the case's resolution,

Trafigura refused to accept responsibility and only paid compensation to continue its business practices. Trafigura's impunity can only make sense if we link it to the view of Africa as trash.[17]

Electronic waste comes as part of used devices to be resold in Africa. They come presented as commodities that are indispensable for Africa's digital revolution. These and other items, such as used clothes and other household goods, have been shipped to the continent since the 1990s. The used-clothes business is popular across the continent, including at the Katangowa market in Lagos, Nigeria, where buyers jostle for clothes already worn in Europe and America. Likewise, containers bringing computers, cell phones, and other electronics are shipped to Africa, including to Lagos, Nigeria, and Ghana. While some of these electronics are in fine shape and are ready to be sold as is, others need repairing before they can be marketed, while the irredeemable ones gain value because of their retrievable parts. It is for this last function that Agbogbloshie has become best known, even though sales and repairs take place there as well. It is where e-waste is sent and where impoverished people work as metal-gatherers collecting scrap for sale. This process raises ecological problems that make Hugo's photographs relevant as an eco-media project.

Hugo underscores fire as a mechanism for understanding the ecological significance of his project. In her foreword to Hugo's collection, Federica Angelucci writes of the "striking convolutions of toxic smoke in the pale sky," and of the "reality of stench, heat, and disease" in Agbogbloshie.[18] Angelucci's observation approximates Ato Quayson's, who describes the "near-permanent fires of e-waste disposal mounds" in Agbogbloshie.[19] These commentators highlight the social and environmental problems festering in this urban space. The greatest achievement of Hugo's photography is his effort to orient viewers to the toxicity that is hardly perceptible with a camera lens.[20] By foregrounding the fire motif throughout the collection, Hugo elevates the toxicity of Agbogbloshie to the senses of his viewers. Hugo's collection also adumbrates the laborers that are mostly left out of discussions of the cyber network.

As in Monteiro's case in chapter 1, the crime scene here indicts humans for their consumption practices. Planned obsolescence is part of the design process of electronics, especially cell phones and computers, which means that they are rapidly and easily discarded, especially in the throwaway culture of the Global North. We can activate a list of crimes that would include that of waste, but also a lack of consideration for the lives and environments that are on the receiving end of discarded technological gadgets. If the shipment of e-waste to places like Agbogbloshie is meant to register their disappearance and oblivion, Hugo's work, intended to circulate in Western circles and among privileged Africans, makes sure to remind viewers that out of sight does not equal out of mind. Hugo's photographs, like Monteiro's earlier, gnaw at the senses of viewers, imploring them to find a correlation between their use practices and the endangerment of people and ecosystems across the world.

However, there is a major distinction between Hugo's and Monteiro's work worth highlighting before delving deeper into *Permanent Error*. Michael Fried has consistently written of artworks that celebrate their artifice and constructedness by their theatricality and their distinction from those works that practice absorption and effacement.[21] The latter kind of work, in Fried's reading, seems indifferent to the camera and the artist. The illusion of reality is greater in such works than in those texts that call attention to their fabrication as works of art. This difference can be brought to bear on Monteiro's and Hugo's work. Monteiro's project smacks of theatricality. The supernatural being, the weaving of the images, the clothing and the entire staging of the photographs announce their artifice, their "to-be-seenness."[22] Monteiro's project would fall within the sublime waste photography that can be contrasted with the documentary type.[23] The photographs in *Permanent Error*, in contrast, fit the documentary mode; they create the illusion of the real. The documentary feel is accentuated by images that suggest indifference to the camera. As we will see shortly, it is as if Hugo is an unobtrusive observer merely capturing things as they are.

Take the first picture in the book for instance, a photograph of casually arranged objects, including a semi-buried keyboard, clothes, and other forms of waste (figure 2.1). There is no order to their presentation; it is as if they appear as he found them. Why would Hugo include such an image and put it as the first of a range of photographs collected in *Permanent Error*, especially when there are more interesting photographs in the collection that he could begin with? I would argue that such an image allows Hugo to elevate a sense of the naturalness of the images. Considering the political function of the photographs, a point I return to subsequently, it seems that Hugo wants to hide his hands and the presence of his camera. He wants to foreground the documentary status of his work and thus puts an image with the least sense of manipulation at the beginning.

Besides its documentary value, this image is also effective for capturing the ecological work of the photograph. Another reason that a photographer would begin with an image portraying a partly buried keyboard is to under-

2.1 Computer detritus in dirt, *Permanent Error* © Pieter Hugo, 2011

score the fundamental impact of toxicity in this environment. The keyboard and other forms of waste, partly buried, indicate that mere removal of the waste is not a solution as it has seeped into the land, from where its detrimental effects can enter food and water sources and constitute a danger to generational health. Although this image denies theatricality, it does enable the artist to foreground the crime against ecology in Agbogbloshie.

If we can visualize the waste seeping into the land from the first image in the book, the one immediately following it heightens the sense of toxicity by introducing fire (figure 2.2). We are shown here a discarded central processing unit (CPU) on fire. Fire "is more likely to speak to us of disruption and

Networks, Toxicity, and Labor

71

2.2 Burning computer unit, *Permanent Error* © Pieter Hugo, 2011

chaos," which means that this image is an early registrant of the problems in Agbogbloshie.[24] The burning object is positioned very close to the camera, which makes it look as if it is about to jump out at the viewer. The camera work here facilitates proximity, a form of nearness between the image and the viewer. The viewer can also see smoke rising into the atmosphere at the photograph's edges. The nearness of this image to the viewer's body invites a bodily reaction. Because we are affected by what we are near to, Hugo's photograph invites a bodily response to the fire and the smoke. In its first two images, the book highlights its real aura, visualizes the contamination of the earth by electronic waste, and demonstrates the transportation of toxic ma-

Chapter Two

terial to the proximate body but also to the atmosphere where it can potentially cause more harm.

Hugo's collection follows this photo of fire with others portraying still burning fires or the lingering smoke that affects the visibility of the photographs' background. It is significant that in the other images including fire, Hugo couples the fire or smoke with human beings and/or waste littering the environment. This would not be noteworthy except that it highlights the exceptional status of the first image that includes fire—that is, the second photograph in the book. This image contains nothing of note except the burning CPU, which invites undivided attention to the burning unit. It is possible that the photographer is aware of the subsequent fatigue that may result from the preponderance of fire imagery and wants the viewer to stay with it the first time by itself, to achieve the already discussed effect, but also to register it as a crucial motif of the work.

From the first image of the buried keyboard to the fire-engulfed CPU, and throughout the collection, Hugo wants the viewer to sense the dangers that metal-gathering poses to human and nonhuman beings in Ghana. Hugo, in other words, is demonstrating a "melancholy black ecology" marked by precarity.[25] Precarity is discernible in Hugo's work, and it is obvious from the photographs that the discarded items are detrimental to human health, but the photographer does not stop there. He heightens the scale of the impact by including animals as well. In *Picture Theory*, W. J. T. Mitchell states that "the animal can see what we see."[26] Hugo goes further to show that the animal can suffer what we suffer. To further understand the functioning of the depicted animals, we may need to revisit Sean Cubitt's claim that "the task of depicted animals [is] to supply: an other subjectivity, not an absence."[27] Hugo's first animal image features a cow resting (figure 2.3). In this photograph, which shows the animal indifferent to the camera, there is no fire, but we see charred items strewn across the ground, suggesting residue from previous fires. This image suggests that the fire's victims are not only the humans but also the nonhumans as well. I take up the human-animal relationship in detail in chapter 4, but the positioning of the cow in this ecosystem is particularly significant here. The animal's body is on the potentially contaminated ground, making it easy to imagine toxic transfer.

There is a valid question that can be raised here, which is why fire is crucial to the operations of the e-waste site. Burning enables the retrieval of copper and other metals from the gadgets, metals that are themselves toxic. Summarizing the retrieval process, Kenneth W. Harrow states: "the plastics were burned off, the metal extracted, and the carcinogenic dioxin fumes in-

2.3 Cow resting on ground, *Permanent Error* © Pieter Hugo, 2011

haled as the recycling led to the recuperation of value."[28] Sean Cubitt explains that the "labor of recycling is dirty, dangerous, and bitterly underpaid; the places where it is conducted are polluted beyond belief, and require a transport and logistics operation of global span."[29] Similarly, Richard Maxwell and Toby Miller assert that "e-waste generates serious health and safety risks for salvage workers."[30] Stephen Rust goes further to acknowledge that "the environmental and health issues facing countries like Ghana and China as a result of e-waste salvaging can be directly linked to our collective consumption of media technology and content."[31] These scholars agree on the toxicity of these metals, which is further heightened by the noxious smell and chemicals emitted as a result of burning.

Taken together, then, when the fire combines with the chemical and other toxic materials, the process instantiates "trans-corporeality." According to Stacy Alaimo, trans-corporeality captures the ways "in which the human is always intermeshed with the more-than-human world," and how "the bodies of all living creatures intra-act with place—with the perpetual flows of water, nutrients, toxicants and other substances."[32] Alaimo's project can be understood within the materialist strand of ecocriticism that seeks to understand the intra-actions, interactivity, and agency of matter in assemblages.[33] The cell phones, laptops, and iPads ultimately leave the bodies they were glued to in America and Europe or more privileged areas of Ghana to find other bodies to attach to. The devices that do not make it as functional equipment are then opened in a process whereby chemicals and other toxic materials combine with fire to poison the bodies of humans and animals who work and live around Agbogbloshie. The abbreviations preceding the photographs in Hugo's book introduce the metals and other "actants" operative in the technological infrastructure, many of which have the agentic ability to transfer and transform matter into poison in human and other-than-human beings. The interbody relationship exhibits a toxic landscape, one at risk of being irremediable.

Lest it seem that only men and animals are affected in this space, women exist there as hawkers and sellers of wares to the men and the neighboring community. Girls and women, including Amama Suleiman and Naasra Yeti, appear in the photographs as hawkers of water sachets and other goods.[34] From the images, there is a gendered division of labor where the men work with the electronic items while the women sell items to them. This division would be consistent with the cultural logic of such societies, where technical tasks are often reserved for men. This does not mean that these cultural expectations are not transgressed, but this does not appear to be the case in Hugo's photographs. However, while there may be division of labor, Hugo's work makes it clear that no one can escape the toxic landscape and waterscape of Agbogbloshie.

The extent of the toxic network of Agbogbloshie can be deciphered in a special set of landscape photographs in *Permanent Error*. Most spreads of the book include an image on the right-hand page while leaving the left one blank. Around the middle of the book, both pages contain photographs. However, in one exceptional case the viewer encounters a triple-page spread,

with the extra page folded backward to maintain the book's symmetry (figures 2.4, 2.5, and 2.6). When the spread is fully opened, we find a panoramic view over three pages. In the foreground of the triptych of photographs electronic parts are strewn across the ground while in the background we can spot the lagoon and neighboring settlements. Together all three pictures depict discarded objects, the lagoon, and houses from different perspectives, offering a fuller picture of the environment. In the middle picture, the background view is obstructed by the image of a boy posing in a black sleeveless shirt and pants, with a necklace dangling from his neck. The other two images do not include any humans. What is the significance of this exceptional spread?

In these three images Hugo utilizes devices of landscape photography and the triptych form of European altar art while complicating the original design of these forms. Landscape art, including photography, tends to prioritize nature's beauty. Often excluding humans, it presents the landscape as beautiful, majestic, grand, and sublime. Landscape art aestheticizes the environment for human consumption and to create a feeling of awe. A prominent example would be the photographic depiction of the American West as a vast wilderness, so erasing the cultural-cum-historical presences that shape such spaces. In the American West this means the elision of the displacement of indigenous peoples for the spectacular image of "unspoiled nature" aimed at human pleasure and reverence. A similar reverential awe marks the original use of the triptych in Christian art depicting religious figures and icons in European altarpieces. The depicted figures would include one or

Chapter Two

2.4–2.6 "Zakaria Salifu," *Permanent Error*
© Pieter Hugo, 2011

some of the following in three panels: Christ, his disciples, the Virgin Mary, and the saints.[35]

Hugo's adaptation of these art forms, however, complicates their original designs. In the African context, Hugo's intent is not to demonstrate the sublime but the ordinary, not the sacred but the secular, not the profound but the profane. Rather than depicting unsullied nature, the form of landscape photography enables his visualization of a toxic environment, while foregrounding the monotony and stasis of Agbogbloshie, the banality of life here and the absence of progress. Unlike the traditional landscape photograph that excludes humans, Hugo puts a young male at the center to orient viewers to a social ecology. He also includes other reminders of human presence, including the settlements in the background, the smoke making its way into the atmosphere, and the electronic waste on the ground. The triptych actualizes the representation of a toxic network, one that extends the figuration of the casualties of the e-waste site. If the other photographs limit the visible casualties to the men who work here and the few women hawkers, this group of photographs foregrounds scale by linking the site to its surroundings, including the lagoon and those who make a home in the settlement behind.

Critics of media representations of Agbogbloshie often differentiate the site from the neighboring slum, noting their separation by the Odaw River.[36] They argue that the electronic market be separated from the neighboring settlement in critical analyses, a separation that is impossible from an ecological angle. The water may separate the strewn objects from the informal settlements, but it can also carry the toxic elements to the neighboring com-

2.7 "Abdulai Yahaya," *Permanent Error* © Pieter Hugo, 2011

munity and beyond. The unusual spread of similar photographs denotes the continuous spread of toxicity and disease across this ecological community. A comprehensive account of the toxic network here must accommodate the extent of its flows and impacts across space.

Having discussed the toxicity that electronic waste introduces into Agbogbloshie and Hugo's documentary representation, it is important to turn to the metal-gatherers themselves, the mostly young men featured in the photos. The most haunting picture in the book features a young male crouched low as he poses for the camera (figure 2.7). Whereas the background is visible in most of the images, this one zooms in on the human

Chapter Two

figure. We see flickers of fire in the background, but except for those, what is visible is mostly the body of this young man holding a wooden staff. Water dribbles down the left side of his face; perhaps this is sweat from the fire, or tears, or even both. His face and body glitter from perspiration, which in turn accentuates his blackness.

Allan Sekula teaches us that photography is "a system of representation capable of functioning both honorifically and repressively."[37] Both functions described by Sekula are present in this image of Abdulai Yahaya. By presenting his image in an international publication, foregrounding his body and naming him and the other subjects in the captions section at the end of the book, Hugo's work satisfies the honorific function of the photograph. Moving chronologically through the book on my initial viewing, I was disappointed that we get no information about the subjects, especially those who ostensibly posed for the camera. On getting to the captions segment at the end, however, it was gratifying to put names to some of the faces. The act of naming accentuates the visibility afforded by the photograph while foregrounding individuality. As T. J. Demos puts it, Hugo's "practice of titling his images after the names of his sitters" ensures that the "emphasis falls on the singularity of his given subjects," thereby counteracting the homogeneity usually ascribed to Africa.[38] Moving from anonymity in the images themselves to naming at the end parallels a move from absence to presence, from object to subject, and from obscurity to prominence.

Yet we can glimpse repression in this photograph. The crouched positioning suggests Abdulai's subordination by the global system of exploitation. This close-up image accentuates the physical effects of the toil and smoke on Abdulai's body. In this image, the closest close-up image in the series, the viewer is abruptly confronted with another body. The closeness of this body is meant to bridge the gap between the viewer and the viewed, to bring our bodies closer (albeit uncomfortably) to Abdulai's as a way of appreciating the gap between the privileged users of technology and people like Abdulai, stuck with the detritus. The camera thus functions as witness to the repression of Abdulai. Nevertheless, the camera also transcends this witnessing role to become the repressive instrument when it fixes one particular image of Abdulai in our minds. Of relevance here is John Tagg's declaration that a camera does not merely represent reality but "inflect its context."[39] The inflectionary role of the camera is what is at stake in this discussion of the apparatus's repressive function. Like the rest of us, Abdulai is a complex human being with many sides to his personality. However, "by turning the diverse aspects of foreign life into a single narrative," the camera denies us the

2.8 "Mohammed Musam," *Permanent Error* © Pieter Hugo, 2011

opportunity to appreciate Abdulai's complexity.[40] The viewer can only work with one view of the subject made possible by the photograph.

Hugo's *Permanent Error* also includes photographs of other metal-gatherers. A prominent example features three young men (figure 2.8). While the focus of the camera is on the boy in the center, positioned sideways and nearer to the camera, with arms crossed and eyes looking at the camera, the other males are positioned on either side. The one to his left is hardly visible except for his head and face and one hand holding his gathering tool. His eyes focus intently on the fire before him, while the figure on the other side is hardly visible in his bent posture as if he is looking for something. He is likely scanning the ground for valuable items that he can pick up. Thus, while the young male at the center seems to be posing for the camera, the other figures appear focused on their work so that they seem oblivious to the camera's presence. Agbogbloshie appears in this framing as a site for work and self-fashioning.

Speaking of self-fashioning, some images in this collection dispense with absorption in favor of the performative role that photography has played for Africans over time.[41] Emerging from the colonial situation with its elision of African subjectivity, Africans took to photography to present their own images and demonstrate their subjectivity. We can see a similar inclination in the images where the young men pose for the camera. In most cases, they are holding their gathering tools, which suggests the inseparability of their identity from their labor. In one fascinating photograph, Ibrahim Sulley stands in a pose, legs apart, wearing a hat, a Puma-branded shirt, and baggy jeans (figure 2.9). Behind him is a fire, which he possibly took a break from tending in order to have his picture taken, while further behind him is a cow that seems poised for the camera. Human and animal separated by the fire look into the camera. The human-animal entanglement that is visible here aside, there is a vulnerability on the face of this young male. As worldly as his dress seems, his face is expressionless, perhaps defiant in its refusal to smile for the camera.[42] Ibrahim's dress and pose may suggest that he is a participant in a youth culture linking him to other lovers of designer apparel across the world, but he is different from his counterparts in more privileged environments, those spared the toxicity and vulnerability he faces in "a place called away."[43]

There are pictures of other workers with different dress styles and poses, but their grave faces reveal no smile; the graveness of their faces is symbolic of the harsh conditions within which they live. For these people, Agbogbloshie is a work site, but it is also a place to pose, sleep, and defecate. This site, to use Trebor Scholz's words from his introduction to *Digital Labor*, shows the "intertwining of labor, leisure, consumption, [and] production."[44]

• • •

The manual labor that powers Agbogbloshie is crucial to the functioning of the global digital network and thus deserves to be understood as digital labor. Seamless telecommunication is made possible by the ease with which malfunctioning and old gadgets can be replaced with new and updated ones. Even if we do not ask, Hugo has done the work of showing us where the discarded items go. Digitality has always been associated with smart, geeky

2.9 "Ibrahim Sulley," *Permanent Error* © Pieter Hugo, 2011

labor, so it is easy to discount manual work that is nevertheless pertinent to digital processes. Scholz's conceptualization of digital labor links it to "social life on the internet."[45] Within this perspective, it becomes difficult for other practices to count if they manifest outside the internet. This emphasis around being "on" the internet favors "immaterial labor," "the labor that produces the informational and cultural content of the commodity."[46] The "informational" has a remarkable currency as a critical and analytical tool, which means that it can easily overshadow the heavy and dirty work involved in electronic waste disposal and recycling.

Furthermore, the location of Agbogbloshie in Africa, far away from the

Chapter Two

cities driving the current global order, contributes to its marginalization in discussions of the digital sphere and labor. Maurizio Lazzarato's influential work on immaterial labor explores the benefit of allying the informational and the infrastructural analyses of labor. By rejecting the separation of manual from intellectual labor, and making a case for their imbrication, Lazzarato paves the way for the work of bringing together content creation, curation, and consumption on the internet with the recycling of electronic waste as integral aspects of digital labor. Within this integrated frame, we can modify Andrew Ross's point about how "each rollout of online tools has offered ever more ingenious ways of extracting cheaper, discount work from users and participants."⁴⁷ Each rollout is a potential boost to informational practices and Ross is correct that users heavily subsidize the practice of digitality. But there is more to be said about each rollout: it also means the obsolescence of older tools, their disposal, and their arrival in spaces such as Agbogbloshie. The workers visible in *Permanent Error* facilitate the introduction of new gadgets since they make it easy for the previous devices to disappear and stand ready to absorb the relatively new as it makes room for the introduction of even newer tools. The list of users and participants whose labor is exploited includes these pickers and recyclers in Agbogbloshie, the caretakers of digital debris. The visibility of their work in Hugo's collection is useful for connecting their labor to the constellation of events in the cybersphere.

We need to adopt what Lisa Parks and Nicole Starosielski term an "infrastructural disposition" to enrich our understanding of media processes and to capture the inequality of their materiality.⁴⁸ If we attend seriously to the infrastructural logic of digital tools, then we should include within the category of digital laborers the workers depicted in *Permanent Error*. Digital labor, as it is presently theorized, hardly takes cognizance of workers outside the workings of Euro-America.⁴⁹ And when it does, it is often the workers in the Asian factories producing cell phones under grueling conditions who are included. But the workers in Agbogbloshie, whose efforts contribute to the functioning of the digital system, are also participants in digital labor.

Moreover, the health hazards and vulnerabilities connected to their work compel a rethinking of free labor. In her discussion of "free labor," Tiziana Terranova describes it as: "voluntarily given and unwaged, enjoyed and exploited, free labor on the Net includes the activity of building web sites, modifying software packages, reading and participating in mailing lists and building virtual spaces. Far from being an 'unreal,' empty space, the Internet is animated by cultural and technical labour through and through, a continuous production of value which is completely immanent in the flows of the network society at large."[50]

Terranova and many others who have theorized free labor focus on work that happens on the internet. Mark Andrejevic, for instance, takes aim at the exploitation that occurs when user-generated information is sold by Google and other web corporations. Although Andrejevic is careful to disaggregate forms of exploitation online and distinguish them from the more insidious practices in sweatshop factories and other workplaces, he notes that bringing these forms of abuse together can "add depth and urgency to the critique of exploitation in the information economy."[51] But who is keeping record of the exploitation of workers who handle discarded internet infrastructure in Agbogbloshie? This is the perspective I foreground by including these workers, many of whom have lost their youth, in the category of free laborers. Like the laborers in Terranova's schema, the recycling work of these pickers is unwaged. Unlike the workers we encounter in the discussion of Bieleu's film below, these workers receive no payment from the users of discarded gadgets, and neither are they paid by the telecommunications companies. Yet the work of these laborers is part of the "cultural and technical labour" that animates the internet.

It can be objected that these workers get remunerated, unlike the users of the internet, but this is a faulty assumption. As Marx reminds us in the *Grundisse*, "wages are the product of the exchange between worker and capital."[52] It is also a virtue of Marx's work that he stresses the "predetermined" nature of wages for rendered labor.[53] The paltry financial reward, coming from the production of value from the sale of retrieved metals, is not a wage. It is unguaranteed as it depends on the retrieval of valuable material and is not contingent on the amount of invested labor. The worker in Agbogbloshie "takes high risks, [and] puts in long hours without any guaranteed reward."[54] The risks of engagement and the unguaranteed reward provide the basis for conceptualizing the work at Agbogbloshie as free labor.

Considering the hazardous work environment of these workers, it is possible to adapt insights from Lauren Berlant's discussion of "cruel optimism" to this analysis of free labor:

> "Cruel optimism" names a relation of attachment to compromised conditions of possibility whose realization is discovered either to be *im*possible, sheer fantasy, or *too* possible, and toxic. What's cruel about these attachments, and not merely inconvenient or tragic, is that the subjects who have *x* in their lives might not well endure the loss of their object or scene

Chapter Two

of desire, even though its presence threatens their well-being; because whatever the *content* of the attachment is, the continuity of the form of it provides something of the continuity of the subject's sense of what it means to keep on living on and to look forward to being in the world.[55]

Berlant may not have mentioned Ghana or Agbogbloshie and her work focuses on people with choices, but some of her insights are pertinent for the African context, where there are no viable alternatives for these laborers. For the critic who wonders why anyone would continue in a toxic profession as the workers in Agbogbloshie do: this e-waste site, as toxic as it may be, enables these workers to be in the world, be productive members of society, form communities, and make a living, no matter how fraught. For Berlant, one characteristic of cruel optimism is "suppression of the risks of attachment," a point that maps well onto our context, where labor is intertwined with toxicity.[56] Like other young hustlers in Africa waiting for a break, these laborers expend their youth while hoping for a better future.

The risk of attachment has been documented by successive scholars who have found elevated exposure to toxic chemical compounds in the bodies of workers in Agbogbloshie. One study observes the highest levels of "elemental biomarkers"[57] in those workers who reported working near sites where e-waste is burned, while another concludes that "soils from the open e-waste burning areas in Agbogbloshie were heavily contaminated by chlorinated and brominated DRCs [dechlorane-related compounds]."[58] The elevated exposure to toxicants is due to the use of fire, discussed earlier as crucial for retrieving copper and other metals in the crude recycling processes employed in Agbogbloshie. Anthropogenic fire has been crucial for human evolution and progress. It enables agriculture and cooking and is instrumental for many industrial processes; fire's value extends from the secular sphere into religious ones, where it denotes the presence of the holy spirit. It is the elemental symbol for the Christian Pentecost, while the burning of candles and incense generates a divine aura in religious ceremonies. "Fire generates humanity."[59] In fact, "fire and humanity have become inseparable and indispensable. Together they have repeatedly remade the earth."[60] Fire "is our most radical environmental shaper, our premier instrument of habitat conversion, and one of our most important elemental media."[61] Yet this elemental media also contains contradictions.

Fire enables the retrieval of metals, valuables on which recyclers subsist, and it promotes the culture of repair and reuse just as it has enabled agricultural practices on the continent over time. Yet just as bush-burning often exceeds the intent of the people who set fires, the productive value of fire surpasses the desire of workers in Agbogbloshie. The side effects of fire is manifest in the elevated exposure to toxic chemicals produced from the burning of discarded electronic items. When I asked a worker there if he was aware of the risk of his labor, he responded in the affirmative, and turning to face me, asked what else he should be doing. He had come from the northern part of the country, like many who migrate to Accra, to find gainful employment. Many who fled the interethnic conflicts in northern Ghana from 1994 onward also found refuge in the Agbogbloshie area, originally named Fadama by earlier settlers from the north in the 1960s and 1970s.[62] These workers have to repress their knowledge of the risk of cancers and other ailments in order to continue their struggle. They do so hoping for the next big thing, as they told the Ghanaian-British photographer Asare Adjei. As Adjei reports, "many of the children dream of becoming footballers, in spite of their ill health. Many of the adults hope to find steady employment in other fields such as taxi driving or cooking." It is significant that "virtually all of them dreamed of escaping their surroundings to the western world, settling into life there and one day owning the same computers that they process every day in Sodom and Gomorrah."[63]

Sodom and Gomorrah is the informal designation used by locals for the larger area encompassing Agbogbloshie.[64] Derived from Abrahamic religious traditions, the name harkens back to the cities destroyed in the Book of Genesis for their unrepentant sinfulness. The cities were destroyed by fire and brimstone, and since then the name has continued to be used to mark sites of perversion. The name sticks because of the urban perversions in Agbogbloshie, or as Quayson explains, "what it really signifies is the inexplicability of urban transformations that can produce such a slum right in the core of the capital city itself."[65] But the name also resonates due to the unending fire from recycling in the area, as Hugo's work repeatedly shows. For the workers in Hugo's photographs and others who toil in Agbogbloshie, hell is already loose on earth as they are surrounded by unending fire burning electronic gadgets and their bodies. In Christian and Islamic belief systems, the dominant religions in Ghana, the Sodomites were punished for their sins, which raises the question of the sins of laborers in Agbogbloshie, subject to unceasing fire. What sin have they committed? What is the offence for which they are suffering? Their sin seems to be the accident of birth in a geography marked by enduring legacies of slavery, colonialism, and postcolonial underdevelopment, all working together to stunt the achievement of a good life. If the infernos recorded in the religious books were brought about by individual and collective sins, the Agbogbloshie case appears fore-ordained. To rewrite the oft-quoted scriptural passage "before you were born I knew you" for our context, these are people marked by race and class before they were born.

The constant fire on display in Hugo's collection represents the risk of attachment that manifests in disease and death, lethal consequences outweighing the unguaranteed reward that the metal-gatherers receive for retrieving metals. My case for free labor in Agbogbloshie rests on the fact that these workers have no predetermined wage and only get rewarded afterward for the items they retrieve. The constant fires—resulting in exposure to carcinogens—produces an ecology of risk that outweighs whatever benefits these workers derive. Furthermore, the recompense is so little that many cannot afford to leave the area at the end of the day. One study reports that "most (96.6 percent) of the participants indicated that they slept near Agbogbloshie, 70.7 percent reported sleeping inside their work shed, and the mean (SD) number of years lived near Agbogbloshie was 6.0 (4.2). More than half (68.9 percent) of the respondents reported earning less than 20 Ghana cedis per day," which amounts to less than \$5.[66] Unable to afford shelter elsewhere, these gatherers work in Agbogbloshie by day and sleep there by night, thus having no respite from the harsh conditions. They are like those consigned to hell, a perpetual fire from which there is no break.

This is the place to revisit Marx's question: "where is the profit to come from, if no unpaid labour is performed?"[67] Many of Marx's conclusions have become obsolete in the contemporary economy, and critique of his work for its Eurocentrism and insufficient attention to race remains relevant.[68] Nevertheless, Marx's analysis of the free labor generated by surplus populations resonates here. In the first volume of *Capital*, Marx posits that "the great beauty of capitalist production consists in this—that it not only constantly reproduces the wage-worker as wage-worker, but produces always, in proportion to the accumulation of capital, a relative surplus-population of wage-workers."[69] Marx builds on this point—the indispensability of surplus population—in the *Grundisse* where he writes that "it requires a part of the population which is unemployed . . . i.e. a relative surplus population, in order to find the readily available population for the growth of surplus capital."[70]

Agbogbloshie provides an instance where "capital extracts value from a distance."[71] The workers captured in Hugo's collection may be tangential to the shiny worlds of Apple and Microsoft, but their labor subsidizes the cost of the capitalist who produces phones and computers cheaply because the cost of disposal is low or nonexistent. This little or non-existent cost also serves the planned obsolescence of technological gadgets: consumers do not have to worry about the cost of disposal and so can easily replace their devices, which encourages further production, and the cycle continues. An ideal scenario where electronic devices last longer and are recycled in an environmentally friendly manner will result in reduced demand and higher cost of disposal, both of which will diminish production and profit. Subsidizing the status quo, marked by the quick turnaround of gadgets disposed of easily, are those left out of the robust gains of capitalism: the paupers, as Marx describes them. Like the free laborers that Marx describes, the gatherer in Agbogbloshie toils in "conditions which are accidental for him, and indifferent to his organic presence. He is thus a virtual pauper."[72] It is significant that Marx uses the "colonies sent out in antiquity" to illustrate surplus population and free labor, suggesting the international and colonial dimensions of this exploitative practice.[73] Agbogbloshie contains the surplus population producing the free labor that generates value based on the calculus of disposability.

Achille Mbembe's theory of the superfluous may have been conceived with the South African mines in mind, but its overarching theme of the expendability of black life accords with conditions in Agbogbloshie.[74] I have considered metal-gathering and the recycling of electronic devices in Agbogbloshie as free labor because it is unpaid and is rife with risks that undermine future reward. Free labor is also apropos here because it is produced by a surplus, expendable population. There is no health insurance or life or injury insurance available to the people that Hugo photographed. Both indispensability and disposability—characteristics of Mbembe's superfluous laborers— are apprehensible in this context; this surplus population is easily replaceable with the battalion of the unemployed seeking food, clothing, and shelter. Their life, like their labor, is free.

One implication of the foregoing discussion of labor is the need to probe the extent to which the labor expended by the workers in Hugo's photographs or that of internet surfers (discussed by Terranova) is "free" or offered voluntarily. I do not intend to return us to slavery, but how many of these contemporary forms of labor are given willingly as the capitalist system refines ways of obtaining labor from workers with little or no compensation? Beyond Agbogbloshie, take the time spent on the internet in the Global North and those parts of the Global South with access. The voluntary nature of internet navigation is undermined by the constant pull of algorithms and codes. To this end, Frank Pasquale has described ours as a "black box society" where illusions of control mask the sway that technology has over us.[75] John Cheney-Lippold explains human disembodiment in the face of data imprints that feed and generate "our digital selves." Cheney-Lippold concludes that "as everything we do becomes datafied, everything we do becomes controllable."[76] These scholars are getting at what Antoinette Rouvroy terms "algorithmetic categorization"—which "simply ignores the embodied individuals it affects and has as its sole 'subject' a 'statistical body.'"[77] At stake in these studies is the loss of subjectivity in online environments as a result of "algorithmetic" permutations that dehumanize computer users, seeing them instead as data to be manipulated and controlled. In the face of the de-subjectivization that these scholars foreground, the idea that online free labor is freely given deserves reconsideration.

Moreover, the reorganization of work in the digital economy, to the detriment of workers and to the benefit of corporations and shareholders, has expanded free time that would have been channeled into productive labor with commensurate reward if more just and equitable systems existed.[78] Screen time has become an attractive means of expending free time. Furthermore, accessing preferred websites and pages such as YouTube channels is oftentimes contingent on watching advertisements and/or performing some online tasks, which calls into question the voluntary nature of such activities. The existing critique of free labor and its attendant exploitation is important, but that critical attention needs to be extended to labor performed in offline sites in Africa that are nevertheless crucial for the functioning of the internet. It is equally important to consider the degree to which what we call free labor is unfree.

Although I position the Agbogbloshie example alongside the exploitation of online laborers in the discussion of free labor, it should be clear that these are different processes: "We should be careful not to talk about free labor as if this was one distinctive category of labor." It is worth underscoring that "free labor comes in many forms that obey to different logics."[79] Some of it may be voluntarily given and actually enjoyed, but there are those forced into free labor by extenuating circumstances. An individual who browses the internet for play is remarkably different from the metal picker who is precluded from alternative modes of subsistence, even if both produce value in the digital economy. There is also the need to distinguish between workers in Agbogbloshie and internet users whose labor may be unwillingly given. Although both sets of laborers may appear indirectly coerced into producing value, the exposure of Agbogbloshie's metal-gatherers to extreme environmental and economic risks separates them from their counterparts in more protected places. Free labor is a global phenomenon, but the hierarchy of exploitation and exposure to ecological risks demands a careful segmentation of these laborers. In other words, the statistical or datafied body is radically different from the toxified body, which makes it imperative to consider the hierarchy of exploitation and toxic exposures for any serious scrutiny of free labor and the extent to which it is offered voluntarily or coerced.

The scale of unfreedoms demands that we pay attention to those workers forced by the absence of viable alternatives into labor conditions that destroy more than they improve their lives. Yochai Benkler teaches us that a "person whose life and relations are fully regimented by external forces is unfree," and it is that unfreedom that is reflected in the faces of the subjects of Hugo's photographs.[80] A performative masculine swagger may conceal the risks of their labor, but it is clear from the crouching, the sweat and vulnerability on their faces, and their overall demeanor, that these are people unhappy with their lot. Their facial expressions, in many cases, showcase anger and defiance at systems that have kept them down and deprived them of the autonomy to choose a risk-free or less risky way of earning a living. They may not be in chains like enslaved people, but we can read the smoke and fire encircling them throughout Hugo's collection as indicators of their unfreedom—as signs of their entrapment. The fact that their life station is predetermined before birth by their epidermis and by geography says much about their lack of choice.

In closing this examination of Hugo's work, I want to engage with *Permanent Error* as a constructed artifact despite its documentary appeal. John Berger's reminder that "every time we look at a photograph, we are aware, however slightly, of the photographer selecting that sight from an infinity of other possible sights" proves useful for remembering that selectivity and arrangement are features of Hugo's work.[81] Here is the appropriate place to comment on the choice of presenting the work in book form as opposed to the internet site that Monteiro adopts for his spectacular images. What is the value of presenting photographs in a physical book rather than in other forms, especially with the new tools afforded by new media? In her well-known work *On Photography*, Susan Sontag reflects on the value of encountering photographs in book form. According to her, the book guarantees "longevity, if not immortality."[82] The book form is also favored in *Regarding the Pain of Others*, where she contends that it allows for reflection, for staying longer with the image. In her words, "up to a point, the weight and seriousness of such photographs survive better in a book, where one can look privately, linger over the pictures, without talking."[83] When read in relation to the ongoing analysis of Hugo's work, this reflective and contemplative affordance is especially important for the culture of change that *Permanent Error* hopes to instigate. As opposed to film, where the viewer cedes control of the modalities of watching to the filmmaker and where the image stays onscreen for a defined brief duration, the viewer of *Permanent Error* retains considerable agency to determine the length of time they devote to each image and the sequence of viewing those images. In film, by contrast, not only the temporality but also the sequence is determined in advance.

The viewer of Monteiro's photography online has some flexibility, but then is susceptible to the distractions of the web, the lure of other tabs and windows, and of pop-ups and advertisements. In other words, the multitasking enabled by the online experience can hinder the contemplative viewing required by ethico-politico-ecological projects such as Hugo's. Moreover, the (illusion of) immediacy that the printed text offers is counteracted by the hypermediacy of digital representation. Media forms try "to achieve immediacy by ignoring or denying the presence of the medium and the act of mediation."[84] As a printed text in the documentary mode, *Permanent Error* depends on the quality of immediacy. The text's manipulation of the represented body put in proximity to that of the viewer is crucial for bridging distance just as the reality effect that the collection exudes with its documentary characteristics are meant to hide its constructedness, its role as representation.

Immediacy serves Hugo's ethico-politico-ecological project just as the textual material accompanying the photographs does. We should understand the textual framing of Hugo's photographs by experts as a strategy to avoid the danger of misreading, as a corroborating device, and as an effort to streamline the meaning of the work. In *Permanent Error*, the photographs reinforce the verbal text and vice versa. In his afterword, Puckett will not let us get away from "a place called away."[85] By providing a historical overview of the place, its functioning and the existing laws governing toxic waste disposal, Puckett produces a rich context for understanding the photographs. It is as if the creator of *Permanent Error* subscribes to Rosalind Krauss's idea that "a meaninglessness surrounds it [a photograph] which can only be filled in by the addition of text."[86] Yet there is a conscious effort that the photographs be appreciated on their own. Texts are omitted from the pages on which the images appear; not even page numbers are permitted alongside the images, and the rich framing text by Puckett is placed at the end of the book to be encountered after the viewing exercise.

Puckett's text would make for an excellent introduction considering its detailed statement of the problem and articulation of possible solutions; yet the project begins with a single-page foreword by Angelucci followed by a list of abbreviations from the United Nations' e-waste guide. These materials orient the viewer toward the photographs to come but they fall short of the historical and critical energies of Puckett's text. Puckett's text, appearing where it does, encourages viewing the images more than once, offering both a preliminary exercise and the possibility of other viewing(s) after gaining a deeper appreciation of the issues from the concluding afterword.

Permanent Error, in its title and content, demonstrates the lasting effect of toxicity, but it does not foreclose the possibility of transformation or change. Puckett lists what has been done and what is still needed to transform the electronic recycling process. It is productive to read "permanent error" not as a fait accompli but as a title that invites urgent action to arrest ecological annihilation. To further understand the title, we can turn to computing, where "permanent error" usually denotes the failure to transmit an email message to its potential receiver. The sender who receives such a message does not immediately abandon the email address, but rather troubleshoots, and when this fails contacts the email provider to escalate the issue. Hugo's work invites a similar problem-solving approach. While the photographs elucidate the problem, Puckett, at the end, provides a roadmap for change. His essay has done the troubleshooting for us, noting the progress made, and delineating what remains to be done.

The images that precede Puckett's words indicate that it is inadequate to reduce our electronic waste and stop transporting it to faraway places. To be sure, recycling, repair, and reuse are crucial components of sustainability. In addition to thwarting capitalism's throwaway culture and cultivating environmentally friendly practices for necessary waste (I discuss African examples in the epilogue), these activities constitute a source of income in places with limited employment possibilities. The innovative recycling practice in Ghana also broadens access to digital technologies in low-income societies.[87] Shutting down the recycling business in Agbogbloshie would therefore be a mistake. The responsibility of governments and nongovernmental organizations is to provide and scale recycling strategies that attend not only to the health but also the social and environmental well-being of workers. Alongside these steps, detoxifying the environment of Agbogbloshie and making it habitable for human and nonhuman beings are crucial.

Chapter Two

Poisonous Fruit: *The Big Banana*, Africa, and World-Making

The demand for an alternative imaginary in Hugo's project arises from a disaffection with the world as it is—a disaffection with rising inequality that breeds poverty, conflict, disease, and other aberrations of contemporary social life. Hugo's collection of photographs crystallizes one such problem in its illumination of the impacts of throwaway culture and planned obsolescence in Ghana. Drawing attention to the problem and including essays by Angelucci and Puckett that foreground possibilities for fixing the problem, Hugo's project participates in the process of world-making. This kind of world-making draws on but insists on transcending the confines of the nation-state. Puckett, in his essay, wants nation-states to ratify legislation banning the improper disposal of toxic waste and its export to developing countries of the world. This move is a recognition of the persistence of the nation-state in sociopolitical life. However, the essays and the photographs they frame equally speak to individuals and collectivities beyond the nation. Inviting contemplation of the consumption associated with our digital practices, Hugo's project expands our repertoire of recognition and identification beyond the frames of locality and nation. The plight of those in faraway places is brought closer to us by the close-up shots and other techniques on display in Hugo's work on toxicity. Hugo's world-making process evinces a vision of transnational solidarity, of which there are other examples. For another instance of a world-making project that goes further than Hugo's in articulating transnational social imaginaries, we can turn to Bieleu's film *The Big Banana*.

Besides its development of the post-national formation decipherable in Hugo's project, *The Big Banana* makes manifest the implications of toxicity that remain latent in Hugo's still photographs. *The Big Banana* is a documentary and as such positions itself as a moving image allied with history.[88] The history the film explores is of an agricultural economy in the Moungo region of Cameroon. This region, according to the film's voice-over, has been exporting bananas and other fruit to Europe since at least the sixteenth century, revealing its imbrication in global processes for a long time. However, the images of the community in the film convey suffering. Moungo's case is no different from other parts of the developing world, where small businesses have been dethroned by mega corporations. Where in the recent past small-scale farmers leased and rented land from the government for commercial agriculture and pooled resources to export their yield, the multinational corporation the Société des Plantations du Haut Penja (PHP) has taken control of agribusiness in Moungo in the film's present. Taking advantage of economies of scale, its European provenance, as well as the bribery of public officials and coercion, PHP displaced local farmers, entrenched poverty, and poisoned the ecosystem, all while maximizing profits. Because it thematizes "cross-border collaboration and concerns with imbalances and inequalities of power in global society," *The Big Banana* falls within the ambit of "transnational ecocinema."[89] This film, utilizing a mix of expository and reflexive styles of documentary filmmaking, indicts PHP for its corrupt and endangering practices while not sparing the corrupt politicians and elites who are in the pay of the company. In the process, the people who work for and have worked for PHP as well as residents of the community dissect the impacts of the agricultural plantation serving consumers in Europe and America.

In a recent essay, Rachel Gabara provides an overview of the documentary film genre in Africa that is relevant for contextualizing *The Big Banana*:

> French colonial documentary begins with the newsreels of the earliest years of the 20th century and continues with the colonial adventure films of the 1920s and 1930s. The 1940s saw the rise of French colonial ethnographic documentary and then, in the 1960s and 70s, a postcolonial ethnographic response from the first generation of independent African filmmakers. In the early 1990s, a new generation of postcolonial African filmmakers began to experiment with documentary style and form, rejecting ethnography in favor of reflexive nonfiction film. In a range of modes, African documentary filmmakers have fought back against a colonial filmic tradition, rejecting the images that had been created of them and their continent and transforming a genre that had as its goal the capture of Africa on film.[90]

The Big Banana would fall under the latest category, where experimentation with form and anti-colonial sensibility are crucial. The operations of PHP in Moungo instantiate the fact that "the afterimage of the colonial episteme lives on, reasserting itself in forms of neocolonialism every bit as reprehensible as their odious forebears."[91] As is to be expected, PHP is not given the last word in Bieleu's film, in which the people mount a rigorous challenge to the unconscionable practices of the company. Bieleu's work in *The Big Banana* extends his investment in the use of the camera for documenting and critiquing social ills. Born in Paris, he grew up in Cameroon before studying film at London Metropolitan University. His other social documentaries include *What Hope for the African Youth*, which examines the migration of African youth toward European countries, and *Herakles Debacle*, on the social and ecological impacts of a palm-oil plantation in Cameroon.[92]

Scholars working on the documentary genre in Africa and elsewhere have pushed back against the classical distinction between the "real" documentary genre and fiction film considered as imagined and constructed. It is now commonplace to agree with the view that documentary filmmaking is also an artistic practice hinged on constructedness, even when the filmmaker attempts to conceal their artifice.[93] The pioneering documentarist John Grierson captures the creative and constructive work of the documentary filmmaker when he writes that "you photograph the natural life, but you also, by your juxtaposition of detail, create an interpretation of it."[94] Focusing on the reflexive character of contemporary African documentary films, critics have drawn attention to the "hand" of the filmmaker and to the filmmaker's role in the representation of historical reality in documentaries.[95] To acknowledge this genre's constructedness is not to collapse its difference from fiction films. The limited control that the documentary filmmaker has in the process of achieving "fidelity" to a historical reference is an area of departure from fiction film where the filmmaker has a broader leeway to produce his/her images.[96]

What can be called the hand of the filmmaker appears in the animated prologue to Bieleu's *The Big Banana*. The animation opens on an agricultural landscape followed by rapid scenes of workers on the plantation, of a truck carrying the produce to the port, and of cranes and shipping containers, suggesting shipment overseas. The final image of the animated sequence is of bananas in a grocery store abroad. These opening scenes move at a fast pace, with fast drumming that foregrounds the African context of the film. It is as if the filmmaker wants to quickly move through this sequence in order to get us to the "real" thing. The fast pace can also mirror the pace of the labor involved, of how PHP's employees must work in order to meet the demands of their exacting jobs. If we can read the documentary as a filmic essay with an argument, then the animated sequence at the film's beginning serves as its thesis statement. Here the filmmaker brings together the issues animating the film: labor; the network or assemblage that makes food production, distribution, and consumption possible; and the theme of the outward flow of resources from Africa.

The sense of animation as summation of the film's argument is buttressed in the only other animated scene, which appears after the film's first sequence. Whereas the animated prologue moves quickly, this single moving image renders the slow movement of a worker bent from carrying a single banana fruit as he moves from the right side of the screen to the left, from the inside to the outside. Here slowness serves to foreground arduous labor. This figure seems exhausted from carrying the banana in an image that suggests things are more difficult for people in the Moungo region than they appear. The second animated sequence also reinforces the first by depicting an outward movement of the bananas, suggesting that the people lose more than they benefit from the current network order. Taken together, the animated scenes capture the filmmaker's artistic intent even as they introduce the major issues addressed by the film. I would also argue that the animated sequences serve to reinforce the realness of the documentary proper. Clearly differentiated from the part dealing with the inhabitants of Moungo and their experiences with PHP and the government, the artificiality of the animation underscores the closeness of the rest of the film to the historical real. If documentaries are often judged by their success in depicting their historical referents, then we can say that this animated series works to burnish *The Big Banana*'s credentials as a documentary. By highlighting its own artificiality and constructedness, the use of animation draws in the viewer to appreciate the verisimilitude of the film proper.

The Big Banana makes use of evidentiary editing that is supplemented by the voice-over. To expose PHP's activities, the film focuses on interviews with current and former workers, as well as other residents of the affected communities, politicians, and experts on toxicity. With these interviews, it is as if the filmmaker invites us to imagine his retreat from the scene. Foregrounding the victims as experts, the film gives first-person accounts of their experiences. One former worker, fired after ten years of employment, laments the forged signature on his termination documents and the fact that he was shortchanged in the payment of his severance package. While he is interviewed alone the first time, his wife appears later to corroborate his claims and to articulate the injustice of the company's actions and the enduring impacts on their family. Close-up shots, accompanied by a slow, somber soundtrack, are used to foreground the pain this family is going through. As they sit outside their house for the interview, the camera moves to show us the background. Like most houses shown in the wide shots used to capture the landscape, this is a ramshackle house, suggesting that this man has achieved little after spending ten years with the company.

It is significant that the camera stays mostly outdoors. When the camera follows the retrenched man inside, the film quickly cuts to another scene. This approach suggests that there is nothing to see within the house as this family earns less than they need to make a living. The mise-en-scène is bare, with the camera returning to the same agricultural landscape and shanty houses. This inclination to stay outside where natural light can be used may also be a statement on the infrastructural state of the community, where electricity is hardly available. Early in the film, the voice-over informs the viewer that the average worker earns $52 a month, which is less than the $61 average recommended by the Cameroonian state and much less than the over $200 needed to meet the cost of living. Yet this region is a major exporter of $245 million of bananas, an announcement that is followed by a scene depicting the shanty houses of the community residents. This image of destitution is further contrasted with the well-manicured lawn of the managers' quarters. All these demonstrate the disconnect between the company's upper echelons and the people who work for them, and between the expended labor of the people and the value attached to it by the company.

The Big Banana uses medium and long shots to position people in relation to their environment. For those interviewed outside their houses, such shots allow the viewer to appreciate their poverty, and in cases where the camera turns to the landscape, it is to foreground the labor of cultivating the bananas. Such scenes often show workers cutting or carrying bananas. In other cases, it is to announce a shared vulnerability in the face of toxicity. In one aerial shot, an airplane sprays the bananas with chemicals to eliminate pests and ultimately to keep the bananas in a shape that meets export requirements. The voice-over and a PHP employee notify viewers that workers do not receive notice of the crop-dusting and so get sprayed along with the crops. The positioning of the human and the environment in long and medium shots intertwines their toxified bodies.

While Hugo's still images can only gesture to toxicity with their fire motif and textual accompaniment, Bieleu's moving images foreground the aftermath of exposure to toxic chemicals. In the film, toxicity is everywhere: aerial crop-dusting conveys that air carries the chemicals to food and water sources. The viewer may still be processing this thought when the film cuts to scenes of witnesses testifying to indiscriminate spraying of chemicals affecting places outside the plantations. Pesticide-infused water used for washing the bananas is disposed of improperly, easing its entry into the community's water sources. Money may be scarce in this region, but toxicity abounds, as it does in the town of Arlit, discussed in the next chapter. Asked about the impact of toxic waste, the chief of one village participates in the production of doubt. Asked whether agrochemicals used by PHP cause diseases, Chief Daniel Nsonga of Mpoula village equivocates: "maybe they cause disease, maybe they don't." But Bieleu does not let this chief, who is clearly on the side of the government, have the last word.

He produces evidence of toxicity by zooming in on health hazards in the region. A doctor who worked at PHP's hospital explains the medical risks to the workers, and the film presents one such worker losing his sight to the ravages of the chemical sprayed on the plantations. The close view of the man's poor sight is meant to move the viewer. As he explains his condition, the camera zooms in and lingers on his deformed right eye. Positioning his head to foreground that eye, the close-up shot invites the viewer to touch the "skin of the film."[97] This inclination to touch follows from the premise that "ethical or other environmental arguments will only have force if we physically feel them."[98] Bieleu's focus on the man's eye, at the risk of voyeurism, is meant to provoke a response from the audience, to move them to touch the film's skin, the screen, and to reach for the skin of the film's subject. The camera's attentiveness to the diseased eye can also be an invitation to the viewer to clear their eyes, to see beyond the confines of their comfort and to probe the provenance of their food. Voice-over and interviews are calibrated to buttress this filmic image, telling the viewer that four out of every five workers are afflicted by eye problems. Documentaries do not just inform but they attempt to elicit action. In this particular case, statistical, medical, and visual evidence combine with the emotional manipulation wrought by the close-up shot of the eye and film's sound to move the viewer.

Before continuing, it may be necessary to ponder who the audience of this film is. A film distributed by New York-based ArtMattan is meant to circulate in Western circles, especially in educational settings and other spaces interested in the affairs of Africa and the diaspora. I can access the film courtesy of my institution's subscription to the Kanopy streaming site. It is also available on Amazon and other streaming platforms. This distribution structure makes sense for *The Big Banana*, which directly addresses a Western audience in Europe and America. Inaccessible in Cameroon, where it is banned for criticizing the government-company alliance, the digital networked sphere makes the film available to viewers across the world. Put differently, the film's mode of address sculpts its network form in anticipation of the content.

Starting with the animated sequence, the film orients the viewer to an away—the bananas' destination. The shipping containers in the film's prologue and later, as the film describes the process of exporting the banana, are symbolic of its embeddedness in a network. Those shipping containers make possible the comingling of Africa and Euro-America in the film. As the film progresses, however, its audience becomes clearer. In an early scene showing the bananas in a grocery store somewhere in Europe, the camera zooms in on the fruit, the phallic object of desire in Bieleu's film. Its positioning as the object is intensified with the intrusion of a hand trying to pick up the banana. Significantly the camera focuses on this hand and the banana, leaving out the body to which the hand is affixed. In this moment the anonymous hand introduces the audience of the film, which is anyone who relies on places like Cameroon for their bananas and other food produce. In this scene, the Western consumer, "the citizen food consumer," touches hands with the Cameroonian worker(s) who prepared the banana for export.[99] In this meeting of hands that the film stages, we can detect a reminder that what we eat "passes through a set of human practices and material processes that do the translating from food production to food consumption."[100]

Subsequently the camera cuts to actual residents of Europe, to the Asian importer who admits that the banana business is a very profitable one, and to the group of consumers who respond to PHP's activities in Moungo. Most of the European interviewees call the impoverishment and endangerment of the Africans "disgusting," while one tellingly likens the process to slavery. The outward flow of resources involving PHP is reminiscent of the flow of human capital from Africa during the slave trade. Considering the coevalness of the slave trade and banana exports—the latter began in this region in the sixteenth century—the comparison resonates.

For viewers yet to be moved by the film's "deliverance of others" through logical evidence and appeal to the senses, identification with familiar film subjects provides an alternative for persuasion.[101] When foreign consumers describe PHP's activities as disgusting and liken them to slavery, they are interpellating foreign viewers like themselves to reevaluate their food politics. The film's aim of reaching beyond territorial and cultural boundaries relies not only on portraying the suffering of those who produce the food imported to Euro-America, but also on enlisting people who live in Europe and America to join their voices in persuading others to condemn PHP's activities and bring about a difference.

As the camera shuttles between its African, European, and American scenes, the film makes a case for what Arjun Appadurai calls "nonterritorial principles of solidarity."[102] This post-national formation is concretized in the latter part of the film with the partnership between Partners for Just Trade and RELUFA, representing agricultural cooperatives comprised of small farmers in Moungo. If this film is about the antics of global agribusiness, why focus at all on the activities of small farmers? In a society where the principles of checks and balances do not work, where most elected representatives serve on the board of PHP, and where the national government is headed by an autocrat who has been in power since the 1980s, bringing these farmers into the film's focus is a process of empowerment, letting them tell their stories where their representatives have failed. The presence of RELUFA in the film manifests an alternative mode of transnational relationship and cooperation.

Bieleu's film concretizes the failures of the nation-state as well as the winners and losers in the current global system. The winners, in the film's telling, include PHP, the local elite, and government officials. To move the farmers and residents of Moungo from losers to empowered subjects would require active collaboration along transnational lines. The subjects interviewed in *The Big Banana* do not advocate for PHP's departure from their community but advise that it change its ways. Despite their awful experiences, they are not opting for isolationism. The film's "farm worker futurism" or "farm worker visions" call for a reformed system of being in the world alongside the company, the government, and the consumers of their produce.[103] *The Big Banana* is "about the limits of interconnection, about the areas where capital cannot go, and about the specificity of the structures necessary to make connections work."[104] The imbalance of existing connections calls for the "work of reconnection."[105] *The Big Banana* undertakes that work of reconnection, and its specification for globalization's reformation is centered on the consumer. The energy of Bieleu's film is not expended on the trite demand for changes in governmental behavior in Cameroon. Such changes would be a welcome development, but the film instead channels its power of persuasion toward individuals as consumers. Corporations take notice of drops in their market share, and consumers have the power to make this happen. Hence the official of Partners for Just Trade, based in St. Louis, Missouri, who addresses the camera asserts that "consumers have so much power." This, after all, may be the film's most important message and the point to which it builds.

Ethics are at the heart of documentary filmmaking and *The Big Banana* is no exception, as it raises the question of the viewer's ethics toward the film's subjects. Michael Renov may as well be speaking of Bieleu's film when he writes of "an investment in otherness, in the necessity of responsibility and of the ethical encounter, directing our consideration to moral concerns."[106] Partners for Just Trade buys their produce from RELUFA and other organizations that favor the welfare of their employees, which means that the cost of production is higher when compared with prices offered by anti-worker

Chapter Two

behemoths such as PHP. This higher cost creates a problem for pricing, a problem acknowledged when the film demands that the viewer make a choice between buying a cheaper product that impoverishes the worker or one sourced from pro-labor and environmentally friendly sources that costs slightly more. To enable the consumer, its audience, to reach a decision, the film withholds the presentation of choices until it has clarified the social, environmental, physical, and psychological costs of companies like PHP.

One achievement of Bieleu's network form is to reveal the cost of paying the cheaper price or ignoring where one's fruit comes from. Multinational corporations such as PHP want to keep the production process away from their consumers in the same way that phone and computer companies prefer to be less transparent about the sourcing of their metals or the disposal of their waste. Just as Hugo's work connects consumers to an e-waste site and its impact on the ecosystem, Bieleu's film argument is that the cost of ignoring the source of one's food or preferring to buy the cheaper option is being borne by the poor, low-waged, poisoned worker in far-flung places such as Cameroon. The archaeology of spatial network forms in this chapter unearths the invisible hands taken for granted or elided. These would include those of the pickers who plow through digital waste in places like Agbogbloshie and the workers in Cameroon who work on the plantations on which the bananas we consume are grown.

Bieleu's commitment to foreground these male workers, however, renders almost invisible the women in this environment. *The Big Banana* instantiates Bill Nichols's claim that as in fiction film, the documentary "camera's gaze can still be treated as gendered and fully implicated in questions of desire as well as control."[107] Women appear mostly in the European spaces of the film, which suggests that they have more voice here than in the African context. Yet closer scrutiny of their appearance in these settings reveals their connection to domesticity. They function here mostly as grocery shoppers except for the workers at Partners for Just Trade, who are featured as career women. The scenario is worse in the Cameroonian setting, where the women are largely absent. When they do appear, they are subordinate to their husbands, as in the sequence depicting the former employee of PHP terminated after ten years of service with little compensation. He appears by himself initially, but when his wife is to be interviewed he is sitting beside her, as if controlling her script. It could be argued that the documentary's primary task is to represent things as they are and thus that the critique here is of the patriarchal structure of this region of Cameroon and not something of the camera's making.

In fact, we can concede the patriarchal structure of this society but still demand that the camera subvert such a structure. This would mean implicating a culture that foregrounds men, granting them the most fertile land while relegating the women to small lots allocated to gardening. There is confirmation in *The Big Banana* that space is "gendered through and through" and the viewer can also decipher "the limitation of women's mobility, in terms both of identity and space."[108] The vast land on which men work mirrors the freedom they enjoy, while the smaller, less fertile plots closer to home allotted to women are indicative of their limited opportunities and circumscription in the film.

There is a moment where Bieleu's film could have foregrounded female subjectivity, and it involves the pineapple farmer whose land was forcibly taken by PHP and whose wife allegedly left him following his economic woes. From his perspective we learn that his wife left, leaving behind his children. This is an important scene, one in which the film foregrounds the economic and psychological impact of dispossession. This family, in this farmer's telling, is torn apart by PHP. The telling of this story favors the man's account. We see him at close range but also in relation to the land. Nowhere is the view of his wife or children represented, and we do not know if the filmmaker tried to reach them. Representing such voices would have created a more balanced account of this story of dispossession while also broadening the diversity of perspectives to which the viewer is exposed. In the end, *The Big Banana* hardly departs from the "patriarchal visual iconography of female figures in film" that restricts women to the domestic sphere.[109] The representation of the African woman in *The Big Banana* is characterized by the "construction of her inactive silence."[110] Women are physically present in the film, but we hardly hear their perspective or see them represented in a complex way. Take, for instance, the woman mentioned by her husband in absentia as he laments his economic and emotional losses; she is "invoked only to be spoken of as absent, recalled as a reminder of her dispossession, and not permitted her version of her story."[111] Whereas the women in the Euro-American spaces are seen and heard as citizens, shoppers, and professionals, their African counterparts are barely seen and hardly heard except in their roles as wives.

The film's silencing of women notwithstanding, Bieleu's work is articulate in its vision of ethical interconnection for world remaking, represented in the fair-trade model that RELUFA and its American collaborator offer. In an essay about food and global justice, Mark Budolfson asks, "what is it best to do about the disturbingly large harm footprint that is associated with our

Chapter Two

food?"[112] Bieleu's film provides one possible answer when it challenges consumers to concern themselves with the provenance of their food and to consider produce from less problematic sources even if it costs more. As Clark Wolf reminds us, "eating is a political and moral action as well," and as such, "people can make purchasing and lifestyle choices that expressly and intentionally reflect underlying values."[113] *The Big Banana* stresses the ecological footprint of banana plantations in Cameroon to foreground the imperatives of careful deliberation in relation to the political and moral action, lifestyle choices, and underlying values that Wolf analyzes. Where Hugo's photographs problematize the practice of electronic recycling in Ghana, *The Big Banana* visualizes the social and ecological costs of banana production with a view to affecting the Western consumer.

The film's reliance on ethics linked to the consumer raises questions of access: access to the film and to pricier food options. Western consumers are not monolithic; they are differentiated by class among other vectors of difference. Class differences would determine those able to access *The Big Banana* via subscription streaming services such as Amazon or attend resourced institutions with library access to the film. There is also the cost implication of purchasing ethically produced food that responds to the demand for healthy eating as well. The viewer's aspiration to shop at whole food stores will not materialize if they cannot afford the premium prices. Put differently, inequality among Western consumers poses access barriers to the film and to the practice of its individualist consumer ethics. Finally, it must be said that green consumption, however useful, repeats the capitalist ideological orientation that precipitated the environmental crisis in the first place. The individual response to environmental degradation, which green consumption supports, lacks the holistic approach demanded by planetary problems.

Conclusion: From Cyber Network to Food Network

This chapter started with digital technologies that have enabled transformations in communications and interconnections. The cell phone and computer are readily available and accessible instruments of communication. They are also tools that have been used to draw attention to environmental problems. Yet they are complicit in the problems they render visible. Cell phones, computers, and other media have bridged the gaps between cultures, people, and spaces. Even as they expose environmental problems, their making and disposal are tangled in toxic processes. Put differently, whether we consider the mining of the metals that are used in making our technologies in Africa, or the processes of making them in Asia, or their disposal in places like Agbogbloshie, what emerges is a sense of "toxic interpenetration."[114] This chapter demands a recalibration of understandings of digital labor to capture the offline work facilitating the smooth operations of digital processes and put pressure on current conceptualizations of free labor, inviting a reconsideration of its scope and the extent to which such labor is expended willingly.

As the analysis of Hugo's photographs reveals, the process of extracting valuable metal precipitates a movement of toxic material to bodies of human and nonhuman animals as well as to the atmosphere and water, from whence the chemical compounds can be carried further. A similar process plays out in the Cameroon of Bieleu's *The Big Banana*, this time with chemicals used on agricultural plantations. If the impact of toxicity stays at the level of potential in Hugo's project, it is actualized in Bieleu's, where the detrimental aftermath of agrochemical use is inscribed on the body. Hugo's and Bieleu's projects demonstrate the lopsidedness of current networks of global interconnection and initiate the process of remaking them to serve planetary ends.

Images such as Hugo's and Bieleu's are useful for activating optical consciousness, but they also contain blind spots, including the limited visibility of women. I want to conclude with a brief excursus into Julia Dahr's climate change film *Thank You for the Rain*, a film that visualizes spatial networks and foregrounds female labor at the same time. A collaborative project between a male Kenyan farmer in the district of Mutumo and a female Norwegian filmmaker, this film announces its network form early on. Julia asks to film Kisilu as he goes about his farming business and his activist work encouraging members of his community to plant trees; Kisilu agrees on the condition that he be given his own camera as well. This move foregrounds a self-fashioning intent. He wants to tell his story as he deems fit, and the handheld camera he uses throughout the film helps to demonstrate his subjectivity. In *Thank You for the Rain*, Kisilu's image-making is outside Julia's control, and when he returns the camera it is filled "with images and sounds inscribed with a trace of themselves, and of their mode of being in the world."[115] Julia's control and power—due to her race and class—are undermined by Kisilu's control of the camera and the telling of his story and that of his community.

Through his request, Kisilu is also demanding the reconfiguration of the control of the mode of production. Refusing to cede control of his story to Julia and rejecting dependence on her to tell his story, Kisilu makes possible

Chapter Two

a network form at the production level. This collaborative effort presents an alternative figuration of the world order. When he first appears in front of the camera with his family, Kisilu asks, "Why can't we be seen?" On the surface, this question is leveled at the camera's ability to see them, but it can be read at a deeper level too. The question has implications for the intersection of media and race as in instances where certain camera lenses have failed to properly capture darker skin. In the context of the film's involvement in the politics of climate change and carbon reduction, this earlier question takes on further salience by the film's end when the United Nations Conference on Climate Change (COP 21) has failed to achieve the expected level of reduction in carbon emissions. Kisilu himself is a participant at the conference and speaks on panels from the perspective of farmers in African arid environments. In the film, drought has affected their output so much that many men have abandoned farming for the city to seek other forms of employment. For Kisilu and others who stay behind, when the rain comes, it comes with ferocious winds that blow off their roofs, compounding their problems.

Thank You for the Rain depicts poor farmers as the most impacted by climate change, even when they contribute little to the problem. Kisilu can also accept the fact that he is doing his best to sensitize his people to the importance of planting trees against the looming ecological threat. Like his late compatriot Wangari Maathai, who was discussed in chapter 1, Kisilu's campaign is initially met with resistance, but in a later sequence, after Julia receives the video from his camera, we learn that his tree-planting campaign has taken off with several groups working with him on the project. These poor farmers are negatively affected by climate change and want to be part of the solution. Kisilu attends the Paris conference with anticipation of a favorable outcome. He is exuberant when the then US president Barack Obama makes a case for reaching an agreement, and looks downcast as the then presidential candidate Donald Trump criticizes Obama for considering global warming as the United States' biggest challenge. Ultimately a deal is reached, but the Paris Agreement is disappointing for activists who argue that the emission reduction rate is significantly low in comparison to the level needed to slow the ravages of climate change. Kisilu's experience in Paris is not altogether different from Naomi Klein's at the UN climate summit in Copenhagen in 2009, where world leaders failed to reach a significant deal. Her realization then "that no one was coming to save us" is useful for apprehending Kisilu's frustration at the end of the Paris meeting.[116]

When Kisilu asks "Why can't we be seen?" early in the film, we can take it that he is critiquing those leaders ensconced in Paris and other foreign capitals. As the film shuttles between Oslo and the farming community in Kenya, and between this community and Paris, the distinction is clear. Mud houses at one end and skyscrapers at the other. The European settings qualify as examples of Castell's "space of flows," which fosters the creation and cultivation of elite networks and is timeless; the "space of place," on the other hand, would be represented by Kisilu's community, shut off from the main circuits of wealth and privilege.[117] Kisilu's lament at the film's beginning, "Why can't we be seen?," is a plea for recognition and the acceptance of the responsibility to address carbon emissions in the interest of those whose livelihood is already directly threatened.

If the filmmaker's hand is less visible in *The Big Banana*, Julia and Kisilu are visible participants in their work, and if a robust female subjectivity is missing in the former, the latter foregrounds that perspective. Julia is seen in the film as she cooks with Kisilu's family and as she arrives in the village from Oslo. We also see her in Oslo and Paris, and through her voice-overs we get a sense of the film's events and her impressions of Kisilu's work. Kisilu and his wife, Christina, are presented as amiable partners despite their economic woes. But she is not always framed alongside him. We see her alone, with her children, and with other women, such as when she jokes that the wind has humiliated her by exposing her undergarments. Injecting humor about her undergarments into a moment of stress helps to lighten the mood of the film following the removal of their roof by the wind. As in the Central African art context that Z. S. Strother observes, humor functions in Christina's case as "an existential posture of defiance in the face of suffering."[118] The added humor also exposes another side of her personality, one that is not directly tied to her identity as Kisilu's wife. As Kisilu's tree-planting campaign takes off and results in his absence from his role at home and on the farm, the camera does not neglect to include Christina's perspective. In one poignant scene shot in close-up and wide shots, Christina declares herself the "loser" in her husband's success. She is proud of his achievements; but alone and surrounded by the farm presented to us in wide shots that amplify the magnitude of the work to be completed, she laments the difficulties that Kisilu's absence poses for the family. *Thank You for the Rain*'s portrayal of the female voice does not stop with Christina, as we see other women in meetings with Kisilu.

To be sure, networks facilitate the collaboration between Kisilu and Julia, but then Kisilu and other residents of African communities are also victims of the vicissitudes of global interconnections. Network forms breed toxicity from electronic waste and from the operations of a banana plantation in

Cameroon. I turn in the next chapter to uranium and oil. We derive energy from oil, a commodity that crisscrosses the world through undersea and oversea networks and that is crucial to the functioning of the global networked economy: "oil moved by pipeline rather than rail, was light enough to carry across oceans, followed more flexible networks, and created a great separation between the places where energy was produced and those where it was used."[119] Oil's transnational and transoceanic portability, its slipperiness and ability to bridge and widen the gulf between the sites of its drilling and the privileged environments of its use render it an example of a network form. Oil's network credentials are burnished by the fact that its exploration spews toxic waste that travels across spaces and between human and nonhuman bodies in a similar manner to the metal recycling and banana plantation processes discussed in this chapter. Chapter 3 examines the impact of oil and uranium production in the Niger Delta, Nigeria, and Arlit, Niger, respectively, with an eye toward the trauma caused by energy extraction.

ecologies of oil and uranium

extractive energy and the trauma of the future

This chapter concentrates on the traumas associated with oil extraction and uranium mining in Africa. Heeding Michael Rothberg's call for trauma studies that attend to "the linked examples of globalized industrial pollution and human-induced climate change," I examine here the traumas resulting from resource extraction in the Niger Delta region of Nigeria (oil) and Arlit, a town in Niger (uranium).[1] While trauma studies tend to foreground the past and present, I reorient the temporality of postcolonial trauma toward the future, toward the suffering that is yet to come. Reading Michael Watts and Ed Kashi's *Curse of the Black Gold* alongside Idrissou Mora-Kpai's film *Arlit* for this chapter, I consider the link among energy drilling, the traumas induced by atmospheric and social climate change, and migration.[2] While *Curse of the Black Gold* allows me to establish the connection between oil extraction and trauma in the early part of the chapter, I interrogate the link among uranium mining, climate change, and migration in the last two sections, where *Arlit* comes into central focus. Focusing on the considerable tax of uranium and oil (resource media) on the ecosystem (elemental media), as depicted in film and a book composed of poetry, essays, and photographs (representational media), while also attending to the footprint of these media arts, this chapter underscores my encompassing sense of ecomedia. In so doing, it discloses the considerable infrastructural cost of our "mineral rites" in Africa.[3]

The Niger Delta, known as a site of contestation for resource control, is a prime example of an "extraction zone" marred by degradation from oil exploration.[4] As in the Venezuelan context that Fernando Coronil considers, "control over oil money enabled . . . [the Nigerian state] to transform itself as it expanded the range of its rule." Yet due to its kleptomaniac greed and scandalous ineptitude, the Nigerian state failed to become a responsible "mediator between the nation and the foreign oil companies" or to deliver the gains of modernity that would earn it the status of "the magical state."[5] Describing the situation in the Niger Delta, the activist and writer Nnimmo Bassey contends that "the scramble for the wealth does produce the pillaging of the public sector by private interest."[6] The region is "exemplary of frontier capitalism with speculative, spectacularized, and violent forms of enclosure, dispossession, and profit-taking."[7]

Exploitation is the currency of the Niger Delta, and it predates the oil economy. The exploitation of the region started not with the discovery of oil but with slavery in the fifteenth century and the oil-palm business that replaced it in the nineteenth century.[8] This account returns us to the fifteenth century, a period of global expansion, of the "discovery" of the New World and other parts of the globe and the tremendous loss that followed. The point is that the story of the Niger Delta has been of the "theft of the body," one that from the beginning denied the humanity of people, one that ultimately resulted in millions of bodies taken forcefully, separated from kin at home, and for those who arrived in the New World, further separated from newly reconstituted family and friends.[9] Add to the foregoing forms of violence physical flagellation, and it makes sense that a considerable amount of scholarship is devoted to the traumatic effects of slavery.[10]

In Cathy Caruth's influential definition, "trauma describes an overwhelming experience of sudden or catastrophic events in which the response to the event occurs in the often delayed, uncontrolled repetitive appearance of hallucinations and other intrusive phenomena."[11] Caruth's definition privileges individual psychological manifestations of trauma and links the phenomenon to a catastrophic event. A singular traumatic stressor and a psychological focus also underline Dori Laub's claim that "massive trauma precludes its registration; the observing and recording mechanisms of the human mind are temporarily knocked out, malfunction."[12] These pioneering contributions to humanistic conceptualizations of trauma have been critiqued for a restricted psychic orientation tied to a Western understanding of the self and suffering, and the emphasis they place on catastrophic events such as the Holocaust.[13]

Postcolonial scholars have especially objected to the undue focus on the individual and on a catastrophic event when articulating trauma. Stef Craps, for instance, rejects the "traditional event-based model of trauma, according to which trauma results from a single, extraordinary, catastrophic event" for "a model of trauma which . . . can account for and respond to collective, ongoing, everyday forms of traumatizing violence."[14] As he reminds us, "current trauma discourse has difficulty recognizing that it is not just singular and extraordinary events but also 'normal,' everyday humiliations and abuses that can act as traumatic stressors."[15] For Craps, this decolonized view of trauma is crucial for apprehending "traumas of non-Western or minority populations for their own sake."[16] Postcolonial trauma encompasses "individual trauma—which may include physical injury (including the experience of rape), the experience of living through instances of displacement, conflict, violence, and environmental disaster, and the psychic trauma that often result from one or more of the foregoing—and the collective trauma of a given postcolonial region at a specific historical moment."[17] Trauma, in this framing, is psychic and physical, and it is anchored in a collective. Even when trauma is apprehended in individual terms, it is often done in relation to the collective or community.[18]

Postcolonial trauma broadens the parameters of trauma theory so that it speaks to the multiplicities of violence, suffering, and abuse that ensue from various forms of colonialism: slavery, formal colonialism proper, and the neocolonial manifestations of subjugation. For the reader wondering why trauma is the privileged framework for this chapter, it is so because Watts and Kashi's rendition of the Niger Delta as well as the depiction of Arlit in Mora-Kpai's film situate them as sites of multigenerational violence inflicted on people and the nonhuman—land, water, animals, and so forth—by oil and uranium mining operations in West Africa. The violence inflicted on communities in the Niger Delta and Arlit have resulted in environmental degradation, loss of human and nonhuman lives, displacement, among other characteristics of postcolonial trauma mentioned earlier. What makes *Curse of the Black Gold* particularly insightful for my analysis is that it emphasizes the multiplicities of traumatic stressors by demonstrating the link between oil exploration and previous forms of traumatic violence, such as slavery and

Chapter Three

colonialism, while orienting us to ongoing wounding from petro-violence and attuning us to the aftermath that is to come.

Curse of the Black Gold: Five-Hundred Years of Trauma in the Niger Delta

A collaboration between an eminent Africanist and professor emeritus of geography at the University of California Berkeley and an award-winning photographer and filmmaker whose work spans diverse topics such as the protestant community in Northern Ireland, the lives of Jewish settlers in the West Bank, the plight of Syrian refugees, and the Iraq War, Watts and Kashi's work sculpts the "'timeless' duration, relentless repetition, and narrative splitting off associated with trauma."[19] One fruitful place to commence this investigation of *Curse of the Black Gold* is its fragmentary form, which attests to the complexities of articulating trauma. Composed of essays, photographs, and fiction, but also of poetry, interviews, and a letter, this work challenges generic boundaries. To an extent it can be described as a photographic essay, but what do we do with the fiction and poetry that it includes? The photographs and essays appear as documentary material, but isn't this will-to-nonfiction thwarted by the obviously constructed poetry? Disparate genres collected in the book announce a search for an appropriate form to carry the weight of the Delta experience. The disparate items in the collection attest to the plurality of factors engendering trauma in the Delta. In short, Watts and Kashi's work bears the mark of trauma at the level of form.

In *Picture Theory*, W. J. T. Mitchell states that the text of the photo-essay, "like the photograph . . . admits its inability to appropriate everything that was there to be taken and tries to let the photographs speak for themselves or 'look back' at the viewer."[20] Mitchell adds that "it is at such moments of inadequacy, perhaps, that a mixed, hybrid discourse like that of the photographic essay emerges as a historical necessity."[21] I take from Mitchell's discussion "inability" and "inadequacy" in order to register the enormity of oil violence in the present context. To return to the primary text here, the incorporation of multiple genres represents the inadequacy of each form to capture the magnitude of the violence brought about by oil in the Niger Delta. Neither essay nor photograph is adequate to the task. It does not even seem that both are enough to capture the outcome of the dangerous liaisons between the oil companies and the government in Nigeria. The book needs additional materials in the form of poems on the Delta, interviews, and a letter by Nobel laureates decrying the devastation wrought there. Formal heterogeneity is fundamental to *Curse of the Black Gold*. The various genres in the collection register the multiplicities of stressors and their impacts, including the displacement that is central to the workings of postcolonial trauma.

The essay form is one vehicle of accounting for trauma in this multimedia project. G. Ugo Nwokeji, Ukoha Ukiwo, and Watts, in their essays, locate the current Delta crisis in a longer narrative of exploitation.[22] In the title of Nwokeji's piece he links slave ships and oil tankers, and in the essay he makes the connection clearer by suggesting that "the long and violent passage of the slave ship . . . may help us understand the deeper and multiple meanings of the oil tanker."[23] The ship and tanker stand here for two axes of evil, slavery and petro-capitalism, which share certain similarities despite their differences. In both economies, the inhabitants of the Niger Delta have been at the losing end, with their geography supplying the "commodities"—human and nonhuman—that flow outward to other climes. The flow to other parts of the world, in both cases, happens by water. Slavery and petro-capitalism represent massive gains for other places but have brought ecological devastation and other forms of loss to the region. The local beneficiaries in both slavery and the oil business are a small elite profiting from the status quo. Both economies violently extract energy from the Delta. It is relevant for this analysis of the link between oil and slavery that people in the region believe that oil emanates from the bodies of their kin sold into slavery.[24] Whatever we may think of this perspective, it makes clear the connection between the two economies in the Delta milieu.

Conceived in socioeconomic or mythical terms, the crude oil business manifests traumatic repetition, albeit a different one that does not necessarily emanate from the victim. Scholars of trauma from Freud to Caruth have analyzed the repetitive compulsion in trauma victims that make them relive their experience in dreams, nightmares, and other symptoms. This form of repetition, the "experience of hypnotic imitation or identification" in the victim marks a mimetic trauma theory.[25] Repetition works differently in this postcolonial rendition of trauma. First there is a pluralizing of traumatic events and activities that shifts the agentive focus of repetition to the perpetrator(s). I am not suggesting here that postcolonial subjects do not suffer the kind of intrusive symptoms that characterize psychological trauma; my point rather is the need to appreciate the multiple kinds of violence enacted on the region by external actors as well as the internal violence that they catalyze. Emphasizing structural causes also deepens the opportunity for social transformation to remove traumatizing events rather than merely encouraging individual healing in a repressive status quo.

In Watts and Kashi's work, repetition appears in the connection among slavery, the oil-palm business, and the carbon economy, as well as in the fact that this point is repeated by many of the book's interlocutors. Where Nwokeji writes of the slave ship's connection to the oil tanker, Watts posits that "oil tankers lined the Cawthorne Channel like participants in a local regatta, plying the same waterways that, in the distant past, housed slave ships and palm oil hulks."[26] Ukiwo similarly notes, "The Niger Delta stands today—as it has for five centuries and more—at the epicenter of a violent economy of extraction."[27] Just from this sentence, one can notice that the author cannot do away with the past. He wants to write of the Delta today, of the contemporary moment, but the em dash formally breaks his thought and returns us to earlier moments of violence and displacement. Ukiwo is finally able to return to the present as it manifests in oil exploration, but the future horizon is unclear, which explains the uncertainty in the questions with which he ends his essay: "Might the glory days of the Oil Protectorates be made anew? Could black gold—the fuel of modern capitalism—hold the key to the future prosperity of the Niger Delta?"[28]

The questions with which Ukiwo ends his reflection capture the high expectations following the discovery of oil in Oloibiri in the present-day Nigerian state of Bayelsa in 1956. Andrew Apter has written of the spending spree that the Nigerian state embarked upon and which derived from oil money. Apter writes of "Nigeria's goal as a developing country, to build an efficient and productive industrial economy."[29] In short, oil appears early on as a "happy object," a kind of object "imbued with positive affect."[30] Despite the early promise of oil earnings, unfortunately the answer to Ukiwo's questions remains negative. The Nigerian government promoted "relatively little domestic production" while oil wealth mainly enriched public officials and their cronies.[31] Moreover, as some of the images shown below demonstrate, the area that has produced the oil wealth remains marginalized and extremely underdeveloped, while oil earnings are transferred to Nigerian cities outside the Niger Delta and abroad. The Niger Delta's devastation contrasts with the transformation of Abuja, the federal capital, "from a rural village into a wealthy modern city, embodying a spectacle of oil wealth."[32] The expectations of oil modernity were summarily dashed with the Niger Delta's exclusion from the benefits of oil. The negative turn from the blessing of petro-modernity to the curse of primitive accumulation has also precipitated other traumatic events: the Nigeria-Biafra civil war that had oil as the unspoken undertone; incessant national and regional conflicts stoked by the slick oil; and the martyrdom of Ken Saro-Wiwa, killed for his activism against exploitation and degradation in the Delta, among others.

In the aftermath of Saro-Wiwa's death at the hands of General Sani Abacha's military junta in 1995, Ato Quayson persuasively argued for extending the protocols of literary tragedy to understanding everyday suffering.[33] It is telling that Quayson's example is drawn from the Niger Delta, where the discovery of oil has resulted in ecological degradation and political repression. Where oil from the Delta has enriched local and national elites and swelled the profit column of the oil companies' accounting books, the region still lacks basic infrastructure including schools, roads, and medical facilities.[34] What the region has gained in abundance is environmental pollution, both to land and water, as well as the suppression of dissent by successive governments in Nigeria.[35] To counteract these devastating consequences of oil modernity, Saro-Wiwa mobilized his Ogoni people to push for self-determination and the control of oil resources.[36] His actions precipitated his arrest and ultimate death on the trumped-up charge of inciting the murder of rival Ogoni leaders.[37] Following Saro-Wiwa's martyrdom by the Nigerian state, "his transformation into a potent symbol for resistance against petro-capitalism became even more pronounced."[38] Saro-Wiwa, before his death, warned that his nonviolent approach would be superseded by violent means of protesting against the Nigerian state and oil companies' mistreatment of the Delta. It took less than ten years after Saro-Wiwa's death for the materialization of violent resistance in response to state violence and the marginalization of the region.[39]

All these interlinked events corroborate the fact that we cannot assume a singular traumatic event in the postcolony. Stef Craps's suggestion that "traumas sustained by the formerly colonized and enslaved are collective in nature and impossible to locate in an event that took place at a singular, historically specific moment in time" should guide us.[40] In terms of the Niger Delta, we have to speak of multiple events that persist in the everyday. We can categorize the "performance of violence" in the region into two groupings: those caused "by acts of community protests" and those directly emanating from oil production.[41]

If the texts clothed in scholarly garb foreground the repetition of traumatic events in the Delta, as already been argued, the photographs in *Curse of the Black Gold* evidence oil's contamination of the everyday. Where elites appear as authors of written text and as interview subjects, images recode the

Chapter Three

3.1 Front cover, *Curse of the Black Gold* © Ed Kashi/VII, 2008

lives of ordinary people, script the fractious intimacy of humans with non-human hydrocarbon technologies, and expose assaults on everyday life. On the book cover is an image of a local woman captured in motion while another, going about her business, can be seen in the background with her back to the camera (figure 3.1). Also in the background we barely see the outlines of three schoolchildren and we can make out three thatch huts, obviously homes of community members. Looming large in the image are massive oil installations—"carbon energy machine[s]"—that dwarf humans.[42] From these installations, smoke billows, making for a cloudy sky and a dimly lit picture. Through the smoke, we can see outlines of a brighter sky; oil pollution obstructs the climatic rhythm. Oil is the ostensible king while humans look cowed before it. This is a panoramic image that wraps over onto the back cover, which shows the extent to which oil has overtaken everything, including more-than-human lives. On the back we find a grouping of goats, which suggests that oil impacts livestock too. The looming oil infrastructure overwhelms the ramshackle houses alongside the various life forms in this image.

The conditions of the homes are pitiable, returning us to the thatch huts in Chinua Achebe's early fiction. The difference, of course, is that the setting

3.2 Inside front cover, *Curse of the Black Gold* © Ed Kashi/VII, 2008

is not the nineteenth or early twentieth century, a time predating oil modernity. This picture is the scorecard from the Niger Delta, fifty years after the discovery of oil in commercial quantity. These people live every day with smoke and pollutants from the infrastructure of the oil business, while they remain in extreme poverty. We only have to turn the pages to encounter more images of the rot and ruin of the Delta.

It is significant that the first two spreads make use of a black background, therefore foregrounding the scene on the cover. The first spread, which is repeated at the end of the multimedia work, is a map of the Niger Delta (figure 3.2). As this book is "extroverted," which means it is geared toward a Western reader, some form of geographical orientation seems necessary.[43] Yet we can barely decipher this map with the black background and the faint contrastive light on it. Sites of trauma are darkened sites; they remind us of the violence that has scarred the land and its people, as well as our inability to fully account for the magnitude of the suffering. We can thus interpret this spread as enacting trauma. This initial spread reminds us that the Niger Delta is a site of traumatic events that go back centuries.

The darkness of the initial pages continues on the next spread of *Curse of the Black Gold*, which contains an excerpt from a 2006 United Nations Development Programme report (figure 3.3).[44] Printed in orange above the black background, the message registers the disjuncture of a region that "produces the oil wealth that accounts for the bulk of Nigeria's earnings," but where the earnings "have barely touched the Niger Delta's own pervasive poverty."[45] This message appears in orange as a reminder of the uninterrupted gas flares in the region; the color also alludes to Shell, the major oil company in the region, whose operation in Ogoniland was fundamentally responsible for Saro-Wiwa's murder. In the color coding of the message can also be found echoes of the fires from oil spills that have rocked the Delta over the years.

We need to turn only one more page to see further evidence that oil is seared into the lives of these communities. The fog has lifted on this colored spread but the pictorial perspective foregrounds oil pipelines that are just a few feet away from people's houses (figure 3.4). One must look beyond the

"The Niger Delta produces the oil wealth that accounts for the bulk of Nigeria's earnings. Paradoxically, however, these vast revenues from an international industry have barely touched the Niger Delta's own pervasive poverty.... For most people, progress and hope, much less prosperity, remain out of reach.... If unaddressed, these do not bode well for the future of Nigeria or an oil-hungry world."

United Nations Development Program, Niger Delta Human Development Report, Abuja, 2006

3.3 Excerpt from United Nations Development Programme Niger Delta Report, *Curse of the Black Gold*, 2008

3.4 Children playing on oil pipelines in the Niger Delta,
Curse of the Black Gold © Ed Kashi/VII, 2008

oil infrastructure to catch glimpses of domestic life in the houses and shops. This relegation of people's life to the background links this spread to the book cover, where again the prominence of the oil machinery dwarfs the inhabitants of this space. On the pipelines we can see a little boy who seems to be finding his balance while an older girl earnestly runs across them. To leave pipes exposed as they are here, and in residential areas, heightens the risk of spills and fires even as it denotes the fractious intimacy or the dangerous entanglement of human and machine.

In this spread and in others that follow, the viewer can decipher "the devastating material effects and unimaginable disproportionalities" that Jennifer Wenzel marshals as evidence of "petro-magic realism." Whereas "petro-magic offers the illusion of wealth without work," Wenzel describes how "petro-magic realism pierces such illusions, evoking a recognizably devastated, if also recognizably fantastic, landscape."[46] The devastated landscapes evoked in the photographs demonstrate the violence of petro-modernity. As the reader flips through the pages, taking in further examples of the incredible human-machine intimacy, the brutal realism confirms Allan Sekula's description of photographs as "documents of the 'microphysics' of barba-

Chapter Three

3.5 Women baking *krokpo-garri*, or tapioca, in the heat of a gas flare,
Curse of the Black Gold © Ed Kashi/VII, 2008

rism."[47] In some images, the women are drying the local staple, *garri*, with heat from nearby gas flares. In others, combustible refined oil is sold by the roadside, with cars and motorcycles driving by; the waterscape of the region is also overwritten with oil structures competing for space with human swimmers and fish. I have focused on toxicity at length in chapter 2 and do not intend to repeat myself here, yet we must note the enmeshment of bodies here—of the human and the technological, and the corrosiveness of such intermingling.

The captions accompanying the photographs remind readers of the numerous diseases in this region, many of which are connected to oil. It is no surprise that the book includes more than one picture of women baking *garri* with gas flares. On the one hand, this repetition foregrounds the prevalence of the practice, but it also forces viewers to confront the health implications of the activity. According to Susan Sontag, "while the image . . . is an invitation to look, the caption, more often than not, insists on the difficulty of doing that."[48] There is always the possibility that the images of the women surrounded by cassava and gas flares may attract some viewers, captivate them with its symmetry and stunning quality (figure 3.5). The caption that follows, however, undercuts such notions when it illuminates the health dimension of the women's activities: "Life expectancy is short for the Urhobo people, as pollutants from the flares cause serious health problems."[49] Not only are the women directly exposed to the flare, but this danger extends to members of their family and others who will purchase the staple and consume it. In the example of the image with the women baking *garri*, the caption moves it away from aesthetic pleasure, something for enjoyment, instead orienting us to the health challenges and the infrastructural lack—amid plenty—that informs their action.

Although *garri* processing is highlighted as a form of female labor in the text, the men are also engaged in manual forms of labor no less arduous and hazardous. While "oil encourages fetishistic representations of its value as a magical property detached from labor,"[50] *Curse of the Black Gold* visualizes the toxic labor of oil exploration. There are images of bare-chested men engaged in menial labor, often in the oil industry. Two images stand out in this regard. In one, two young men roll a visibly heavy barrel of liquid gas, their sweat, bulging and defined muscles, as well as their facial contortion, expressing the enormity of their task (figure 3.6). In the second, two "oil-soaked workers take a break from cleaning up a spill in the swamps near Oloibiri," to quote the original caption (figure 3.7).[51] While the men rolling the barrel of gas appear bent, the oil-soaked workers are standing up, their heads cropped out of the image as the camera zooms in on their bodies. Each of the men is holding a machete in one hand and a stick in the other. They are wearing only pants, and their upper bodies appear shiny and glistening from the oil and perspiration.

To be sure, Kashi's images of the men in *Curse of the Black Gold* are erotic in the sense that they capture not only the men's toned torsos but foreground their loins in one image crammed with phallic resonances. They form the figure of "the delectable Negro," here being sexually exploited not by transatlantic slave traders but global fossil-fuel capitalism.[52] However, these images also paradoxically hold within them tensions undermining sexual gratification if we apply the notion of insightful reading to them. To apprehend these tensions is to consider the surface and depth of these images alongside other components of *Curse of the Black Gold* with attentiveness to the history of the region.

There is in the images a shared link between the form of the male body and oil form. Oil is attractive because it generates wealth and energy powering the current global order. As we consider its materiality, however, its stench, sludge, and toxicity dislodge pleasure as the animating impulse of this commodity form. The same logic applies to Kashi's erotic images of men drenched in oil. The close-up views of the men's bare bodies appear poised to stimulate the viewer, to attract them to take in the shiny, muscular bodies. Shirtless male bodies appear covered in oil and sweat, in black skin, black masks, with broad chests and bulging muscles for the consumptive pleasure of the viewer (see figures 3.6 and 3.7). Like the oil being rolled toward the viewer (figure 3.6) for consumption, the images offer the proximate skin for the viewer's pleasure. The frontal view of the bodies particularly announces that they are to be looked at.

However, drawn in by the pleasurable bodies, the stimulation is unsettled by the smell of oil, its toxic infringement, and the images' evocation of slavery. The complexity of these images ensures that erotic pleasure is not an end. In figure 3.6, for instance, the two men intently focus on the oil barrel, which nudges the viewer's gaze away from their tense muscles to their labor. Redirecting focus to the exacting labor compels attention on the men's discomfort with the weight and smell of oil, therefore reordering the erotic investment. The body stands for itself in representation but also echoes prior discourses.[53] One such discourse that *Curse of Black Gold* links to is slavery: its sexualization of the enslaved and "superexploitation of the black body as muscle-machine," to use Kobena Mercer and Isaac Julien's words in this Nigerian context.[54] The earlier discussion of the essays in *Curse of the Black Gold* has already connected the slave ship with the oil tanker. The evocation of slavery in the essays is illuminative for reading these images and undercutting their sexual potential.

These images of black men with bare upper bodies participate in a discursive romance with slavery, where the black body was subject to exploitation. Although the oil workers engage in these tasks voluntarily compared with their enslaved predecessors, the force of their consent is sharply mitigated by the dire socioeconomic condition of the region, the limited employment opportunities there, and the overall precarity. If slavery manifests as "theft of the body," as Spillers reminds us, it can find a parallel in the oil institution in the Delta, where bodies are stolen by the ravages of diseases, hunger, and other toxic material.[55] We need not look further than these black men to see the overwhelming of the body by oil. With their heads cropped out (figure 3.7), they have lost individuality and specificity; their value coheres primarily in the extraction of labor, as was the case with slavery. The sweat mixed with water, the oil on water and salt, recall the physical labor of the Delta forbears taken into captivity and forced to work in the plantation economy. Whether it is the two headless men who appear before us with machetes in hand or the

3.6 *(opposite)* Workers pushing a barrel of gas, *Curse of the Black Gold*
© Ed Kashi/VII, 2008

3.7 *(above)* Oil-soaked workers taking a break from cleaning up an oil spill
in the Niger Delta, *Curse of the Black Gold* © Ed Kashi/VII, 2008

others bent in their struggle to move the barrel of gas, or even their forebears
stuck in sugar and cotton plantations in the days of yore, what is at stake is
the exertion of labor in productive economies that hardly reward the black
body. Foregrounded here is the idea of the Niger Delta as site for energy extraction, which was also the guiding logic of slavery.

The shine aesthetics undergirding Kashi's photographs of oil workers
buttress the connection between the fossil economy and slavery in *Curse of
the Black Gold*. The artistic burnishing of shiny surfaces has been traced to
sixteenth century oil paintings, where the technique drew attention to the
value of commodities.[56] Self-fashioning in this artistic mode is bound to material possessions finely wrought to shine. The polishing of surfaces is meant
to foreground their value and the owner's status. This practice was extended
to enslaved black people in order to enhance their worth. The art historian
Krista A. Thompson eloquently describes how the same bodily shine was
used to move enslaved people away from the boundaries of humanity to the
commodity corridor. Oil and other material were used to hide scars and to

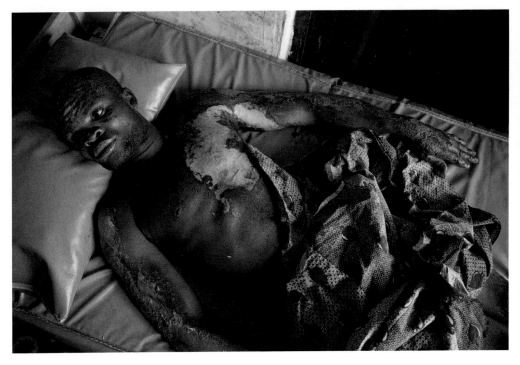

3.8 A man in hospital with burns, *Curse of the Black Gold*
© Ed Kashi/VII, 2008

make these bodies more attractive to buyers.[57] The shiny aesthetics operative in Kashi's photographs link them to the institution of slavery where a similar technique was employed to increase the slave's marketability. Shiny skin promotes the allure of the body while also implicating the labor of Kashi's subjects in the oil economy.

Linking current extractive conditions in the Niger Delta to slavery detracts from the erotic power of the images by inducing a critical engagement with extractive labor, but it is a photograph showing a victim of fire from an oil spill, his entire body covered in burns, that completely reroutes the pictures' libidinal energy (figure 3.8). In this photograph we literally see oil stealing the body where the shiny black skin has disappeared, this time not due to the whip. Whereas figures 3.6 and 3.7 make erotic overtures to the viewer, figure 3.8 disfigures that pleasure by presenting the aftermath of oil's volatility and toxicity. The burnt body, looking to the side, away from the viewer, evokes repulsion at both the degradation of the body that Watts and Kashi's work traces back to slavery and the toxicity that the oil industry represent in the Delta. I have shown figures 3.6, 3.7, and 3.8 to audiences, many of which use "uncomfortable" to register their response. They report being fascinated by the aestheticized images but then that fascination giving way as they dwell on the images and as they approach the burned victim in figure 3.8. It is not surprising that resonances with the tortuous past of slavery (in the consumption of black labor and the eroticized body) would most likely yield feelings of discomfort and disgust that are bound to arrest the erotic dimension of Kashi's photographs.

As oil's pleasures are undermined by its toxic afterlife, there is an under-cutting of the erotic promise of Kashi's images by the disfigured body in figure 3.8 as well as echoes of slavery's commodification and exploitation of black people in figures 3.6 and 3.7. Kashi's images make a connection between the lesser-known Niger Delta labor economy and the well-known exploit-ative horrors of the transatlantic slave trade in order to inspire remediation of the socioecological crisis in the Delta. Therefore, it is simplistic to dismiss these images for their portrayal of bare, black male bodies. With the benefit of insightful reading, Kashi's photographs show that despite slavery being a thing of the past, the world continues to commodify black bodies and exploit their labor, calling into question conventional understandings of linear, pro-gressive temporalities.

Photography has been associated with death, and the images in Watts and Kashi's work are no exception. Barthes's ruminations on his dead mother in *Camera Lucida* and James Elkins's suggestion that "photography fills our eyes with all the dead and deadening stuff of the world" are just two ex-amples.[58] Unlike conventional photographs of atrocity, however, there are no images of dead humans in *Curse of the Black Gold*, although we can say that the inhabitants of the region appear as victims of slow or incremental death. Rather, it is dead nonhumans that appear before us: dead fish as well as the blood and horns of slaughtered animals. The images of fish take on salience at a moment of decline in marine resources. Reports on the Niger Delta, including Watts and Kashi's, lament the dearth of fish stock in a re-gion where people depend on it for food and where fishing and farming are the mainstays of the economy. As fish stocks further decline, Kashi's photo-graphs provide evidence of loss as well as the memorabilia for mourning that which is no longer plentiful, whose decline has increased poverty in the re-gion as well as precipitated migration away from rural communities. But even as Kashi's photographs mourn what is no longer there, as most photo-graphs do since they capture vanishing moments, Kashi's lens also captures continuously existing traumatic experiences in the Delta, where the smoke continues to billow into the atmosphere, suffocating human and nonhuman lives. This is a region where waterways are filled with oil infrastructure jutting out of the waterscape, a geography where oil infrastructure overwhelms the inhabitants daily.[59] The traumas represented in these Niger Delta photographs are not eclipsed after the camera is put away.

Traumas of the Future

Because the physical and psychological wounding in the Niger Delta does not stay in the past or stay contained in the present, it is appropriate to consider traumas of the future. Trauma studies have focused mainly on the past, but in light of the bombing of the World Trade Center and Pentagon in 2001, as well as catastrophic weather events such as Hurricane Sandy in the United States, critical attention has started to shift toward traumas of the future. Jacques Derrida's reflection on the September 11, 2001, attacks in the United States raises the specter of this form of trauma. In his words, "we must rethink the temporalization of a traumatism if we want to comprehend in what way 'September 11' *looks* like a 'major event.' For the wound remains open by our terror before the *future* and not only in the past."[60] With the 9/11 attacks, the traumatic event(s) is/are not located solely in the past but also in the idea that the United States shares the vulnerability that has been associated with less powerful countries of the world. The breach of the homeland sundered the illusion of national security while raising the stakes for surveillance at home and abroad. That the 9/11 attacks happened meant that they could happen again, hence the trauma that Derrida painstakingly articulates in his dialogue with Giovanna Borradori.

Brian Massumi shares Derrida's conviction that 9/11 opened up a new regime of unforeseen threat and thus exploded our sense of security. For Massumi, the "threat is from the future. It is what might come next. Its eventual location and ultimate extent are undefined. Its nature is open-ended."[61] E. Ann Kaplan calls this "pretrauma" in her study of futuristic disaster narratives: "my experiences during Hurricane Sandy reflect the familiar PTSD— that is, I responded to the catastrophe through what it triggered about past traumas. However, having had this experience, I may now suffer from pretrauma—that is, living in fear of a future terrifying event of a similar kind."[62] Locating the source of pre-trauma or trauma of the future in ecological disaster as Kaplan does is interesting and has relevance for the concern of this chapter. What is also interesting is her claim that the "pretrauma genre emerges as Eurocentric cultures become newly aware of the uncertainty of human futurity."[63] This new awareness further demonstrates the privilege of

Western societies, spared the violence that they have directly or indirectly visited on non-Western countries, until recently.

"Prisoners of geography," such as those in the Niger Delta, the territorial features of which have turned into their undoing, do not share this nascent sense of uncertainty.[64] Places such as the Niger Delta have been continuously subject to Eurocentric colonial violence over centuries, long before bombings and climate change became palpable risks. I will argue here that at least three vectors of Watts and Kashi's project raise the question of the trauma of the future, namely the young children whose images appear in the book, the bodies exposed to toxicity at work, and the imagery of wounding that is encoded in a poem by Uche Peter Umez.

In the earlier discussion of the two young men rolling a heavy barrel over the ground, what I declined to mention was the young boy in the background hawking water (figure 3.6). The camera shot freezes him in motion with his face and body turned to the camera and the young men laboring under the weight of the barrel. Considering that the photographer had the option of cropping out the boy but chose not to, this image invites us to read the boy's gaze in light of the men's labor. In her recent work, Tina Campt asks that we embrace "the choice to 'listen to' photographs."[65] In Campt's telling, "listening to images is constituted as a practice of looking beyond what we see and attuning our senses to the other affective frequencies through which photographs register."[66] She concedes photographs' quietude but cautions that "quiet must not be conflated with silence."[67] Fred Moten must have this sonic intensity in mind when he declares that "photographs in general bear a phonic substance."[68] If Campt's insights and Moten's phonic claim are brought to my analysis, we can ask: What does this photograph tell us about the boy? We should also ask what thought is running through the boy's mind as he watches his older compatriots. We don't know if this boy is in school or not. Is he hawking water full time or is this an after-school activity? Even if he is in school, the dilapidated school structure in another spread does not register a solid educational engagement for the kids. In short, to return to the image, the boy's look speaks of his vulnerability.

The boy's presence, the footsteps underpinning his motion, and his gaze are practically audible, distracting us from the noise of the rolling barrel and the "moaning," groaning, and "mourning" of the men laboring behind it.[69] Yet the aural quality that the boy brings to the picture cooperates with the aural-visual image before him to underscore the precariousness of existence in this clime. As he watches the older men from behind, the picture seems to

3.9 A young girl in the Niger Delta, *Curse of the Black Gold*
© Ed Kashi/VII, 2008

be registering the sight before him as the zenith of his ascent. The image suggests that the weight of the boy's labor will not get lighter, that with the passage of time, its heaviness will be akin to the weight borne by the men pushing the oil drum. While he is standing upright in the image, the sight before him gives the impression of a bent posture in the future, indicative of the battering of everyday life in such a place. Perhaps he is asking himself if this is the lot that awaits him and if he can transcend such circumstances. This photograph is an archive of uncertainty and stasis for the boy and for the men, whose hard labor symbolizes the Herculean tasks confronting young people in this environment.

Another image is worth discussing here. It is a close-up shot of a girl's face and shoulder covered in raindrops (figure 3.9). Behind her in the distance is a destroyed building where at least the roof, doors, and windows are missing. The caption for the photograph informs us that the location is Odiama, "a town that was attacked and destroyed by the Nigerian Military Joint Task Force."[70] The girl appears superfluous to the destruction captured in the image and the accompanying caption. But is she really? Although she appears "at the edge of sight"—at the margin of the photograph, she is the focus of the image and thus deserves attention.[71] We see only her face and shoulders, with the rest of her body outside the picture frame. This composition signals the girl's marginality just as the distance between her and the destroyed building indicates her "dislocation from the communal web of kinship."[72] Capturing the face of the child in extreme close-up and with the rain water evoking tears highlight her vulnerability and can be read, in Levinas's terms, as an invitation to respond to the face of the Other.[73] But we can also ask what kind of future awaits children who are subject to the continuous violence in the region. Is anything being done so that these children will not continue to experience the traumatic cycle of violence they witness every day? There is no easy answer to these questions, but unless things change for the better as the contributors to *Curse of the Black Gold* hope, it is not too farfetched to conclude that not only is the future of these kids bleak, the entire region and possibly the entire country are also at risk. If the status quo remains, these kids could constitute "the open threat of an aggression capable one day of striking,"[74] therefore deferring and extending the cycle of trauma in the Niger Delta.

The extension of trauma into the future is inseparable from the potential impact of bodily exposure to oil toxicity. One implication of the materialist turn in the environmental humanities is a consideration of nonhuman agency, or "thing-power."[75] Oil and its infrastructure are agents in the Delta region. Oil, as Juan Pablo Pérez Alfonzo reminds us, "is the most important of the fuels indispensable for modern life."[76] To decipher oil's agency in *Curse of the Black Gold*, we have to heed Imre Szeman's call to probe the "social ontology of oil—the how, why, and wherefore of oil in our social, cultural, and political life."[77] That oil yields money for Nigeria is an established fact, and so is the fact that our modes of inhabiting the earth are contingent on this resource. Its force for good, however, is challenged in the Delta where it sticks on the human body. Whether it is children swimming in the water, or the bodies of fish soon to be consumed by humans and other aquatic creatures, or even the young man with wounds from an oil spill explosion, oil punctures the promise of the future. The men working to clean up oil spills are exposed to toxins that debilitate the body over time, and such is the case for the women who work close to gas flares. *Curse of the Black Gold* paints the image of a future tainted by oil toxicity. Like the threat that Massumi describes, the form or shape of the aftermath of toxic exposure may remain undefined or unforeseen, yet the potential of the threat looms across the pages of Watts and Kashi's text.

The future dimension of trauma being charted also appears in one of the poems in the work, Uche Peter Umez's "Dark Through the Delta."[78] Umez is a contemporary Nigerian poet with a doctorate in English from the University of Alberta, Canada. Isidore Diala contends that Umez's craft is "consumed by a passionate concern for social injustice and ameliorating the miserable lot of the downtrodden" and that he "sheds a sober but always compassionate light on the many inadequacies of the national life that threaten to make Nigeria a pariah nation."[79] Diala describes "Dark Through the Delta" as a "stirring evocation of the mood of continuing cynical despoliation" and as "painting a haunting scene of utter decay and abandonment."[80] The first four stanzas of the poem capture the devastation to the river and land—to elemental media, so to speak. The stanzas also capture fraying of nets, and the rusting of canoes, hoes and cutlasses, all fishing and farming equipment.

The fifth stanza shifts to the kite, a bird of prey, "hovering" in the sky. Hovering here registers a shift in tense from the past and present of earlier stanzas toward the future. The kite is waiting to kill or for some creature to die from oil's effects, therefore constituting the sign of future trauma. The poem attunes us specifically in this stanza to the yet to happen. In my reading, the poem proceeds in the last two stanzas to underscore an itinerary of a traumatic future:

> I see the fat of the land
> being eaten out
> by the burgeoning pollution,
> by the intricate machinery of oil greed

Considering that the Niger Delta is a site of primitive accumulation and the instantiation of what the political scientist Jean-François Bayart terms the "politics of the belly," it makes sense that Umez draws on alimentary imagery, of consumption, of food and eating, to describe the despoliation of the land.[81] The poet's choice of imagery is equally consistent with Achille Mbembe's conclusion that eating and festivities are of primal importance for African rulers and their modes of governmentality.[82] What interests me, though, is the continuity marked by the tense (being eaten). Umez's poem registers the wounding of the land, its evisceration by oil greed, but then this incident is not just located in the past or present as in earlier stanzas. Umez's choice of grammatical tense extends the duration of eating and wounding to the future.

The final stanza continues this attunement to the yet to come:

behold, it is the fortune
of my hapless kin
being eroded, stealthily eroded . . .

The present continuous tense "being" is repeated to foreground the fact that the erosion of fortune lasts beyond the immediate present. The reference to "hapless kin" evokes the children in the photographs, whose future is jeopardized by the primitive accumulation of elites and the devastation in the region. "Hapless" recalls the misfortune in the Niger Delta, but the word can also be read as a phonic approximation of "helpless," which in this case characterizes children's dependence on their parents or guardians. Seen this way, "hapless kin" can be read as dependents of the poem's persona, whose inheritance—the fortune—is repeatedly under attack as present global consumption levels imperil the planet for future generations. But we must not stop here.

Elsewhere, I have challenged the anthropocentric conceptualization of the environment in African literary studies. The study models a critical practice attentive to human-nonhuman entanglement or what I call their proximity.[83] As an example of what I termed the "aesthetics of proximity" in that work, Umez's poem highlights other ecological components including the river, the land, and the clouds imperiled by oil exploration. Focusing on these constituents makes for an expansive understanding of "kin" in the final stanza, one that acknowledges the shared vulnerability on display throughout the poem, linking humans and other aspects of the ecosystem together. Take for instance the "nets frayed and flung away" in the second stanza. The decommissioned nets suggest the unavailability of fish, either killed by the "grime" in the river in the fourth stanza or driven farther into the ocean. Interestingly, fish are not mentioned, underscoring their disappearance or even extinction, a point buttressed by the fact that this stanza has the fewest lines in the poem, only two. The formal economy of the stanza particularly addresses the species scarcity suggested by the discarded nets. My point is that "hapless kin" should be read ecologically, to embrace the various life forms under threat in this ecology of risk. Ultimately, the poem ends in an ellipsis suggesting incompleteness, irresolution, and the continuation of the traumas articulated in the poem. Moreover, the persona is unsure of the future shape of the metaphorical and physical cannibalization of the Niger Delta. The uncertainty registered in the ellipsis thus evokes the threat the future holds for the Delta.

Oil functions as a "hyperobject" in the Delta.[84] With oil in the water, the air, the food, and even in their homes as Watts and Kashi demonstrate, the region's inhabitants cannot possibly give a complete account of their loss. Even the suspension of drilling and closure of oil operations in the region would not reverse the contamination and other calamities that invariably accompany oil exploration and extraction. This inability to consciously give account of losses, combined with the ongoing perpetration of violence in the Delta, postpones the cessation of suffering there. Yet Watts and Kashi make clear that these people are not mere victims but survivors as well.

To attempt a representation of traumas as Watts and Kashi have done almost always engenders the question of ethics in relation to victims and survivors.[85] Bearing ethics in mind, we can probe the cost of Watts and Kashi's attempt to bring recognition to the plight of the Niger Delta. To what extent do they succeed (or fail) to avoid revictimizing their subjects? With Abigail Solomon-Godeau, "we must ask, in other words, whether the documentary act does not involve a double act of subjugation," and, with Martha Rosler, consider the extent to which *Curse of the Black Gold* transcends the "genre of victimhood."[86] While *Curse of the Black Gold* depicts pain and suffering in its representation of the Niger Delta ecoscape, it does so with sensitivity to the complexity and heterogeneity of the people and their ecosystem and in ways that transcend mere victimhood. With the mixture of words and images, we get a glimpse of diverse perspectives in the region, from middle- and upper-class voices to the ordinary people made visible in Watts and Kashi's work.

What can be read as the region's defining motto appears in the form of graffiti on the wall of a zinc house (figure 3.10). Michael Warner's understanding of graffiti as "always a kind of counterpublicity" appropriated as a subcultural media form resonates with this example that reads "TRUST NO BODY IBIMARI MARCUS."[87] A zinc house is a marker of underdevelopment, of the absence of the means to afford a proper house with proper materials. We also see pots and plastic buckets on the floor outside this makeshift house, which suggest lack of privacy for domestic activities. This external space serves as kitchen for the occupants of this house. This house (if we can call it that) and the accoutrements of domesticity in front of it are markers of the failure of the alliance between government and oil companies to meet the needs of the people. As such, "trust nobody," a common saying in Nigerian parlance, takes on a special salience in this spatial economy where the promise of national independence and of oil modernity has been severely broken by successive governments and corporate actors. Lacking the mechanism of official media, the author here, who signs off this message as Ibimari Marcus, takes to graffiti to pen an indictment of those entrusted with the

Chapter Three

3.10 Graffiti on a corrugated metal wall, *Curse of the Black Gold*
© Ed Kashi/VII, 2008

commonwealth. As brief and casual as it appears, the graffiti's eloquence rivals the longer narratives weaved by the polished scholars, writers, and activists whose works appear in *Curse of the Black Gold*. Whereas graffiti is largely anonymous and "abstract away from the given body," making it "difficult to criminalize," the message here is signed like the other documents in Watts and Kashi's book.[88] Conferring individual agency and presence to the author, the graffiti demands to be taken as seriously as the other documents in *Curse of the Black Gold*.

In addition to the graffiti, photographs offer a window into the complex structure of feelings of the Delta's inhabitants. There are photographs of children playing, unperturbed by the underdevelopment around them. It is a virtue of the photographs that there is room for childhood innocence amidst the suffering that pervades the book. The use of color, especially for the photographs, draws in the viewer to appreciate beauty among ruins and "negates the discomfort the viewer might otherwise feel" in looking at the devastated ecoscape.[89] The pictures that particularly come to mind are those of the women dressed in traditional attire. These women, like the others in *Curse of the Black Gold*, are survivors.

3.11 Women marching for peace in the Niger Delta, *Curse of the Black Gold*
© Ed Kashi/VII, 2008

In one spread, we see women of the Anglican Church marching against violence on the street, which highlights their contributions to peace efforts in their community (figure 3.11). These women are beautiful in their white blouses and purple wrappers. They are holding white handkerchiefs, which women usually wave in traditional dancing. Whiteness here can also stand for the peace they crave. They are smiling as they dance and are uncircumscribed by the circumstances of the land. In another spread, we see beautifully dressed women attending a wedding in Port Harcourt, a major city in the Niger Delta. Watts and Kashi's work demonstrates that the region is not just a space of suffering and loss; the images of the women alongside those of the children show that dancing, playing, and even weddings happen here.

The images of graffiti, children playing, and women dancing speak to the presence of life, zest, and vivacity in the Niger Delta. Moreover, the pictures showing kings in their palaces and of Queen Georgina Tenalo of Ogoniland reveal that the Delta is not altogether a lawless space but a place with some form of constituted authority and order. We see a space where women such as the queen and the Anglican women are not mere victims but are agents at the forefront of addressing the violence in the region. In addition to its

Chapter Three

pictorial representations, *Curse of the Black Gold* includes the works of female writers such as Kaine Agary and a panoply of written materials chronicling women's participation in the Delta's struggle.

In the portrayal of women as leaders, as marchers, and as writers in the public sphere, the multimedia text complicates a simplistic understanding of their role as domestic caregivers.[90] As Aili Mari Tripp and Oyeronke Oyewumi, among other scholars, have shown, women in Africa have occupied important roles, including as rulers, since the precolonial era, a fact that gets muted in simplistic depictions of African women as exploited victims.[91] In contrast to these stereotypical representations, *Curse of the Black Gold* presents women in public spaces and in their public roles, thereby demonstrating their participation in social and political processes affecting the Niger Delta. The narrative here is that *Curse of the Black Gold* pushes back against the idea of victimhood, and women play a critical role in forging the image of the Delta as a lived space populated by active agents working toward social transformation.

Embodied Performance and Trauma in the Niger Delta

There is another way to apprehend the photographs of the dancing women and other performance scenes: through the prism of working through trauma. Scholarship on traumatic memory, especially in African and other non-Western cultures, has highlighted the value of nonliterary artistic forms for healing trauma. In *Art and Trauma in Africa*, for instance, Lizelle Bisschoff and Stefanie Van de Peer and their contributors demonstrate that African artists use their projects to address "the violent past in order to establish a more peaceful, secure future."[92] Similarly, Ananya Jahanara Kabir critiques the Eurocentric inclination of trauma studies, which is responsible for its emphasis on narrative in the process of reconciliation and healing. Kabir's indictment affirms Diana Taylor's critique of the Western emphasis on writing and how it trivializes or invalidates the possibility of traumatic healing in embodied performance.[93] While not dismissing the value of narrative in working through trauma, Kabir and Taylor recommend a decolonized process that decenters the written text while foregrounding the place of the body and performance. In Kabir's words, "for a start, trauma theory would have to reengage the psychosomatics of the body in dance."[94] The frameworks of Kabir and Taylor map well onto this analysis of *Curse of the Black Gold*, where narratives remain insufficient to exorcise the traumas of slavery, the palm-oil economy, and crude oil exploration. Dancing, in this image-text, functions as an antithesis to another form of performance, that of the militants who have taken up arms against the government and oil companies whose activities entrap the communities of the Delta. Said differently, if these militants democratize violence in the region with their bodies and with weapons affixed to them, the women use their bodies to demand peace in the region. As they dance in a frenzy, as they exercise their bodies in the process of exorcising their land, they challenge the occupation of their bodies by the state, oil companies, and militants. Performance in this context "privileges body over speech, presence over absence and praxis over product."[95] Where oil threatens bodies in the Delta as discussed earlier, these women reclaim their bodies through performance. By walking they reject the oil-powered automobile: "pedestrianism becomes political action and therapy, a means of moving (literally, physically) against the melancholy of oil dependence."[96] Marching through the community with dance and excitement is a symbolic gesture for reclaiming the space rendered inhospitable by the accumulative violence of the government, oil companies, and militants.

The deployment of the body for therapeutic purpose in *Curse of the Black Gold* recalls Fanon's *Wretched of the Earth* and his description of the stomping of feet, dancing, and other embodied activities that the colonized use to alleviate the stresses of coloniality.[97] Although Fanon's Marxist sensibility does not allow his endorsement of activities that rechannel the aggressiveness that should be mobilized against the colonizer, they provide precursors to the agency activated in performance in *Curse of the Black Gold*. Dancing is a mechanism for psychic and social reclamation and healing. The church-women embark upon this activity to seek peace in a troubled region and to alleviate their suffering just as the colonized did. Religious performances and other bodily enactments are technologies for working through ecotrauma in Watts and Kashi's multimedia project.

Separately from *Curse of the Black Gold*, we can decipher the same practice of emplacement in the video art of Zina Saro-Wiwa, the daughter of the late Ken Saro-Wiwa. It is only fitting that an excursus into the cathartic role of performance in the Delta takes us to the daughter of the man whose name has become synonymous with the region. As mentioned earlier, Saro-Wiwa—businessman, politician, and environmental activist—was executed by the Nigerian government for his activism against the exploitation of the Ogonis on November 10, 1995. At the time, his family lived in England while he spent most of his time in Nigeria tending to his business and activist work. Due to his hurried burial in an unmarked grave to discourage identification, Saro-Wiwa's family was unable to retrieve his body and seek closure until 2002.

Since then, Saro-Wiwa's children have found ways to publicly mourn their father. His oldest son, Ken Wiwa, who took over his father's business and served as adviser to the Nigerian president Goodluck Jonathan, wrote an important memoir, while his sister Noo wrote a travelogue detailing her journey to Nigeria to grapple with her father's death and her attempt to come to terms with the country that martyred him.[98] Noo's twin sister, Zina, whose work I examine here, is not left out of this search for the appropriate form of mourning their deceased father. In addition to establishing the Boys' Quarters Project Space, an art gallery, in her late father's former office space in Port Harcourt, Zina Saro-Wiwa has also created documentaries, video installations, and other artistic projects on the Niger Delta, mourning, oil economies, and Nollywood, among others. Her *Sarogua Mourning* video installation, created in 2011, is relevant for understanding the intersection of trauma and performance.[99]

Sarogua Mourning takes its name from the Delta deity, Sarogua, god of war and of rain. The younger Saro-Wiwa explains that her father's reference to the deity in his poetry is one reason she adopted Sarogua for her project. In the video, Saro-Wiwa sits in front of the camera. Behind her is a red background with black at both the left and right margins. The red here symbolizes her father's martyrdom while the black articulates the unarticulated grief that the video aims to expunge. Saro-Wiwa explains that the video arises because of the inadequacy of the conventional Western mode of mourning for articulating her trauma. Thus the shaved head and the rest of the performance are modeled on traditional conceptions of mourning in the Niger Delta.[100]

The video can be divided into three parts. In the first, Saro-Wiwa is silent, apparently unable to articulate her loss or pain. In the second part, she is finally able to, but her speech rambles a bit. She repeats wanting to "feel pain," seeking "catharsis," and "working through." Silence and narrative having failed, in the third part, the most powerful part of the video, she breaks down in tears, which mix with laughter at intervals. Sometimes the line between weeping and laughter is blurred so much so that only the tears remind the viewer that she is crying. The grieving is punctuated with occasional quiet, after which the weeping and laughter resume. Saro-Wiwa's performance is enhanced by her bodily movement as she bows her head amid sobbing or as she raises it to face the camera. The video locates grief in her physical body and shows that she must work through her grief physically in order to process it.

Sarogua Mourning carries both secular and spiritual connotations. War deities fight on behalf of their supplicants, so we can suppose that the invocation is a call for justice in the Niger Delta. Yet Sarogua is also the god of rain, which means the deity has the transformative power to cleanse Saro-Wiwa's pain while making possible her rejuvenation. As a psychological exercise, the performance is cathartic for her. Like her brother's and sister's writings, this artistic project is calibrated for therapeutic purposes, but its publicness also interpellates the viewer to participate in the work of mourning. As "implicated subjects," whose energy consumption is inextricable from the oil culture that consumed Saro-Wiwa, we are invited to participate in Saro-Wiwa's public mourning, to mourn the devastation and loss that ensue from satiating our consumptive desires.[101] To recapitulate, my foray into Zina Saro-Wiwa's video art is meant to deepen my engagement with the body as a site of healing in the Niger Delta. Performance serves in her work and in *Curse of the Black Gold* as a modality for attending to the stressors of oil culture. In the case of the latter project, performance is also central to its mapping of the Delta as a site of complex significations, of depicting the region not only as a site of suffering and degradation but also as a transformative space for play and pleasure.

Limits of Witnessing

Nevertheless, there is room to argue that *Curse of the Black Gold* courts sensationalism in its portrayal of catastrophe. To flesh out this position, we can turn to the email exchange between the photographer Ed Kashi and Jomo Gbomo, the spokesman of the Movement for the Emancipation of the Niger Delta. In one email to Gbomo, Kashi writes, "I have spoken with my man in Port Harcourt and he sounds a bit skeptical but he told me that a leaking well that he showed us last week has exploded and is on fire. This is exactly what we need for our work."[102] This is a clear demand for an image of disaster. Such stories sell well and enable the quick cultivation of "mass subjectivity."[103] It can be argued that the rhetorical force of a burning well serves the purpose of the book, which Watts explains as being aimed at a "better and deeper understanding of what it will take to defuse and rebuild the violent economies of the Niger Delta."[104] Such an image, however, derives rhetorical power from its provenance in Africa. Sontag is indeed right that such "sights carry a double message. They show a suffering that is outrageous, unjust, and should be repaired" but they also "confirm that this is the sort of thing which happens in that place."[105] The exotic space of the Other on fire can attract empathy, but it also confirms a particular narrative of violence that has shaped the (mis)understanding of the continent for centuries.[106]

In the end the larger question is the extent of the book's immersion in oil. Stephanie LeMenager and Sean Cubitt, among others, have written of the ecological footprint of print and electronic media, of their consumption of a considerable amount of energy. This energy currently comes mostly from oil. *Curse of the Black Gold*, while critiquing the culture of oil in the Delta, relies on oil for its own production and distribution. Both Watts and Kashi record multiple trips to Nigeria and the Delta, travel involving long flights on planes fueled by oil. These flights, no doubt, generate carbon footprints. Moreover, the processing of the film, the making of the paper on which the words and images appear, and the book's journey from its publisher to libraries and private owners make use of petroleum energy. The most troubling aspect of the work's indebtedness to oil, however, is the revelation in the acknowledgments that "the Bayelsa Government, through the services of Von Kemedi and Governor Timi Sylva, also contributed financial support."[107] Sylva, then governor of Bayelsa, is the only elected senior government official whose photograph is in the book. Is his appearance tied to his patronage? *Curse of the Black Gold* is stuck in oil like the people whose lives it illuminates. Because Bayelsa is a major oil producing state with most of its revenue coming from oil rent, it is plausible that Watts and Kashi's book is partly funded by the same oil economy it condemns.

This funding arrangement combines with the processes of production and distribution to highlight the limits of ecomedia. They are crucial for creating awareness of ecological problems, especially those occurring in faraway places, and for mobilizing resistance against the devastation of the ecosphere. However, they can also be tied to the cultural logic of exploitation and degradation. *Curse of the Black Gold* is an outstanding exposé of oil violence and degradation, but it is also indebted to oil at the levels of production and distribution. It demonstrates that culpability is possible at sites of sharp critique.

So far, this chapter has mined the creeks of the Niger Delta in *Curse of the Black Gold* to discover the rich resources they contain for an understanding of trauma. The incubus of the trauma analyzed here is the carbon economy that the Delta supports as a major region of fossil fuel deposits. Considering the dispossession as well as the physical and emotional devastation articulated in Watts and Kashi's work, we can reach at least two conclusions.

One is that sites of energy extraction such as the Delta, especially when they exist in the postcolony, bring about physical, economic, and psychological stress on the inhabitants unfortunate enough to have to make a home there. Another point from the ensuing discussion is that oil itself is a medium linking people and places. It is the mediating object between oil companies and oil communities; between governments and oil companies; but also between governments and host communities. Oil also links the Niger Delta to other parts of the world, such as the United States, which buys Nigeria's crude oil. Watts and Kashi's project demonstrates oil's shortcomings as a medium. In other words, in all the mediating relationships outlined here, communities in the Delta remain at the losing end of their transactions with the oil companies, the government, and the larger world. These conclusions are applicable to other mining sites across the continent—namely, that such communities are left out of the gains of capitalist extraction in their domain while being encumbered with the ensuing ecological catastrophe. In the following reading of *Arlit*, a documentary film about uranium mining in Niger, I show that insights of trauma studies are useful for apprehending the losses—physical, mental, economic—brought about by extractive capitalism, and that like oil, uranium breeds disease, poverty, and displacement for African communities.

Arlit: Climate Change, Trauma, Migration

Idrissou Mora-Kpai, who was born in Benin, has garnered international accolades such as the Dutch Prince Claus Award for his artistic practice. He is a graduate of the Konrad Wolf Film University of Babelsberg in Germany and currently teaches media arts at Ithaca College, New York State. His filmic oeuvre, shuttling between Africa and the diaspora, includes *Indochina: Traces of a Mother*, which focuses on the mixed-race children born to African soldiers and Vietnamese women during the Indochina War (1946–54).[108] He also directed *America Street*, depicting a poor African American community in Charleston, South Carolina, following the 2015 police killing of Walter Scott.[109] In *Arlit*, named after the town it documents, Mora-Kpai's camera is attuned to the environmental impacts of uranium mining and the implications of the economic downturn that followed a decline in uranium prices.

In the film's opening shots, we see buses bringing workers into Arlit. "Welcome to Arlit" is the message on the sign that greets the visitor and the film's viewers. Like Nigeria, discussed earlier, Niger obtained independence in 1960, but its complete entanglement with energy mining started in 1968, ten years after the first oil tanker left the Niger Delta. Niger's independence from France has meant little, as the country's relationship with the French company running the Somair and Cominack mines remains lopsided and exploitative. The French company, Areva, reached an agreement that enabled it to pay little rent and tax for its operation in the "ex-colony." The agreement promoted French interests, and efforts by the then president Hamani Diori to renegotiate it in the 1970s in the face of dwindling government revenue met with little success.[110] This negotiation remained inconclusive when Diori was overthrown in a coup in 1974.[111]

The regulatory mechanisms that would guide mining operations in Euro-America are lacking in Arlit, which means that the company operates with impunity, continuing the colonial subordination of local interests to French ones. A 2017 report on Arlit notes that the two mines in Niger "account for around a third of the multi-billion-dollar company's total global production."[112] Areva generates considerable energy for France's nuclear program but this relationship leaves the Nigeriens at the losing end. This exploitation has been cited as a major factor in Tuareg rebellions in the region, orchestrated mainly by the Mouvement des Nigériens pour la Justice. The nomadic Tuareg people inhabited the northern region of the country in the pre-mining era and have protested their exploitation, especially at the hands of the mining industry and the Nigerien government.[113] As a connector or medium of interaction between France and Niger, uranium is marked by the same disequilibrium that marred colonial relations.

Mining operations in Niger are detrimental to the ecosystem as they contaminate the water and land as well as endanger various life forms. In 2003, Aghir In'Man, a local NGO headed by Almoustapha Alhacen, an employee of the Somair mine, invited CRIIRAD, a French laboratory, and Sherpa, a human rights organization based in France, to measure radiation, and they found dangerous levels everywhere: in contaminated water from community taps and in scrap metal in market stalls.[114] Mining is a water-intensive project and this has implications for Arlit, which is located in the desert. The extensive use of water in the mines has contributed to its scarcity and the further desertification of the region.[115] High rates of radioactivity have been recorded in the available water sources as a result of toxicity from the mining process.[116] Mine workers have also reported various illnesses and many have died from cancers. Scrap metal from mining operations are discarded indiscriminately, and this has also contributed to the spread of radiation among the population, many of whom recycle these discarded objects for domestic use. Unsurprisingly, Areva has done little to educate the citizens on the dangers of radioactive waste, and neither has it done much to decommission the objects and dispose of them properly.[117] Rather, the company has rejected any effort to link cancers to its operation, linking its method to those practiced in South Africa and other places where Gabrielle Hecht observes the same "invisibility of radiological hazards."[118] The impacts of mining take a long time to materialize, which makes it easier for the companies to commit resources to disconnecting these illnesses from mining labor. In fact doctors in Areva's employ are reluctant to diagnose occupational illnesses despite studies linking radon emissions from the mines to cancer and other serious ailments.[119]

This last point is illustrated in *Arlit* where the company's doctor argues that the water-based process makes the Somair and Cominack mines less likely to cause cancer. If the chief in Bieleu's *The Big Banana* attempts to produce doubt about toxicity in the banana plantations by being equivocal about the relationship between toxic materials from the banana plantation and diseases (see chapter 2), this medical expert, in the pay of the mining company, dismisses such concerns entirely, noting that the only sickness caused by the mining operations is eczema. By accepting responsibility for eczema, an easily treatable skin ailment, the doctor and his paymasters trivialize the health of their workers and lay the groundwork for intentionally misdiagnosing serious ailments.

These diseases and the stories of loss—of livelihood, colleagues, family members, and friends—connect *Arlit* to the genre of ecotrauma cinema. Ecotrauma cinema "represents the harm we, as humans, inflict upon our natural surroundings, or the injuries we sustain from nature in its unforgiving iterations."[120] In *Arlit*, we see both the violence wrought on the land and human injuries from the exploitation of nature. The characteristics of trauma films are germane to *Arlit*: "non-linearity, fragmentation, nonsynchronous sound, repetition, rapid editing and strange angles. And they approach the past through an unusual admixture of emotional affect, metonymic symbolism and cinematic flashbacks."[121] As a work of trauma, *Arlit* is nonlinear. Episodic nonlinearity is indeed an appropriate term for capturing the film's structure. As the film opens with establishing shots locating us in place, there is also a notable tracking shot where the camera pans across the desert. I will have more to say about the function of this scene to the film's narrative later, but at this initial point it can be (mis)taken for a landscape scene inviting contemplation. If we follow Martin Lefebvre's distinction between setting and landscape, we can indeed read the desert as landscape, as independent of the film narrative, if only initially and briefly.[122] The overwhelming nature of the desert and human immateriality in the face of its vastness are captured by the camera pan early in the film. As spectacle, this landscape hardly lends itself to the kind of consumerism that film scholars have critiqued.[123] It is more appropriate to see it as "an object that draws the viewer ineluctably to itself and crushes him with the thought of its greatness and ineffability."[124] The landscape shots remind the viewer of the delusions of human grandeur and of the vulnerability of human beings, which can be a trigger for trauma. The extradiegetic music, which vanishes after the early scenes of the film, is nonsynchronous.

When we enter the film narrative proper, we encounter former mine workers, the unemployed, including a former Tuareg rebel, and migrants who found themselves in Arlit as they attempted to travel to North Africa and Europe through the desert. The dominant motif in this section is nostalgia. When we encounter two men who arrived in Arlit in the late 1960s at the beginning of mining operations, they speak of the glories of the old days, when workers earned much more money for working at the mines. The mines boomed and boosted the economy. Some of the residents sold cars and the workers patronized restaurants. Although cinematic flashback is absent, the oral recollection of the past fulfills its function. Family portraits from the period are incorporated into the film to further demonstrate past prosperity. Most of the photographs depict young, fashionably dressed people. For instance, one picture in the montage shows a young man holding a gun, suggesting the influence of the American Western and a shared modernity.

Like "many of the people who appear in environmental documentaries" that "are traumatized by ecological events and devastation," interview subjects in *Arlit* are trauma victims.[125] As the interviewees recollect their experiences of the prosperous past, their voices and their facial expressions carry emotion. These are men beaten and cowed by the passage of time. While they may have been prosperous in the past, they look defeated as they sit for interviews for the documentary. Nostalgic memory serves in the film as a bulwark against the present quagmire.[126] Nostalgia allows for connection and a sense of community in a society riven by disease, poverty, and other aberrations of extractive economies in the Global South. Again and again, interviewees repeat that the past was much better and that Arlit boomed as a cosmopolitan space attracting people from across the world. The film's multiglossia attests to this cosmopolitanism: Hausa, English, and French are some of the languages spoken.

As these residents recount their experiences of the past, of the boom that ended in 1980 with the drop in the price of uranium, the viewer can identify an additional source of pain and loss in the ephemerality of developmental promises. The film's subtitle refers to Arlit as a "second Paris," registering the promise made by the mining companies to develop the town. Just as the inhabitants of the Niger Delta believed that oil exploration in their communities would engender massive infrastructural development, the expectation here was that Arlit would be transformed by money from uranium. It is on this basis that the tracking shot of the desert achieves its first narrative significance. As the camera slowly moves to reveal the vast desert, the place has no resemblance or similarity to ultramodern or postmodern Paris.[127] The flat landscape connotes monotony and the absence of progress. The equivalent of the Eiffel Tower in Arlit is the mining infrastructure littering the film. In a telling scene that foregrounds the irony of the film's subtitle, the man who first explains the "second Paris" appellation is standing before mud houses. At this moment, the irony is not lost on the viewer that this community has benefited nothing from opening the bowels of the earth to the machinations of Areva. As such, when the older men recall the past, there is a tinge of further loss, one that is connected to the unrealized promise of modernity.

This unrealized promise is not unique to Arlit's workers, however; it is what has driven the migrants we meet in the film's first section. They have come from everywhere: Benin, Nigeria, Cameroon. The women who run the restaurant have come expecting the boom of the glory days. As the camera focuses on one with medium and close-up shots, she intimates to the viewer that her journey was in search of economic prosperity to support her family at home. Her Arlit dream ended, now she cannot return due to the travel cost. We also meet a Cameroonian who has come through Nigeria on his way to Marseille, France, where his mother lives. He has a romantic vision of Europe and is committed to reaching it through the desert. On his first try, he was duped and left penniless, which is the reason he is in Arlit, but he is optimistic of success on his next try. The Cameroonian is particularly interesting because apart from the children playing in the streets, he is the only interviewee who seems visibly happy about his prospects. The gloom pervading the earlier portion of the film later reaches its apogee when the older workers report various cancers and we learn of deaths.

In *Moses and Monotheism*, Freud gives an account of trauma and its relation to temporality that is worth recalling in this context. For Freud, someone may leave the scene of an accident unhurt, but that does not mean that the person is unaffected by the incident. In Freud's words, "the time that elapsed between the accident and the first appearance of the symptoms is

Chapter Three

called the 'incubation period,'" which is marked by "latency."[128] Although Freud is primarily concerned with psychological symptoms, his term can be deployed for understanding the time lag between the exposure of the mining workers in Arlit to toxicity and the physical manifestation of that exposure as sickness and death. If we privilege the incubation period and the latency stage, we can interrogate the so-called glorious days when mining sufficiently rewarded the workers. What was the cost of the financial boom? The second segment of Mora-Kpai's film makes it clear that the price of the profits from the Somair and Cominack mines was the toxification of the body, the land, air, and water. As in Agbogbloshie and the Cameroon region discussed in chapter 2, the ecosystem is also at risk in Arlit. This is a place where "the mines leach water from pastoral land and gardens; radioactive dust from the open-pit mines settles over the parched landscape; and the air itself is laden with it."[129] To buttress the violence wrought on the earth and bodies by the mining process, the film depicts a spectacular scene of dynamite explosion. The loud noise and the smoke billowing from the scene ensure that the violence is not only etched on the land but that it is equally sculpted on the lungs of residents. In other scenes, we see the burrowed land, a reminder that mining is a process of excavation and extraction with nothing put back in return.

Defining the responsibility of the spectator of ecocinema, Roberto Forns-Broggi asks for an attunement to the more-than-human world, "whose voices the dominant rationality has traditionally denied."[130] This orientation to nonhuman beings is particularly salient for *Arlit*, which gives viewers a glimpse of the Others in the environment. It is not a coincidence, for instance, that we encounter a flock of birds more than once in the film. In the polluted ecosystem that the film presents, the presence of birds and their twittering orients viewers to other vulnerable creatures caught in the ecological catastrophe that is uranium mining. Another scene features bleating sheep even when the animals are outside the camera's scope. The repetition of such scenes is crucial for highlighting that more than human lives are at stake. Human and animal sounds are endangered by the mining industry concretized by the noise of machinery reverberating in the film. The screeching and sometimes wheezing noise from slow-moving machines in *Arlit* signals uranium's seemingly harmless but gradual disintegration of the body. To attend to the film's acoustemology, to the knowledge produced by its sounds, is to become aware of its "interanimation and interarticulation of human and nonhuman sounds" in order to underscore the risk that the extractive machine poses to ecological plurality in Arlit.[131]

Environmental justice films marshal the sick body for its advocacy and *Arlit* is no exception.[132] In one touching scene, a former employee explains to viewers that they were unaware of the toxicity and that they would wear the same clothes at work and while carrying their children at home. The failure of the mining company and government to sensitize people to the health hazards of mining rings loud here, but what is particularly distressing is one interviewee's comment that the ailments "happened suddenly." Sudden is the operative word in terms of trauma, as it articulates the unexpectedness of the ailments that plague the people. Symptom appearance is sudden or unexpected because of the time lag, because the manifestation does not follow in the immediate aftermath of an event. *Arlit* "create[s] out of images, sounds, geography, and history the narrative of human suffering" building over time.[133] To use Carmela Garritano's words, "Mora-Kpai's documentary extends time to follow the drawn-out temporality of uranium's decay."[134] As the older workers describe sudden falls in the bathroom, joint pains, and the doctors' failure to determine exactly what ails them, we are returned to the scene of the man whose eyes have been damaged by toxic materials from PHP's operations in Cameroon. Like the plantation worker's, the miners' affective states call for the viewer's empathy. As each recalls his ailment sitting down or lying down, or recalls those of others who have not survived, the film's pathos is elevated to draw in the viewer to the calamities resulting from mining operations. It is against this background that the viewer encounters current employees laboring in the mine. They do not address the camera, perhaps out of fear of losing their jobs, but from what we already know from their predecessors, the future does not bode well for them.

In the earlier discussion of *Curse of the Black Gold*, the presence of children is crucial for interrogating the trauma of the future; that claim holds true for *Arlit* as well. In one scene, which should qualify as a "resonant moment," we see children playing in the streets like their Niger Delta counterparts.[135] What interrupts the pleasure of play here is the mise-en-scène: to be precise, the surrounding decommissioned machinery strewn across the dusty ground. Objects, Martin Heidegger writes, are the things "we take in view, what is most immediate, most capable of being grasped by the hand."[136] Discarded, these objects, imbued with toxicity, take on a new life. Far from inert, their "thingness," in Bill Brown's register, compels attention.[137] If in Heidegger's work, humans grasp things, and objects are only useful to the extent that they serve human needs, here we have to join Brown in considering "how objects grasp you: how they elicit your attention, interrupt your concentration, assault your sensorium."[138]

In this scene, the camera moves around, showcasing the objects scattered across the area before resting on the playing children, thereby mirroring the movement of radioactivity from the infrastructural waste to the children's bodies where it settles as a health hazard. This scene resonates because of the immediacy of these gadgets, children's exposure to contamination, and the adverse impact the objects can have on them. These discarded materials may have outlived their usefulness for mining, but they have taken on new roles. As the children play in proximity to the toxic objects and as the contaminated dust enters their bodies when they kick a ball, *Arlit* concretizes an uncertain future rife with health hazards. Because these objects call to us from the film's frame to consider their aliveness, we cannot focus on the kids' play or easily partake of their leisure activity. Beyond the medical implications of the exposure, we must also ask what future awaits these children in this environment, where the major form of employment is the dwindling mine "contaminated with radioactive tailings, effectively forever."[139]

To avoid ambiguity about the significance of the scene of children playing, a subsequent scene shows an environmental activist displaying a discarded object. The camera zooms in and out on the object and then turns to the official explaining about the toxicity of discarded materials and how they make their way into the community as recycled objects. Recycling is toxic here as it is in Agbogbloshie. With contaminated objects becoming part of the assemblages sustaining households in Arlit and its environs, it is immaterial whether a family member worked in the mines or not. Like in Agbogbloshie and the Niger Delta, toxicity seeps everywhere in the world of Arlit. Toxicity is also implicated in deep time as it bridges the past of exposure, the present manifestation, and the lingering impacts on the community's future. Uranium toxicity takes time to manifest, which means that for the children and even their progeny, the hauntings of contamination may be ever present.

As the children play in toxic environments and as their elders die from radiation poisoning, migration takes on a special allure for those eager to escape their predicament. Amadou, a young man whose father worked in the mine, is an example. He is a motor mechanic affected by the economic decline of the community. His father had come from Benin and encourages him as the film ends to return there. Returning home, in the elder's estimation, will not only rescue his son from economic stagnation but will protect him and his family from the effects of radiation. Arlit is a town of migrants, some attracted by the mining economy in its heyday, and others who ended up there as they tried to reach Europe through the desert. Located near the border with Algeria, the area is an attractive point for would-be migrants seeking to enter Europe. One such man in the film is the Cameroonian, who has not given up on his plan to reach Europe. As the film winds down, he maps his impending journey.

It is a fitting nod to the film's intertwining of energy drilling and displacement that its closing scene is a point-of-view shot featuring the Cameroonian. Before him is the vast desert, which returns us to the earlier tracking shot of the desert. I have considered the panning shot of the desert as a landscape shot indicating the overwhelming power of the desert and marking the irony of the promise of modernity ("second Paris"). Here I want to note its value for the film's narrative on migration. It is significant that the shot of the desert early in the film is not static. We can combine the earlier panning shot of the desert with the point-of-view shot with which the film ends. The movement of the camera in the earlier scene recalls the movement of people from across West Africa and beyond to Arlit, and most especially it foreshadows the impending movement of the Cameroonian toward Marseille. At the film's end, we can identify unity in its nonlinear projections of mobility. In other words, the panning shot of the desert combines with other aspects of mise-en-scène to foreground movement: the buses that ferry people in and out of town, the cars that we see in the repair shops, and the repeated shots of birds that fly away as the camera cuts to the next scene. The birds may point to other-than-human presence, but they also serve as an indicator of mobility in combination with the other factors.

All this is to say that geographies of energy extraction such as that of the Niger Delta and Arlit engender climate change and traumas that in turn encourage people to seek opportunities elsewhere. At this point, the reader needs no further convincing that mass utopia—for developmental modernity in both the Delta and Arlit—is "a rusty idea."[140] As seen in *Curse of the Black Gold*, climate change caused by oil exploration results in acid rain and pollution that render farmland infertile and destroy the aquatic environment for fish stock. The threat to livelihood adversely affects the health and well-being of the community.[141] Decline in agricultural yields further puts pressure on these communities to engage in less sustainable practices, and ultimately promotes conflict.[142] In the absence of peace and amidst displacement caused by militant and military attacks in the region, people are bound to seek better climes where they can lead better lives. But where migration remains a latent possibility in *Curse of the Black Gold*, we see its manifestation in *Arlit* with its focus on a town that has attracted migrants due to its uranium deposits and geographical location. More specifically, the film's closing turn to imminent departures from the town further concretizes this link among resource extraction, climate change, and migration.

In Lieu of a Conclusion: Against Closure

As this chapter ends, it is productive to return to the ending of *Arlit* where the point-of-view shot shows the would-be migrant looking into the horizon. How are we to interpret this ending? In other words, are there grounds for his optimism, that Marseille will indeed be his promised land, where it will be like being born again? We can read this ending in at least two ways. The vast desert can symbolize the abundant opportunities that await him beyond Arlit, where he will be free from radioactivity and able to explore more attractive economic opportunities. However, it does not take much to challenge such a positive interpretation. The Sahara Desert, as nonhuman agent, has made migration possible for many Africans, but it has also been the final resting place for those who have succumbed to its tough terrain: its vastness, the scorching sun and dry heat, as well as hunger and dehydration. In this economy of seeing, the vastness represented in that closing shot is more of an impediment to the successful attainment of the migrant dream. Even for those who succeed in reaching Europe's shores, the hostility against African migrants and the obstacles put in the way of successful integration undermine the narrative of progress, the kind woven by the Cameroonian migrant in Mora-Kpai's film.

Arlit ends before we can determine the fate of our migrant, but we can turn to recent African films for a dramatization of the conditions they face. Wanuri Kahiu's *Pumzi*, discussed in chapter 1, is not a film on migration per se but it yields rewards if read from that perspective, especially in connection to *Arlit*.[143] The major preoccupation of Mora-Kpai's film is the degradation connected to uranium mining, while Kahiu's film is a quest for planetary rejuvenation after World War III has resulted in extinction and engendered water scarcity. The world outside Kahiu's Virtual Natural History Museum is contaminated by radioactivity from nuclear weapons used in the war. These nuclear warheads are enriched with uranium, establishing a connection between *Arlit* and *Pumzi*. Both films are linked by uranium and radioactivity. *Arlit* is also joined to Kahiu's film by a shared quest motif. If *Arlit* ends as the Cameroonian is about to begin his journey through the desert in search of greener pastures, Asha in *Pumzi* spends time in the desert in search of a fertile, uncontaminated land. Like the migrants whose quests for visas are denied at embassies and who therefore resort to the desert and the sea,

Asha's request for an exit visa to leave the sealed-off futuristic edifice is denied, and she resorts to an unconventional means of escape. Out of that environment, her perilous journey takes her through the wasteland, where nothing grows and even the river has dried up. Her journey to locate the source of the rich soil sample takes her through the desert. The extended shot of her journey in the vast, barren landscape simulates the journeys of would-be migrants, the kind of journey that the Cameroonian is about to embark upon as *Arlit* ends.

Asha's arrival at area of uncontaminated land recalls the border where the migrant is placed between the space of abjection he/she is renouncing and the promise of happiness that beckons. Again, Asha's experience at this site is illustrative of the migrant experience. Having transferred the plant she is carrying from the nursery to the earth and nourished it with her sweat and remaining water, Asha lies down to rest. As I argued in chapter 1, the promise of positive interspecies relationships, one premised on relationality, is thwarted when Asha disappears to make way for the tree's blossoming. Rather than the more eco-cosmopolitan pairing of woman and tree, the tree thrives in place of the woman. To be sure, the portrayal of Asha improves the representation of black women in the speculative genre of science fiction, yet her disappearance reveals an obvious limitation to the role's success.[144] For this specific analysis, the failure of relationality or eco-cosmopolitanism registers the failure of European countries and citizens to welcome the migrant with open arms. Like Asha, who is supplanted by the tree, the migrant is seen as vermin to be squashed, as a threat to the security of the homeland to be removed. Furthermore, since Asha nourishes the tree with water before it grows to obliterate her, we can say that she drowns in it like the migrants who perish in the sea. The Cameroonian in *Arlit* speaks of being born again, with language alluding to Christianity. If baptism is premised on the promise of rebirth, of rising after the initial submerging, Asha, like the drowned migrants, fails to attain the promise of redemption by water. We arrive at the migrant narrative in *Pumzi* through indirection; yet these experiences— of migrants who make it to Europe and those who die trying—have been directly captured in films and the stories they tell are of suffering, loss, and even death.[145]

Ultimately the work of this chapter requires a rewriting of the story of the "influx" of African migrants, one that accounts for the structural issues driving mobility. Rather than the conventional hysterical denunciation of these migrants as bringing diseases and crime to Europe, we can rebalance the relationship between the continent and the external world, reconstitute the fiscal and ethical exchanges across territories, and promote sustainable practices that will support the flourishing of lives on the continent. With Sontag, we can instantiate "a reflection on how our privileges are located on the same map as" the suffering recounted here.[146] One productive possibility for this reflection is to examine our role as "consumer[s] of pollution."[147]

Africa's resources continue to be siphoned off by European and American companies.[148] China will have to join the list as it expands its role on the continent, such as in Niger where it has broken France's monopoly in the mining business.[149] The illicit practices of these companies—seen in this chapter—alongside the forms of change they precipitate in the atmospheric and social climate contribute to the increasing number of people fleeing the continent. Unfortunately, racism is still the organizing rubric for the treatment of these migrants, who must be cast out of the West.[150] The process of resource extraction in Nigeria, Niger and elsewhere on the continent will have to be overhauled. This will mean, in other words, casting out not the immigrant body but the pollution of landscapes and waterscapes through comprehensive decontamination systems. A post-carbon economy is the ideal outcome of climate activism, but what does this really mean for places like the Niger Delta and Arlit, destroyed and wasted by energy extraction? How do we avoid the scenario where they fall into another form of abandon and neglect when the oil and mining companies turn off the last switch? In this future to come, human and nonhuman lives on the continent will count as much as those of the privileged in the countries of Europe and America, and their well-being will be prioritized over the narrow economic interests that engender the status quo from Niger to Nigeria, from Arlit to the Niger Delta, and from *Arlit* to *Curse of the Black Gold*.

human meets animal, africa meets diaspora

the conjunctions of cecil the lion and black lives matter

In the previous chapter I showed the connection between resource extraction, environmental degradation, and displacement. Africans exploring migratory routes into Europe and other parts of the world are often seeking better socioeconomic conditions, away from the attenuation of the good life for many on the continent. This attenuation is, of course, indissociable from the hauntings of colonialism and from globalizing processes in Africa. But whereas immigrants such as the Cameroonian encountered in chapter 3 struggle to enter Europe, and others like him get stuck in places like Arlit, or die in the desert, or drown in the Mediterranean Sea, African things and objects, such as oil and uranium, easily make their way across the globe. These resource media link the continent to the world, albeit unequally. Images from the continent too enjoy immigrant rights enabled by many factors, one of which is the preponderance of social media. I discuss in this chapter one such image that circulated following the death of Cecil the Lion at the hands of an American big-game hunter in Zimbabwe in July 2015. Many factors contributed to the viral spread of this image, but the "tipping point" of its success in America, I want to argue, was its appearance during the Black Lives Matter activism of the time.

Following Cecil's death, a photo of his killer and a male companion posing with a dead lion from a previous hunt went viral. Analyzing the image as an "active rhetorical agent," alongside Black Lives Matter's attention to decimated black bodies, allows for apprehending vulnerabilities across species.[1] This contrapuntal analysis also opens a space for the much-needed dialogue between African studies and African diaspora studies.[2] Saidiya Hartman anticipates my argument when she writes of a "promise of affiliation" between Africans and African Americans based on shared struggles around the failure of abolition and decolonization.[3] My argument in this chapter is that the "problematic of race" undergirds Cecil's death and the circulation of the image under investigation, and that race remains the underexplored fundament of wildlife media including the CNN film *Trophy*, codirected by Shaul Schwarz and Christina Clusiau.[4]

This chapter builds on wildlife film scholarship while proposing in the final section a model of interspecies entanglement in a time of crisis.[5] My approach foregrounds the experiences of the communities interacting with conservation practices in Africa. Rather than prioritizing the interests of wildlife over the human inhabitants of African communities or ignoring animal interests altogether for human concerns, there is room for what Saskia Sassen calls an "analytical borderland," where competing interests are analyzed and reshaped for the higher purposes of trans-species conviviality and for the achievement of a planetary humanism.[6] I will posit in the concluding section that Orlando von Einsiedel's film *Virunga* activates a borderland for intertwining human-nonhuman interests and cultivating positive interspecies relationships in precarious times.[7]

I am indebted to Paul Gilroy and Achille Mbembe for the articulation of conviviality as well as planetary humanism. Conviviality names a mutual imbrication, a consequence of living together and sharing physical space. This interrelationship, the entanglement "of those who command and those who are assumed to obey," sometimes contentious and violent, defines conviviality for Mbembe.[8] Where the relationship between the ruler and the ruled in Africa exemplifies the concept for Mbembe, Gilroy turns to multiculturalism in Britain. Gilroy uses conviviality "to refer to the processes of cohabitation and interaction that have made multiculture an ordinary feature of social life in Britain's urban areas and in postcolonial cities elsewhere."[9] Gilroy's treatment of the subject acknowledges the frictions and tensions characterizing the practice of multiculturalism. Whereas Mbembe acknowledges the violence often visited on the dominated in the convivial relationship in Africa, Gilroy highlights abuses in Britain, especially as they concern the racialization of minorities, specifically of black bodies subject to police brutality and other signatures of racial aggression. Both thinkers want to undo the violence of intergroup dynamics and ultimately imagine a cosmopolitan rendering of relations.[10] This planetary humanism is "allied to nonracial, transblack histories and imagined here from an assertively cosmopolitan point of view."[11] Transcending race does not ignore race and racism as structural violators in the current world order but is an invitation to turn from racial to moral reasoning as the basis for relationships with the Other.[12]

It can be argued that there is nothing significantly innovative about these articulations of cosmopolitan feeling, but they are relevant for my project because of the possibility of a non-anthropocentric sensibility that they permit. Mbembe predicates the survival of humans and the planet on the ethics of care we exhibit to others, stating, "in opposing itself to the world of nonhumans, humanity opposes itself."[13] Gilroy and Mbembe decry the acrimonious politics of identity among humans—and in Mbembe, across species—which is the reason their works are attractive for a chapter problematizing racial divisions as well as arbitrary, exploitative human-animal distinctions. While the nonhuman remains tangential in the articulations of these scholars and other meditations on planetary humanism, I foreground what Chielozona Eze calls "empathetic cosmopolitanism" in the analysis of relationality across species, making a strong case for the inextricability of the radical Other—animals—in considerations of planetary humanism.[14] Anthropocentric conceptualizations of ethical engagements with the Other may represent an improvement over parochial notions of human solidarities, but they remain insufficient if they maintain the wall of an absolute separation from animals and other beings. In the end, the chapter argues for seeing race as the elephant in the room of wildlife media.

The balance of the chapter is spread across two substantive sections and the conclusion. In the first section, I discuss the circulation of a trophy photograph to explore the opportunities it provides for articulating shared vulnerabilities between black lives and animal lives. The second section examines Schwarz and Clusiau's *Trophy* for its treatment of blackness in the safari business, while in the conclusion I suggest that Einsiedel's *Virunga* underscores human and nonhuman vulnerabilities and lays the ground for the work of bringing about a world of multispecies thriving and belonging.

In considering black people's complex relation to "nature," especially animals, some critics may object to my bringing humans and animals together

Chapter Four

within a racial framework. Addressing this issue, Graham Huggan and Helen Tiffin concede that the "metaphorisation and deployment of 'animal' as a derogatory term in genocidal and marginalising discourses . . . make it difficult even to discuss animals without generating a profound unease, even a rancorous antagonism, in many postcolonial contexts today."[15] This unease is connected to the "intersectional fantasies of racialization and animalization" at the heart of blackness and modernity.[16] The history of blackness has been about the denigration of the Other, and that discursive, material "racial formation" involved naturalizing the black body.[17] The history of the modern world has worked by depicting Africa and people of African descent as aspects of nature, the inhuman, subhuman, beastly, and monstrous.[18] Discourses of slavery and colonialism are replete with examples of these denigrations, which in Stuart Hall's terms amount to "stereotyping as a representational practice."[19] Moreover, during slavery, the Jim Crow era, and even our contemporary moment, aspects of the environment served and continue to serve as technologies for terrorizing black bodies. Trees were used for lynching while dogs were accomplices in the hunt for fugitive slaves and were deployed against civil rights protesters in places like Birmingham, Alabama; more recently, the police set dogs against black protesters in the aftermath of Michael Brown's death in Ferguson, Missouri.[20] In demonstrating their subjectivities against the asubjective claims of white superiority and the physical flagellation enabled by aspects of the environment, many black persons, especially in the diaspora, have sought to distance themselves from animals and nature. This tactical move is understandable and has led many to the conclusion that African Americans have an ambivalent relationship to the environment.[21]

As strategic as the distancing of nature is, it is problematic for the way it implicitly approves the codes of coloniality and racism. To maintain the negativity of nature is to remain stuck within the colonial script. As such, when black people distance themselves from nature because of historical racial experiences, it amounts to ceding ground to the infrastructure of white supremacy. In making this claim, I do not intend to trivialize the experience of blackness, especially in the New World, but to posit that a decolonized ecological framework is possible, a framework that acknowledges and productively memorializes the legacy of slavery and ongoing practices of black subjugation but does not succumb to the logic of these abhorrent systems.

African communities and some in the Americas can provide instances of human-animal interactions that are less exploitative, premised on a relational disposition, which can serve as templates for imagining planetary humanism. Practices in the Andes, and among the Shona of Zimbabwe and the Yoruba of Nigeria, draw on indigenous cosmologies to redefine the cartography of subjectivity so that it includes nonhuman beings, who are treated with respect and care and become worthy of consideration.[22] As Allen F. Roberts reminds us, "many African philosophies posit a culture-to-nature continuum, with interlacing instances of nature-within-culture and culture-within-nature. Animals may have souls, be devious, and know magic; they both deserve and require sacred attention from humans who interfere with them."[23] Pythons, for instance, take on sacred value in my Igbo community in Nigeria and in others, where killing them is prohibited. Marisol de la Cadena has also written of "earth beings" in Latin American societies deserving ethical consideration.[24] These indigenous practices predate the work in critical animal studies and new materialism, which seeks to decenter humans, critique the notion of human superiority, and relativize the degrees of difference between humans and animals.[25] All this is to say that rather than continue to uphold the arbitrary distinctions and denigration of animals that we have inherited from the colonial edifice, we can turn to these inspiring examples of relationality between humans and others offered by indigenous cosmologies and from contemporary critiques emerging from the fields of animal studies and new materialism.[26] That way, animals retain their differences but lose the negative stereotypes that were employed to denigrate humans alongside them. This sense of "conviviality with a difference" is crucial for attaining planetary humanism.[27]

The Migrant Image: Cecil the Lion Meets Black Lives Matter

W. J. T. Mitchell may as well be referring to the image of Walter Palmer standing over a dead lion when he writes: "At a time when actual human bodies are more and more fenced in by actual and virtual borders, fences, checkpoints, and security walls, . . . the digital image can sometimes operate as a kind of 'wild gas' that escapes these restrictions."[28] In 2015, when this image circulated, the migrant crisis was in full swing, with refugees taking unconventional routes to reach Europe from Syria and different parts of Africa while others sought to enter the United States from Mexico. This was also the height of the nationalist agitation tinged with racism that propelled Donald Trump to victory in the United States and led to the success of the Brexit vote in the United Kingdom. All these events have unique dimensions, but they share the fear of contamination and pollution of the nation by black and brown immigrants. It was in the context of this national anxiety that Cecil's death made news at the end of July 2015.

Cecil the Lion was killed by an American dentist in Hwange Park, Zimbabwe, in July 2015. Hwange is the largest national park in Zimbabwe and is the third largest in Africa, following the Serengeti in Tanzania and the Kruger National Park in South Africa.[29] It gained game reserve status through the Game and Fish Preservation Act in 1930 and was proclaimed a national park in 1949.[30] The park is located in northwest Zimbabwe, bordering Botswana to the west.[31] Walter Palmer, big game hunter, traveled to Zimbabwe to hunt and kill a lion. Once Palmer had paid $50,000 to a professional hunting guide in Zimbabwe, all was set for the hunt to begin on July 1. An elephant carcass was positioned to ensnare the lion, and that evening Palmer fatally wounded Cecil as he feasted on the elephant.

According to reports by Oxford University's Wildlife Conservation Research Unit (WILDCRU), a research team that had studied Cecil for years, the lion suffered for hours until Palmer and his crew returned the next morning to kill him and remove the body. In the process, they removed and discarded the collar that had been put on by the Oxford team to monitor Cecil. As Oxford's Andrew Loveridge summarizes it in his book on Cecil: "What I find most difficult about the whole incident is the apparent callousness with which the hunters undertook this hunt. The lion was a commodity to be collected, 'taken' in hunting parlance. Concern for the pain and suffering of the animal never seems to have been a particular consideration. I find the thought of killing any animal purely for sport or pleasure abhorrent, but if it has to happen, it must be done cleanly and without undue stress or suffering."[32] Loveridge's language forces us to pay attention to the language of trophy hunting. "Taken" is particularly instructive as a loaded term that elides the violence committed in the process. Palmer would reproduce the same word in his apology, where he reiterated that he had operated within legal bounds. The concept of legality was thrown around by both pro-hunting and anti-hunting conservationists in the aftermath of Cecil's death. While the latter insisted that there was no approved lion quota that would have permitted the hunt, the proponents of trophy hunting argued that the American had acted legally by working with a professional hunter who guided the process.

In addition to touting its legality, hunting proponents have also argued that revenue from hunting supports conservation efforts in Africa and boosts local economies.[33] As reasonable as these propositions sound, the conversation misses a point: legality is an insufficient barometer for assessing right or

4.1 Walter Palmer and his companion with a dead lion

wrong. The imposition of colonial rule across the African continent and the slavery that rocked the New World were legal at some point. Commodification of the body here resonates with earlier, legal colonization and dehumanization of the black body. I will have more to say about these connections subsequently, but first let us examine the viral image and the politics of its reception (figure 4.1).

As already noted, the lion in this image is not Cecil, which means that the image works by indirection. This is an image from another hunt that Palmer had participated in. It shows him towering above a dead lion, which he probably killed with the support of the other white man beside him. This image is different from the others discussed in this book, which are produced by artists as aesthetic objects. We can say that the professionalism at the heart of those other images is absent from this one.

Death haunts this image. Susan Sontag takes the conjunction of death and photography in an interesting direction when she writes: "Guns have metamorphosed into cameras in this earnest comedy, the ecology safari."[34] If taking pictures of animals replaces killing them in Sontag's framing, in the moment represented by the circulatory image under discussion, shooting pictures and shooting animals go together. In this case, "the technologies of the gun and the camera themselves evolved in lockstep" for shooting and "freezing" the Other.[35] The alliance of gun and camera is still relevant, but it also needs updating as the weapons of choice have proliferated. In Cecil's case, a compound bow, which would enable the hunt to accrue points in the Safari Club system, was used. The lion's suffering would have been minimized had Palmer used a gun, but then such a weapon would have disqualified the hunt from the peer recognition and prestige accruable from the Safari Club point system.

The image of Palmer with the deceased lion is a safari photograph linking the camera to death, but a case can also be made for its constructedness. Constructedness is at the heart of art and this image betrays its artifice. In this image the men strike poses that position them in a dominating relationship with the animal. Their smiles indicate their victory over nature and we can say they look satisfied, assured of having conquered the jungle. To the side of the lion we can glimpse the bow, but it is not foregrounded or emphasized. What is prominent in the photograph is the lifeless body of the lion, the "unanswerable gaze of a fellow creature," arranged in a prone position.[36] But more importantly, the photograph, the "quintessential migratory creature in its refusal of borders," celebrates the exploit of the hunters, revealing in the process the portrait of the hero as a white man.[37] To foreground white masculinity, the weapon facilitating the hunt must be cast aside and the black subjects who assisted the trophy hunters cannot make an appearance.

Even as photography makes visible that which ordinary eyes cannot see, it is also the case that it leaves out other things.[38] What is left out here includes other labor that resulted in this hunt—namely, the black bodies that assisted in the hunt, performing its most tedious tasks, to pave the way for the white man's success. On the (in)visibility of blackness in game lodges, the South African writer and critic Njabulo S. Ndebele writes: "Living somewhere out there, beyond the neatly clipped frontier, the black workers come into the clearing to serve. And then they disappear again." While not granted presence in this space, "the faceless black workers . . . clean the rooms, wash the dishes, make the fire, babysit the children, and make sure that in the morning the leisure refugees find their cars clean."[39] There is also labor involved in the transformation of the dead animal into a valuable trophy, which is mostly performed by black hands. In the case of Cecil, the professional guide who assisted Palmer also enlisted black labor in preparing the animal's body for onward transportation to the United States. The construction of this image, in a nutshell, leaves out traces of black labor. Such absences constitute visible invisibilities necessary for upholding the image of the white man as hero.

In *Why Photography Matters as Art as Never Before*, Michael Fried considers largeness and being made "for the wall" as important characteristics of contemporary photographic art. In his words, there is "an intention that the photographs in question would be framed and hung on a wall, to be looked at like paintings."[40] Even though some of the pictures he analyzes did not begin large, as is the case for Thomas Ruff's head-shots of students, Fried argues that their "frontality" puts them in "a particular mode of relation to the viewer, one of mutual facing."[41] The photograph I am discussing here may be miles apart from the professionally produced images that Fried discusses, but a potential for "wall hanging" joins them together. Part of the allure of the hunting photograph is its role as evidence: it is testimony that the hunt has happened. It is also an object to be looked at and admired, like a work of art, when hung on the wall. Its frontality—manifesting in the way the humans and the lion are situated to face the camera—and staged quality position the image in direct relation to the viewer, who is invited to appreciate Palmer's accomplishment. In the age of social media, the wall of aesthetic contemplation has now extended beyond the physical walls of the home and of the office. Pictures now adorn Facebook walls and other social media spaces where they can be liked, loved, shared, and re-shared. In the case of our image, its availability suggests that Palmer or his partner shared it at some point, inviting admiration and likes for it, and seeking recognition as a trophy hunter.

With this photograph, Palmer intends to strike an exhibitionist pose, to demonstrate his masculinity, and to delight his friends, to locate himself as an upwardly mobile subject who can afford to travel and hunt lions in Africa. We can return to Fried, this time to his distinction between works of absorption and those steeped in theatricality. Artworks in the absorptive mode maintain "the supreme fiction or ontological illusion that the beholder [does] not exist, that there [is] no one standing before the canvas."[42] The subjects of these works appear engaged in activities preventing their apprehension of being beheld by an external gaze. Theatrical pieces, on the other hand, announce their artifice and directly perform for the viewer. Palmer's photograph is a performance for his audience; it announces its "to-be-seenness" and is staged to maximize the demonstration of the hunter's conquest and mastery.[43]

But as it circulated in 2015, the image's affective meaning took on a different valence, one of sympathetic feeling for the animal and outrage against the killer. The receiver of a message is unbound to the intention of the sender.[44] The protesters who occupied the premises of Palmer's dental practice and who left flowers and signs mourning the lion demonstrated their indignation as the image circulated. Against Palmer's intent, this photograph became evidence of brutality and the exploitation of animals, especially endangered ones. The photograph was transformed in function from the self-performative to pedagogical as it was shared and re-shared.

As the image circulated in the aftermath of Cecil's death, it took on art's pedagogical function. As a teaching object, as instantiation of Debord's *détournement*, which disfigures the picture's original role as spectacle, the image registers the violence of Palmer's behavior and the threat to wildlife populations in Africa.[45] Art speaks through the language of indirection, and this image is no exception. While the lion in this picture is not Cecil, viewers have no problem appreciating it as a stand-in for the charismatic animal because of the lions' shared generic classification and vulnerability. The outrage over the killing of Cecil as represented by this image was certainly a response to Palmer's action, but it equally speaks to a broader problem of violence against vulnerable bodies. Palmer becomes a symbolic representation of humans whose actions contribute to the depletion of wildlife.

When the news broke in the American media, there was an overwhelming condemnation of Palmer for causing Cecil's death. Images of the lion and condemnation of the killer saturated social media and various news outlets, making the incident an example of image events that parlay environmental issues into people's consciousness.[46] We find an instantiation of "convergence culture" here, wherein audiences follow the migratory routes of an image over both social and traditional media.[47] The image was shared across multiple social media platforms; the traditional media was not left out as segments were devoted to the news, and analysts representing various sides of the conservation issue took turns dissecting the event. For example, *Trophy*, a CNN film discussed in the next section, includes footage from the coverage of Cecil's death in mainstream news outlets. We see in this event the transformation of "the digital image into a cultural virus," a process involving "a frenzy of circulation, being copied, linked, and forwarded as fast as possible."[48] The Oxford WILDCRU research team seized on the killing of their research subject to raise funds online for their conservation projects, helped in part by late-night host Jimmy Kimmel's impassioned denunciation of Palmer and a call for donations on his show. By September 2015, the Oxford team had raised over $1 million, while "between 1 July and 30 September there were a total of 94,631 hits in the editorial media" on Cecil the Lion.[49]

We ought to ask: What made this image go viral in America at a time when African bodies are policed, when borders are shut to them, and when many have taken unorthodox means to flee the continent? In other words, why did this "migrant image," to use the words of the visual culture scholar W. J. T. Mitchell, make its way across the world in ways that most Africans on the continent cannot?[50] We can start with a simple answer, which is that the age of digital media makes it easier for information and images to travel with accelerated speed. All it takes is multiple shares for media content to go viral. In other words, technological sophistication in the social media era partly engendered the dispersal of this image. In *Spreadable Media*, however, Henry Jenkins, Sam Ford, and Joshua Green caution that "we must all be careful not to suppose that a more participatory means of circulation can be explained solely (or even primarily) by this rise of technological infrastructure."[51] These authors are among those who have acknowledged that there is more to spreadability and virality than technology per se. Jenkins and his team ask that we pay attention as well to the "social logics and cultural practices" shaping the circulation and sharing of media resources.[52]

One cultural factor driving spreadability was the fact that Cecil had attained notoriety during his lifetime as a subject of research carried out at Oxford University. The Oxford research had already turned him into what we can call an animal celebrity. Pictures and videos of the lion had already gained traction from the research of this elite institution. It helped too that Cecil loved humans, which probably was also part of his undoing. His comfort in proximity to humans endeared him to many, raised his profile among visitors to the park, and increased traffic to the area. Many went to Hwange for the opportunity to view Cecil. The cultural capital that the Oxford team bequeathed to the lion was also enhanced by his species. Lions are charismatic megafauna, one of the big cats that excite the Western imagination. Over time, Westerners have cultivated affective connections with such creatures, to the point that their endangerment or extinction sends cataclysm across the world. As the image and its accompanying discourse circulated, they brought together a fragmented and complex population into an impermanent, flexible assemblage to express moral concern over Cecil's killing and the brutal fact of the disposability of certain forms of life.

Members of the Oxford team, David W. Macdonald and his coauthors, underscore the affective dimension in their explanation of why Cecil's death made news as it did, even though many lions had been "taken" before him with little or no outrage: "The lion in question was majestic, rather well-studied, bore an English nickname (more memorable than its data code of MAGM1); it was allegedly lured to its death (although it routinely left the park of its own volition), was wounded with an arrow and endured a lingering death, was killed in apparently dubious circumstances, by a client who was identifiable (as opposed to amorphous villains such as polluting industries in the case of climate change), wealthy, white, male and American and who, to judge by media reports, had previously been associated with problematic hunting episodes."[53] The emotional investment was deepened by a rumor that Cecil had suffered for forty hours before his death. In a Western economy concerned with animal welfare, it makes sense that the suffering of the lion, "the passion of the animal," would generate outrage.[54] Of course, the circulatory function of the internet and its role as mobilizer of affective economies facilitated the effect. Yet there is more to this event. Macdonald and his fellow authors anticipate my move here with the reference they make to the race, nationality, and class of the perpetrator: Palmer's whiteness, his Americanness, and his social status contributed to turning this moment into an event. In other words, we see here the functioning of race as technology.[55]

Sassen's work is worth recalling for apprehending the racial atmospherics of Cecil's death and for facilitating the flourishing of black lives across African and black diasporic spaces. In her project on the transformations that resulted in the global epoch in the late twentieth century, Sassen outlines the concepts of capabilities, tipping point, and organizing logic that enabled the shifts from the feudal to the national and then to the global age. These three concepts nourish this section with heuristic devices for analyzing the significance of Cecil's death. Capabilities can be "conceived of as intermediating in the move from one to another whole or master formation."[56] They are attributes of the previous epoch that make transition or transformation possible. In our example, digital portability, cultural affection for animals, and Cecil's celebrity status were important capabilities that facilitated the circulation of the image of Palmer from another hunt. In other words, the migration of the image was made possible by the rise of social media, and by the sociocultural logics that invest charismatic animals with value. It helps too that conservation is central to social discourses of the twenty-first-century global era.[57] Yet only specific animal species make the cut, usually large and endangered ones such as lions. The image under investigation surely benefited from the public interest in conservation and the other factors listed here.

Yet there is one more factor at work, the tipping point: "a particular combination of dynamics and resources that can usher [in] a new organizing logic."[58] The tipping point is that which interacts with capabilities to bring about a different organizing logic. In this case, I consider as a tipping point the violence against black bodies inaugurated by slavery, but which has manifested in other insidious forms since the "demise" of that institution.[59] "The afterlife of slavery" latches onto black bodies in many forms, including "skewed life chances, limited access to health and education, premature death, incarceration, and impoverishment."[60] Not even the election of the first African American president, Barack Obama, has altered the calculus of black expendability. In fact, the fungibility of black life—which gained center stage with the circulation of real time evidentiary videos in an age of social media—intensified during Obama's tenure and led to the mobilization of the Black Lives Matter movement.

The movement was founded by three black organizers in 2013, with the aim of being "an ideological and political intervention in a world where Black lives are systematically and intentionally targeted for demise."[61] Founded following the acquittal of the murderer of Trayvon Martin in 2013, the movement gained global recognition with its work in Ferguson and St. Louis in the wake of Michael Brown's death there in August 2014. In his appraisal of the intellectual, political, and ethical genealogy of the Black Lives Matter movement, Christopher J. Lebron considers the "three words a touchstone for our American lives today—the struggle to insist that black lives are indeed lives and therefore not candidates for cursory or careless or hateful or negligible elimination."[62] The movement created a space of "appearance" for black lives to be seen and affirmed.[63]

Unfortunately, Michael Brown's was not the last wrongful black death. Three months later, in November 2014, Tamir Rice, a twelve-year-old boy, was killed by police in Cleveland, Ohio, for playing with a toy gun. Fast forward to June 2015, and the senseless massacre of African American worshippers occurred in a church in Charleston, South Carolina. Sandra Bland's death followed on July 13, 2015, galvanizing the Say Her Name movement, which rejected the elision and underreporting of black female victims of police violence. It pains me to agree with Lebron that "this list is far from complete. In fact, it's short by hundreds of names that are the damning evidence of the level of violence against black bodies in America."[64] Lest the reader come away with the erroneous impression that the missing hundreds of names harken back to America's distant history, they are of black people decimated only since 2012.[65]

So, the image of Palmer and the lion circulating after the killing of Cecil on July 1, 2015, a few days before Sandra's unfortunate death in Texas, arrived in a nation reeling from these deaths and many others left out here. Within this context, Cecil's demise was an example of the same white privilege permitting the extreme exposure of nonwhite bodies—human and animal—to what Hortense Spillers calls the "hieroglyphics of the flesh."[66] In other words, Cecil's killing evokes the racial formation of the world that puts white bodies at the apex and black and animal bodies underneath.[67] It is difficult not to read the Cecil incident as the case of a white man walking into a country populated by black people and taking any life he desires.

Despite the differences, it is possible to visualize parallels between this indiscriminate killing and the murdering of black bodies in America by police and individual beneficiaries of white supremacy. We have to say their names: Sandra Bland, Renisha McBride, Trayvon Martin, Michael Brown, Eric Garner, Walter Scott, George Floyd, Breonna Taylor. Unfortunately, the list goes on. Like most of the police officers and individuals who have killed black people, Walter Palmer faced no consequences for his action. Palmer's (mis)deed was considered legal, just as the murderous violence of police officers against black men and women in America has been.

But it is not only recent history that Palmer's hunting image evokes. It is important to link new images with historical ones because "'new' images become legible against the ground of previous visual genealogies, both acknowledged and repressed."[68] Hazel Carby asserts that "there is a direct, but hidden, line connecting Abu Ghraib, the Rodney King video, and the photographs and 'postcards' of lynching that circulated widely in the early twentieth century."[69] We can extend Carby's list to include the image under discussion. The photograph of a grinning Palmer standing over the body of a lion, specifically an African lion, takes us back to the history of white supremacy and its catastrophic effects in Africa and the diaspora. The careful display of the trophy, of the dead lion, recalls the display of lynched black bodies and the postcards that were created from and sold at such events.[70] Commodification of bodies links lynching to this case, where the animal body retains value for its socioeconomic worth.

Not only is there a parallel in the destruction of human and animal bodies, but also in these bodies's functioning as technology for inflating white masculinity. If, in lynching, the emasculation of the black male is crucial for shoring up white masculinity, Cecil's death was also important not only for maintaining white supremacy or enshrining the racial class that can kill without consequence, but also for fueling a destructive masculinist tendency.[71] The conquering of the African jungle has been at the heart of the colonial enterprise and remains crucial for demonstrating white hypermasculinity. In the particular case of the United States, its imperial ambitions in Africa cannot be disconnected from the macho tendencies of explorers such as Theodore Roosevelt, whose well-publicized expedition to the "heart of darkness" resulted in his book *African Game Trails*.[72] As Roderick P. Neumann notes of Roosevelt's expedition and the former president's writings on the subject, "the ideas of race, nature, and national identity intersect in the construction of Roosevelt's imaginary geography of Africa."[73] Neumann contextualizes the colonial ordering of Roosevelt's trip and shows how his imperial vision reinforces the derogatory view of Africans as savages and of the environment as a wild phenomenon requiring white mastery.[74] The colonial orientation of Roosevelt's trip was also buttressed by the express permission he received to kill whatever wildlife he desired. One account of Roosevelt's year-long trip reports a "final shipment of more than eleven thousand vertebrate specimens," and that "expedition members had killed an unprecedented average of forty animals a day for an entire year."[75] Roosevelt's game hunting is relevant because it provides a pretext for Palmer's twenty-first-century micro-reenactment. Thus, a grinning Palmer standing over a dead lion evokes memories not only of lynching but also of colonial violence against African bodies—human and nonhuman.

There is one more connection between the historical antecedent that Roosevelt furnishes and Palmer's twenty-first-century reiteration: Palmer's trip echoes Roosevelt's concern, expressed in a letter to the prominent hunter and conservationist Frederick Selous, that the comforts of his expedition could undermine his masculinist valor.[76] As Gregg Mitman explains this anxiety, "Roosevelt felt that men of his class were threatened by the physical and moral effeminacy of modern times," and so "by combating wilderness, and living the strenuous life that such a struggle entailed, they could reinvigorate themselves with the prowess and republican virtues of their pioneer ancestors."[77] Sidelining the black assistants and the weapon that facilitated the lion hunt in Palmer's case removes the obstacles to the burnishing of his masculine credentials. It matters too that the prey is a lion, an animal with the moniker of king of the jungle. Killing a lion "iconicized masculinity and the conquest of nature."[78] The staging of the lion is considerably important for demonstrating the efficiency and mastery of the hunters. As is typical for trophy photographs, there is no trace of blood or wounds, which hides the infringement of the nonhuman body.[79] Just as in the Kenyan context that Grace A. Musila writes about, "wildlife tourism" assists in the "performance of whiteness" in Southern Africa just as the lynching of black bodies did in the United States.[80] It matters for this argument that memes such as "I am Cecil" and "CatLivesMatter," echoing the "I am Trayvon" and "Black Lives Matter" slogans, surfaced online following the lion's death.

However, it is also true that for those who did not consider black lives grievable or mournable, either because they considered black bodies outside the cartography of the human or because they had written off these particular black bodies as criminals unworthy of being grieved, Cecil provided a mournable alternative in a period of national upheaval. The questions that Judith Butler poses in *Precarious Life* are fitting here: "Who counts as human? Whose lives count as lives? And, finally, what makes for a grievable life?"[81] In the controversy over the expendability of black life, Cecil's death was a crime many could agree with, his loss one they could lament and express outrage over. The online sharing of the image made for an imagined community of mourners and grievers. The internet here made collective mourning possible at a time when the national fabric was fragile.

The fragility of animal life in the face of the law following Cecil's death is isomorphic with "the ritualistic and repetitive murder of the [black] flesh" on the continent and in the United States.[82] With its tactics of subjugation and prevalence, police brutality against black bodies has been regarded as a new form of lynching, as the perpetuation of the "death-bound-subject," that is, "the subject, who is formed, from infancy on, by the imminent and ubiquitous threat of death."[83] Even when direct coercion is not imprinted on the black body, other forms of violence have been visited on black communities, such as the contamination of water with lead in Flint, Michigan, and the deprivation of inner city schools of adequate resources.[84]

We have already seen the mobilization of collective emotions in the wake of Cecil's death, so this is a good place to further underscore the impacts of this image in the United States. As is typical of iconic images, the "visual eloquence" of our primary text "and its wide circulation [provided] figural resources for subsequent communicative action."[85] Cecil's death and the image that followed it spurred a participatory culture, wherein people created their own images on YouTube critiquing Palmer. What changes did Cecil bring about and what are the potential possibilities left to be explored?[86] The event precipitated some changes at the governmental and private sector levels. For example, the US government, following the outrage over Cecil's death, included lions on the Endangered Species List, which made the process of importing them into the country more rigorous.[87] Airlines also responded, prohibiting the transport of animal trophies from Africa as a result of Cecil's death and the viral image. The unraveling of some of these policies under Obama's successor notwithstanding, we can trace their creation and implementation in the first place to the affectivity of the circulatory image following Cecil's death.

Meanwhile in Zimbabwe, many wondered why the death of Cecil should elicit such outrage. Their surprise is traceable to the contestation over nature in Africa, where colonialists categorized the practices of Africans as antithetical to the demands of conservation.[88] Pitting nature against humans this way and denigrating humans by pejoratively linking them to beasts and monsters, as was done during the era of slavery and the colonial economy, engendered an apathy toward animals in some Africans.[89] There are also real, existential problems such as the fact that people have been displaced to make room for game reserves and parks, especially in Southern Africa.[90] Many African communities have also fallen victim to attacks by lions and other animals who have killed kith and kin and trampled upon crops and other vectors of economic viability.[91]

Thus, when Goodwell Nzou, a Zimbabwean living in America, says in the pages of the *New York Times* that Zimbabweans do not mourn lions, he is hinting at the history of dispossession on which the nation was built, alongside the necessity of dealing with more pressing human issues, issues of hunger, poverty, disease, and other aberrations of the postcolonial state.[92] Nzou and other respondents were also aware that the death of a Zimbabwean human would not elicit the same kind of response across the world. However, in their focus on human concerns, the Zimbabweans do not sufficiently attend to the inextricability of the manner of Cecil's death from the continuous legacy of settler colonialism in their country. The name of the dead lion takes us right to that history: "Cecil's name in fact served as a constant reminder of the association between nature, colonial power, privilege, and injustice."[93] Cecil Rhodes, after whom the country of Southern Rhodesia was named, until the switch to Zimbabwe following independence, was a propagator of British imperialism. He made his fortune from the decimation of black lives working in the mines and from their displacement to pave the way for development. He instigated the British South African Company expedition that conquered the Ndebele people and led to the occupation and subsequent colonization of the territory we now know as Zimbabwe.[94] Rhodes's colonizing class "not only violently conquered the indigenous black people, but also dispossessed them of land and denied them citizenship rights, ruling over them as 'rightless' subjects."[95]

Rhodes was an unapologetic believer in white supremacy and extolled the belief that his race must lead the rest of the world. From South Africa to Zimbabwe, Rhodes led or participated in colonial practices that subjugated local populations. No wonder, then, that the Rhodes Must Fall movement, demanding the decolonization of the curriculum in the University of Cape Town in South Africa and the removal of Rhodes's statue at the center of that campus, took shape just before Cecil's death. Analyzing both the Black Lives Matter and Rhodes Must Fall student movements together, Akosua Adomako Ampofo argues that they "show us clearly the historical ties to slavery, colonialism, and racism that exist in the everyday lives of Black people."[96] Colonialism underwrote the Zimbabwean nation and its conservation discourses and practices. Colonialism was also the guiding logic of Cecil's death, and it underpins other exploitative activities that we have seen in this book.

To summarize the foregoing discussion, Cecil's death generated outrage in the United States and across the West, while there was little attention to the incident in Zimbabwe and elsewhere in Africa. Many Westerners care very much for lions and tigers but ignore the deaths of black people who live around them and do not mind displacing black bodies in Africa and elsewhere to make room for these animals. Also, many Africans are not oblivious to the fact that their lives matter less to such Westerners than those of the lions and elephants on the continent. The binary opposition that Mbembe critiques in the analysis of conviviality carries through here, with black/white, human/animal, and Western/African distinctions. This binary division also underpins the demarcation in the study of the black diaspora and the continent proper. The coincidence of the Black Lives Matter movement with the circulation of Palmer's photograph occasions the possibility of a new organizing logic, to follow the final step in Sassen's schema, one which recognizes the continuities between Africa and its diaspora and replaces the current problematic order with a desired or hoped-for planetary humanism.

An organizing logic is the "dynamic and the relational system that constitute . . . a social and geopolitical order."[97] Sassen's work identifies three successive orders, the feudal, national, and global, while also illuminating the capabilities and tipping points enabling the transition from one epoch to the next. Space does not permit an elaboration of these dynamics here, but what interests me is the inadequacy of these orders to the project of conferring legitimacy to black and animal lives, and the necessity of a new epoch. Differences abound among the premodern feudalist, modern nationalist, and the postmodern global ages, but they share a currency, which is the exploitation of the Other.[98] To put this differently, the various eras produced a surplus on whose abjection the self and collective formations depend: the serf in the case of feudalism; minorities and the poor in the case of the nation; and developing countries as well as the minorities of Western countries in the time of globalization. To take our contemporary moment for instance, the benefits of globalization have yet to spread evenly in the way that its constitutive violence has severely impacted the world. And in all three systems, animals have occupied the lowest rung of the social order, considered valuable to the extent that they serve instrumental purposes.

How then do we overturn the precarity characteristic of these epochs, underlined in the discussion of Cecil and the Black Lives Matter movement's campaign against the killing of black people? To address the precarity of vulnerable bodies—human and nonhuman—requires the ascendancy of a new organizing logic, a planetary one. In other words, the proportion of exploitation across species and across black diasporic spaces made visible by Cecil's death and the Black Lives Matter movement provides an opportunity to transform the world order. The transition from the feudal to the national and to the global phases has not addressed the issues of inequality and the vulnerable state of the planet. In fact, these negativities have intensified with each succeeding epoch for black people, which has made some scholars conclude that blackness resides in a zone of nothingness.[99]

While conceding the violence against the black body that underpins the nihilist orientation of Afro-pessimist thought, I am drawn more to the possibilities in the space of nothingness, of the possibility of freedom despite the fact of flagellation.[100] With Alexander Weheliye, I "ask what it might mean to claim the monstrosity of the flesh as a site for freedom."[101] It is productive to read "the subaltern body in pain as a (de)tour . . . to a version of the human unburdened by shackles of Man."[102] This version of unburdened humanity is in keeping with the demands of the planetary humanism sketched earlier in the chapter, predicated on the "radical overturning of the ground that we are under."[103] A radical overturning of our ground on the way to a recalibrated human subjectivity should not leave the conventional species hierarchy in place. The Other of Man has always been defined in animalistic terms, which means that smashing the pedestal of Man provides an opportunity to reconstitute human relationship to animals. I am

Chapter Four

aware that Weheliye would take exception to my proposal, considering his critique of the common rhetorical strategy of bringing together exploitation of black and animal bodies by post-humanists and animal rights scholars.[104] His anxiety is understandable within the bloodied history referenced early in the introductory section of this chapter, but as I already mentioned there, there are alternative conceptions of human-animal relations that disavow colonial framings of their nexuses.

While maintaining the right to difference between humans and animals, the appearance of a recalibrated human in relation to the Other occasions reconstituting the ground for an ethical relation to the animal. That is the crux of the planetary humanism being unveiled in this chapter. Sassen underscores the fact that each epoch derives some of its capabilities from the preceding period, and the proposed planetary time is no exception. Space-time compression, a significant characteristic of the global era, registers the period's distinction from the national epoch preceding it. This common-sense of globalization, as it opens territories and boundaries beyond nationally defined lines, allows for the incubation of a different era that undermines borders across spaces and species. In other words, the arrival of a planetary order will be met with the removal of barriers to relational dispositions between humans across geographies and between human and nonhuman beings. To that end, the protests, agitations, and robust critical thought precipitated by Cecil's death and the Black Lives Matter movement can be seen as prerequisites for the calibration of sociality toward an alternative future.

A glimpse of this ideal intersectional politics can be seen in the conclusion of Nzou's article, cited earlier: "please, don't offer me condolences about Cecil unless you're also willing to offer me condolences for villagers killed or left hungry by his brethren, by political violence, or by hunger."[105] We see captured here the non-sympathy for the lion that has been discussed as marking the reaction of Zimbabweans, and Africans more broadly, who feel that lions have more value than black people in the Western imagination. Nzou, however, leaves the space open for sympathetic feelings across species when he requests recognition and sympathetic consideration for the plight of Africans as a result of the condition of postcoloniality. In insisting that sympathy for the animal must go along with a recognition of the human condition, Nzou is establishing the basis for coexistence while illustrating the parameters for a planetary humanism cognizant of the interests and conditions of various life forms across spaces. Nzou could have eliminated the animal from consideration, but "unless you're also willing" ties the human to the Other. Their inseparability, which parallels the inseparability of African communities from black diasporic ones, is at the core of wished-for planetary humanism.

Trophy and the Return of the Repressed

One impact of Cecil's death has been renewed attention to conservation in the public sphere. We have also witnessed a proliferation of photographs and films lamenting the endangered status of animals. That list of films would include *Virunga*, discussed later, Dereck Joubert's *The Last Lions*, and Nick Chevallier and Bruce Young's *Blood Lions*.[106] Schwarz and Clusiau's *Trophy* also belongs on that list. Originally screened at the Sundance Film Festival, the film later premiered on CNN on Sunday, January 14, 2018. The film's "production ecology" encompasses the broader conservation debate that followed Cecil's death and the declining numbers of wildlife as well as the heightened focus on climate health.[107] Another impetus of course was the proposal by the Trump administration to remove the ban on trophy imports imposed by the Obama administration following Cecil's death. As such, CNN's interest in the film underscores the alignment of public-interest programming with commercial viability.[108] The environment and animals are marketable, and so it makes sense that CNN devoted the eve of a national public holiday to airing *Trophy*. That holiday is Martin Luther King Day, which implicates the film in a racial economy even before viewers encounter its content. By devoting two hours of airtime to the film on the eve of a national holiday commemorating the life of a man who fought for civil rights for African Americans, CNN invites the kind of racial looking that I bring to the analysis of the film. *Trophy* further cements Schwarz's role as a filmmaker invested in exploring controversial yet topical social issues. His earlier film *Narco Cultura*, for instance, focuses on the dynamics of drug trafficking between Mexico and the United States.[109] Presenting the intimate workings of the drug business, this documentary explores the connection between trafficking, money, and violence. The issues explored in the latter film may be altogether different from the preoccupations of Schwarz's earlier project, but the triad of trafficking, money, and violence links them.

Trophy opens with a scene depicting Philip Glass, big-game hunter and sheep breeder, and his teenage son hunting a doe in Texas. The son's shot is followed by his father's, which kills the animal. The son poses with the remains, the first trophy in the film. The father tells the boy that his days hunting small animals are over and encourages him to concentrate henceforth on big game. This scene of father-son bonding marks an initiation into manhood and transports us to South Africa, Namibia, and Zimbabwe, where viewers learn of conservation efforts and obstacles to them, including poaching. The film informs the viewer that over 60 percent of wildlife has been lost since 1970, particularly singling out elephants and rhinos as facing extinction. The filmmakers had set out to produce an exposé of the hunting industry, but their critical examination revealed a more complex situation.[110]

When the film shifts from Texas to South Africa, we meet John Hume, who owns the largest rhino-breeding ranch in the world. To protect rhinos, he saws off their horns, which makes them unattractive to poachers. As Hume explains, a 4 kilogram rhino horn fetches about $250,000 on the black market in Vietnam. In Vietnam and other parts of Asia, rhino horn is believed to have potent medicinal value, which drives up the price, making it worth more than gold and heroin, to use Hume's analogy. But since 2009, the government of South Africa has placed a moratorium on the sale of horns to save the rhinos. Hume argues that the ban has resulted in increased poaching of rhinos, unlike his conservation practice, which harvests the horn while keeping the rhino alive. Hume states early in the film that no species can face extinction if breeders can earn money from them.

Much of the film is devoted to depicting pro-hunting and anti-hunting perspectives. As seen in the debate that ensued following Cecil's death, hunting interest groups argue that the proceeds support conservation efforts, while anti-hunting groups condemn the commodification of animal bodies. In the film, we learn of the different price tags of the "big five" species, with buffalo fetching the lowest price of approximately $8,000, while the rhino tops the pack at over $300,000. Poaching is a big problem in the film, and repeatedly we encounter rhinos that have fallen victim to poachers. The film draws the viewer into its affective dimension at such moments as the camera closes in on the animal body. Hume is shown in one instance trying to suppress his emotions over the loss of an animal. In one poignant scene, a living rhino cries over a dead one and scampers around the body. On one occasion, where the carcass is that of an elephant, the manipulation of the camera to produce a close-up shot and later a zoomed-out perspective that positions the elephant within the larger environment is accompanied by a melancholy soundtrack. The viewer is invited by such scenes to identify with the animals. Such scenes also humanize the players in the conservation business. Hume, for instance, is shown as genuinely caring for the rhinos.

However, at a debate with Will Trevor, of the group Born Free USA, the opposition tries to paint Hume as a businessman only interested in profit.

Early in the film, Adam Roberts, Born Free's CEO, eloquently links contemporary safari hunting to the colonial exploitation of wildlife by Roosevelt and others. For Roberts and other anti-hunting activists, the gains of hunting are nullified by the violence against animals, and they argue that the practice does not necessarily protect animals from extinction. This position is echoed in writings by Michele Pickover and others who condemn animal exploitation in whatever form. Pickover condemns all brutality against animals, arguing instead for photographic safaris. In her words, "the number of ecotourists far outstrips the number of trophy hunters. Photographic tourists can 'shoot' an animal an unlimited number of times while a hunter can only shoot it once."[111] Pickover argues for seeing humans and animals in relational terms as she stresses their interconnectivity, even in exploitation. Here she echoes John Berger, who has written that almost "all techniques of modern social conditioning were first established with animal experiments."[112] For Pickover and for Berger before her, continuing to sanction violence against animals in whatever form can potentially enliven the possibility that similar treatment will be extended to humans.

While *Trophy* exposes the viewer to the intricacies of conservation and uses cognitive and emotional appeals to draw in the audience, the fact of blackness does not receive the sophisticated treatment it deserves in the film. As I indicated earlier, the film's premiere on the eve of Martin Luther King Day already positions it within the discourse of race. We can develop the race thematic further by discussing the film's content and what it excludes. It is significant to this reading that the film transports the American hunters directly to wildlife in Africa without encountering the continent's modernity. It is as if Africa remains frozen in the past of Roosevelt's expedition, depicted with found footage. Except for image quality, nothing much has changed in the representation of the African bush. One must ask: What will it take to showcase the complexity of, say, South Africa, since much of the film is devoted to conservation efforts there? Except for an Air Namibia plane from which the passengers alight, there is little to orient the viewer to lived life in African countries. Even the shot of the plane blocks the surroundings, so that it may as well be in the middle of the bush that the carrier lands: "Once again, the power balance is in favour of displaying the African as naturally natural. This way, attention is drawn away from South Africa as a functioning [twenty-first]-century society."[113]

This image of wildness pervades the film so much that while the film introduces us to Las Vegas, whose skyscrapers host the Safari Club International Convention, and the Texas countryside, it does very little to showcase

Chapter Four

the larger ecosystem of its African countries. The film adopts a "selective gaze that mediates the practices of African tourism . . . that only picks up wildlife, wilderness and 'noble savages.'"[114] This naturalistic image of Africa as something to be feared and tamed is further reinforced by a hunting instructor interviewed in the film, who explains that his trainees come to him nervous before embarking on their trip "because in Africa it is dangerous." This position may not correspond with the filmmaker's, but the film's portrayal of the continent does nothing to complicate or challenge it. It does not help that the film has CNN's imprimatur, which means the validation of this image of Africa for its wide audience.

If blackness entirely disappears in Palmer's photograph, discussed earlier, we see it present, albeit in a marginal form, here. *Trophy* is an appropriate film with which to reflect on Mitman's question: "what place [do] humans occupy" in the depiction "of wildlife through a wide-angle lens?"[115] Africans hardly speak in *Trophy*, appearing mostly to support hunting expeditions. They are the porters who unpack the plane carrying the hunters. They also guide the hunting sessions, even though they are left out of the picture when the animal is "taken." This point, already made in the discussion of Palmer's photograph, bears further analysis in the context of *Trophy*. James Murombedzi's observation that the "majority of black employees in the safari industry are cooks and camp attendants" resonates here.[116] Murombedzi further adds that Africans are mostly left out of the skilled labor group and that their efforts in the hunting process are not properly recognized. In his words, "these trackers are treated as unskilled labourers, rather than being recognized as qualified guides."[117] Misnaming or misappropriation matters because the black workers are particularly exposed to the dangers of the hunt. Early in the film, for instance, they entrap some crocodiles as the white supervisor commands the operation from a safe distance. Later in the film, as Philip Glass embarks on the lion-hunting trip, we see him in the company of the black workers as they track the animal. Interestingly, the editing of the scenes where the animal has been killed and the American poses with it leaves out traces of black help. As Glass and his white companion approach the dead animal and congratulate themselves on their achievement, blackness disappears. Here, as in Palmer's case, the black hands are relegated to the backroom to guarantee the "dramatic interest" characteristic of wildlife film. The emotional drama that appeals to the audience of wildlife film involves a considerable degree of fabrication and exclusion, including of the labor provided by black people.[118]

In the case of *Trophy*, it is more significant that people of color are mainly absent from the conservation business except as manual laborers. The owners of ranches and reserves as well as the clientele and the patrons of the Safari Club convention are mostly white. Even anti-hunting protests in the United States, featured in the film, hardly include people of color. What does it mean that black bodies are marginal in this business? We are returned to the inseparability of conservation from imperialism and the exploitation of blacks. As Jane Carruthers reports in her seminal history of Kruger Park in South Africa, conservation means different things for different races in Southern Africa. While the park represents the beauty of nature and retreat for whites, she writes that for black Africans, "particularly those in areas adjoining the Park, who live in extreme poverty . . . the Park's name and ethos have come to symbolize strands in the web of racial discrimination and white political and economic domination."[119] Although Carruthers is writing of Kruger here, her conclusions are portable across Southern Africa, where people have been displaced to make room for animals and/or prohibited from cultivating land that their ancestors farmed for centuries. Beyond Southern Africa, there are other examples of such people, who would fit the category of "conservation refugees," "who are removed from their homelands."[120] They are removed often because of "a perceived threat to the biological diversity of a larger geographical area."[121] Any list of conservation refugees would include the Maasai in Kenya, who are pitted against the conservationists whose projects impede the pastoralist work of the local population.[122]

To return to Schwarz and Clusiau's work and to Southern Africa, the film's penetrating interrogation of conservation fails to delve into the question of access to land that is the bane of interracial relations in the region. The viewer remains uneducated about the history of white expropriation of land in the seventeenth century, the 1913 Natives Land Act that restricted black people to approximately 10 percent of South Africa's land, how John Hume came into possession of his ranch, and even the fact that wildlife conservation is a recent phenomenon that has supplanted livestock and crop farming in the country. Like the game reserve in South Africa that Rob Nixon writes of, "history's corrugations have been Botoxed from nature's visage" in the representation of the continent in *Trophy*.[123] To return this eclipsed history to the frame, we need to consult William Beinart's work on conservation in South Africa and explore its connection to settler colonialism:

> Dutch settler conquest of the midlands was largely complete by 1806, when the British took control of the Cape, and most of the Khoisan population had been displaced as independent landholders. Africans proved

more difficult to dislodge. Their political and demographic weight under-pinned a long military resistance throughout the nineteenth century. Boer and British settlers were eventually able to secure a major portion of Xhosa territory, west of the Kei river and the margins of Thembu-land, around what became Queenstown. But Africans retained substan-tial settlements, which later became the basis for reserved land in the Transkei and Ciskei.[124]

There is no space for an elaborate discussion of settler colonialism here, but Beinart's work demonstrates the violence that accompanied settlement by the Afrikaners and the British in South Africa. Differences abound within South Africa and across the subcontinent, but the process mostly involved the displacement of the local inhabitants to make room for white settle-ment.[125] The Zimbabwean example discussed in the previous section con-forms to this model of displacement, too. As they settled, Europeans' early conservation efforts concentrated on livestock management and land culti-vation. As Beinart explains, early intervention consisted of conserving water and preventing land desiccation. The initial conservation effort was particu-larly hostile to wildlife, much of which was considered vermin and killed. Lions fell into this category. Things started changing in the 1950s and 1960s when landowners started to make the shift to wildlife management to ad-dress the problem of dwindling revenue from livestock and crop cultivation.

The market has always been central to conservation in Africa. Yet the Europeans, themselves fond of hunting for sport, would accuse Africans of destroying the environment and wildlife. This accusation of cruelty against animals was the pretext for the first hunting legislation in the Transvaal (passed in 1858), designed "to control and restrict African access to wildlife. Blacks were only allowed to hunt if they were 'trusted servants,' in posses-sion of 'passes,' and accompanied by whites who were in charge of the fire-arms."[126] This legislation and successive laws controlled black ownership of firepower and limited access to wildlife.

Schwarz and Clusiau's film, while eliding racial histories of Southern Africa with significant implications for conservation, is useful for critiquing the limitations on black access to guns and wildlife. A scene where a wildlife security squad invades the home of an alleged elephant poacher late at night is useful for underscoring this critique. The accused's wives and children are ordered out of the house, made to sit or lie on the ground, and threatened to confess the crime of their husband and father. The white anti-poaching official expresses worry about the children's future, exhorting them to stay away from the bush to avoid being shot. His worry that the sons will take after their father seems genuine, but the film's opening scene figuring the white Texan and his son complicates this view. While the teenager's initiation into manhood is complete when his father recommends big-game hunting to him, which will presumably take the young lad to Africa, black youths on the continent are denied that luxury under threat from the barrel of a gun. Where the white kid's money will ensure that he follows in the footstep of his father, poor African kids are warned to stay away from hunting to save their lives.

The film demonstrates "the structural inequalities and associated power differentials" that determine the beneficiaries of wildlife conservation and bearers of the cost.[127] Inequality is particularly apparent in the demonstration of power over the black body. We do not hear directly from the accused poacher, but the viewer is presented with a stack of bullets allegedly recovered from the house as evidence. The invasion is reminiscent of colonial police raids. Indeed, the search for the firearm, its role in establishing guilt, and the larger restriction of Africans connect this scene to the colonial moment, when black ownership of guns and access to game were limited. Guns are preponderant in *Trophy*, both on the continent and at the Safari Club convention in Las Vegas. They are the primary weapons for hunting animals, but in the scene under discussion, they have been turned against black bodies. Although distance separates the continent from the United States, there is a parallel in the exposure to gun violence that connects the US context, already explored in the previous section, to the African one. In both spaces, the black body is the site of discursive and material violence. The invasion scene in *Trophy* illuminates the militarization of conservation.[128]

In the end, Schwarz and Clusiau's film complicates the notion of criminality in the wildlife business. Those arrested and sometimes killed in anti-poaching operations are community members seeking livelihood opportunities in an environment where there is limited land for cultivation and drought has affected crop yields. Moreover, such communities have seen their crops and livestock destroyed by wildlife, threatening food security. In the film, for instance, the few shots allowing for local perspectives do show the villagers lamenting the destruction of their crops. In one case a lion has eaten goats and a cow, leading one family to keep its remaining cow indoors. The anti-poaching official explains that the lion may attack the family indoors if it smells the cow there, which altogether foregrounds the dangers that such communities face. Considering these developments, the film problematizes the label "bad guys" used by one official for people whose crime is to seek a means of surviving under a capitalist system. Such labels are problematic because they "do not resolve the underlying reasons why people poach in the first place; and they do not tackle either the role of global trading networks or the continued demand in end-user markets."[129]

Although scholars advocate community involvement as a way of reforming conservation in the twenty-first century, we see in *Trophy* that the local population remains vulnerable within such arrangements. In the film, the community receives an elephant carcass, but the scene of sharing the meat becomes the occasion of subtle protest. While one community member identifies the animal as the elephant that destroyed his crops, many others complain of its size, indicating that they are only allowed a smaller share. One vocal man goes so far as to state in English that they want a bigger animal next time. This scene confirms that community involvement programs favor "the outsider and government who make the decisions."[130] The complaints by the community members in *Trophy* suggest that the conservation business favors outsiders over them just as is the case with the Zimbabwean CAMP-FIRE program that Murombedzi analyzes.[131] While small elephants are allocated to the poor villages for food, the bigger ones are made available to the moneyed hunters who fly in from across the world.

Critics of meat eating would condemn both the killing of the elephant for food and its aesthetic use by the wealthy, but we need to be careful to remain sensitive to the subsistence needs of host communities like the ones portrayed in *Trophy*. Deane Curtin's reflection on the subject is apropos here, as he emphasizes contextual conditions, noting that his privileged white American subjectivity permits vegetarianism and veganism in ways difficult or impossible for others.[132] Curtin's position contrasts with that of others such as Pickover, who "recommends vegetarianism and veganism as antidote to the suffering caused animals in the meat industry."[133] Although this point is less developed in her work, she also argues that meat eating fuels inequality and hunger for the poor.[134] Anat Pick echoes Pickover when he argues that veganism is also central to "creaturely ethics." For Pick, the kind of interspecies worlding recommended by Donna Haraway cannot cohabit with eating animals. In his words, "while I agree that hunters, for example, may relate to their prey in complex ways, I have difficulty conceiving this as a relation of love."[135] While these authors provide compelling ethical and intellectual justifications for veganism, they do not differentiate between a Western style of luxurious consumption and the subsistence of poor communities across the world, who have lived on the land for ages.

We see here the tension between the tenets of multispecies ethnography and the demands of environmental justice. Multispecies ethnography decenters the human while establishing relationality between humans and others, including animals, while environmental justice is concerned with differential power distribution that disproportionately allocates resources, often on the basis of race, class, gender and other social vectors.[136] How can we reconcile these seemingly competing needs of nonhumans and those humans who are economically disadvantaged and whose livelihood depends on other life forms? The challenge is "how we can articulate human rights and human aspirations to a good life together with the claims of nonhuman species on our moral consideration?"[137] The concluding section broaches this conundrum with Einsiedel's film *Virunga* as a navigational guide.

Virunga, Becoming-With, and Planetary Futures

Planetary humanism imagines a world where race is immaterial and where moral considerations guide relation to the Other, which means that the denigration of nonhumans or the perpetuation of "hyper-separation" between them and humans is untenable in this new vision.[138] One important step to realizing this vision is to confront the "rhetorical animal sacrifice" that marks the current order.[139] Whether it is in Palmer's treatment of animals, which I connect to the decimation of black lives in Africa and the diaspora, or the engagement with animal conservation in *Trophy*, where black people retain marginal positions and animals are mostly framed in commodity terms, we are returned to a centuries-old distancing and instrumentalization of various life forms. These exploitative practices undermine the emergence of the ethical relationality that is at the heart of planetary humanism. Monetization and the commodification of life characterize the scenes of subjection in both Palmer's photograph and Schwarz and Clusiau's film, and they further postpone the realization of the principles of interspecies ethics.

I turn to *Virunga* in this closing act because of the possibility it holds for co-articulating the worlds of humans and animals and for its investment in their conviviality. The film, which has the backing of executive producer Leonardo DiCaprio, garnered an Oscar nomination and clinched many film awards. Although DiCaprio does not feature in the film, his role as producer is exploited in the film's marketing, which portrays him as a conservationist celebrity.[140] Promotional material for this Netflix film foregrounds DiCaprio due to his celebrity appeal, but the credit for film director goes to the British filmmaker Orlando von Einsiedel, who rose to prominence with *Virunga*, an account of efforts to conserve gorillas in the Virunga National Park in the

Democratic Republic of the Congo. Subsequently he directed *The White Helmets*, a short documentary on first responders serving civilians in war-torn Syria, for which he won an Academy Award, and *Lost and Found*, a powerful portrayal of the process of reuniting children separated from their parents in Rohingya Muslim communities displaced from Myanmar.[141] Although *Virunga* has garnered several accolades including an Academy Award nomination for best documentary feature, it has generated some critiques as well. Critics have argued that it "normalize[s] and legitimize[s] the militarization of conservation," and that its heroic portrayal of park rangers elides the violence they inflict on members of surrounding communities.[142]

Virunga National Park, like others across the continent, is a product of colonialism, established in 1925 as Albert National Park, in honor of the then king of Belgium.[143] The area of the park was expanded considerably in the 1930s in a process that further displaced communities whose communal lands were expropriated. This expansion was achieved under the guise of a state of emergency declared in response to the spread of sleeping sickness so that removal was framed as being in the interest of people's safety. Areas unaffected by the disease also saw the forceful removal of inhabitants by colonial armed forces. As in South Africa and elsewhere, the people, perceived as a threat to wildlife, were removed and denied access to the environment, therefore dismantling their customary mode of communal land ownership.[144] Despite independence, not much has changed and Belgians retain important positions in managing the park. Emmanuel de Merode, who took over the administration of the park as warden in 2008, is a Belgian. Before 2005, the park was managed by the underfunded and ill-managed state agency, the Congolese Institute for the Conservation of Nature (ICCN). Following reports of corruption and inefficiency, the park's administration was taken over by a public-private partnership between the ICCN and the African Conservation Fund (now the Virunga Foundation). Since 2010, the park has been solely managed by the Virunga Foundation, which obtains some of its funding from Western donors, therefore retaining the park's European ties.[145]

The film makes sure to foreground the country's colonial heritage early on by showing archival footage of the exploitation of human and nonhuman resources early in the twentieth century. If, as Nancy Rose Hunt states, "it is no longer tenable to imagine one can write an urgent, effective history about violence in Leopold's Congo without tethering it to the present," *Virunga* insists that a history of the present is incomplete without accounting for Leopold's Congo.[146] The brutalities of King Leopold, whose ivory and rubber businesses in Congo set the stage for the contemporary violent extraction of minerals, are also recorded in the film.[147] As Kevin Bales puts it, "wild rubber, as well as elephant ivory for piano keys and decoration, was ripped out of the forests at an incredible human cost."[148] Torture and murder were part of the arsenal deployed by the colonial regime to force local people into the forest, and estimates put the loss of human lives at about 10 million.[149] The viewer is also introduced to Patrice Lumumba, the prime minister of Congo whose anti-colonial sensibilities led to his assassination by Western-backed forces. With this background, the film achieves what *Trophy* fails to do: a historicizing that contextualizes the continuous violence in Congo and the longue durée of exploitation there.

It is tempting to see the film's depiction of contemporary violence in the country as responding to the demand of the Western gaze. In other words, the film's presentation of the waves of violence in Congo since the Rwandan genocide could be seen as feeding the Western imagination for a barbaric Africa—but the issue is more complex.[150] To be sure, Congo saw an influx of refugees from Rwanda, many of whom sought refuge in the park.[151] It is also true that the region has been destabilized since then and that militias such as the M23 rebel group shown in the film have occupied areas of the park. Yet the film's project of historical recuperation invites a more complex reading, just as its framing of vulnerability rewrites the typical conservation script in Africa. *Virunga* includes close-ups and long takes of beautiful landscapes like other nature films. Its cinematography is superb as it presents various animals in their splendor. But the film does not remain stuck in the image of untouched, pristine nature.

Culture is introduced in the first scene, showing a procession of mourners carrying the corpse of a slain ranger. This early interjection shows the interaction of culture and nature and the dangers of protecting the park from poachers, warlords, and oil explorers, among others. At least 130 rangers have died serving the park since 1996.[152] The rangers' deaths parallel the decimation of wildlife, which has left species such as the mountain gorilla endangered. The population of hippopotamuses too has reduced significantly, and with them the stock of fish in Lake Edward.[153]

The extended shot of the procession stands by itself as a moving event, but then it takes on further significance when paired with a later shot of a procession carrying a slain gorilla. The procession with the slain animal recalls the opening scene of the film, where the deceased is a ranger. Both animals—human and nonhuman—are being mourned as victims of violence. As the film reveals, the park is threatened by poachers and by SOCO International, a British oil company granted rights to explore for oil. The park administration opposes the potential endangerment of the mountain gorillas and other wildlife in the park, and pressures the government in Kinshasa to suspend the concession. De Merode's administration employs a media campaign that catches the attention of international organizations and SOCO is forced to suspend its activities in the area.[154] But before that, the company bribes rangers and sponsors violent aggression against uncompromising ones. Even the warden suffers an attack, although he survives the gunshot wounds. Human and nonhuman lives are threatened by the various armed groups operating around the park, and the processions in the film concretize their shared vulnerability.

We see further evidence of what Haraway would consider living and dying with animals in the film's parallel editing. In one sequence we encounter Kaboko, a gorilla who eventually dies, writhing in pain on the floor, and then the film cuts to humans displaced by the invading rebel group, fleeing to escape the violence. That both scenes follow each other foregrounds the film's work of linking human and animal suffering. In another sequence we find a gorilla holding on to a caregiver as the sound of an explosion rends the air, while another seeks comfort by the wall. These scenes are followed by another depicting a human visibly anxious from the disturbing noise. The camera also cuts to other animals scampering for safety in the same way that it reveals human members of the community trying to escape. The film refuses to privilege either suffering with its utilization of crosscuts. Einsiedel's film decenters human beings, but it does not elide them in order to enthrone the animals. By showing various life forms occupying vulnerable spaces and demonstrating their shared animality, *Virunga* makes a strong case for interspecies entanglement in a moment of crisis.

One of the film's achievements is that its account of tragedy is tempered with a portrayal of interspecies life, love, and play. To affirm life, the film provides intimate views of the inhabitants of the gorilla orphanage in Rumangabo. Although Derek Bousé would argue that it is a "false intimacy" that we feel when the camera brings an animal close to us, the viewer of *Virunga* feels drawn into the gorillas' world.[155] We meet not only Maisha and Kabako but also Ndeze and Ndakasi. The affective pull of the scenes depicting these young gorillas is enhanced by their play with their human caregivers. Brian Massumi locates play as the site of an "integrally animal politics" distinct from a "human politics of the animal" that privileges the human.[156] Play is the constitutive site of Massumi's animal politics because, in this activity, "the humans enter a zone of indiscernibility with the animal," and play "dramatizes the reciprocal participation of the human and the animal, from both sides."[157] Indiscernibility and reciprocal participation are contingent on communicative action, all features of human-animal play in *Virunga*. There is communication between humans and animals as they hold each other affectionately, walk, and play. The human potential for becoming animal is evident in scenes of interspecies play, just as those moments manifest prime opportunities for recuperating gorillas from degraded animality.

The human-animal relationship in *Virunga* permits the making of "odd-kin."[158] One of the caregivers even says he sees himself as not just father but also mother to the orphaned gorilla. He is seen, at one point, carrying the gorilla on his back, and the animal returns the favor by clasping his arms around his human "parent." It is interesting to recognize the kinship being established here and how its oddness disrupts species and gender boundaries. Students of Africa will recognize in this film image the same method that women use in carrying their children on the continent. Attuned to a "praxis of care and response," and mindful of "shaping conditions of multispecies flourishing in the face of terrible histories," *Virunga* depicts an ethics of care and responsibility to the Other despite the stressful social and economic conditions of the film's setting.[159]

The film wants to transcend mere entertainment and so provides a complex history of the region and stories of admirable interspecies belonging amid a climate of strife. In the end, it implores the viewer who wants to support Virunga National Park to visit the film's website.[160] This invitation requires some action of the viewer. *Virunga*, by asking for citizen action at the end, attempts to produce "environmental subjects."[161] One tab on the website says, "Take Action," under which is a link to donate, or spread information about Virunga, or even visit the park. Another interesting option asks visitors to check their investments, and for those with stakes in SOCO International (now Pharos Energy) to pressure the company to commit to staying away from Virunga permanently.

Virunga invites viewers to connect human health to ecological well-being, which is important for planetary humanism. Oil is not the only problem. The hazards of mineral mining in the region are worth considering as well, to ensure that our gold and cell phones are not produced from blood minerals: "we don't have to give up gold; we just have to give up the slavery and environmental destruction that make gold so ugly in its beauty."[162] A vision of planetary humanism invites consideration of the Other, broadly conceived to include humans and more-than-humans, at the receiving end of our living practices. I will give the last word here to Sean Cubitt, who in a chapter on "drawing animals" has this to say of consideration: "what those who survive must learn is that the consequences are still there: that actions have reverberations. It is not that each from henceforth will give up action—far from it. But that each must take account of the others, and of debts and responsibilities owed to the world."[163]

african urban ecologies

transcriptions of precarity, creativity, and futurity

In previous chapters I have shown the network forms that constitute African ecomedia. In their layering of time, past, present, and future; their contraction of space through linking African territories to transnational and transcontinental geographies; and their reconstitution of the human in an assemblage that includes animals and things—these cultural artifacts reject linearity and insularity while promoting trans-territorial, transoceanic, and transhuman solidarities and exchanges. I turn in this final chapter to media representations of the environments of African cities. The African city is a rich site for apprehending the dimensions of networks that we have seen so far in this book. It is a site where the old and the new are always in dialogue and contestation.[1] The African city, as a site of innovation and creativity, also lends itself to perorations on the future.[2] Urban space on the continent is also a worldly or global space where the demarcations between rural and urban and between local and global are constantly being erased.[3] It is also a space of meetings and transitions that make AbdouMaliq Simone consider "people as infrastructure."[4] But the African city is also the place to complicate Simone's sense of infrastructure because humans are always in relational arrangements with nonhuman forms such as plant and animal life as well as other technologies.

Despite its promise, the African city has yet to receive the scholarly attention it deserves in the environmental humanities, which tends to focus on rural contexts and spaces of resource extraction on the continent. These are important and legitimate areas of inquiry, but marginalizing the African city results in the elision of the affective lives of millions of Africans and their interactions with their environments. In foregrounding the African city in this chapter, I intend to address a gap in environmental humanities scholarship while also recuperating urban life in its complexity and messiness for insights into ecological relations. Extant studies of African cities have also not sufficiently addressed these spaces in ecological terms, leaving room for an analysis of the dimensions of degradation and reclamation in urban Africa. My claim is that photography and film offer windows for appreciating daily lives of ordinary people in the city and proffer the imaginative means for transforming African urbanity toward more just and sustainable futures. My specific claim is that ecomedia that focuses on urban space in Africa constitute the urban as a site of everyday precarity, a space for geopolitical-cum-ideological contestation that endangers the human and nonhuman biosphere, and a space for articulating future possibilities.

Aiding my task of elaborating this three-tier argument are Guy Tillim's collection of photographs, *Jo'burg*, Wu Jing's film *Wolf Warrior 2*, Femi Odugbemi's film *Makoko: Futures Afloat*, and Olalekan Jeyifous's Afrofuturist 3D architectural images *Shanty Megastructures*.[5] Immediately following this introductory segment, I examine Tillim's photographs for their portrayals of the precarity that constitutes everyday life for many in postapartheid Johannesburg. Next, I explore Jing's film for its deployment of the African city as a site for the ideological enthronement of China as a benevolent superpower. Jing's work returns the colonial gaze to the African space, which is portrayed as a site of violence, disease, and other markers of Africanness in the racial economy. Turning to Odugbemi's and Jeyifous's projects in the final section, I discuss the consecration of urban space in Africa as the terrain of future possibilities. This concluding section interrogates ecomedia focusing on the African city for renditions of eco-conscious futures.

Cities have always been points of intersection and relationality in Africa, a place of cosmopolitan mixing and mooring. This is to say that worldliness characterizes even those cities predating the colonial moment on the continent.[6] In old Benin City and Kano, to use two examples from West Africa, the city infrastructure brought people together from far and wide to engage in trade and other socioeconomic activities.[7] We can understand the African city as a palimpsest that has evolved with subsequent iterations of writing and overwriting. The temporal and spatial conjunctions that occur and recur in the African space make it amenable to the kind of inquiry undertaken in this chapter.

In broad terms, scholarship on African cities emphasizes the dual presence of "privation [and] invention" as well as "catastrophe and creativity."[8] This trend is consistent with developments in the study of cities of the Global South, which can be categorized into irreparable pessimism or "irrepressible optimism" about these cities.[9] As we will see in the following sections, much more is at stake in this terrain, where people's lives "may be radically incomplete but continues to be . . . busy with activity, noisy with stories, garrulous with grotesquerie, gossip, humor, aspirations, fantasies."[10] The multifaceted stimulations that Georg Simmel sees as features of the metropolis are fundamental to African urban configurations, some of which are textualized in the cultural forms analyzed in subsequent sections.[11]

The Everyday in the African City

The African city may be a "space of possibles," but it is also a site of precarity, clearly foregrounded in Guy Tillim's photographic projects.[12] Tillim was born in Johannesburg in 1962 and studied at the University of Cape Town. He started his professional career as a photojournalist relaying the realities of apartheid South Africa to the world by doing freelance work for Reuters and Agence France-Press. The social commitment of his early work carries into his later documentary photographs on different parts of Africa. His series *Jo'burg,* which won the Leica Oskar Barnack Award in 2005, documents the enduring legacies of apartheid in the Hillbrow area of Johannesburg. He has produced and exhibited other works such as *Avenue Patrice Lumumba*, on the urban geography of the Democratic Republic of the Congo, and *Museum of the Revolution*, detailing the transformations of major African cities because of decolonization.[13] Tillim's work primarily concentrates on city spaces and their architecture.

African cities index the hauntings of colonial and postcolonial societies' unequal access to space. Studies of urbanity across colonial Africa have shown geographical divisions that restricted the access of Africans to the city or at least to its European parts. In the well-known case of South Africa, for instance, Africans were confined to Bantustans and were required to show

Chapter Five

permits to enter the city. Even those who made it into the city with passes or by surreptitious means were domiciled in hostels and squatter settlements that still dot the national landscape as reminders of the past. The endurance of these colonial vestiges in postapartheid South Africa is a clear reminder that the urban poor remain entrapped in the nonfulfillment of the promise of freedom.[14] The unequal geographies of colonialism have widened from South Africa to Sudan even as the continental urban cartography significantly contributes to the "planet of slums."[15] Henri Lefebvre does not have Africa in mind when he writes of "dominated spaces," but an examination of the continent's urban ecology shows the preponderance of spaces mediated by violence.[16] As elsewhere, the dominated space often sits in contiguous relation with the space of the dominant class or the elite in Africa.[17] Pockets of wealth dotted with "garrison architecture" are scattered across Africa, sitting next door to slums and shanties.[18]

Tillim's *Jo'burg* provides intimations of precarity for those left behind by the neoliberal agenda pursued by successive governments in South Africa. Johannesburg is the only African city featured on the world city list due to the concentration of financial hubs of global capital there. World or global cities are financial centers of global capitalism and neoliberalism, housing headquarters of transnational and multinational corporations, serving as nodes for the service sector, and hosting a concentration of large media and telecommunication companies. To be part of this elite grouping is to be a city that plays a big role in the economic configuration of the world, especially in the areas of trade and business services.[19] This economic configuration of the city leaves out most urban spaces in the world and highlights the inequality of global relations.

This inequality in economic power grounds social relations and spatial organization in Johannesburg. Superfluous spaces have risen in the city to service the moneyed class—Melrose Arch and Montecasino are two examples.[20] These postmodern spaces are indicators of South Africa's postapartheid success and integration into the global economy. As shiny as these parts of Johannesburg are, the story they tell of the city is at best partial. The boutique hotels and ultramodern malls and plazas springing up across the city are enthralling spaces of consumerism and global performativity; they also index "splintering urbanism."[21] Splintering urbanism generates and sustains uneven geographies, with the rich able to access faster internet that bypasses congestion, better roads, water, and other social services, leaving the poor and minorities unconnected or less connected to these necessities. In the hotels, malls, and the gated communities walled off from the reach of the

majority of people who live in the city, the private takeover of the responsibilities of the defunct or weakened welfare state has further fragmented
space, sharpening the divide between the elite and ordinary people. Where
do these other people live? And what does life look like for them?

We can find answers to these questions in Tillim's work, in which he
turns his camera on decrepit multistory buildings housing the urban poor.
In Tillim's shots, we encounter the nervousness that Loren Kruger identifies
as characteristic of Johannesburg, which she terms an "edgy" city.[22] Nothing is permanent here and violence can quickly erupt among residents, between residents and landlords, or between residents and state agents fixated
on evicting them. The founding of the city itself is entwined with violence,
considering that Johannesburg emerged from the underbelly of the mining
economy of the 1930s and 1940s. As Achille Mbembe and Sarah Nuttall explain it, "this is a city born out of a ruthless, extractive, mining economy."[23]
On the eve of the formal installation of the apartheid state, black bodies were
lowered into the mines to excavate the gold that placed the city on the global
commodity map. These bodies endangered their health as they churned out
the gold that built the city that they would never fully inhabit. Coming from
all across South Africa and from across the region in search of wealth, or coerced "to supply the sweat of their labor in extracting the thin but lucrative
seams of gold," these workers were housed in hostels and saw their mobility
restricted in the city as apartheid limited black occupation of space.[24] As we
move from this twentieth-century gold economy into the twenty-first century, the fact that much has not changed for the black inhabitants of the
city is a sobering lesson of Tillim's work: these Africans still occupy the precarious position that made them expendable as gold miners and as a people
whose "right to the city" was severely curtailed.[25]

From just the title and form of Tillim's *Jo'burg*, the viewer can decipher
its role as a hymn to everydayness, ordinariness, and informality. Johannesburg is the official name of the city, but it is Jo'burg for those familiar with
its labyrinths, the many who live there. In emphasizing the city's informal
nomenclature in the title, Tillim foreshadows the fact that we are about to
encounter images not of Melrose Arch and other symbols of the city's membership of a global consumerist network, but of structures housing those left
out of the hypercapitalism of this African space. Additionally, the form of
the book, its continuous concertina-style format, resembling the compact
photo albums of my childhood years in Lagos, Nigeria, adds to the informality of the images that follow. Like the family album that sat on the center
table of our living room, holding memories of baptisms and birthdays, the

5.1 View of Hillbrow looking north from the Mariston Hotel, *Jo'burg*
© Guy Tillim, 2005

familial album-like form of Tillim's collection demonstrates its preoccupation with everyday life. Moreover, the form here speaks of the scarcity that is
its thematic preoccupation. Unlike his project *Avenue Patrice Lumumba*, produced under the auspices of Harvard University's Peabody Museum, which
features large photographs, the compactness of *Jo'burg* underscores the compactness of space in Johannesburg's inner city and the limited opportunities
for the residents there. The continuous flow of the concertina-like album
gestures to the lingering effects of apartheid in inner-city Johannesburg,
where residents have not witnessed significant material transformations of
their living conditions since democracy arrived in 1994.

Although the first spread in Tillim's work provides an elevated shot of the
city skyline and telecommunications masts (figure 5.1), subsequent pages and
spreads undermine the promise of this first view. To understand the bulk of
the photographs, it is important to analyze this first spread, with its panoramic view of the city. In it, the city of gold springs up without inhibition.
The tall buildings and expansive view suggest infinite possibilities. At the
center of the image is a telecommunications mast rising above the buildings.
This marker of communication frames the city in relation to the world. It

5.2 A young woman on a roof, *Jo'burg* © Guy Tillim, 2005

signals the city's positioning as the African node of global financial circulation, linking the space to others across the world. There is much promise in this image, but unfortunately that promise is not carried through in the rest of the photographs. The panoramic view may promise infinite opportunities, but the cloudy, gray, overcast sky can be read as an ominous indicator of what is to come. In other words, grayness here preempts the view of those to whom the city's sense of promise does not apply.

Turning the page, we can begin appreciating what it means to be left out (figure 5.2). The image is of a literal outside, a rooftop with dirt on the floor and clothes hung to dry. A woman with her back to us is captured in motion. On the next spread, two men are sleeping on a roof (figure 5.3). These men are left out in at least two ways. Sleeping outside in this way suggests the absence of shelter, the lack of rooms of their own. Louise Meintjes captures the condition of homelessness in Johannesburg where migrant Zulu men "live in decrepit conditions, in men's hostels, informal settlements, shared rooms in inner-city apartments, or in backyard rentals in the townships." These men, in Meintjes's words, "are poorly, partially, or temporarily employed, if they have work at all."[26]

The precarious employment that Meintjes underscores brings me to an-

5.3 Two young men sleeping on the roof of Sherwood Heights, *Jo'burg*
© Guy Tillim, 2005

other issue represented in Tillim's photograph. The caption provided at the end of the collection describes this image as one of Mathews Ngwenya sleeping with a friend in the winter sun. Studies of free time across the continent are worth recalling here, of young people "'simply sitting,' 'killing time,' and having 'too many thoughts.'"[27] As Ato Quayson shows in the case of Accra, Ghana, as a result of under- and unemployment, young people in the city resort to various practices, including the creative improvisation of gym equipment for bodybuilding, in order to expend their abundant free time.[28] In Ethiopia, they drink coffee, smoke *khat*, and watch films to keep themselves occupied.[29] These insights on free time are relevant here, where two men are sleeping fully dressed in broad daylight—and outside, too. One way to read this is as an image of men passing their free time. With the absence of work to engage their productive abilities, these men sleep to while away the time and to mitigate boredom. The next spread stays outside, with one man, whose only visible features are his shoulder and hand, holding a cigarette, and another facing away from the viewer, looking down into the street from the roof (figure 5.4). In these images taken on roofs, none of the photographic subjects are looking at the camera. They either have their backs turned to

5.4 On the roof of Jeanwell House on Nugget Street, *Jo'burg*
© Guy Tillim, 2005

us, or have their faces and bodies cropped out except for an arm and hand. I read this distancing as a sign of the dissolution of individual subjectivity mirroring the exclusion of these bodies from the bounds of proper urban living in the African city. In other words, the estrangement of these people from the camera and the viewer parallels their estrangement from the promise of postapartheid progress.

The sight of destitution in these rooftop images follows the viewer into the indoor scenes of Tillim's photographs. At least three signs of precarity can be deciphered from those photographs shot inside: claustrophobia, bareness, and decay. Against the opening scene of plenitude and infinity, the photographs of indoor space in the collection showcase claustrophobia: narrow corridors, small rooms, and metal barricades are some of the elements of compactness in Tillim's work. In one photograph, a man is trying to open the door to his room (figure 5.5). This shot provides a view of a narrow hallway, while to the right is the metal bar separating the corridor from the stairs. All lines in the image lead down the hallway—the perspective points to the end of the hall, as does the descending line of the stairs and the man's gaze (directed away from us). But rather than opening up to any possibility, those lines and the man's gaze converge on closure.

It is interesting that in the spread following this one, we see a small child to one side of the image and barbed wire on the other (figure 5.6). Bars are a constant motif in this series, and when combined with the narrowness of rooms and hallways, and the barbed wire, the viewer is faced with prison-like imagery. To think of prison here is relevant because Tillim's settings are spaces of confinement just as detention centers are. These inner-city spaces are abodes for those frozen in time. They cannot return to a precolonial or pre-apartheid past, but they cannot enter the present either. Like prisoners, their ambitions and opportunities are curtailed by the state and the workings of neoliberalism, which make such bodies expendable. Operative in the South African context is "the neoliberal narrative of 'space as a fluctuating commodity' and 'consumable product'" that consigns the majority of urban dwellers to the margins of the city, where they are forced to live in unsanitary, compact spaces.[30]

In addition to claustrophobia, bareness and decrepitude are other characteristics of Tillim's indoor spaces that speak of the inhabitants' precarity. The compact rooms mostly feature necessities: in some cases beds almost cover the entire room; in others, near-empty rooms contain little in terms of furniture and the accoutrements of daily life. Besides beds, kitchen utensils, and pictures on the wall, there is little else in the form of household goods in these photographs. The people who live here own so little a decade after the first democratic election ushered in the Nelson Mandela government in 1994, and they lack suitable housing. In these "bad buildings," as the government describes some of them, bricks are falling off and glass is broken in places. Paint is peeling off and walls are stained. The rooms too are poorly lit, which makes the photographs less clear. Poor lighting combines with the aforementioned factors to indicate underdevelopment. In short, Tillim's photographs present the misfortune of decay that overwhelms these inhabitants of inner-city Johannesburg.

Architectural decay serves as a marker of stunted progress or underdevelopment in Tillim's oeuvre. In his collection *Avenue Patrice Lumumba*, for instance, which captures buildings and sculptures in the Democratic Republic of the Congo, Tillim shows architecture losing its shine to the ravages of age.[31] Temporal decay is at work in *Avenue Patrice Lumumba* as it is in *Jo'burg*. An abandoned swimming pool surrounded by weeds, a headless sculpture, broken doors and windows, as well as dilapidated furniture are all signs of

5.5 Man opening a door at Cape Agulhas, *Jo'burg* © Guy Tillim, 2005

decay in *Avenue Patrice Lumumba*. Introducing the collection, Tillim describes his photographs as "a walk through avenues of dreams." Tillim recognizes "Patrice Lumumba's dream, his nationalism" in these "structures," but he is also quick to acknowledge the demise of Lumumba's dream.[32] Tillim invites his viewers to imagine the former life of these buildings and artworks, the glory of their early days, and their promise. Lumumba's dream of a prosperous nation decoupled from Belgium's strangulation would die with him in the hands of the same Belgian state, which killed him in collaboration with a compromised local elite and the CIA. If Lumumba's dream was snuffed out quickly in 1961, the dream of urban progress has taken more time to fizzle out, as shown in the photographs collected in *Avenue Patrice Lumumba*. Whether it is in *Jo'burg* or the other collection, Tillim invites viewers to recognize architectural decay as a sign of the deterioration of postcolonial life and as an index of the failure to realize the promise of urban modernity.

Claustrophobia, bareness, and decay may constitute some of the characteristics of urban living in Tillim's *Jo'burg*, but the climactic scenes of precarity in the collection are the photographs of displacement. Some photographs feature men in red overalls and helmets. Described as members of Wozani Security, also known as the Red Ants, these men connote danger

5.6 A child and barbed wire at Milton Court, *Jo'burg* © Guy Tillim, 2005

with their uniforms and it is manifest in their actions (figures 5.7 and 5.8). In these images they have come to evict residents of these buildings whose few belongings are thrown out. The last photographs in the collection are devoted to eviction, with objects removed from their places and scattered across rooms and, in the penultimate image, outside (figure 5.8). If there is some form of order in the arrangement of domesticity in the earlier images, chaos reigns with the arrival of the Red Ants. The images of eviction are from different buildings, which suggests the preponderance of the practice, but the exercise looks the same: the removal of poor urbanites without providing alternative accommodation. We should bear in mind the failure to keep the promise of housing provision at the dawn of independence. As the displaced persons wade through their belongings, exposed to the elements in the penultimate image, we are confronted by those who cannot dwell, in Martin Heidegger's terms.

Tracing the etymology of the concept in Old English and German, Heidegger posits that to dwell is "to remain, to stay in a place."[33] Continuing, he identifies building as central to dwelling. In the work of the German philosopher, building as it relates to dwelling has two intertwined connotations: "Both modes of building—building as cultivating, Latin *colere*, *cultura*, and

5.7 Members of Wozani Security, popularly known as the Red Ants, *Jo'burg*
© Guy Tillim, 2005

building as the raising up of edifices, *aedificare*—are comprised within genuine building, that is, dwelling."[34] Glossing Heidegger's work for the global age, one can say that "the acts that 'attain to dwelling' are rather those that build a life, a sense of belonging to a place, a culture, a way of life—in short, a world—that we have a hand in helping to build or maintain."[35] The essential conditions for dwelling are edifices that shelter humans as well as the opportunity to cultivate the earth, to be productive members of society and to pursue meaningful ways of life. These essential conditions are missing in Tillim's photographs. Whether it is the men sleeping outside or those occupying ramshackle buildings, these people cannot dwell, since the actualization of dwelling is "to be set at peace, . . . to remain at peace."[36] In the absence of a suitable abode, within the context of eviction that is chaotic and negates peace, these occupants of urban space cannot possibly cultivate. As Heidegger himself puts it, "only if we are capable of dwelling, only then can we build."[37] It is significant that the photographs offer a limited glimpse of the productive activities of these people and contain little evidence of homeliness, stability, and community: Are they even employed? How can they cultivate or till the earth without the necessary infrastructure to support

5.8 The Red Ants evicting residents, *Jo'burg* © Guy Tillim, 2005

a productive and fulfilling life in the city? To return to that penultimate photograph then is to behold a testament to the state of un-dwelling.

Heidegger describes the preservation of the fourfold—namely the earth, the sky, the divinities, and mortals—as the essence of dwelling. As he puts it, this essence includes "to save the earth, to receive the sky, to await the divinities, to initiate mortals."[38] Heidegger's account of dwelling links humans to a cosmic whole, connecting mortals (living and unborn) to the earth (that nourishes them and houses their ancestors), to the divine, and to the elements (sky), a linkage that echoes practices of many African societies where communal well-being is contingent on cosmological harmony. There is an echo of Heidegger's fourfold in Wole Soyinka's staging of the African world to include the "realm of infinity" comprising "the natural home of the unseen deities, a resting-place for the departed, and a staging house for the unborn."[39] Soyinka conceives of the world of the living, of the dead, of the unborn, and the transitional abyss as constitutive of the cosmological plane. Human coexistence with the rest of the cosmos necessitates ritual, which is the occasion for communal regeneration. On these occasions, humans invoke the divine to imbue their community with new

strength.⁴⁰ There is no singular South African culture but scholars working on the cosmological systems of the various ethnicities document similar
interactions across spheres of existence. Writing on the Zulu, Harriet Sibisi
records belief in a "Supreme Being or God" who "lives up above . . . with
the Goddess often referred to as the 'Princess of the Sky.'" Sibisi adds that
"the spirits of the deceased live down below" with the "unborn spirit," and
that "the passage of the spirit from the world below to this world, and vice
versa, is effected through married women."⁴¹ Although the particularities
of Cape Nguni cosmology is different from that of the Yoruba or Zulu, the
broad outline of W. D. Hammond-Tooke's description of it conforms to the
interrelationship between divinity, humans, animals, and ancestors, and in
all of the aforementioned cultures ritual is a precondition for cosmological
equilibrium.⁴² From Soyinka's Yoruba culture to various South African traditions, humans cherish land that gives them food and water, and which provides links to their dead ancestors and the divine. Kwasi Wiredu's discussion
of communal ownership of land among the Akan of Ghana applies to African cultures in South Africa and elsewhere: "land was supposed to belong to
the whole lineage, conceived as including the ancestors, the living members,
and those as yet to be born," and "for this reason, in traditional times the
sale of land was prohibited."⁴³ To preserve the earth, these Africans tended
the land and related with other humans within and outside their lineage. To
care for mortals also involves relationality across species, making room for
the kind of human-animal entanglement that Wendy Woodward illustrates
in her study of animal subjectivities in Southern Africa.⁴⁴ In these cultures,
people perform rituals at the start of the planting season, during harvest,
and throughout the year in supplication and thanksgiving for favorable elemental conditions, for human and animal fertility, as well as for a bountiful
harvest. To dwell, in this sense, means to maintain cosmic balance akin to
Heidegger's fourfold.

However, the history of land expropriation in South Africa, leading to
urban migration for black Africans, sundered the relationship to land, communal ties to mortals, the sky, and to the divine. If in the past communal
ownership vested the chief with authority to allocate land to community
members for housing and farming, the colonial expropriation of land for
white settlement and conservation, already discussed in chapter 4, significantly reduced the amount of land owned by black people.⁴⁵ Whether it
is in the Bantustan reserves into which they were herded or the suffocating space they occupied in the townships during apartheid, these Africans
lost access to land and the opportunity to cultivate it. As "the population of

Chapter Five

the reserves increased from approximately 4.5 million to 11 million" between 1960 and 1980, population pressures led to soil erosion and desertification.[46] Underscoring the dire conditions, Mamphela Ramphele posits that "marginal land was ploughed by people trying to eke out a living under desperate circumstances, leading to desertification of large parts of rural areas formerly covered by sweetveld (good grazing)."[47] Unable to properly tend the land in the reserves, many were forced into the urban wage economy, which meant further disconnection from land, from the wherewithal to tend it, and the ability to commune with their ancestors. The loss of land interrupted the connection among the living, the dead, the earth, the sky, and the divine.

Heidegger's diagnosis that the "proper dwelling plight lies in this, that mortals ever search anew for the essence of dwelling, that they must ever learn to dwell" must be revised for this African context to foreground the racial exclusions undermining the attainment of dwelling.[48] What is missing is the institutional and material means of dwelling denied them by the workings of race.[49] The institution of apartheid as official policy in 1948, three years before Heidegger delivered his paper "Building Dwelling Thinking," continued the process of depriving black people in South Africa of the prerequisites of dwelling. In other words, racial considerations undergirded the exclusion of South Africans from land ownership and cultivation starting with the earlier allocation of land in favor of whites, to official segregation based on race in 1948, and the later Group Areas Act of 1950 and pass laws. Deprived of land and in some cases forced into the money economy to support themselves and their families, these South Africans lost the opportunity to preserve the fourfold. Leaving families, their ancestors, and gods behind as they journeyed to the city in search of economic opportunities, they were unable to re-create the cosmological totality that earlier sustained them. Cultural considerations, including social and religious practices, should guide architectural decisions, a protocol that colonial planners ignored in land allocation and urban planning in South Africa and across the continent.[50] The delinking of urban spatial distribution and architectural designs from culture served the interests of the colonizers for whom the black subject was primarily a means to economic and political ends. The architecture of race is responsible for the non-realization of the essence of dwelling for many black South Africans, including those captured in Tillim's penultimate photograph.

That penultimate photograph's depiction of eviction contains the hauntings of a problematic colonial past, thereby rendering the city as a "palimpsestual" form of writing.[51] In his work on spatial practices in the city, Michel de Certeau writes that "objects and words also have hollow places in which a past sleeps," and that "places are fragmentary and inward-turning histories."[52] Looking inward to South African history, this photograph can be read as a receptacle of history, as an object "in which a past sleeps." Colonial occupations "contextualize enclosure, exclusion, domination, [and] disciplinary control," and the South African experience was no exception.[53] Apartheid involved an architectural design of spaces to avoid interracial mixing and to deprive blacks of land. Nevertheless, confining black people to the native reserves did not stop them from finding their way into the city and making a claim on it. In Johannesburg and Cape Town, squatter communities arose that challenged the colonial script in South Africa. The practice of persistently holding space through squatter camps became a means of "making freedom."[54] Eviction notices were rampant and were often followed by forced removal and demolition, such as the removal of a vibrant black community in Sophiatown and of colored people in District Six. Thus in Tillim's eviction image we find not only the ruins of people's property, for also present here is the ruin from a colonial past that continuously haunts the city.[55]

In her introduction to an edited collection on colonial ruins, Ann Laura Stoler offers "a provocative challenge to name the toxic corrosions and violent accruals of colonial aftermaths, the durable forms in which they bear on the material environment and on people's minds."[56] Stoler adds that the effects of the colonial past "reside in the corroded hollows of landscapes, in the gutted infrastructures of segregated cityscapes, and in the microecologies of matter and mind."[57] Although an artifact of the present, Tillim's *Jo'burg* carries the echoes of the colonial past in its depiction of the "intransigence of apartheid."[58] It is significant that the collection begins and ends with panoramic views of a broader Johannesburg urban landscape (figures 5.1 and 5.9). The skyscrapers proclaim the city's prosperity and membership of a global financial circulatory network. Yet the images sandwiched in between them tell a different story, of those left out of the city's success.[59] The everyday connotes precarity for the people memorialized in Tillim's photographs. If we recall the tightness of space, the bareness of belongings, and the decrepit state of infrastructure the photographs present, and compare those qualities with the set of possibilities offered by the opening and closing images taken from atop the Mariston Hotel in Johannesburg, we can begin to see the architecture of segregated urban spaces that Stoler writes about.

Stoler's insistence that the effects of the colonial ordering of space manifest not only in material terms but also in people's minds is relevant for dis-

5.9 The view from the top of the Mariston Hotel looking south, *Jo'burg*
© Guy Tillim, 2005

cussing the psychological imprint of spatial segregation on the inner-city residents of Tillim's work. Granted that we know little about them from that work, yet the content of their inner thoughts is worth probing. There is little evidence of sociality in Tillim's collection, where most of the urban residents appear withdrawn and engaged in self-contemplation.

In one image taken at a building in the area of Johannesburg known as Central Business District (figure 5.10), the viewer can see three different generations in one room. There is a schoolgirl in uniform who is in the center of the shot. There is a woman who is probably her mother and then two elderly people, perhaps her grandparents. I am struck by the difference between the girl's confident pose—her legs are wide apart and she looks ahead—and the way that the older subjects in this photograph look withdrawn. The woman who may be the child's mother has her arms folded as she appears in deep thought in her sitting position; the grandfather figure appears absentminded too. It is as if the weight of the moment bears heavily on the minds of the older subjects of this photograph, who cannot clearly distinguish their precarious situation from the conditions of the colonial era. To cite the title of one short story by the Ghanaian writer Ama Ata Aidoo, evident before view-

5.10 Three generations in one space, *Jo'burg* © Guy Tillim, 2005

ers are those "for whom things did not change."[60] The absence of change maps onto the presentation of the photographs in a concertina style, suggesting that the visual narrative is a continuous one from the apartheid days into the post-segregation era just as the series' compact form speaks to the scarcity underpinning the lives of residents. Denied full rights to the city, unable to properly dwell in decrepit structures from which they face the threat of eviction, these urban residents have not seen significant improvements from the apartheid days.

It is important though that we do not write off these city inhabitants. Their appearance and their occupation of urban space is a stubborn refusal to accept the logic of South Africa's neoliberal order. By holding on to the city they participate in everyday forms of resistance.[61] As a reminder of the incompleteness of the postapartheid project of redistribution, Tillim's project demands a recalibration of the social system and more specifically a re-imagination of the urban. Tillim's photographs are helpful instruments for the process of reimagining and reconstituting the city and the nation in South Africa. He critiques precarity in order that it might be upstaged by a fairer spatial arrangement.[62]

The Space of Geopolitics: China in the African City

Up to this point, we have seen the African city as a site of precarity as well as a worldly space that enmeshes the rural and the urban alongside the local and the global. As a crossroads of culture and economic exchange, the African city is not immune to the dynamics of global relations and the inequality that accompanies them. Although formal colonialism has ended in most parts of the continent, Africa remains tethered to the strictures of Europe and the far-reaching hand of US influence. There are also new relationships and alliances that recalibrate older forms of subjugation. To speak of novel forms of subjugation and imperial reach is to create the space for introducing a global power whose presence is reshaping the continent's ecology and economics in significant ways: China. In an earlier chapter, I mentioned China as another place where toxic waste goes, but that description of the country does not provide the complete picture. The truth is that China's extensive manufacturing economy requires raw materials for its industries and markets for its mass-produced commodities. Africa has become a strategic destination for Chinese investment.

For some critics, China's projects in Africa—oil and mineral exploration, manufacturing, and other economic activities—constitute the new scramble for Africa.[63] In this mode of seeing the relationship, China is the contemporary incarnation of the European powers that balkanized and looted the continent in the nineteenth and twentieth centuries. Proponents of this position quickly cite the expanding footprint of the East Asian country in key sectors of Africa's economies, including oil and mining, and its acquisition of large tracts of land at negligible prices.[64] Many African states now owe their largest debt to China even as Chinese businesses and factories dominate the economic scene. Another point adduced by those sympathetic to the colonial argument is the racism and discrimination that Chinese employers and citizens practice against Africans, while yet another is the ecological devastation that Chinese businesses and construction projects leave in their wake.[65]

On the opposite side of the spectrum are those who perceive a mutually beneficial relationship, interpreting the colonial argument as sensationalist and unsupported by empirical and factual evidence.[66] Ching Kwan Lee especially argues that China's reach on the continent is always checked by the contestation of African governments, civil society, labor unions, and even ordinary citizens. In her words, "Chinese state interests must contend with local African political economic and social pressures."[67] Drawing attention to the absence of "the coercive means of military conquests or monopolistic chartered companies" that characterize colonial and imperial regimes, Lee avers that China must always seek consent for its operations, therefore engendering a reciprocal relationship.[68] This kind of development is the "win-win" development paradigm repeatedly touted in Nick Francis and Marc Francis's film *When China Met Africa*, which tracks Chinese investment in agriculture, mining, and infrastructural projects in Zambia.[69]

The pro-China argument goes this way: China is primarily interested in reciprocal bilateral and multilateral relationships on the continent. Supporters of this position insist that unlike European countries, China's primary interest is in a South-South development paradigm that provides raw materials and markets for Chinese goods while the African countries receive substantial infrastructural development and cheap loans in return. The South-South dynamic is linked to the 1955 Bandung Conference, at which China pledged cooperation and support for African countries and other nonaligned nations.[70] Tracking the evolution of the relationship between the continent and the Asian global power, formally institutionalized by the formation of the Forum on China-Africa Cooperation in 2000, Drew Thompson writes: "In the 1960s and 1970s, China supported liberation movements in several African countries, gave aid to socialist nations to build stadiums, hospitals, railroads and other infrastructure, and cemented relations through a steady stream of expert engineers, teachers, and doctors. Today, Chinese officials travel to Africa accompanied by bankers and businesspeople, promoting political and economic commerce that expands China-Africa ties in a sustainable fashion. While trade and diplomacy are driven by China's newfound economic strength and subsequent demand for raw materials, China continues to support longstanding programs that deliver aid to underserved African citizens."[71] One of China's first major projects in Africa was the TAZARA Railway, completed in 1974 and linking the coastal port of Dar es Salaam in Tanzania with Zambia's Copperbelt region.[72]

Wherever one falls on the scale of gauging China's relationship with Africa, the environmental impacts of Chinese engagement in Africa and land concessions hold ominous signs for Africa's future. Even Deborah Brautigam, whose writing dismisses the colonial framing of China's presence in Africa, agrees that "Chinese companies are clearly implicated in illegal harvesting of old-growth timber and illegal fishing, and in obtaining concessions without regard to the rights of local communities."[73] She also expresses concern for the long-term impact of signing away large tracts of land to foreigners.[74] Focusing on the environmental implications of the relationship helps to complicate the binary conceptualization of the subject.

China has worked very hard to distance itself from the European exploitation of Africa. Since the decline of the Soviet Union at the end of the Cold War, China has positioned itself as a benign alternative to the colonial powers that plundered the continent. China provides aid to African governments, invests in industries and infrastructure, and sponsors scholarship opportunities for African students to study in China.[75] More recently, the country has extended its sphere of influence to the cultural arena.[76] Alessandro Jedlowski confirms that "Chinese media companies are in fact signing major deals all over the continent in an explicit bid to develop soft power strategies . . . and to counter the bad image of the People's Republic [of China] that much Western media have circulated."[77] Against charges of racism and discrimination, corruption and environmental degradation, Chinese media producers have stepped into the scene with images and projects demonstrating China's superpower status as well as its benevolence and its differences from the hegemonic West.

For the reader wondering what these perspectives on the Asian superpower have to do with African cities, I argue in this section that the African city is the stage for the ideological battle between the Chinese East and the US-led West in cultural media, and as in every battle in which elephants fight, the grass—in this case African space and the continent's inhabitants—suffers. The opportunity cost for projecting the image of a strong and charitable Chinese state in Wu Jing's *Wolf Warrior 2*, for instance, is the destruction of African urban space and the massive death toll of inhabitants. In the following reading of the film, the "heart of darkness" has literally been moved from the African countryside to the city, where we see unbridled violence perpetrated by a rebel group intent on seizing power. In the end, the African city is a necessary sacrifice for the triumph of a benevolent China, a superpower that resists intervening militarily in Africa until the arrival of United Nations approval, an unsubtle dig at the history of unilateral interventions by the United States, of which the invasion of Iraq is a prime example.

My intention is not to single out a particular film, especially since Jing's film draws antecedents from Chinese martial arts films and even Western moving images depicting Africa in negative terms. It is easy to dismiss these works as popular cultural expressions that should not be taken seriously, but to do so would be to ignore the ideologies that they normalize. Popular films such as *Wolf Warrior 2* perform ideological work with racial implications. The Africa of such films often requires the white (or brown) savior to save the barbaric natives from violence and self-destruction, but there is more to such representations than has yet received critical attention. Besides the racial ecologies of these texts, it is important to consider their representations of the physical environment and their reinstatement of the colonial treatment of African space as a wasteland needing external intervention. As I demonstrate in what follows, the ideological orientation of popular cultural media such as Jing's film has racial and ecological implications for apprehending urban space in Africa.

Set in China and featuring an elite military unit led by Leng Feng (Wu Jing), the first *Wolf Warrior* film takes as one of its key themes the military might of the Chinese state.[78] Whether through its portrayal of training missions with sophisticated weaponry, first-grade war planes, missiles, explosives, and other gadgets, or the takedown of an international drug and arms syndicate threatening the territorial integrity of the nation, this patriotic film makes clear that China's enemies will be crushed. Even the head of the syndicate warns his white mercenaries early in the film not to underestimate Chinese might in a move that foreshadows his arrest and the death of the mercenaries as the film ends. The film ends soon after the leader of the mercenaries engages Feng in a battle that the Chinese soldier wins. This may be an individual triumph, but in a film charged with patriotic overtones, Feng's victory begs to be understood as a triumph over the West. Considering the United States' position as the chief global power since the end of World War II, the film signals the arrival of another hegemon on the world stage. As *Wolf Warrior* closes, the commanding officer in charge of Feng's unit declares that there will be no hiding place for anyone testing China's resolve. The sequel, to which I now turn, also ends with similar nationalist rhetoric, encouraging the Chinese not to lose hope when in danger in a foreign country because the strong Chinese state will deliver them.

What is the cost of the patriotic rhetoric and action in *Wolf Warrior 2*? "Is it conceivable that the exercise of hegemony might leave space untouched?"[79] Clear answers to these pertinent questions do not emerge until in the sequel, where the action shifts to Africa. It is telling that no African country is named, locating the film and the Chinese influence in a continental frame, even though the African scenes were shot in Alexandria and Soweto, townships that extend South Africa's geography of precarity beyond the inner city shown in Tillim's photographs. While the decision to set the film in a fictitious African territory may be a way to avoid criticism from citizens appalled by the violent representation of their country, the careless and easy use of the generalized Africa moniker hearkens back to a troubled colonial past that the Chinese want to dissociate themselves from. In one early scene in *Wolf Warrior 2*, Feng, seeking the source of the bullet that supposedly hurt his Chinese lover, vows to traverse the entire continent in order to find the culprits. The continental search recalls the scramble for Africa and the exploration of its interiors by European powers in search of resources and territories to conquer. Echoes of a colonial script abound in *Wolf Warrior 2*, a script that only deepens as the film progresses.

The opening scenes of the film foreshadow the role Africa and Africans will play as foils to the Chinese. The film credits appear over a scene of water that brings into view a ship being surrounded by Somali pirates. Hollywood watchers are already familiar with the trope of Somalis as pirates from *Captain Phillips*, in which an American vessel is commandeered by pirates.[80] In this case, however, the pirates fail and are dislodged by Feng, who happens to be onboard. He has taken to sea life after being dismissed from the Chinese military. Following the killing of the pirates, the film moves to the African city where Feng offloads the goods he has brought to trade. Here the film recognizes China's vast economic reach. The focus on Chinese products in the film is a reminder of the extent to which the continent depends on the Asian country for finished goods. But economics is not the paramount issue animating the film.

More important is China's military might, which becomes prominent as a rebel group spreads mayhem across the city. The state of emergency declared by the prime minister does not stop the armed group from entering the city with tanks and guns, destroying property and taking human lives. Feng is in a park with Tundu, his "godson," when the first shot is fired. He later finds himself in a Chinese shop attacked by militants and engages them in a firefight. As the militia regroups to mount a bigger assault, Feng and the Chinese shop owner reason that they should find their way to the Chinese embassy. Though they wonder at first if the non-Chinese among them will find refuge there, the Africans present at the scene go with the two men as they make their way amidst extreme violence on the city street. The violence here and throughout the film reinstitutionalizes the Eurocentric view of Africa as a violent space and of Africans as bloodthirsty. It is particularly significant that there is no indication of the cause of the violence. The only hint the film provides is that a power-hungry rebel leader has enlisted the aid of mercenaries to help overrun the city.

The prime minister and soldiers guarding the city are no match for the rebels, and with the destabilization of the state, China steps in to rescue the Africans and Chinese residents. When Tundu insists on finding his mother rather than leaving for China with Feng, and the Chinese shop owner confesses that the mercenaries at the Chinese-run hospital are responsible for hurting Feng's lover, Feng decides to stay behind too. His subsequent journey takes him across the city and beyond, where he engages in battles against the rebels. In his account of informal urban settlements, Mike Davis argues that "the 'feral, failed cities' of the Third World—especially their slum outskirts—will be the distinctive battlespace of the twenty-first century."[81] Davis's conclusion is prescient for understanding Feng's fight across the African city and the ideological battle that the film discourse participates in. For what the African city provides is a space for the ideological positioning of China as the eminent, benevolent, smart, and efficient superpower. In this journey, which first takes Feng to the hospital where Dr. Chen, who has found a cure for Lamanla disease, works, and later to a Chinese factory where the film's final battles occur, Feng and the Chinese come out triumphant. Even carnivorous animals are set against the Chinese to foreground the latter's strength. While Feng and his fellow soldiers dislodged a pack of wolves in *Wolf Warrior*, in the sequel, Feng's vehicle outruns a lion that chases after it as he moves from the hospital to the factory: Feng, and by extension his country, have triumphed over jungle and urbanity, over country and city.

The film's use of special effects and stunts embellishes its aesthetics and theatricality. These technical details animate the continuous fast-paced fighting that becomes monotonous because of its frequency and duration. Special effects and stunts combine to produce a technological sublime, positioning the Chinese in a superior position to the Africans and as competitors and ultimate victors over the West. The Chinese has conquered technology too. When an American doctor, Rachel, who assists Feng in rescuing Prasha, an African girl, from the hospital, proudly announces that she has sent a tweet to the American embassy and help will soon come, Feng sneers at her optimism. In an interesting scene, when she tries to call the embassy, she reaches a recorded message saying it is closed. Enjoying her anger over US irresponsibility, Feng tells her that the Americans left as the fighting commenced. This moment speaks to the retreat of the United States as China takes charge of humanitarian aid and military assistance. Unlike the US and Europe, China does not evacuate only its own citizens, taking on board Africans and offering them the protection that their own state cannot. As the city is reduced to rubble, the Chinese flag flies triumphantly on the rescue ship.

For the viewer wondering why the film moves from China to Africa, and about the choice of the latter among other possibilities, the continent's negative connotation makes it conducive for the geopolitical realignment that the film is invested in. The African space in *Wolf Warrior 2* is not only violent; it is also the site of disease, bringing the colonial narrative of the continent to completion: all the ingredients are featured, including poverty, war, and disease. Feng is exposed to Lamanla when he encounters quarantined Africans suffering from the disease. At the time of his death, Dr. Chen is on the verge of finding a cure, which Rachel appropriates for treating Feng after his exposure to the dangerous disease. We should not lose sight of the casting of Africa as a site of deadly diseases, or of the positioning of the Chinese doctor to provide medical care to Africans. *Wolf Warrior 2* demonstrates China's superior power by deploying its diplomatic arm (embassy), military might, economic potency (factory), and social services (hospital) to save the Africans.

The Chinese intervention in Jing's film degrades the African city, engendering environmental destruction. The factory fight scene, for instance, comes to mind. Both sides of the conflict fire various weapons, with the Chinese fleet firing missiles to aid Feng. As weapons hit the factory, dust-like particles are emitted into the atmosphere, raising the specter of environmental pollution. There are other physical markers of destruction too: the explosions and gunfire as well as the destroyed cars and armored tanks release pollutants into the atmosphere. As examples of the "slow violence" that Rob Nixon theorizes, the impact of these pollutants may not be as immediately obvious as the more immediate death and injuries in the film. Nevertheless, the fact that their environmental impacts "are slow in the making" or that their effects may take a longer period to materialize does not diminish the risk of these pollutants to the biosphere. As the smoke slowly makes its way into the atmosphere and into the soil in the film, we are reminded of the "incremental and accretive" process that Nixon describes and "calamitous repercussions playing out across a range of temporal scales."[82] The temporality of Jing's film is insufficient for these repercussions to emerge but the possibility demands a consideration of the immediate and long-term environmental consequences of the film's action. In its thematic representations of environmental destruction and in the carbon expenditure of its making, *Wolf Warrior 2* actualizes the "combustible disorder" of film ecology.[83]

An archaeology of film ecology—especially of the commercial genre— reveals considerable energy consumption.[84] The kind of large-scale production that Jing's film is part of makes "massive use of electricity and petroleum and release[s] . . . hundreds of thousands of tons of deadly emissions."[85]

Moreover, the waste of resources characterizing large-scale filmmaking applies to *Wolf Warrior 2*. Nadia Bozak singles out long takes, which she reads as a "signal of material excess and an ideology of material decadence."[86] Although generalizations do not always work, Bozak's insight on the long take is apropos for the fighting scenes in Jing's film. Material excess is at stake in the demonstration of China's technological prowess in these scenes, deploying the extended take to mesmerize viewers. And with excess goes the expenditure of resources, including energy. Additionally, considering its sophisticated use of special effects, its transnational shooting, and the scenes of devastation, the making of *Wolf Warrior 2* certainly leaves a tremendous carbon footprint. The film's production and its thematic preoccupation buttress the critique of China as a polluter of African space and suggest that the Asian superpower achieves its economic and military leverage at great environmental cost.

The rapid disintegration of the lawless city in *Wolf Warrior 2* parallels the ascendancy of a law-abiding China. In a telling scene where the survivors of the factory attack join Feng, Rachel, and Prasha in a truck heading to the UN camp, the Chinese flag is all they need to gain passage at a military checkpoint. This moment in the film is powerful and warrants scrutiny. It is significant that the truck's occupants discard their guns as Feng hoists the Chinese flag and keeps it flying until they reach the UN compound. The film seems to be stating that even in a context of war, what one really needs is not guns but the acceptance of China's role as a superpower. The hoisting of the Chinese flag on various occasions in the film concretizes a takeover of the country by Chinese interests. This takeover is foreshadowed in the battle over Prasha, an African girl captured by the mercenaries. One of the fighters declares that whoever gets Prasha gets to control the state. Prasha's gender suggests the feminization of the nation, but what is of utmost interest is that as the film ends, Prasha is in the custody of Feng, which represents the takeover of the African territory, including its urban space, by China. Films like *Wolf Warrior 2* are players in the zone of geopolitical construction of the Other in relation to a powerful, benevolent, and charitable self. These projects must be seen within China's plan to expand its global role and extend its geographical influence, especially in Africa, where the raw materials needed to power its factories are readily available. As China takes over in *Wolf Warrior 2*, we must not lose sight of the destruction wrought on the African city, or of China's ongoing transformation of the continent outside the world of the film.

China's incursions into Africa have meant that an increasing number of

Africans now live in the Asian country. Adams Bodomo estimates that about 500,000 Africans live in China as of 2012.[87] Like those on the continent who have reported racial discrimination from their Chinese employers, Africans in China have reported abusive practices predicated on skin color.[88] Media artifacts such as *Wolf Warrior 2* may be useful for raising Chinese national consciousness, but they do not educate Chinese people about their African hosts and guests. By promoting violence as characteristic of African life and failing to positively develop any African character in the film, the makers of *Wolf Warrior 2* perpetuate the stereotypical view of the continent that is responsible for the denigration of its people and environment. The film's depiction of the continent accords with the stereotypical depiction of a generic Africa in Chinese cultural productions.[89]

Watching *Wolf Warrior 2*, I could not resist connecting its depiction of Africans to Howard W. French's disturbing observation that China infantilizes Africans: "China had not so much broken with the paternalism of the West . . . . Africans were not really brothers. Not at all. Behind the fraternal masks, Chinese officials thought of them as children, capable only of baby steps, to be brought along with sugary inducements and infantilizing speech."[90] When French's text is read alongside the fact that the only likeable Africans in *Wolf Warrior 2* are children—Tundu and Prasha—it is difficult not to agree with French or at least with the idea that from the film's point of view, the only good Africans are children who need China's assistance to mature into proper human subjects. Tundu is presented as a godson to Feng, who instructs him on proper etiquette before the fighting begins, while Prasha owes her life to Dr. Chen's treatment. It must be pointed out, in closing, that Jing's film was released to popular acclaim in China, where it shattered the box office record. Thus it matters what view of Africa it presents to its primary audience, many of whom are potential employers and neighbors of Africans on the continent and abroad.

The City of the Future

Tillim's photographs and Jing's film demonstrate the challenges of the African city: its grinding poverty and the degraded living conditions for many who make homes there. The violence and inequality that characterize these cultural artifacts demand the reconstitution of urban space on the continent. How can we remake African cities so that they become equitable terrains for multispecies flourishing? African ecomedia are valuable materials to think with in the process of recalibrating the city. The value of these cultural productions coheres in their imaginative breadth, their ability to conjure realms beyond the immediately possible. The urban geographer Garth Myers recognized this potential when he included a chapter on Somali literature in his book on African cities. For Myers, literary texts "point toward more imaginative, creative African alternative visions of cities."[91] Myers shows the transformation of Somalia in Nuruddin Farah's fiction into a site of possibility. Fiction's ability to restore hope in the case of Somalia, often cited as an instance of a failed state, registers its pertinence for reimagining degraded and blighted cityscapes.[92] The imaginative work of fiction will not replace the important "practical, activist work" needed to bring about the city of the future, but it is a condition of possibility, a spur for praxis.[93]

We can locate that spur for praxis in Femi Odugbemi's *Makoko: Futures Afloat* and in Olalekan Jeyifous's Afrofuturist *Shanty Megastructures*. Odugbemi studied film and television production at Montana State University. He worked with the Nigeria Television Authority and in advertising before branching into directing documentaries such as the award-winning *Bariga Boy*, on young street performers in the Bariga area of Lagos, and *Makoko*, as well as producing television dramas including *Tinsel* and *Battleground*.[94] Odugbemi is founder of the annual iRepresent African documentary festival in Lagos and has juried international film festivals. An interest in Lagos and Makoko is not the only link between Odugbemi and the New York–based visual artist Jeyifous. They share Yoruba ancestry, which inspires some of their creative projects. Jeyifous grew up in Nigeria, where his father was a university professor, before relocating to the United States. He attended Cornell University for his undergraduate degree in architecture, a subject matter that shapes his art, including his 3D architectural drawing series *Shanty Megastructures*, which was first exhibited at the Shenzhen Biennale of Architecture and Urbanism in China. The spectrum of Jeyifous's work covers drawings, sculptures, and murals.

The projects of Jeyifous and Odugbemi under consideration here emerged from Africa's largest metropolis, Lagos, which is increasingly becoming an art-world city, and home to various artistic renditions of the future. Lagos, the economic capital of Nigeria and West Africa, is a city of approximately 20 million people, attracting inhabitants from across Nigeria and the region. Like other geographies of exploitation in Africa, Lagos is also a city of inequality, with extreme wealth concentrated in certain parts of the city, while others manifest evidence of extreme poverty. These areas are often in close contiguity, so much so that the observer can easily glimpse the distinction within a short distance. The power of Odugbemi's film of Lagos comes precisely from focusing on one such area, around Third Mainland Bridge, connecting the Lagos mainland to the Island, the site of shiny skyscrapers housing the corporate headquarters of various financial services firms and institutions. Underneath the bridge linking the two areas is a third space—Makoko—housing the Ogu people, many of whom migrated from Badagry in the early twentieth century. This fishing community lives on makeshift houses raised on stilts and jutting out of the water, a few kilometers away from downtown Lagos with its vibrant economic powerhouses. Not too far away also is Eko Atlantic City, the postmodern city being erected on land reclaimed from the ocean, which will host corporate offices, high-rise residential buildings, and ultramodern shopping and entertainment multiplexes.[95]

Odugbemi's film opens with aerial views of Lagos Island, with its high-rise buildings, "signifiers of economic, political and cultural power."[96] The viewer can make out the logo of the United Bank of Africa, one of the biggest banks in Africa, cresting the top of one of the skyscrapers. Those familiar with the area can also make out the Catholic Holy Cross Cathedral on Broad Street in downtown Lagos Island. If this film is about the riverine Makoko community underneath the bridge, why does it begin with an aerial view of the center of hypercapitalism in Lagos? In other words, why does a documentary that is interested in the view from below open with an aerial view of the world of the upper class? The film's opening shots link it to Tillim's collection of photographs of Johannesburg discussed earlier, which also opens with a panoramic view of Johannesburg's skyline. Odugbemi's opening, like Tillim's, orients its audience to the bifurcation of space. We see how inequality plays out even within a short distance. Makoko may be very close to Lagos Island, but the precarious existence of its inhabitants is radically different from the lifestyle of the people occupying the offices and residences in the buildings seen in the opening of Odugbemi's film.

The settlement of Makoko manifests the characteristics of the "encroachment of the ordinary," Asef Bayat's term for the "silent, patient, protracted, and pervasive advancement of ordinary people on the propertied and powerful in order to survive hardships and better their lives."[97] From its beginnings in the early twentieth century, the settlement has established itself at the edge of the city. Denied government support and recognition, the inhabitants have taken up space despite the will of the authorities and have found ways to provide necessities for their survival. Like the Iranian poor whom Bayat describes, the residents of Makoko "are driven by the force of necessity—the necessity to survive and live a dignified life" and they "move directly to fulfil their needs by themselves," including the education of their children.[98] More recently, however, the government has attempted to displace the residents of Makoko, citing health hazards and the disfiguration of the metropolis by shanty structures. Makoko may be a site of Bayat's "encroachment of the ordinary," but it also manifests what can be described as an encroachment on the ordinary by the repressive arm of the state and capitalist interests.

What makes *Makoko* a film relevant for an exploration of "city futures" is the value placed by the people who live there on education.[99] The interviews that comprise the bulk of this short documentary focus on the community's efforts to educate its children, first at a school donated by a visiting foreign group and later at the popular floating school that the Nigerian architect Kunle Adeyemi envisioned and designed. As the film shows, the first school built on reclaimed land was donated to the community in response to their demand for an educational facility for their children. Asked by a foreign group what they needed help with, the community chose a school. By their choice, this lagoon community is investing in its future by investing in its children. Noah Shemede, a teacher at the school who later became its headmaster, informs the viewer that the school's name Whanyinna translates as "love" in English. Noah and his fellow teachers work for a pitiable stipend, provided briefly by a local government that refuses to grant them official recognition as part of the school system, and raised mostly from community donations. As the community members express their pleasure at supporting their children's education and as the teachers take turns to articulate the importance of educating the kids, we see an already impoverished people making further sacrifices to guarantee their future. Seen here is the manifestation of the do-it-yourself attitude that Bayat recognizes in informal communities across the Global South. One teacher speaks of how parents are convinced to send their children to school so that they can become doctors and presidents in the future, while another expresses a desire that the children will become great in the future.

Odugbemi's *Makoko* offers a glimpse of the "city of generosity," and the community it depicts evidences a "patchwork of self-organization."[100] In the film, community members make financial contributions to the educational development of their children, and high-school graduates suspend their own aspirations to lay the foundation for a better future for the children of Makoko. Makoko is a bleak space, with few resources and little support; its residents are under constant threat of eviction by a state government that sees it as an eyesore undermining the nearby infrastructural signs and symbols of Lagos's participation in the project of global modernity; furthermore, its floating school, which garnered international awards, and promised the rejuvenation of the community, collapsed just three years after its construction during a heavy storm in 2016. Nevertheless, the centrality of the children and the community's pursuit of educational opportunities for them in Odugbemi's film keep the hopes of this urban space afloat. The film proposes that amidst the gloom, the children's future and that of their community will be secured through education.

Makoko is also the context for Olalekan Jeyifous's Afrofuturist project, *Shanty Megastructures*, which supplies a vision of what the Lagos Lagoon community could be in 2050 (figures 5.11 and 5.12). In their study of urban development, Karen Ching-Yee Seto and Meredith Reba ask: "How can we build and operate cities while preserving the natural environments in which they coexist?"[101] Of all the projects studied in this chapter, Jeyifous's contains the most features of an eco-conscious urban space and is illustrative of "fictions of cities of the future," imbued with the mechanism for reimagining the city.[102] Whereas the skyscrapers that open Odugbemi's film tower over Makoko's shanty structures, in the 2050 vision that Jeyifous maps, the shanties have been remade as towering megastructures outfitted with solar panels, connected with skywalks, and spruced with greenery.

In this setup, Makoko retains the communal life that is evident in Odugbemi's work while undergoing an infrastructural overhaul that makes it more livable. Water is not the only infrastructure connecting people in this community. The skywalks also enable movement and transitions between buildings. While green spaces continue to be lost in Lagos and other cities as they compete against the human need for housing and other modern conveniences, *Shanty Megastructures* makes greenery an aesthetic and functional aspect of its composition. By halting the "historical 'conquest' of nature that has attended urban growth," Jeyifous remakes this urban space as a site of ecological relations between humans, who are connected by both water and skywalks, as well as between humans and nonhumans.[103] We have here the alternative "practice of urban theory" that Ash Amin and Nigel Thrift recommend, one that is "based on the transhuman rather than the human."[104] It is significant that Jeyifous's artistic vision does not relocate Makoko's residents away from their community but remakes it for improved living while enabling them to retain their identity as a riverine and fishing community. If colonial visions of architecture usually foreground the designer's desires and the state's, in Jeyifous work we are faced with a design that aligns with users' cultural habits. Simply put, depicted in Jeyifous's work is an instance of "future-oriented narratives of urban sustainability, which try to balance

5.11 Futuristic image of Makoko, *Shanty Megastructures* © Olalekan Jeyifous, 2015

natural and cultural resource preservation and enhancement, development, and public and economic health."[105] Development, in this context, does not involve the usual displacement of people away from their acculturated space and habits. It also does not imply the eradication of green life to accommodate the niceties of technological progress. The people can still depend on water for fish and there is also room for cultivating plants in this vision of the future.

The turn to solar energy is the most radical move in *Shanty Megastructures*, making the project an example of the "revolutionary infrastructure" that must upend our carbon-based modernity.[106] In *Taming the Sun*, Varun Sivaram imagines a future powered by solar energy that highlights the revolutionary potential of Jeyifous's work.[107] Sivaram desires a time when "Solar PV isn't just powering glamourous urban buildings or massive industrial plants," and looks forward to a time when solar equipment will become "light enough to be supported by flimsy shanty roofs in the slum outskirts of megacities in the developing world," and "even the poorest of the poor [will] easily afford solar power."[108] *Shanty Megastructures* visualizes in an artistic form what Sivaram believes massive investment in solar energy innovation can make

5.12 Nightview of Makoko's futuristic image, *Shanty Megastructures*
© Olalekan Jeyifous, 2015

possible.[109] At the moment, access to solar power remains the preserve of a privileged few in Lagos, but Jeyifous rewrites that script. By thinking and visualizing it, *Shanty Megastructures* brings us closer to its realization.

Not only is Jeyifous democratizing solar energy as an attribute of the commons by making it a fixture of a future Makoko, but the abandonment of dirty fuels also envisions a post-carbon world. As the catalogue of the ravages caused by the oil industry in Nigeria's Delta discussed in chapter 3 demonstrates, the dependence on oil is not sustainable within the context of climate change and in light of other negative consequences for producing communities. Sivaram, like other scientists, recommends solar energy for various reasons, but the pertinent rationales include its abundant availability, its functioning as "the planet's best hope for confronting climate change," and the added advantage of its rapidly declining cost.[110] Sivaram's reminder that the failure to curb carbon emissions from fossil fuels will spell doom for the planet highlights the significance of Jeyifous's vision and its imaginative siting of alternative energy in one of the poorest locales in Africa's largest metropolis. *Shanty Megastructures* democratizes the "right to the city" and fosters "spatial justice."[111]

Ultimately, Jeyifous proposes a vision of the city where poor humans have access to improved living conditions, are surrounded by green life, and share intimacy with the aquatic world. If Makoko and other poor parts of Lagos currently present dark voids at night due to the erratic power supply in the city, Jeyifous's nighttime view of the city is lit by solar power supplied by Lagos's fierce and fiendish sun. In her work on urban environmentalism, Jenny Price articulates characteristics of a sustainable urban sphere: "the quality and equality of life in the places we make our homes depend fundamentally on how sustainably and equitably we use, move, change, manage, and preserve nature inside and outside of cities."[112] Jeyifous's work may be centered on Lagos, far away from the Los Angeles that grounds Price's essay, but its eco-sensibility, its prioritization of human and nonhuman coexistence, makes it an aspirational model of the city of the future.

epilogue
Toward Imperfect Media

African ecomedia, including film and photography, deliver the world to us, allow us to visualize the impacts of ecological degradation, and urge us to reorient our cultural habits to address the problem of climate change. Resource media, including oil, uranium, and bananas, are also useful for linking spaces of production on the continent to consumptive endpoints, often in the Global North. Media forms brought together here share the purpose of connection. They enrich our world and make it possible to see and adopt things from parts of the globe we otherwise would not have access to. Yet they share one more similarity: they are purveyors of ecological degradation that disproportionately imperil Africa's ecologies. Media, as Siegfried Zielinski notes, "have contributed their share to the gigantic rubbish heaps that cover the face of our planet or to the mobile junk that zips through outer space."[1] What he didn't say is that Africa is a primary location of these gigantic rubbish heaps, which contaminate elemental media such as water, earth, and air for the continent's inhabitants. *African Ecomedia* is an accounting sheet of how Africa continues to be the disposable factory and junkyard for these contaminative practices.

Recent Intergovernmental Panel on Climate Change reports spell out the doomsday scenario for the planet if carbon emissions are not dramatically reduced. Unfortunately, the countries responsible for the biggest emissions—in Euro-America and Asia—remain reluctant to significantly reduce their consumption levels and make substantial investments that will enable a radical shift to renewable energy. The major media industries replicate this unsustainable practice. Hollywood, for instance, has been described as one of the largest polluters in Los Angeles, and although the industry is embracing green strategies, including carbon offsetting, its primary paradigm remains excessive consumption through the making of capital-intensive films and the use of high-energy technologies with a considerable ecological footprint.[2]

Not even the acclaimed Afrofuturist film *Black Panther*, with which I opened this book, escapes the problems of overconsumption and the promotion of resource extraction. These problems complicate the film's claim to ethical ecological futures.[3] While the film's racial politics and its alternative imaginary that centers Africa and black people have been celebrated, the continent remains the place of resource extraction that engenders the film's conflict. *Black Panther* has been hailed as "a movie unique for its black star power and its many thoughtful portrayals of strong black women," and continental Africans deeply appreciate its "representation of pan-African culture."[4] Yet I agree with Christopher Lebron: *Black Panther* is not the movie we deserve. Lebron critiques the criminalization of the black American male posed against noble African royalty, a division undermining the possibility of global black solidarity in the film. We can begin to understand my reservations by pausing over Lebron's description of the object of the film's conflict. To him, vibranium is "a substance miraculous in ways that the movie does not bother to explain."[5] Lebron is right that vibranium's source and the retrieval process are not properly historicized. In fact, the miraculous depiction of the mineral recalls the magical sensibilities of oil culture, which Fernando Coronil captures in his work on Venezuela.[6] Such magical thinking elides the exploited labor as well as the incredible ecological devastation and socioeconomic conflict left behind at scenes of extraction.

Resource extraction fuels wars in various parts of Africa already, so it is problematic that the film's imagined future is also implicated in the Africa-in-crisis economy. The film's conflict revolves around control of vibranium. In fact, vibranium is associated with violence, resulting in environmental destruction throughout *Black Panther*. We learn from T'Challa's father's visit to N'Jobu that Ulysses Klaue triggered an explosion that resulted in the death of many as he tried to steal vibranium from Wakanda. The flashback reveals devastation, with the vegetation in the foreground representing the non-human lives caught in the fire that scars the ecosystem. The sequence moves from the actual explosion to foregrounding the vegetation as the fire burns in the background, to a scene totally covered in smoke and fire, with debris suspended in the air. The royal family too is scarred as the king kills his brother for betraying Wakanda, a traumatic act of violence that is repeated when Killmonger fights T'Challa for the throne and for the control of vibranium. As Killmonger's death repeats his father's and as the film shuttles from Wakanda to the British Museum and to South Korea, the struggle to control vibranium leaves behind bodies—of humans and of destroyed environments. The resource curse follows vibranium, the medium connecting the transnational characters and scenes in *Black Panther*.

Moreover, vibranium evokes other dirty extractive processes endangering ecosystems in Africa. Its phonic resemblance with uranium aside, vibranium is also used for weapons development, just as uranium enriches weapons of mass destruction with consequential implications for African communities where it is mined (see the analysis of *Arlit* in chapter 3), and for the larger world threatened with nuclear annihilation (see the discussion of *Pumzi* in chapter 1). In other words, while vibranium may be responsible for improved living conditions in the film, it perpetuates the logic of extractive capital that is responsible for social and ecological crises on the continent. Moreover, it does not prove itself "a reliable long-term source of non-carbon emitting energy supplies."[7]

Ultimately, the film's vision of infinite resources is not in tandem with the realities of a finite planet.[8] Wakanda's vision of infinite resources replicates the Hollywood tendency toward excess and promotes unrestrained consumption. In its refusal to contend with the exhaustion of resources and in its failure to reimagine a radical, revolutionary energy source, Coogler's film points to its limit in the work of articulating a sustainable future. I take the favorable representation of blackness in *Black Panther* seriously, but its treatment of Africa as a site of conflict and resource extraction and its Hollywood pattern of consumption disqualify it as contender for the media future we need. What is needed is less carbon offsetting, where film productions invest in planting trees and other "green" practices, and more of a radical overhauling of an industry that needs to reconsider its commitment to excessive accumulation and consumption.

As *Black Panther* ends, a white delegate interrupts T'Challa's speech at the United Nations to sarcastically ask what a nation of farmers (Wakanda) can offer the world. T'Challa's unspoken answer is vibranium, but there is a more sustainable response. *African Ecomedia* contends that the continent should be seen not only as the site of ecological degradation but also as a generative site for alternative media practices, which I call *imperfect media*. Imperfect media describes the poor media aesthetics that I recommend in place of the media of excess. My use of "poor" is inspired by Ngũgĩ wa Thiong'o's work on poor theory. According to the Kenyan novelist, playwright, and theorist, "poor theory and its practice imply maximizing the possibilities inherent in the minimum."[9] He remarks that "in social life, poor means being extremely creative and experimental in order to survive."[10] Like Ngũgĩ, I do not romanticize poverty, which continues to devastate lives and communities across Africa. However, I am interested in the creative, improvisational, and experimental impulses that scarcity engenders. It is interesting for my purposes that Ngũgĩ uses the improvisational traveling theater in Kenya to illustrate poor theory: "A traveling theater cannot carry a stage and auditorium, it cannot have the luxury of choosing! It does with whatever is handed to it, making an aesthetic under circumstances not chosen by them."[11] Ngũgĩ gestures to media practices that are necessary for readjusting expenditure toward a more sustainable mode.

African media productions contain examples of the infinite resourcefulness that is crucial for making poor or imperfect media in a time of finite resources. Recycling and minimalism are some of the characteristics of this kind of media. In chapter 1, I discussed various artistic projects that emerged from waste. There I argued that recycling is a means of producing beauty in a space of scarcity and scars. I also examined recuperative art as a sustainable practice facilitating the transformation of the environment and modeling an ethic of reuse. The throwaway culture and planned obsolescence built into media devices such as computers and cell phones are also thwarted in Africa, where these gadgets are repaired at low costs to retain use value and postpone their demise. I have been amazed at the quick pace and cheap cost at which devices are fixed across the continent, which helps to reduce turnover and minimizes the need for new equipment. The exploitation of labor and pollution in Agbogbloshie aside, the location is also a site for the exemplary, creative repair and reuse of electronic gadgets. Samuel Shearer records "repairmen" who fix "handsets for resell [sic]" in Kigali, Rwanda. He also observes "men and women" who "hunch over pump sewing machines patching up used clothes, breathing fresh value into garments with their labor."[12] These examples speak of the prevalence of reuse across the continent and the way the practice permeates various facets of life.

The commonality of this recycling practice is not unique to contemporary African art and life. We can trace it as far back as the emergence of African cinema in the 1950s. Explaining his filmic practice, the "father" of

African cinema, Ousmane Sembène, describes what he calls *mégotage*, the making of film from cigarette butts.[13] The filmmaker emphasizes the constrictions placed on his work by limited funding, resulting in an improvisational film practice that maximizes the use of film stock, outdoor lighting conditions, and other resources at the filmmaker's disposal. Recognizing the limited reach of his literary output in a continent with low literacy at the time, Sembène turned to film to reach a wider audience, and was undaunted by infrastructural challenges as he made what became seminal films such as *Xala* and *Mandabi*.[14]

The same commitment to reaching a wider African audience, in spite of limited funding opportunities and an overall economy of scarcity, led to the emergence of the widely known Nollywood industry in Nigeria.[15] Since its humble beginnings in the early 1990s, Nollywood has grown to become a major film industry rivaling Hollywood and Bollywood in terms of output. Despite the dismissal of Nollywood by some critics who differentiate it from the more "serious" African cinema,[16] the industry deserves serious consideration because of its popular appeal not only in Nigeria but across the continent and the diaspora. The reach of Nollywood is tremendous despite its challenges, including funding. Limited resources have inspired Nollywood filmmakers to apply resourcefulness to producing their films, as Carmen McCain's interview with a filmmaker demonstrates:

> The only light I knew that heavy was HMI's. Coming to the location, I already built something with iron, and some plywood, cut in different dimensions so I could use it to create a flicker. Once I slide it up and down, it creates a lightning effect, but it wasn't working properly because it continued to leak light. It wasn't giving me the darkness and the lightning effect that I needed. On set, we constructed a flag, a plywood, that we used to cover the light. We kept taking it off and putting it back, kept taking it off and putting it back. When we tried it, it was amazing. That is how we consistently pulled off the lightning effect.[17]

Chris Eneaji, the filmmaker here, is describing the process of creating a lightning effect in the absence of Hollywood's advanced technologies. Like Sembène before him, he must improvise and make do with available resources to produce imperfect media.

I derive the term *imperfect media*, which names media artifacts that make judicious use of limited resources and thereby lead us in the direction of more sustainable media, in part from Julio García Espinosa's "imperfect cinema" manifesto:

Imperfect cinema is no longer interested in quality or technique. It can be created equally well with a Mitchell or with an 8mm camera, in a studio or in a guerrilla camp in the middle of the jungle. Imperfect cinema is no longer interested in predetermined taste, and much less in "good taste." It is not quality which it seeks in an artist's work. The only thing it is interested in is how an artist responds to the following question: What are you doing in order to overcome the barrier of the "cultured" elite audience which up to now has conditioned the form of your work?[18]

As García Espinosa explains in a follow up essay, this theorization of imperfection is not necessarily about making bad film, but instead warns against well-made film that supports the dominant ideologies.[19] In the Cold War era characterized by anti-colonial struggles, García Espinosa was critiquing aesthetic excellence without consideration of the politics of oppression. As he puts it, "perfect cinema—technically and artistically masterful—is almost always reactionary cinema."[20] Brought into my context, perfect media names the typical Hollywood production; it is beautiful, promotes resource depletion, and leaves a significant ecological footprint. If in García Espinosa's term film must be committed to a radical politics of emancipation, it seems to me that the commitment to ecological sustainability must now be at the forefront of filmmaking and other media practices. Seen this way, Eneaji's improvisation will not be a marker of the low quality often attributed to Nollywood but an instance of what I call imperfect media.[21]

The concept of imperfect media shares characteristics with what Jacob Smith calls "eco-sonic media": they both "manifest a low-impact, sustainable infrastructure; . . . foster an appreciation of, or facilitate communication with, nonhuman nature; . . . provide both a sense of place and a sense of planet; and . . . represent environmental crisis."[22] However, my conceptual coinage is not restricted to sound, as Smith's is; I propose it as a comprehensive term to accommodate various media possibilities, and the conjunctional possibilities of sound, words, and image. The term's inclusiveness is an acknowledgment that all media forms—with their various capabilities—have a role to play in tackling the environmental crisis and climate change. Ecology is relation; as such, media relationality must be the methodological principle of ecomedia studies.

The formal economy that produces imperfect media is not restricted to film; it equally manifests in African music production. Louise Meintjes's work on a South African local recording studio explains the production of "lo-fi sound" from meager resources. Attending to the interactions of improvisation and precarity in music-making, Meintjes reveals how the artists can maintain creative autonomy by resisting the dictates of the mainstream music industry.[23] Tsitsi Ella Jaji identifies the same improvisational practice in the "noise and static, reverberation and echo, feedback and interference" in black diasporic music.[24] The technical "difficulties" in Jaji's archive and the low production quality in Meintjes's are also indicators of imperfect media. It is easy to simply dismiss these encumbrances as instantiations of amateurism or deviations from aesthetic excellence; I argue that these interferences manifest the creativity and resourcefulness called for in a time of finite resources, and demand the cultivation of a disciplinary protocol that listens intently and slowly to decipher the composition amidst the noise, echo, static, and other seeming distractions. Imperfect media requires adjustment or sacrifice from media producers and consumers.

A radical reassessment of taste and pleasure is required given that the well-made, perfect film or song runs the risk of being ecologically reactionary. For if we cannot sustain current consumption levels, it becomes imperative that we reconstitute our pleasure principles to be attuned to the demands of a diminished planet. Writing on the necessity of a low-carbon energy culture, Harold Wilhite believes that humans must proceed on the "understanding that sustainable ways of consuming energy does not imply regression or sacrifice but rather readjustments that also offer opportunities to improve quality of life."[25] Although I think that sacrifice may be necessary to achieve the desired change, Wilhite is correct that we should embrace the possibilities for an improved quality of life that reorienting our energy use offers. In this sense, the Hollywood culture of excess will not be the barometer of filmic or media excellence. In fact, the irony is not lost on me that many Nollywood filmmakers currently orient their practice toward the American film industry and that many critics of these Nigerian films use Hollywood standards to evaluate it.

I argue for the opposite of extant practices by insisting that Eurocentric media practices, with their characteristic high consumption models, have much to learn from their African counterparts premised on recycling and minimalist aesthetics. Making do with little has not made African artifacts less attractive to their audiences. African media are made under difficult circumstances and are not immune from carbon emissions. Yet, in their production and content, the works studied in this book evince the social commitment for which African cultural productions are known.[26] The creativity exhibited in these films and other media artifacts demonstrates ways of living and making art in economies of scarcity, while the suffering they archive should invite a reflection on the exorbitant costs of maintaining the current architectures of our existence.

As someone who comes to this project with a background in literary studies, I cannot conclude it without a brief mention of its significance for the study of literature and other book-based disciplines. This project resonates with our work as scholars of literature and other book-based disciplines since it compels us toward reflection on literature—in the broadest sense of the term—as a material practice. The textual object, the printed book that grounds our work, is an outcome of processes with serious ecological import at the levels of production, distribution, consumption, and disposal. And so is the proliferation of literature in digital spaces. The same media infrastructure I have been discussing supports literature on digital platforms. As we opt for digital reading to save trees, it becomes imperative to underscore the ecological consequences of the use and disposal of computers, cell phones, and other media devices. This book offers a critical template for scrutinizing digital and print books for their complicities in ecological decline, and for apprehending the environmental impact of the act of reading itself. We cannot jettison physical books and digital devices entirely, but an awareness and sensitivity to their ecological entanglements should guide our work as readers and writers.

The notion of insightful reading also has relevance for studying postcolonial and other minoritarian literature. The commonsense approach to studying contemporary postcolonial narratives seeks to determine the extent to which they commodify their characters and non-Western locales. One problem with such a fixation is the denial of the complexity of these literary texts. In the African literary field, for instance, social commitment is primarily measured against the style of Chinua Achebe's generation, and contemporary writers are censured for departing from the glorious era when African writers put their art at the service of political engagement.[27] It may be that political commitment needs a rethinking in the twenty-first century and that a productive engagement of recent narratives with insightful reading can deliver a result different from hasty dismissals for catering to the Western gaze. Instead of condemning such literary works, we can uncover their transgressive potential by examining their surface and probing their depths, while also employing deep contextualization and appropriate theoretical paradigms.

Insightful reading proposes that we pay attention not only to how the text is positioned for the Western gaze but also to how it discloses the complicity of that gaze in the suffering it represents. This eclectic approach re-

Epilogue

jects the singularity of existing reading models in favor of accumulating their most productive insights. Readers should not have to choose between a symptomatic and surface reading or between a deep reading and a descriptive approach. The war over contextualization and decontextualization is irrelevant here and combatants in the theory and anti-theory camps can happily sheath their swords. Insightful reading takes what is relevant from these approaches, without the need for firm allegiance. Its goal remains to move away from the tendency to dismiss the image of suffering as exploitative in order to apprehend its complexities.

This study is, thus, both an ethical invitation to behold the Other and a call for future studies of images of ecology and the ecology of images in Africa. The ethical demand is for what the Akan philosopher Kwasi Wiredu terms the "principle of sympathetic impartiality," by which he means the manifestation of "due concern for the interest of others," or the ability to put oneself "imaginatively" in the position of others.[28] Wiredu marshals the principle of sympathetic impartiality as a universal value binding people everywhere. People in Africa and elsewhere disproportionately affected by the distribution of ecological risks deserve the moral consideration underpinning Wiredu's work, and with them the exploited nonhuman lives and their fragile ecosystems. Viewers confronted with the heap of waste in chapter 1, the close-up shots of toiling and diseased bodies in chapter 2, and of the bodies rolling the barrel of liquid gas to consumers in chapter 3, as well as the animal and human bodies under threat in chapters 4 and 5, are invited to undertake empathetic labor. In other words, a different kind of free labor is called for. Unlike the oppressive forms on display in the preceding chapters, this kind is given willingly, is nonexploitative, and is calibrated around the flourishing of various life forms in Africa and beyond. I have only scratched the surface of African ecomedia and will have succeeded if others accept my invitation to dig further, not for gold but for the golden opportunities that the continent's cultural artifacts present to expand the scope of media studies and to confront the climate crisis.

notes

Introduction

1   Ryan Coogler, dir., *Black Panther* (2018), 134 min.

2   Andrew Ross, "The Ecology of Images," in *Visual Culture: Images and Interpretations*, ed. Norman Bryson, Michael Ann Holly, and Keith Moxey (Hanover, NH: Wesleyan University Press, 1994), 325–46.

3   Brian Larkin, *Signal and Noise: Media, Infrastructure, and Urban Culture in Nigeria* (Durham, NC: Duke University Press, 2008); Lisa Parks and Nicole Starosielski, eds., *Signal Traffic: Critical Studies of Media Infrastructures* (Champaign: University of Illinois Press, 2015); Jussi Parikka, *A Geology of Media* (Minneapolis: University of Minnesota Press, 2015); John Durham Peters, *The Marvelous Clouds: Toward a Philosophy of Elemental Media* (Chicago: University of Chicago Press, 2015).

4   Nikhil Anand, Akhil Gupta, and Hannah Appel, eds., *The Promise of Infrastructure* (Durham, NC: Duke University Press, 2018).

5   Peters, *The Marvelous Clouds*, 2.

6   Phaedra Pezzullo analyzes examples of virtual toxic tours that can be useful for drawing attention to ecological problems and creating empathy for their victims in *Toxic Tourism: Rhetorics of Pollution, Travel, and Environmental Justice* (Tuscaloosa: University of Alabama Press, 2007), 168.

7   Stephanie LeMenager, *Living Oil: Petroleum Culture in the American Century* (New York: Oxford University Press, 2014), 6.

8   Parikka, *A Geology of Media*, 3.

9   Richard Maxwell and Toby Miller, *Greening the Media* (Oxford: Oxford University Press, 2012), 104; Kenneth Harrow, *Trash: African Cinema from Below* (Bloomington: Indiana University Press, 2013), 90.

10   Ross, "The Ecology of Images," 336.

11   Peters, *The Marvelous Clouds*, 3.

12   Mehita Iqani, *Consumption, Media and the Global South: Aspiration Contested* (London: Palgrave Macmillan, 2016), 30.

13   Sean Cubitt, *Finite Media: Environmental Implications of Digital Technologies* (Durham, NC: Duke University Press, 2017), 54.

14   Michael Watts, "Oil Frontiers: The Niger Delta and the Gulf of Mexico," in *Oil Culture*, ed. Ross Barrett and Daniel Worden (Minneapolis: University of Minnesota Press, 2014), 189–210; Paul Ugor, "The Niger Delta Wetland, Illegal Oil Bunkering and Youth Identity Politics in Nigeria," *Postcolonial Text* 8, no. 3 (2013): 1–18.

15   Melody Jue, *Wild Blue Media: Thinking through Seawater* (Durham, NC: Duke University Press, 2020), 4.

16   Sean Cubitt, *EcoMedia* (Amsterdam: Rodopi, 2005); Parikka, A Geology of Media; Hester Blum, *The News at the Ends of the Earth: The Print Culture of Polar Exploration* (Durham, NC: Duke University Press, 2019), 29.

17   Peters, *Marvelous Clouds*, 1, 5, 12.

18   Peters, *Marvelous Clouds*, 33, 36.

19   Larkin, *Signal and Noise*, 6.

20   Paul J. Crutzen and Eugene F. Stoermer, "The Anthropocene," *IGBP Newsletter* 41 (2000): 17–18.

21   Bill McKibben, *The End of Nature* (New York: Random House, 2006), xviii.

22   Joni Adamson, "We Have Never Been Anthropos: From Environmental Justice to Cosmopolitics," in *Environmental Humanities: Voices from the Anthropocene*, ed. Serpil Oppermann and Serenella Iovino (Lanham, MD: Rowman and Littlefield, 2017), 162.

23   Richard Kerridge, "Foreword," in *Environmental Humanities: Voices from the Anthropocene*, ed. Serpil Oppermann and Serenella Iovino (Lanham, MD: Rowman and Littlefield, 2017), xv–xvi.

24   Kathryn Yusoff, *A Billion Black Anthropocenes or None* (Minneapolis: University of Minnesota Press, 2018), xii.

25   Elizabeth DeLoughrey, *Allegories of the Anthropocene* (Durham, NC: Duke University Press, 2019), 2; Steve Mentz, *Break Up the Anthropocene* (Minneapolis: University of Minnesota Press, 2019), 1.

26   Yusoff, *A Billion Black Anthropocenes*, 72.

27   Siegfried Zielinski, *Deep Time of the Media: Toward an Archaeology of Hearing and Seeing by Technical Means*, trans. Gloria Custance (Cambridge, MA: MIT Press, 2006), 2.

28   Melinda Cooper, *Family Values: Between Neoliberalism and the New Social Conservatism* (New York: Zone Books, 2017), 9.

29   Moradewun Adejunmobi, "African Media Studies and Marginality at the Cen-

ter," *Black Camera* 7, no. 2 (2016): 125–39; Noah Tsika, "Introduction: Teaching African Media in the Global Academy," *Black Camera* 7, no. 2 (2016): 94–124.

30   Manthia Diawara, *African Film: New Forms of Aesthetics and Politics* (Munich: Prestel, 2010); Carmela Garritano, *African Video Movies and Global Desires: A Ghanaian History* (Athens: Ohio University Press, 2013); Anjali Prabhu, *Contemporary Cinema of Africa and the Diaspora* (Chichester, UK: Wiley-Blackwell, 2014); Jonathan Haynes, *Nollywood: The Creation of Nigerian Film Genres* (Chicago: University of Chicago Press, 2016); Lindsey B. Green-Simms, *Postcolonial Automobility: Car Culture in West Africa* (Minneapolis: University of Minnesota Press, 2017).

31   Erin Haney, *Photography and Africa* (London: Reaktion Books, 2010); Chika Okeke-Agulu, *Postcolonial Modernism: Art and Decolonization in Twentieth-Century Nigeria* (Durham, NC: Duke University Press, 2015); Joanna Grabski, *Art World City: The Creative Economy of Artists and Urban Life in Dakar* (Bloomington: Indiana University Press, 2017).

32   Larkin, *Signal and Noise*.

33   Cubitt, *EcoMedia*; Stephen Rust, Salma Monani, and Sean Cubitt, eds., *Ecocinema Theory and Practice* (New York: Routledge, 2012); Stephen Rust, Salma Monani, and Sean Cubitt, eds., *Ecomedia: Key Issues* (New York: Routledge, 2016).

34   John Parham, *Green Media and Popular Culture: An Introduction* (London: Palgrave Macmillan, 2016); LeMenager, *Living Oil*; Ursula Heise, *Imagining Extinction: The Cultural Meanings of Endangered Species* (Chicago: University of Chicago Press, 2016).

35   DeLoughrey, *Allegories of the Anthropocene*, 2.

36   Scott Slovic, "Seasick among the Waves of Ecocriticism: An Inquiry into Alternative Historiographic Metaphors," in *Environmental Humanities: Voices from the Anthropocene*, ed. Serpil Oppermann and Serenella Iovino (Lanham, MD: Rowman and Littlefield, 2017), 110.

37   Rob Nixon, *Slow Violence and the Environmentalism of the Poor* (Cambridge, MA: Harvard University Press, 2011), 2.

38   The prominent postcolonial ecocritical texts are Graham Huggan and Helen Tiffin, *Postcolonial Ecocriticism: Literature, Animals, Environment* (London: Routledge, 2010), 135; Elizabeth DeLoughrey and George Handley, eds., *Postcolonial Ecologies: Literatures of the Environment* (New York: Oxford University Press, 2011); Nixon, *Slow Violence*; Byron Caminero-Santangelo, *Different Shades of Green: African Literature, Environmental Justice, and Political Ecology* (Charlottesville: University of Virginia Press, 2014).

39   Jean Comaroff and John L. Comaroff, *Theory from the South: Or, How Euro-America Is Evolving toward Africa* (London: Routledge, 2012).

40   Imre Szeman and Dominic Boyer, eds., *Energy Humanities: An Anthology* (Baltimore: Johns Hopkins University Press, 2017).

41   Dipesh Chakrabarty, "The Climate of History: Four Theses," *Critical Inquiry* 35, no. 2 (2009): 208.

42	Chakrabarty, "The Climate of History"; Timothy Mitchell, *Carbon Democracy: Political Power in the Age of Oil* (London: Verso, 2011).

43	Bob Johnson, *Mineral Rites: An Archaeology of the Fossil Economy* (Baltimore: Johns Hopkins University Press, 2019).

44	Nicholas Mirzoeff, *An Introduction to Visual Culture* (London: Routledge, 1999); David Morgan, *The Sacred Gaze: Religious Visual Culture in Theory and Practice* (Berkeley: University of California Press, 2005).

45	Stuart Hall, "Introduction to Part 3," in *Visual Culture: The Reader*, ed. Jessica Evans and Stuart Hall (London: SAGE, 1999), 309.

46	William J. T. Mitchell, *Picture Theory: Essays on Verbal and Visual Representation* (Chicago: University of Chicago Press, 1994), 5.

47	Marita Sturken and Lisa Cartwright, *Practices of Looking: An Introduction to Visual Culture* (Oxford: Oxford University Press, 2001), 345.

48	Francis B. Nyamnjoh, "De-Westernizing Media Theory to Make Room for African Experience," in *Popular Media, Democracy and Development in Africa*, ed. Herman Wasserman (London: Routledge, 2011), 19.

49	Deborah Poole, *Vision, Race, and Modernity: A Visual Economy of the Andean Image World* (Princeton, NJ: Princeton University Press, 1997), 10.

50	Graham Huggan, *The Postcolonial Exotic: Marketing the Margins* (London: Routledge, 2001).

51	Ariella Azoulay, *The Civil Contract of Photography* (New York: Zone Books, 2008).

52	Azoulay, *The Civil Contract of Photography*, 14.

53	See Stephen Best and Sharon Marcus, "Surface Reading: An Introduction," *Representations* 108, no. 1 (2009): 1–21; Heather Love, "Close Reading and Thin Description," *Public Culture* 25, no. 3 (2013): 401–34.

54	Best and Marcus, "Surface Reading," 9.

55	Robert Stam, *Film Theory: An Introduction* (Malden, MA: Blackwell, 2000), 1.

56	Herman Wasserman, "Introduction: Taking It to the Streets," in *Popular Media, Democracy and Development in Africa*, ed. Herman Wasserman (London: Routledge, 2011), 14. For further discussion of popular culture as site of politics, see George Ogola, *Popular Media in Kenyan History: Fiction and Newspapers as Political Actors* (London: Palgrave Macmillan, 2017).

57	Stephanie Newell and Onookome Okome, "Introduction," in *Popular Culture in Africa: The Episteme of the Everyday*, ed. Stephanie Newell and Onookome Okome (London: Routledge, 2013), 19.

58	David Ingram, "The Aesthetics and Ethics of Eco-Film Criticism," in *Ecocinema Theory and Practice*, ed. Stephen Rust, Salma Monani, and Sean Cubitt (New York: Routledge, 2012), 58.

59	Fabrice Monteiro, *The Prophecy*, 2015, series of photographs, https://fabrice monteiro.viewbook.com/; Idrissou Mora-Kpai, dir., *Arlit, deuxième Paris* (2004), 75 min.; Femi Odugbemi, dir., *Makoko: Futures Afloat* (2016), 30 min.; Wu Jing, *Wolf Warrior 2* (2017), 123 min.

60	John Peffer, "Introduction: The Study of Photographic Portraiture in Africa," in *Portraiture and Photography in Africa*, ed. John Peffer and Elisabeth L. Cameron (Bloomington: Indiana University Press, 2013), 13.

61 Paul S. Landau, "Empires of the Visual: Photography and Colonial Administration in Africa," in *Images and Empires: Visuality in Colonial and Postcolonial Africa*, ed. Paul S. Landau and Deborah D. Kaspin (Berkeley: University of California Press, 2002), 141–71.

62 Peffer, "Introduction," 13.

63 Kobena Mercer, *Travel and See: Black Diasporic Art Practices since the 1980s* (Durham, NC: Duke University Press, 2016), 157.

64 Adéléké Adéèkó, *Arts of Being Yoruba: Divination, Allegory, Tragedy, Proverb, Panegyric* (Bloomington: Indiana University Press, 2017), 153.

65 Haney, *Photography and Africa*; Teju Cole, *Known and Strange Things* (New York: Random House, 2016), 128.

66 Larkin, *Signal and Noise*, 43.

67 Manthia Diawara, *African Cinema: Politics and Culture* (Bloomington: Indiana University Press, 1992); Frank Ukadike, *Black African Cinema* (Berkeley: University of California Press, 1994).

68 Diawara, *African Cinema*, 4.

69 Ukadike, *Black African Cinema*, 91.

70 Safi Faye, dir., *Kaddu Beykat* (1975), 98 min.

71 Kath Weston, *Animate Planet: Making Visceral Sense of Living in a High-Tech Ecologically Damaged World* (Durham, NC: Duke University Press, 2017).

72 Pooja Rangan, *Immediations: The Humanitarian Impulse in Documentary* (Durham, NC: Duke University Press, 2017), 4.

73 Rangan, *Immediations*, 7.

74 Manuel Castells, *The Rise of the Network Society* (Malden, MA: Wiley-Blackwell, 2010), 13.

75 David Harvey, *The Condition of Postmodernity* (Cambridge, MA: Blackwell, 2000).

76 Frederick Cooper, "What Is the Concept of Globalization Good For? An African Historian's Perspective," *African Affairs* 100, no. 399 (2001): 189–213.

77 Saskia Sassen, *Territory, Authority, Rights: From Medieval to Global Assemblages* (Princeton, NJ: Princeton University Press, 2006).

78 Castells, *The Rise of the Network Society*, 13.

79 Simon Gikandi, "Globalization and the Claims of Postcoloniality," *South Atlantic Quarterly* 100, no. 3 (2001): 629.

80 Tanure Ojaide, "Migration, Globalization, and Recent African Literature," *World Literature Today* 82, no. 2 (2008): 43.

81 Patrick Jagoda contends that "network imaginary" encompasses "the complex of material infrastructures and metaphorical figures that inform our experience with and our thinking about the contemporary social world." For Jagoda, as well as for Alexander R. Galloway and Eugene Thacker, networks occupy the opposite end of the spectrum from centralized structures with unidirectional roots and flows. See Patrick Jagoda, *Network Aesthetics* (Chicago: University of Chi-

cago Press, 2016), 3; Alexander R. Galloway and Eugene Thacker, *The Exploit: A Theory of Networks* (Minneapolis: University of Minnesota Press, 2007).

82 Jagoda, *Network Aesthetics*, 4.

83 Serpil Oppermann and Serenella Iovino, "Introduction: The Environmental Humanities and the Challenges of the Anthropocene," in *Environmental Humanities: Voices from the Anthropocene*, ed. Serpil Oppermann and Serenella Iovino (Lanham, MD: Rowman and Littlefield, 2017), 12. On networks and strangers, see Kwame Anthony Appiah, *Cosmopolitanism: Ethics in a World of Strangers* (New York: Norton, 2006).

84 Ursula Heise, *Sense of Place and Sense of Planet: The Environmental Imagination of the Global* (Oxford: Oxford University Press, 2008).

85 Jagoda, *Network Aesthetics*, 3.

86 Caroline Levine, *Forms: Whole, Rhythm, Hierarchy, Network* (Princeton, NJ: Princeton University Press, 2015), 113.

87 Niall Ferguson, *The Square and the Tower: Networks and Power, from the Freemasons to Facebook* (New York: Penguin, 2017).

88 Yochai Benkler, *The Wealth of Networks: How Social Production Transforms Markets and Freedom* (New Haven, CT: Yale University Press, 2006).

89 Benkler, *The Wealth of Networks*, 273–300.

90 Kate Soper, *What Is Nature? Culture, Politics, and the Nonhuman* (Oxford: Blackwell, 1995), 7.

91 Lev Manovich, *The Language of New Media* (Cambridge, MA: MIT Press, 2002); Lisa Gitelman, *Always Already New: Media, History, and the Data of Culture* (Cambridge, MA: MIT Press, 2006).

92 Gitelman, *Always Already New*, 5.

93 Wanuri Kahiu, dir., *Pumzi* (2009), 21 min; Monteiro, *The Prophecy*.

94 Pieter Hugo, *Permanent Error* (Munich: Prestel Verlag, 2011); Franck Bieleu, dir., *The Big Banana* (2011), 85 min.

95 Rahul Mukherjee, *Radiant Infrastructures: Media, Environment, and Cultures of Uncertainty* (Durham, NC: Duke University Press, 2020), 5.

96 Mukherjee, *Radiant Infrastructures*, 7.

97 Michael Watts, ed., *Curse of the Black Gold*, photographs by Ed Kashi (Brooklyn: powerHouse, 2008); and Mora-Kpai, dir., *Arlit*.

98 Shaul Schwarz and Christina Clusiau, dir., *Trophy* (2017), 108 min. On the "problematic of race," see Jemima Pierre, *The Predicament of Blackness: Postcolonial Ghana and the Politics of Race* (Chicago: University of Chicago Press, 2013), 186.

99 Orlando von Einsiedel, dir., *Virunga* (2014), 100 min.

100 Guy Tillim, *Jo'burg* (Johannesburg: STE Publishers, 2005); Wu Jing, dir., *Wolf Warrior 2*; Odugbemi, dir., *Makoko*; Olalekan Jeyifous, *Shanty Megastructures*, 2015, series of digital photographs of 3D architectural drawings, http://vigilism .com/filter/Drawings/Improvised-Shanty-Megastructures.

101 Maxwell and Miller, *Greening the Media*, 7; Allan Stoekl, *Bataille's Peak: Energy, Religion, and Postsustainability* (Minneapolis: University of Minnesota Press, 2007), 193.

102　George Osodi, *De Money*, n.d., series of photographs, https://georgeosodi
　　　.photoshelter.com/portfolio/G0000vg60HC6G7LQ; George Osodi, *Oil Rich
　　　Niger Delta*, 2003–7, series of photographs, https://georgeosodi.photoshelter
　　　.com/portfolio/G0000ns8MS37FfZU.

103　Victor Ehikhamenor, *Wealth of Nations*, 2019, series of photographs, http://
　　　victorehi.com/portfolio-item/wealth-of-nations/; Jeta Amata, dir., *Black Gold*
　　　(2011), 120 min.

104　Timaya, "Dem Mama," on *True Story* (DM Records, 2006), https://www.you
　　　tube.com/watch?v=v8mIahgNLPY.

105　Zina Saro-Wiwa, dir., *Sarogua Mourning* (2011), 12 min. Saro-Wiwa's video instal-
　　　lation was first shown as part of the exhibition *What We Talk About When We
　　　Talk About Love* at the Stevenson Gallery, Cape Town; *Niger Delta: A Documen-
　　　tary* (2015). Zina Saro-Wiwa's broader oeuvre can be accessed at http://www
　　　.zinasarowiwa.com/video/.

106　Andrew Esiebo's work is available at http://www.andrewesiebo.com/new
　　　-page-1; Neill Blomkamp, dir., *District 9* (2009), 112 min; Miguel Llansó, dir.,
　　　Crumbs (2015), 68 min.

107　Bruce Young and Nick Chevallier, dir., *Blood Lions* (2015), 84 min; Kate Brooks,
　　　dir., *The Last Animals* (2017), 92 min; Susan Scott, dir., *Stroop: Journey into the
　　　Rhino Horn War* (2018), 134 min.

CHAPTER ONE. Waste Reconsidered

Epigraphs: Souleymane Bachir Diagne, *African Art as Philosophy: Senghor, Bergson
and the Idea of Negritude*, trans. Chike Jeffers (Calcutta: Seagull Books, 2011), 3;
Matt Hern, *What a City Is For: Remaking the Politics of Displacement* (Cambridge,
MA: MIT Press, 2016), 45.

1　Tejumola Olaniyan, "Africa, Post-Global: A Reaffirmation," *Cambridge Journal of
　　Postcolonial Literary Inquiry* 4, no. 2 (2017): 323–31.

2　Aimé Césaire, *Discourse on Colonialism*, trans. Joan Pinkham (New York:
　　Monthly Review Press, 1972), 42.

3　James Ferguson, *Global Shadows: Africa in the Neoliberal World Order* (Durham,
　　NC: Duke University Press, 2006), 198–99.

4　*Economist*, May 13, 2000.

5　Kodwo Eshun, "Further Considerations on Afrofuturism," *CR: The New Centen-
　　nial Review* 3, no. 2 (2003): 292.

6　Ian P. MacDonald, "'Let Us All Mutate Together': Cracking the Code in
　　Laing's *Big Bishop Roko and the Altar Gangsters*," *Cambridge Journal of Postcolonial
　　Literary Inquiry* 3, no. 3 (2016): 328.

7　Mark Dery, "Black to the Future: Interviews with Samuel R. Delany, Greg
　　Tate, and Tricia Rose," *South Atlantic Quarterly* 92, no. 4 (1993): 736.

8　Frantz Fanon, *The Wretched of the Earth*, trans. Richard Philcox (New York:
　　Grove Press, 1963), 167.

9　Magalí Armillas-Tiseyra, "Afronauts: On Science Fiction and the Crisis of Pos-
　　sibility," *Cambridge Journal of Postcolonial Literary Inquiry* 3, no. 3 (2016): 273–74.

10 Wanuri Kahiu, dir., *Pumzi* (2009), 21 min.; Fabrice Monteiro, *The Prophecy*, series of photographs, 2015, https://fabricemonteiro.viewbook.com/.

11 Friedrich A. Kittler, *Discourse Networks 1800/1900*, trans. Michael Metteer with Chris Cullens (Stanford, CA: Stanford University Press, 1990).

12 Gilles Deleuze and Félix Guattari, *A Thousand Plateaus: Capitalism and Schizophrenia*, trans. Brian Massumi (Minneapolis: University of Minnesota Press, 1987).

13 Okeke-Agulu, *Postcolonial Modernism*, 11.

14 Ian Baucom, "History 4°: Postcolonial Method and Anthropocene Time," *Cambridge Journal of Postcolonial Literary Inquiry* 1, no. 1 (2014): 140.

15 Wanuri Kahiu, dir., *From a Whisper* (2009), 79 min; Wanuri Kahiu, dir., *For Our Land* (2009), 49 min.

16 Wanuri Kahiu, dir., *Rafiki* (2018), 83 min.

17 Srinivas Aravamudan, "The Catachronism of Climate Change," *Diacritics* 41, no. 3 (2013): 10.

18 Jennifer Fay, *Inhospitable World: Cinema in the Time of the Anthropocene* (Oxford: Oxford University Press, 2018), 66, 78.

19 Alondra Nelson, "Introduction: Future Texts," *Social Text* 20 no. 2 (2002): 1.

20 Moradewun Adejunmobi, "Introduction: African Science Fiction," *Cambridge Journal of Postcolonial Literary Inquiry* 3, no. 3 (2016): 265–72; Hugh Charles O'Connell, "'We Are Change': The Novum as Event in Nnedi Okorafor's *Lagoon*," *Cambridge Journal of Postcolonial Literary Inquiry* 3, no. 3 (2016): 291–312; Brady Smith, "SF, Infrastructure, and the Anthropocene: Reading *Moxyland* and *Zoo City*," *Cambridge Journal of Postcolonial Literary Inquiry* 3, no. 3 (2016): 345–59.

21 See, e.g., John Rieder, *Colonialism and the Emergence of Science Fiction* (Middletown, CT: Wesleyan University Press, 2008).

22 Lisa Yaszek, "Rethinking Apocalypse in African SF," *Paradoxa* 25 (2013): 49.

23 Diawara, *African Cinema*; Ukadike, *Black African Cinema*.

24 Olivier Barlet, *Decolonizing the Gaze* (London: Zed, 2000); Roy Armes, *African Filmmaking: North and South of the Sahara* (Bloomington: Indiana University Press, 2006).

25 Alexie Tcheuyap, *Postnationalist African Cinemas* (Manchester, UK: Manchester University Press, 2011).

26 Safi Faye, dir., *Kaddu Beykat* (1975), 98 min.; Assia Djebar, dir., *La nouba des femmes du Mont-Chenoua* (1977), 115 min.

27 Pat Brereton, *Hollywood Utopia: Ecology in Contemporary American Cinema* (Bristol, UK: Intellect Books, 2005), 191.

28 Robin L. Murray and Joseph K. Heumann, *Ecology and Popular Film: Cinema on the Edge* (Albany: State University of New York Press, 2009), 100.

29 MaryEllen Higgins, "The Winds of African Cinema," *African Studies Review* 58, no. 3 (2015): 87.

30 Mark Bould, *Science Fiction* (New York: Routledge, 2012), 187.

31 Jeffrey Jerome Cohen and Julian Yates, "Ark Thinking," in *Ecologies, Agents, Ter-*

rains, ed. Christopher P. Heuer and Rebecca Zorach (Williamstown, MA: Clark Arts Institute, 2018), 254.

32 Matthew Omelsky, "'After the End Times': Postcrisis African Science Fiction," *Cambridge Journal of Postcolonial Literary Inquiry* 1, no. 1 (2014): 38.

33 Cajetan Iheka, *Naturalizing Africa: Ecological Violence, Agency, and Postcolonial Resistance in African Literature* (Cambridge: Cambridge University Press, 2018), 163.

34 Kahiu, dir., *For Our Land*.

35 Higgins, "The Winds of African Cinema," 82.

36 The two quotes are taken respectively from Ernst Bloch, *The Principle of Hope*, vol. 1, trans. Neville Plaice, Stephen Plaice, and Paul Knight (Cambridge, MA: MIT Press, 1986), 8; Frederic Jameson, *Archaeologies of the Future* (London: Verso, 2005), 312.

37 Besi Brillian Muhonja, *Radical Utu: Critical Ideas and Ideals of Wangari Muta Maathai* (Athens: Ohio University Press, 2020), 28. Grounding the communal, noncapitalist orientation of Maathai's work in a Kenyan decolonial framework, Muhonja argues that she was guided by a "radical utu": an indigenous philosophy and praxis, "rooted in ethics and values of equity and honor for the humanity of others and for their environments" (Muhonja, *Radical Utu*, x).

38 Noah Tsika, "Projected Nigerias: *Kajola* and Its Contexts," *Paradoxa* 25 (2013): 94–95; Adejunmobi, "Introduction: African Science Fiction."

39 Darko Suvin, "On the Poetics of the Science Fiction Genre," *College English* 34, no. 3 (1972): 373.

40 Darko Suvin, *Metamorphoses of Science Fiction* (New Haven, CT: Yale University Press, 1979), 64.

41 Omelsky, "After the End Times," 47.

42 Pamela Phatsimo Sunstrum, "Afro-Mythology and African Futurism: The Politics of Imagining and Methodologies for Contemporary Creative Research Practices," *Paradoxa* 25 (2013): 117.

43 Molara Ogundipe-Leslie, *Re-Creating Ourselves: African Women and Critical Transformations* (Trenton, NJ: Africa World Press, 1994), 230.

44 Amina Mama, *Beyond the Masks: Race, Gender and Subjectivity* (London: Routledge, 1995), 66.

45 Juliana Makuchi Nfah-Abbenyi, *Gender in African Women's Writing: Identity, Sexuality, and Difference* (Bloomington: Indiana University Press, 1997), 5, 35.

46 Achille Mbembe, *On the Postcolony* (Berkeley: University of California Press, 2001), 8.

47 Nicholas Mirzoeff, *The Appearance of Black Lives Matter* (Miami: Name Publications, 2017), 28.

48 Cole, *Known and Strange Things*, 177.

49 Jonathan Crary, *Suspensions of Perception: Attention, Spectacle, and Modern Culture* (Cambridge, MA: MIT Press, 1999), 2, 13–14.

50 Fabrice Monteiro, *Marrons*, 2015, series of photographs, https://fabricemonteiro .viewbook.com/marrons; Fabrice Monteiro, *The Way of the Baye Fall*, n.d., series

of photographs, https://fabricemonteiro.viewbook.com/the-way-of-the-baye -fall.

51 Larkin, *Signal and Noise*, 35–43.

52 Okwui Enwezor and Octavio Zaya, "Colonial Imaginary, Tropes of Disruption: History, Culture, and Representation in the Works of African Photographers," in *In/Sight: African Photographers, 1940 to the Present*, ed. Clare Bell, Okwui Enwezor, Olu Oguibe, and Octavio Zaya (New York: Guggenheim Museum, 1996), 17.

53 Christraud M. Geary, "Roots and Routes of African Photographic Practices from Modern to Vernacular Photography in West and Central Africa (1850–1980)," in *A Companion to Modern African Art*, ed. Gitti Salami and Monica Blackmun Visonà (Malden, MA: Wiley, 2013).

54 For a discussion of these preceding representational practices, see Olu Oguibe, "Photography and the Substance of the Image," in *In/Sight: African Photographers, 1940 to the Present*, ed. Clare Bell, Okwui Enwezor, Olu Oguibe, and Octavio Zaya (New York: Guggenheim Museum, 1996), 231–50.

55 Rowland Abiodun, "Ako-graphy: Owo Portraits," in *Portraiture and Photography in Africa*, ed. John Peffer and Elisabeth L. Cameron (Bloomington: Indiana University Press, 2013), 341–62.

56 Clare Bell, "Introduction," in *In/Sight: African Photographers, 1940 to the Present*, ed. Clare Bell, Okwui Enwezor, Olu Oguibe, and Octavio Zaya (New York: Guggenheim Museum, 1996), 11.

57 Candace Keller, "Framed and Hidden Histories: West African Photography from Local to Global Contexts," *African Arts* 47, no. 4 (2014): 36–47.

58 Erin Haney, "Lutterodt Family Studios and the Changing Face of Early Portrait Photographs from the Gold Coast," in *Portraiture and Photography in Africa*, ed. John Peffer and Elisabeth L. Cameron (Bloomington: Indiana University Press, 2013), 67–101; Jurg Schneider, "Portrait Photography: A Visual Currency in the Atlantic Visualscape," in *Portraiture and Photography in Africa*, ed. John Peffer and Elisabeth L. Cameron (Bloomington: Indiana University Press, 2013), 35–66.

59 Roland Barthes, *Camera Lucida: Reflections on Photography*, trans. Richard Howard (New York: Hill and Wang, 1981), 87.

60 Oguibe, "Photography," 247.

61 A robust discussion of the constructedness of photographs and the social production of their meanings can be found in John Tagg, *The Burden of Representation: Essays on Photographies and Histories* (Amherst: University of Massachusetts Press, 1988).

62 For an excellent analysis of Atget's work, see Abigail Solomon-Godeau, *Photography at the Dock: Essays on Photographic History, Institutions, and Practices* (Minneapolis: University of Minnesota Press, 1991), 28–51.

63 Walter Benjamin, *On Photography*, trans. Esther Leslie (London: Reaktion Books, 2015), 93.

64 Susan Sontag, *On Photography* (New York: Picador, 2001), 5.

65   Siegfried Kracauer, *Theory of Film: The Redemption of Physical Reality* (Princeton, NJ: Princeton University Press, 1997), 54.

66   Theo Petroni and Fabrice Monteiro, "Ariadne's Thread—Fabrice Monteiro," *Aere View*, August 1, 2013, https://aereview.tumblr.com/post/57094966440 /ariadnes-thread-fabrice-monteiro?fbclid=IwAR3buXTfI3w0vMU5mHdPsp37I r9bkLd4hA3xsTbD_F4eGIC_2SIFlkiP3Yo.

67   Jacques Derrida, "The Animal That Therefore I Am," trans. David Wills, *Critical Inquiry* 28, no. 2 (2002): 369–418; Matthew Calarco, *Zoographies: The Question of the Animal from Heidegger to Derrida* (New York: Columbia University Press, 2008); Cary Wolfe, *Before the Law: Humans and Other Animals in a Biopolitical Frame* (Chicago: University of Chicago Press, 2013).

68   Evan Mwangi, *The Postcolonial Animal: African Literature and Posthuman Ethics* (Ann Arbor: University of Michigan Press, 2019).

69   Elspeth Probyn, *Eating the Ocean* (Durham, NC: Duke University Press, 2016).

70   Nicole Starosielski, "Beyond Fluidity: A Cultural History of Cinema Under Water," in *Ecocinema Theory and Practice*, ed. Stephen Rust, Salma Monani, and Sean Cubitt (New York: Routledge, 2012), 152.

71   Nicholas Mirzoeff, "The Sea and the Land: Biopower and Visuality after Katrina," *Culture, Theory and Critique* 50, nos. 2/3 (2009): 290.

72   Elizabeth DeLoughrey, "Submarine Futures of the Anthropocene," *Comparative Literature* 69, no. 1 (2017): 42.

73   Tobias Menely and Margaret Ronda, "Red," in *Prismatic Ecology: Ecotheory beyond Green*, ed. Jeffrey Jerome Cohen (Minneapolis: University of Minnesota Press, 2013), 32.

74   Probyn, *Eating the Ocean*, 5.

75   Kerry Bystrom and Isabel Hofmeyr, "Oceanic Routes: (Post-It) Notes on Hydro-Colonialism," *Comparative Literature* 69, no. 1 (2017): 3.

76   Harrow, *Trash*.

77   Naomi Klein, *This Changes Everything: Capitalism vs. the Climate* (New York: Simon and Schuster, 2014), 310–15.

78   Nicole Starosielski, *The Undersea Network* (Durham, NC: Duke University Press, 2015); Nicole Starosielski, "Fixed Flow: Undersea Cables as Media Infrastructure," in *Signal Traffic: Critical Studies of Media Infrastructures*, ed. Lisa Parks and Nicole Starosielski (Champaign: University of Illinois Press, 2015).

79   Ytasha L. Womack, *Afrofuturism: The World of Black Sci-Fi and Fantasy Culture* (Chicago: Lawrence Hill Books, 2013), 103.

80   Cole, *Known and Strange Things*, 128–33.

81   Tom Gunning, "The Long and Short of It: Centuries of Projecting Shadows, from Natural Magic to the Avant-Garde," in *Art of Projection*, ed. Stan Douglas and Christopher Eamon (Ostfildern, Germany: Hatje Cantz, 2009), 23–35.

82   Henry John Drewal, "Local Transformations, Global Inspirations: The Visual Histories and Cultures of Mami Wata Arts in Africa," in *A Companion to Modern African Art*, ed. Gitti Salami and Monica Blackmun Visonà (Malden, MA: John Wiley, 2013), 24–25.

83 Christian Niedan, "The Photographic Confrontations of Fabrice Monteiro: An Interview," *The Mantle*, June 24, 2015, https://www.themantle.com/arts-and-culture/photographic-confrontations-fabrice-monteiro-interview; Zahra Jamshed, "'The Prophecy': Photographer captures terrifying vision of future," *CNN*, November 17, 2015, https://www.cnn.com/style/article/photographer-fabrice-monteiro-the-prophecy/index.html.

84 Georges Didi-Huberman, *Images in Spite of All: Four Photographs from Auschwitz* (Chicago: University of Chicago Press, 2008), 133, emphasis in original.

85 Immanuel Kant, "Critique of Judgment," trans. James C. Meredith, in *Basic Writings of Kant*, ed. Allen W. Wood (New York: Modern Library, 2001), 273–366.

86 Laura Mulvey, "Visual Pleasure and Narrative Cinema," *Screen* 16, no. 3 (1975): 6–18; Kaja Silverman, "The Subject," in *Visual Culture: The Reader*, ed. Jessica Evans and Stuart Hall (London: SAGE, 1999), 340–55.

87 Tom Gunning, "To Scan a Ghost: The Ontology of Mediated Vision," *Grey Room* 26 (2007): 99.

88 Gunning, "To Scan a Ghost," 99.

89 Teju Cole, *Blind Spot* (New York: Random House, 2016), 42.

90 Green-Simms, *Postcolonial Automobility*, 8–11.

91 Jane Bennett, *Vibrant Matter: A Political Ecology of Things* (Durham, NC: Duke University Press, 2010), 28.

92 Harry Garuba, "Explorations in Animist Materialism: Notes on Reading/Writing African Literature, Culture, and Society," *Public Culture* 15, no. 2 (2003): 261–85.

93 Barthes, *Camera Lucida*, 85.

94 Fanon, *The Wretched of the Earth*, 167.

95 Barthes, *Camera Lucida*, 26.

96 Abiola Irele, "A Defence of Negritude," *Transition* 13 (1964): 9–11; Diagne, *African Art as Philosophy*.

97 For an overview of these critiques, see Enwezor and Zaya, "Colonial Imaginary," 27–28. Other critics have defended Senghor's concept of Négritude against the charge of black essentialism and anti-racist racism. Diagne, for instance, argues that "underneath what we may call Senghor's 'strategic essentialism' the discourse of hybridity is always at work, rendering fluid the identities on display" (Diagne, *African Art as Philosophy*, 15).

98 Joanna Grabski, "The École des Arts and Exhibitionary Platforms in Postindependence Senegal," in *A Companion to Modern African Art*, ed. Gitti Salami and Monica Blackmun Visonà (Malden, MA: Wiley, 2013), 278.

99 Léopold Sédar Senghor, "Black Woman," in *West African Verse*, ed. Donatus I. Nwoga (London: Longman, 1967), 96–97.

100 Léopold Sédar Senghor, "The Function and Meaning of the First World Festival of Negro Arts," *African Forum* 1, no. 4 (1966): 8.

101 I am grateful to Celina de Sa for bringing the Set Setal movement to my attention.

102 Mamadou Diouf, "Wall Paintings and the Writing of History: Set/Setal in Dakar," *Gefame: Journal of African Studies* 2, no. 1 (2005).

103 Diouf, "Wall Paintings"; Fiona McLaughlin, "Dakar Wolof and the Configuration of an Urban Identity," *Journal of African Cultural Studies* 14, no. 2 (2001): 153–72.

104 Grabski, *Art World City*, 5.

105 Diouf, "Wall Paintings."

106 Robert Stam, "From Hybridity to the Aesthetics of Garbage," *Social Identities* 3, no. 2 (1997): 275–90.

107 Julia Kristeva, *Powers of Horror: An Essay on Abjection*, trans. Leon S. Roudiez (New York: Columbia University Press, 1982), 1–3.

108 Dominique Laporte, *History of Shit*, trans. Rodolphe el-Khoury (Cambridge, MA: MIT Press, 2000).

109 Stephanie Newell, "Dirty Familiars: Colonial Encounters in African Cities," in *Global Garbage: Urban Imaginaries of Waste, Excess, and Abandonment*, ed. Christoph Lindner and Miriam Meissner (London: Routledge, 2016), 37.

110 Lea Vergine, *When Trash Becomes Art: Trash, Rubbish, Mongo* (Milan: Skira, 2007), 9.

111 Grabski, *Art World City*, 136.

112 Patricia Yaeger, "The Death of Nature and the Apotheosis of Trash; or, Rubbish Ecology," *PMLA* 123, no. 2 (2008): 327.

113 Laporte, *History of Shit*, 31.

114 As Julietta Singh puts it, these "images tell us about ourselves, about what it is we have laid to waste and about what the present-futures of our waste might be." Julietta Singh, "Disposable Objects: Ethecology, Waste, and Maternal Afterlives," *Studies in Gender and Sexuality*, 19, no. 1 (2018): 52.

115 For an overview and analysis of this contestation, see Rosalind Fredericks, *Garbage Citizenship: Vital Infrastructures of Labor in Dakar, Senegal* (Durham, NC: Duke University Press, 2018).

116 Fredericks, *Garbage Citizenship*; Brenda Chalfin, "Public Things, Excremental Politics, and the Infrastructure of Bare Life in Ghana's City of Tema," *American Ethnologist* 41, no. 1 (2014): 100.

117 Karl Schoonover, "Documentaries without Documents: Ecocinema and Toxins," *NECSUS: European Journal of Media Studies* 2, no. 2 (2013): 483–507.

118 Bennett, *Vibrant Matter*, vii.

119 Fredericks, *Garbage Citizenship*, 18.

120 See M. Cabral et al., "Low-Level Environmental Exposure to Lead and Renal Adverse Effects: A Cross-Sectional Study in the Population of Children Bordering the Mbeubeuss Landfill near Dakar, Senegal," *Human and Experimental Toxicology* 31, no. 12 (2012): 1280–91.

121 For further discussion of Ocean Sole, see "About Us," Ocean Sole.co.uk, accessed December 2, 2020, https://www.oceansole.co.uk/pages/about-us.

122 For an introduction to El Anatsui's work, see *El Anatsui: When I Last Wrote to You about Africa*, ed. Lisa Binder (New York: Museum for African Art, 2010).

123 El Anatsui, "Statements," El-Anatsui.com, accessed March 31, 2018, http://el-anatsui.com/exhibitions/upcoming/.

124 Brian Neville and Johanne Villeneuve, "Introduction: In Lieu of Waste," in *Waste-Site Stories: The Recycling of Memory*, ed. Brian Neville and Johanne Villeneuve (Albany: State University of New York Press, 2002), 20.

125 Gillian Whiteley, *Junk: Art and the Politics of Trash* (London: I. B. Taurus, 2011), 9.

126 Emmanuel Acheampong, *Drink, Power, and Cultural Change: A Social History of Alcohol in Ghana, c. 1800 to Recent Times* (Portsmouth, NH: Heinemann, 1996); Chima J. Korieh, "Alcohol and Empire: 'Illicit' Gin Prohibition and Control in Colonial Eastern Nigeria," *African Economic History* 31 (2003): 111–34.

127 Wangechi Mutu, *Suspended Playtime*, 2008/2013, packing blankets, twine, garbage bags, and gold string, dimensions variable. For more details, see the exhibition organized by the Nasher Museum of Art at Duke University, https://nasher.duke.edu/exhibitions/wangechi-mutu-fantastic-journey/.

128 Chelsea Mikael Frazier, "Thinking Red, Wounds, and Fungi in Wangechi Mutu's Eco-Art," *Ecologies, Agents, Terrains*, ed. Christopher P. Heuer and Rebecca Zorach (Williamstown, MA: Clark Arts Institute, 2018), 171, 182.

129 For an overview of Mutu's work, see Cole, *Known and Strange Things*, 104–7.

130 For a sample of Kabiru's work, see Kate Sierzputowski, "Kenyan Artist Digs through Electronic Refuse and Found Metal to Create Dazzling Sculptural Eyewear," *Colossal*, July 17, 2015, http://www.thisiscolossal.com/2015/07/eyewear-from-found-trash-cyrus-kabiru/.

131 Jennifer Wenzel, *Bulletproof: Afterlives of Anticolonial Prophecy in South Africa and Beyond* (Chicago: University of Chicago Press, 2009), 127.

132 Wenzel, *Bulletproof*, 145.

133 Yaeger, "The Death of Nature," 335.

134 For further discussion of Kabiru's artistic process, see Teo Kermeliotis, "Artist's Spectacular Glasses Give Trash a Second Chance," *CNN*, December 11, 2017, https://www.cnn.com/2013/04/23/world/africa/cyrus-kabiru-glasses-kenya/index.html.

135 Anne McClintock, "The Angel of Progress: Pitfalls of the Term 'Post-Colonialism,'" *Social Text* nos. 31/32 (1992): 85.

136 Mbembe, *On the Postcolony*, 17.

CHAPTER TWO. Spatial Networks, Toxic Ecoscapes, and (In)visible Labor

1 Pieter Hugo, *Permanent Error* (Munich: Prestel Verlag, 2011); Chris Carroll, "High Tech Trash: Will Your TV End Up in a Ditch in Ghana?," *National Geographic*, January 2008.

2 Ato Quayson, *Oxford Street, Accra: City Life and the Itineraries of Transnationalism* (Durham, NC: Duke University Press, 2014), 227–28.

3 For a discussion of Ouedraogo's work, see Karen E. Milbourne, "African Photographers and the Look of (Un)Sustainability in the African Landscape," *Africa Today* 61, no. 1 (2014): 114–40.

4   Maja van der Velden and Martin Oteng-Ababio, "Six Myths about Electronic Waste in Agbogbloshie, Ghana," *Africa Is a Country*, March 28, 2019, https://africasacountry.com/2019/03/six-myths-about-electronic-waste-in-agbogbloshie-ghana.

5   Jenna Burrell, "What's the Real Story with Africa's E-Waste," *Berkeley Blog*, September 1, 2016, https://news.berkeley.edu/berkeley_blog/whats-the-real-story-with-africas-e-waste/.

6   Pieter Hugo, *Nollywood* (Munich: Prestel Verlag, 2009); Pieter Hugo, *La cucaracha* (Barcelona: RM, 2019). Hugo's work can also be viewed at https://pieterhugo.com/.

7   For one such critique of the Nollywood project, see Nomusa Makhubu, "Politics of the Strange: Revisiting Pieter Hugo's Nollywood," *African Arts* 46, no. 1 (2013): 50–61.

8   Prices of Hugo's work are available on the website of the international auction house Phillips. See https://www.phillips.com/artist/1268/pieter-hugo.

9   Franck Bieleu, dir., *The Big Banana* (2011), 85 min; Julia Dahr, dir., *Thank You for the Rain* (2017), 87 min.

10 Castells, *The Rise of the Network Society*, 53.

11 Levine, *Forms*, 113.

12 Galloway and Thacker, *The Exploit*, 6.

13 Noémi Tousignant, *Edges of Exposure: Toxicology and the Problem of Capacity in Postcolonial Senegal* (Durham, NC: Duke University Press, 2018), 6.

14 Jagoda, *Network Aesthetics*, 177.

15 Nelson Goodman, *Ways of Worldmaking* (Indianapolis: Hackett, 1978).

16 For an excerpt of the leaked memo, see Paul Gilroy, *Postcolonial Melancholia* (New York: Columbia University Press, 2004), 10.

17 Harrow, *Trash*, 84.

18 Federica Angelucci, "Foreword," in Hugo, *Permanent Error*, 9–10.

19 Quayson, *Oxford Street, Accra*, 228.

20 Schoonover, "Documentaries without Documents."

21 Michael Fried, *Why Photography Matters as Art as Never Before* (New Haven, CT: Yale University Press, 2008), 63.

22 Fried, *Why Photography Matters*, 35.

23 Jill Gatlin, "Toxic Sublimity and the Crisis of Human Perception: Rethinking Aesthetic, Documentary, and Political Appeals in Contemporary Wasteland Photography," *Interdisciplinary Studies in Literature and Environment* 22, no. 4 (2015): 718. For Gatlin, the toxic sublime photograph "disturbs primarily viewers' aesthetic sensibilities, not their identities as consumers, polluters, or political agents."

24 Adam O'Brien, *Film and the Natural Environment: Elements and Atmospheres* (New York: Columbia University Press, 2018), 34.

25 Levi R. Bryant, "Black," in *Prismatic Ecology: Ecotheory beyond Green*, ed. Jeffrey Jerome Cohen (Minneapolis: University of Minnesota Press, 2013), 303.

26 Mitchell, *Picture Theory*, 303.

27 Cubitt, *EcoMedia*, 31.

28 Harrow, *Trash*, 90.

29 Cubitt, *Finite Media*, 120.

30 Maxwell and Miller, *Greening the Media*, 104.

31 Stephen Rust, "Overview: Flow—An Ecocritical Perspective on Broadcast Media," in *Ecomedia: Key Issues*, ed. Stephen Rust, Salma Monani, and Sean Cubitt (New York: Routledge, 2016), 95.

32 Stacy Alaimo, *Bodily Natures: Science, Environment, and the Material Self* (Bloomington: Indiana University Press, 2010), 2, 157–58.

33 See the essays in Serpil Oppermann and Serenella Iovino, eds., *Material Ecocriticism* (Bloomington: Indiana University Press, 2014).

34 In her ethnographic study of internet users in Ghana, Jenna Burrell writes of "young women with plastic bags of chilled water observed, sitting on overturned plastic computer monitor cases reappropriated as impromptu stools. They sold the sealed plastic bags of water they carried to these scraps processors who used them to suffocate the fire." See Jenna Burrell, *Invisible Users: Youth in the Internet Cafes of Urban Ghana* (Cambridge, MA: MIT Press, 2012), 178.

35 Lynn F. Jacobs, "Rubens and the Northern Past: The Michielsen Triptych and the Thresholds of Modernity," *Art Bulletin* 91, no. 3 (2009): 302–24.

36 Van der Velden and Oteng-Ababio, "Six Myths."

37 Allan Sekula, "The Body and the Archive," *October* 39 (1986): 6.

38 T. J. Demos, *Return to the Postcolony: Specters of Colonialism in Contemporary Art* (Berlin: Sternberg, 2013), 126.

39 Tagg, *The Burden of Representation*, 119.

40 Nicholas Mirzoeff, *The Right to Look: A Counterhistory of Visuality* (Durham, NC: Duke University Press, 2011), 297.

41 Haney, *Photography and Africa*.

42 Karen E. Milbourne highlights the defiant attitude of the youth captured in Hugo's work: the "series reveals youth who do not bother to disguise their annoyance at being disturbed, or young men who are not bothered at all" (Milbourne, "African Photographers," 123).

43 Jim Puckett, "A Place Called Away," in Pieter Hugo, *Permanent Error* (Munich: Prestel Verlag, 2011), 97.

44 Trebor Scholz, "Introduction: Why Does Digital Labor Matter Now?," in *Digital Labor: The Internet as Playground and Factory*, ed. Trebor Scholz (New York: Routledge, 2013), 5.

45 Scholz, "Introduction," 1.

46 Maurizio Lazzarato, "Immaterial Labor," in *Radical Thought in Italy: A Potential Politics*, ed. Paolo Virno and Michael Hardt (Minneapolis: University of Minnesota Press, 1996), 133.

47 Andrew Ross, "In Search of the Lost Paycheck," in *Digital Labor: The Internet as Playground and Factory*, ed. Trebor Scholz (New York: Routledge, 2013), 15.

48 Lisa Parks and Nicole Starosielski, "Introduction," in *Signal Traffic: Critical Studies of Media Infrastructures*, ed. Lisa Parks and Nicole Starosielski (Champaign: University of Illinois Press, 2015), 5.

49 See the essays in Trebor Scholz, ed., *Digital Labor: The Internet as Playground and Factory*, ed. (New York: Routledge, 2013).

50 Tiziana Terranova, *Network Culture: Politics for the Information Age* (London: Pluto Press, 2004), 74.

51 Mark Andrejevic, "Estranged Free Labor," in *Digital Labor: The Internet as Playground and Factory*, ed. Trebor Scholz (New York: Routledge, 2013), 162.

52 Karl Marx, *Grundisse*, trans. Martin Nikolaus (New York: Penguin Books, 1973), 221.

53 Marx, *Grundisse*, 248.

54 Karin Fast, Henrik Örnebring, and Michael Karlsson, "Metaphors of Free Labor: A Typology of Unpaid Work in the Media Sector," *Media, Culture* and *Society* 38, no. 7 (2016): 969.

55 Lauren Berlant, "Cruel Optimism," in *The Affect Theory Reader*, ed. Melissa Gregg and Gregory J. Seigworth (Durham, NC: Duke University Press, 2010), 94.

56 Berlant, "Cruel Optimism," 116.

57 Roland Kofi Srigboh, Niladri Basu, Judith Stephens, Emmanuel Asampong, Marie Perkins, Richard L. Neitzel, and Julius Fobil, "Multiple Elemental Exposures amongst Workers at the Agbogbloshie Electronic Waste (E-Waste) Site in Ghana," *Chemosphere* 164 (2016): 72.

58 Nguyen Minh Tue, Akitoshi Goto, Shin Takahashi, Takaaki Itai, Kwadwo Ansong Asante, Tatsuya Kunisue, and Shinsuke Tanabe, "Release of Chlorinated, Brominated and Mixed Halogenated Dioxin-Related Compounds to Soils from Open Burning of E-Waste in Agbogbloshie (Accra, Ghana)," *Journal of Hazardous Materials* 302 (2016): 155.

59 Anne Harris, "Pyromena Fire's Doing," in *Elemental Ecocriticism: Thinking with Earth, Air, Water, and Fire*, ed. Jeffrey Jerome Cohen and Lowell Duckert (Minneapolis: University of Minnesota Press, 2015), 44.

60 Stephen J. Pyne, *World Fire: The Culture of Fire on Earth* (Seattle: University of Washington Press, 1997), 4.

61 Peters, *The Marvelous Clouds*, 115–17.

62 Quayson, *Oxford Street, Accra*, 227. *Fadama* is the Hausa word for "swampy."

63 Asare Adjei, "Life in Sodom and Gomorrah: The World's Largest Digital Dump," *Guardian*, April 29, 2014, https://www.theguardian.com/global-development-professionals-network/2014/apr/29/agbogbloshie-accra-ghana-largest-ewaste-dump.

64 I am grateful to an anonymous reviewer for useful contextual information on Agbogbloshie and the surrounding area.

65 Quayson, *Oxford Street, Accra*, 228.

66 Srigboh et al., "Multiple Elemental Exposures," 70.

67 Marx, *Grundisse*, 495.

68 Cedric Robinson, *Black Marxism: The Making of the Black Radical Tradition*, 2nd ed. (Chapel Hill: University of North Carolina Press, 2000), xxix.

69 Karl Marx, *Capital: A Critique of Political Economy*, vol. 1, trans. Samuel Moore and Edward Aveling (Moscow: Progress Publishers, 1887), 545.

70 Marx, *Grundisse*, 533.

71 Armin Beverungen, Steffen Böhm, and Chris Land, "Free Labour, Social Media, Management: Challenging Marxist Organization Studies," *Organization Studies* 36, no. 4 (2015): 475.

72 Marx, *Grundisse*, 527.

73 Marx, *Grundisse*, 527.

74 Achille Mbembe, "Aesthetics of Superfluity," *Public Culture* 16, no. 3 (2004): 374, 381.

75 Frank Pasquale, *Black Box Society: The Secret Algorithms that Control Money and Information* (Cambridge, MA: Harvard University Press, 2015).

76 John Cheney-Lippold, *We Are Data: Algorithms and the Making of Our Digital Selves* (New York: New York University Press, 2017), 262.

77 Antoinette Rouvroy, "The End(s) of Critique: Data Behaviourism versus Due Process," in *Privacy, Due Process, and the Computational Turn: The Philosophy of Law Meets the Philosophy of Technology*, ed. Mireille Hildebrandt and Katja de Vries (London: Routledge, 2013), 157.

78 Andrew Ross, *Nice Work If You Can Get It: Life and Labor in Precarious Times* (New York: New York University Press, 2009), 4.

79 Fast, Örnebring, and Karlsson, "Metaphors of Free Labor," 973.

80 Benkler, *The Wealth of Networks*, 20.

81 John Berger, *Ways of Seeing* (London: BBC and Penguin Books, 1972), 10.

82 Sontag, *On Photography*, 4.

83 Susan Sontag, *Regarding the Pain of Others* (New York: Picador, 2003), 121.

84 Jay David Bolter and Richard Grusin, *Remediation: Understanding New Media* (Cambridge, MA: MIT Press, 1999), 11.

85 Puckett, "A Place Called Away," 97.

86 Rosalind Krauss, "Notes on the Index: Seventies Art in America," *October* 3 (1977): 77.

87 Burrell, *Invisible Users*, 161.

88 Bill Nichols, *Representing Reality: Issues and Concepts in Documentary* (Bloomington: Indiana University Press, 1991), ix.

89 Pietari Kääpä and Tommy Gustafsson, "Introduction: Transnational Ecocinema in an Age of Ecological Transformation," in *Transnational Ecocinema: Film Culture in an Era of Ecological Transformation*, ed. Pietari Kääpä and Tommy Gustafsson (Bristol: Intellect, 2013), 19.

90 Rachel Gabara, "War by Documentary," *Romance Notes* 55, no. 3 (2015): 409.

91 Peter Hitchcock, "Risking the Griot's Eye: Decolonisation and Contemporary African Cinema," *Social Identities* 6, no. 3 (2000): 263.

92 Franck Bieleu, dir., *What Hope for the African Youth* (2008), 71 min.; Franck Bieleu, dir., *Herakles Debacle* (2012), 21 min.

93 John Grierson, "First Principles of Documentary," in *The Documentary Film Reader: History, Theory, Criticism*, ed. Jonathan Kahana (Oxford: Oxford University Press, 2016), 217–25; Bill Nichols, "The Voice of Documentary," in *The Documentary Film Reader: History, Theory, Criticism*, ed. Jonathan Kahana (Oxford: Oxford University Press, 2016), 639–51; and Michael Renov, "Toward

a Poetics of Documentary," in *The Documentary Film Reader: History, Theory, Criticism*, ed. Jonathan Kahana (Oxford: Oxford University Press, 2016), 742–57.

94 Grierson, "First Principles of Documentary," 219.

95 Gabara, "War by Documentary"; and Yifen Beus, "Authorship and Criticism in Self-Reflexive African Cinema," *Journal of African Cultural Studies* 23, no. 2 (2011): 133–52.

96 E. Ann Kaplan, "Theories and Strategies of the Feminist Documentary," in *The Documentary Film Reader: History, Theory, Criticism*, ed. Jonathan Kahana (Oxford: Oxford University Press, 2016), 688.

97 Laura U. Marks, *The Skin of the Film: Intercultural Cinema, Embodiment, and the Senses* (Durham, NC: Duke University Press, 2000), 173.

98 Pat Brereton, *Environmental Ethics and Film* (Oxford: Routledge, 2016), 15.

99 The phrase *the citizen food consumer* comes from Belinda Smaill, *Regarding Life: Animals and the Documentary Moving Image* (Albany: State University of New York Press, 2016), 50. On the link between food producer and consumer, see Emma Roe, "Things Becoming Food and the Embodied, Material Practices of an Organic Food Consumer," *Sociologia Ruralis* 46, no. 2 (2006): 105.

100 Roe, "Things Becoming Food," 109.

101 David Palumbo-Liu, *The Deliverance of Others: Reading Literature in a Global Age* (Durham, NC: Duke University Press, 2012).

102 Arjun Appadurai, *Modernity at Large: Cultural Dimensions of Globalization* (Minneapolis: University of Minnesota Press, 1996), 165.

103 Curtis Marez, *Farm Worker Futurism: Speculative Technologies of Resistance* (Minneapolis: University of Minnesota Press, 2016), ix.

104 Cooper, "What Is the Concept of Globalization Good For?," 189.

105 Ash Amin and Nigel Thrift, *Arts of the Political: New Openings for the Left* (Durham, NC: Duke University Press, 2013), 74.

106 Michael Renov, *The Subject of Documentary* (Minneapolis: University of Minnesota Press, 2004), 167.

107 Nichols, *Representing Reality*, xi.

108 Doreen Massey, *Space, Place, and Gender* (Minneapolis: University of Minnesota Press, 1994), 179–86.

109 Julia Lesage, "The Political Aesthetics of the Feminist Documentary Film," in *The Documentary Film Reader: History, Theory, Criticism*, ed. Jonathan Kahana (Oxford: Oxford University Press, 2016), 676.

110 Abena P. A. Busia, "Silencing Sycorax: On African Colonial Discourse and the Unvoiced Female," *Cultural Critique* 14 (1989/1990): 86.

111 Busia, "Silencing Sycorax," 86.

112 Mark Budolfson, "Food, the Environment, and Global Justice," in *The Oxford Handbook of Food Ethics*, ed. Anne Barnhill, Mark Budolfson, and Tyler Doggett (Oxford: Oxford University Press, 2018), 67.

113 Clark Wolf, "Sustainable Agriculture, Environmental Philosophy, and the Ethics of Food," in *The Oxford Handbook of Food Ethics*, ed. Anne Barnhill, Mark Budolfson, and Tyler Doggett (Oxford: Oxford University Press, 2018), 50.

114 Lawrence Buell, "Toxic Discourse," *Critical Inquiry* 24, no. 3 (1998): 649.

115 Rangan, *Immediations*, 194.

116 Klein, *This Changes Everything*, 12.

117 Castells, *The Rise of the Network Society*, 497.

118 Z. S. Strother, *Humor and Violence: Seeing Europeans in Central African Art* (Bloomington: Indiana University Press, 2016), xi–xii.

119 Mitchell, *Carbon Democracy*, 237.

CHAPTER THREE. Ecologies of Oil and Uranium

1 Michael Rothberg, "Preface: Beyond Tancred and Clorinda—Trauma Studies for Implicated Subjects," in *The Future of Trauma Theory: Contemporary Literary and Cultural Criticism*, ed. Gert Buelens, Sam Durrant, and Robert Eaglestone (New York: Routledge, 2014), xvii.

2 Michael Watts, ed., *Curse of the Black Gold*, photographs by Ed Kashi (Brooklyn, NY: powerHouse, 2008); Idrissou Mora-Kpai, dir., *Arlit: deuxième Paris* (2004), 75 min.

3 Bob Johnson uses "mineral rites" to describe the "various rituals—from the morning shower to online shopping, from freeway commuting to breathing near a petroleum refinery—by which we naturalize these energies, taking them into our bodies in ways we recognize and ways we don't." Johnson, *Mineral Rites*, 2.

4 Extraction zones refer to "regions of high biodiversity" reduced to geographies of "capitalist resource conversion" and exploitation. See Macarena Gómez-Barris, *The Extractive Zone: Social Ecologies and Decolonial Perspectives* (Durham, NC: Duke University Press, 2017), xvi.

5 Fernando Coronil, *The Magical State: Nature, Money, and Modernity in Venezuela* (Chicago: University of Chicago Press, 1997), 4.

6 Nnimmo Bassey, "Oil Fever," in *Curse of the Black Gold*, ed. Michael Watts (Brooklyn, NY: powerHouse, 2008), 91.

7 Watts, "Oil Frontiers," 190.

8 Ike Okonta and Oronto Douglas, *Where Vultures Feast: Shell, Human Rights and Oil* (London: Verso, 2003), 6.

9 The phrase *theft of the body* comes from Hortense Spillers, "Mama's Baby, Papa's Maybe: An American Grammar Book," *Diacritics* 17, no. 2 (1987): 67. On slavery and familial alienation, see Orlando Patterson, *Slavery and Social Death: A Comparative Study* (Cambridge, MA: Harvard University Press, 1982), 5.

10 See Spillers, "Mama's Baby"; Saidiya V. Hartman, *Scenes of Subjection: Terror, Slavery, and Self-Making in Nineteenth-Century America* (Oxford: Oxford University Press, 1997).

11 Cathy Caruth, *Unclaimed Experience: Trauma, Narrative, History* (Baltimore: Johns Hopkins University Press, 1996), 11.

12 Dori Laub, "Bearing Witness or the Vicissitudes of Listening," in Shoshana Felman and Dori Laub, *Testimony: Crises of Witnessing in Literature, Psychoanalysis, and History* (New York: Routledge, 1992), 57–74.

13   Susannah Radstone, "Trauma Theory: Contexts, Politics, Ethics," *Paragraph* 30, no. 1 (2007): 9–29.

14   Stef Craps, *Postcolonial Witnessing: Trauma Out of Bounds* (New York: Palgrave Macmillan, 2013), 4.

15   Craps, *Postcolonial Witnessing*, 45.

16   Craps, *Postcolonial Witnessing*, 19.

17   Jay Rajiva, *Postcolonial Parabola: Literature, Tactility, and the Ethics of Representing Trauma* (New York: Bloomsbury Academic, 2017), 4.

18   Jeffrey C. Alexander, *Trauma: A Social Theory* (Cambridge: Polity Press, 2012), 1.

19   Mieke Bal, "Introduction," in *Acts of Memory: Cultural Recall in the Present*, ed. Mieke Bal, Jonathan V. Crewe, and Leo Spitzer (Hanover, NH: University Press of New England, 1999), ix.

20   Mitchell, *Picture Theory*, 289.

21   Mitchell, *Picture Theory*, 321.

22   See G. Ugo Nwokeji, "Slave Ships to Oil Tankers," in *Curse of the Black Gold*, ed. Michael Watts (Brooklyn, NY: powerHouse, 2008), 62–65; Ukoha Ukiwo, "Empire of Commodities," in *Curse of the Black Gold*, ed. Michael Watts (Brooklyn, NY: powerHouse, 2008), 70–73; and Michael Watts, "Sweet and Sour," in *Curse of the Black Gold*, ed. Michael Watts (Brooklyn, NY: powerHouse, 2008), 36–47.

23   Nwokeji, "Slave Ships," 65.

24   Omolade Adunbi, *Oil Wealth and Insurgency in Nigeria* (Bloomington: Indiana University Press, 2015), 168–69.

25   Ruth Leys, *Trauma: A Genealogy* (Chicago: University of Chicago Press, 2000), 8.

26   Watts, "Sweet and Sour," 36.

27   Ukiwo, "Empire of Commodities," 70.

28   Ukiwo, "Empire of Commodities," 73.

29   Andrew Apter, *The Pan-African Nation: Oil and the Spectacle of Culture in Nigeria* (Chicago: University of Chicago Press, 2005), 8.

30   Sara Ahmed, "Happy Objects," in *The Affect Theory Reader*, ed. Melissa Gregg and Gregory J. Seigworth (Durham, NC: Duke University Press, 2010), 29–51.

31   Apter, *The Pan-African Nation*, 8.

32   Adunbi, *Oil Wealth*, 20.

33   Ato Quayson, "Anatomizing a Postcolonial Tragedy: Ken Saro-Wiwa and the Ogonis," *Performance Research* 1, no. 2 (1996): 83–92.

34   Adunbi, *Oil Wealth*, 8.

35   Cyril Obi and Siri Aas Rustad, eds., *Oil and Insurgency in the Niger Delta: Managing the Complex Politics of Petro-Violence* (London: Zed, 2011).

36   Quayson, "Anatomizing a Postcolonial Tragedy," 92.

37   Quayson, "Anatomizing a Postcolonial Tragedy," 90–91.

38   Caminero-Santangelo, *Different Shades of Green*, 134.

39   Cyril Obi and Siri Aas Rustad, "Petro-Violence in the Niger Delta: The Complex Politics of an Insurgency," in *Oil and Insurgency in the Niger Delta: Managing*

the Complex Politics of Petro-Violence, ed. Cyril Obi and Siri Aas Rustad (London: Zed, 2011), 2.

40 Craps, *Postcolonial Witnessing*, 63.

41 Philip Aghoghovwia, "Nigeria," in *Fueling Culture: 101 Words for Energy and Environment*, ed. Imre Szeman, Jennifer Wenzel, and Patricia Yaeger (New York: Fordham University Press, 2017), 238–39.

42 Mitchell, *Carbon Democracy*, 244.

43 Eileen Julien, "The Extroverted African Novel," in *The Novel: History, Geography, and Culture*, ed. Franco Moretti (Princeton, NJ: Princeton University Press, 2006), 681–83.

44 United Nations Development Programme (UNDP), "Niger Delta Human Development Report," 2006, http://hdr.undp.org/sites/default/files/nigeria _hdr_report.pdf.

45 UNDP, "Niger Delta Human Development Report," quoted in Watts, *Curse of the Black Gold*, 3.

46 Jennifer Wenzel, "Petro-Magic Realism Revisited: Unimagining and Reimagining the Niger Delta," in *Oil Culture*, ed. Ross Barrett and Daniel Worden (Minneapolis: University of Minnesota Press, 2014), 219.

47 Sekula, "The Body and the Archive," 64.

48 Sontag, *Regarding the Pain of Others*, 45.

49 Watts, *Curse of the Black Gold*, 20.

50 Ross Barrett and Daniel Worden, "Introduction," in *Oil Culture*, ed. Ross Barrett and Daniel Worden (Minneapolis: University of Minnesota Press, 2014), xxiv.

51 Watts, *Curse of the Black Gold*, 69.

52 Vincent Woodard uses the term *the delectable negro* to name the literal and metaphoric consumption of enslaved people in the United States through acts of cannibalism and homoeroticism. Vincent Woodard, *The Delectable Negro: Human Consumption and Homoeroticism within US Slave Culture* (New York: New York University Press, 2014).

53 Nicholas Mirzoeff, *Bodyscape: Art, Modernity and the Ideal Figure* (London: Routledge, 1995), 3.

54 Kobena Mercer with Isaac Julien, "Black Masculinity and the Sexual Politics of Race: True Confessions," in Kobena Mercer, *Welcome to the Jungle: New Positions in Black Cultural Studies* (New York: Routledge, 1994), 138.

55 Spillers, "Mama's Baby," 67.

56 Berger, *Ways of Seeing*, 84–87.

57 Krista A. Thompson, *Shine: The Visual Economy of Light in African Diasporic Aesthetic Practice* (Durham, NC: Duke University Press, 2015), 232–33.

58 Barthes, *Camera Lucida*; James Elkins, *What Photography Is* (New York: Routledge, 2011), xii.

59 Stefan Helmreich, "Nature/Culture/Seawater: Theory Machines, Anthropology, Oceanization," in *Environmental Humanities: Voices from the Anthropocene*, ed. Serpil Oppermann and Serenella Iovino (Lanham, MD: Rowman and Littlefield, 2017), 217–36.

60   Jacques Derrida and Giovanna Borradori, "Autoimmunity: Real and Symbolic Suicides—A Dialogue with Jacques Derrida," in *Philosophy in a Time of Terror: Dialogues with Jurgen Habermas and Jacques Derrida*, ed. Giovanna Borradori (Chicago: University of Chicago Press, 2003), 96.

61   Brian Massumi, "The Future Birth of the Affective Fact: The Political Ontology of Threat," in *The Affect Theory Reader*, ed. Melissa Gregg and Gregory J. Seigworth (Durham, NC: Duke University Press, 2010), 53.

62   E. Ann Kaplan, *Climate Trauma: Foreseeing the Future in Dystopian Film and Fiction* (New Brunswick, NJ: Rutgers University Press, 2016), xix.

63   Kaplan, *Climate Trauma*, 28.

64   Tim Marshall, *Prisoners of Geography: Ten Maps that Explain Everything about the World* (New York: Scribner, 2015), 1. For Marshall, our geographical location and its characteristics can be advantageous or constitute a hindrance. In the case of Africa, which he lumps under one chapter, the disadvantages outweigh the advantage. In his words, "the land on which we live has always shaped us. It has shaped the wars, the power, politics, and social development of the peoples that now inhabit nearly every part of the earth."

65   Tina Campt, *Listening to Images* (Durham, NC: Duke University Press, 2017), 6.

66   Campt, *Listening to Images*, 9.

67   Campt, *Listening to Images*, 6.

68   Fred Moten, *In the Break: The Aesthetics of the Black Radical Tradition* (Minneapolis: University of Minnesota Press, 2003), 197.

69   For Moten, "moaning" and "mourning" are constitutive of the sound or phono-character of photographs, especially of black subjects. See Moten, *In the Break*, 196–98.

70   Watts, *Curse of the Black Gold*, 113.

71   Shawn Michelle Smith, *At the Edge of Sight: Photography and the Unseen* (Durham, NC: Duke University Press, 2013).

72   Ogaga Okuyade, "Negotiating Identity in a Vanishing Geography: Home, Environment and Displacement in Helon Habila's *Oil on Water*," in *Natures of Africa: Ecocriticism and Animal Studies in Contemporary Cultural Forms*, ed. F. Fiona Moolla (Johannesburg: Wits University Press, 2016), 219.

73   Emmanuel Levinas, *Ethics and Infinity: Conversations with Philippe Nemo*, trans. Richard A. Cohen (Pittsburgh: Duquesne University Press, 1985), 85.

74   Derrida and Borradori, "Autoimmunity," 98.

75   Bennett, *Vibrant Matter*.

76   Juan Pablo Pérez Alfonzo, *Oil: The Juice of the Earth* (Caracas: Editorial Arte, 1961), 83.

77   Imre Szeman, "Crude Aesthetics: The Politics of Oil Documentaries," in *Oil Culture*, ed. Ross Barrett and Daniel Worden (Minneapolis: University of Minnesota Press, 2014), 352.

78   Uche Peter Umez, "Dark Through the Delta," in *Curse of the Black Gold*, ed. Michael Watts (Brooklyn, NY: powerHouse, 2008), 69.

79   Isidore Diala, "Nigeria and the Poetry of Travails: The Niger Delta in the Poetry of Uche Umez," *Matatu* 33 (2006): 320.

80 Diala, "Nigeria and the Poetry of Travails," 321.

81 Jean-François Bayart, *The State in Africa: The Politics of the Belly* (Cambridge: Polity Press, 2009).

82 Mbembe, *On the Postcolony*, 102–41.

83 Cajetan Iheka, *Naturalizing Africa: Ecological Violence, Agency, and Postcolonial Resistance in African Literature* (Cambridge: Cambridge University Press, 2018), 21–56.

84 Timothy Morton, *Hyperobjects: Philosophy and Ecology after the End of the World* (Minneapolis: University of Minnesota Press, 2013).

85 Dominick LaCapra, *Writing History, Writing Trauma* (Baltimore: Johns Hopkins University Press, 2001), 98.

86 Solomon-Godeau, *Photography at the Dock*; Martha Rosler, "In, Around, and Afterthoughts (On Documentary Photography)," in *3 Works* (Halifax: Press of the Nova Scotia College of Art and Design, 1981), 61–93.

87 Michael Warner, *Publics and Counterpublics* (New York: Zone, 2002), 181.

88 Warner, *Publics and Counterpublics*, 184.

89 Pamela Allara, "Zwelethu Mthethwa's 'Postdocumentary' Portraiture: Views from South Africa and Abroad," in *A Companion to Modern African Art*, ed. Gitti Salami and Monica Blackmun Visoná (Chichester, UK: Wiley-Blackwell, 2013), 481.

90 Ogundipe-Leslie, *Re-Creating Ourselves*, 13.

91 Aili Mari Tripp, "Women and Politics in Africa," in *Holding the World Together: African Women in Changing Perspective*, ed. Nwando Achebe and Claire Robertson (Madison: University of Wisconsin Press, 2019), 145–65; Oyeronke Oyewumi, *The Invention of Women: Making an African Sense of Western Gender Discourses* (Minneapolis: University of Minnesota Press, 1997).

92 Lizelle Bisschoff and Stefanie Van de Peer, "Representing the Unrepresented," in *Art and Trauma in Africa: Representations of Reconciliation in Music, Visual Arts, Literature and Film*, ed. Lizelle Bisschoff and Stefanie Van de Peer (London: I. B. Taurus, 2013), 8.

93 Diana Taylor, *The Archive and the Repertoire: Performing Cultural Memory in the Americas* (Durham, NC: Duke University Press, 2003).

94 Ananya Jahanara Kabir, "Affect, Body, Place: Trauma Theory in the World," in *The Future of Trauma Theory: Contemporary Literary and Cultural Criticism*, ed. Gert Buelens, Sam Durrant, and Robert Eaglestone (New York: Routledge, 2014), 70.

95 Liedeke Plate and Anneke Smelik, "Performing Memory in Art and Popular Culture: An Introduction," in *Performing Memory in Art and Popular Culture*, ed. Liedeke Plate and Anneke Smelik (New York: Routledge, 2013), 1–22.

96 LeMenager, *Living Oil*, 141.

97 Fanon, *The Wretched of the Earth*, 20.

98 Ken Wiwa, *In the Shadow of a Saint* (London: Black Swan, 2001); Noo Saro-Wiwa, *Looking for Transwonderland: Travels in Nigeria* (London: Granta, 2013).

99 Zina Saro-Wiwa, dir., *Sarogua Mourning* (2011), 12 min. Saro-Wiwa's video instal-

lation was first shown as part of the exhibition *What We Talk About When We Talk About Love* at the Stevenson Gallery, Cape Town.

100 Saro-Wiwa, dir., *Sarogua Mourning*.

101 Rothberg, "Preface," xv.

102 Ed Kashi, "Shadows and Light in the Niger Delta," in *Curse of the Black Gold*, ed. Michael Watts (Brooklyn: powerHouse, 2008), 25–27.

103 Warner, *Publics and Counterpublics*, 177.

104 Watts, "Sweet and Sour," 47.

105 Sontag, *Regarding the Pain of Others*, 71.

106 Valentin Mudimbe, *The Invention of Africa: Gnosis, Philosophy, and the Order of Knowledge* (Bloomington: Indiana University Press, 1988).

107 Watts, *Curse of the Black Gold*, 223.

108 Idrissou Mora-Kpai, dir., *Indochina: Traces of a Mother* (2011), 71 min.

109 Idrissou Mora-Kpai, dir., *America Street* (2019), 74 min.

110 Gabrielle Hecht, *Being Nuclear: Africans and the Global Uranium Trade* (Cambridge, MA: MIT Press, 2012), 109–17.

111 Pearl T. Robinson, "Niger: Anatomy of a Neotraditional Corporatist State," *Comparative Politics* 24, no. 1 (1991): 7–11.

112 Lucas Destrijcker and Mahadi Diouara, "A Forgotten Community: The Little Town in Niger Keeping the Lights On in France," *African Arguments*, July 18, 2017, http://africanarguments.org/2017/07/18/a-forgotten-community-the -little-town-in-niger-keeping-the-lights-on-in-france-uranium-arlit-areva/.

113 Jeremy Keenan, "Uranium Goes Critical in Niger: Tuareg Rebellions Threaten Sahelian Conflagration," *Review of African Political Economy* 35, no. 117 (2008): 454.

114 Hecht, *Being Nuclear*, 322–23.

115 Greenpeace, "Left in the Dust: Areva's Radioactive Legacy in the Desert Towns of Niger," 2010, https://www.greenpeace.org/archive-international /Global/international/publications/nuclear/2010/AREVA_Niger_report.pdf, 21–22.

116 Greenpeace, "Left in the Dust," 24–27.

117 Greenpeace, "Left in the Dust," 51.

118 Hecht, *Being Nuclear*, 261.

119 Hecht, *Being Nuclear*, 323.

120 Anil Narine, "Introduction: Eco-Trauma Cinema," in *Eco-Trauma Cinema* (New York: Routledge, 2015), 1–24.

121 Janet Walker, "Trauma Cinema: False Memories and True Experience," *Screen* 42, no. 2 (2001): 214.

122 Setting is tied to film narrative, what Lefebvre calls "eventhood or narrativity," while landscape transcends the story and invites apprehension on its own terms. See Martin Lefebvre, "Between Setting and Landscape in the Cinema," in *Landscape and Film*, ed. Martin Lefebvre (New York: Routledge, 2006), 26.

123 See David Ingram, *Green Screen: Environmentalism and Hollywood Cinema* (Exeter, UK: University of Exeter Press, 2000), 31–33.

124 Jane Tompkins, *West of Everything: The Inner Life of Westerns* (Oxford: Oxford University Press, 1992), 76.

125 Charles Musser, "Trauma, Truth and the Environmental Documentary," in *Eco-Trauma Cinema*, ed. Anil Narine (New York: Routledge, 2015), 46–71.

126 Leo Spitzer, "Back through the Future: Nostalgic Memory and Critical Memory in a Refuge from Nazism," in *Acts of Memory: Cultural Recall in the Present*, ed. Mieke Bal, Jonathan V. Crewe, and Leo Spitzer (Hanover, NH: University Press of New England, 1999), 96.

127 For Sheila Petty, "the interviews evoke a sense of abandonment that reflects the stark isolation of the landscape shots." See Sheila Petty, "*Sacred Places* and *Arlit: deuxième Paris*: Reterritorialization in African Documentary Films," *Nka* 32 (2013): 76.

128 Sigmund Freud, *Moses and Monotheism*, trans. Katherine Jones (New York: Vintage Books, 1939), 84.

129 Cubitt, *Finite Media*, 54.

130 Roberto Forns-Broggi, "Ecocinema and 'Good Life' in Latin America," in *Transnational Ecocinema: Film Culture in an Era of Ecological Transformation*, ed. Pietari Kääpä and Tommy Gustafsson (Bristol: Intellect, 2013), 98.

131 Steven Feld, *Sound and Sentiment: Birds, Weeping, Poetics, and Song in Kaluli Expression*, 3rd ed. (Durham, NC: Duke University Press, 2012), xxiv.

132 For a detailed discussion of the deployment of illness testimonies in environmental justice films, see Cory Shaman, "Testimonial Structures in Environmental Justice Films," in *Framing the World: Explorations in Ecocriticism and Film*, ed. Paula Willoquet-Maricondi (Charlottesville: University of Virginia Press, 2010), 83–100.

133 Martin Mhando and Keyan G. Tomaselli, "Film and Trauma: Africa Speaks to Itself through Truth and Reconciliation Films," *Black Camera* 1, no. 1 (2009): 31.

134 Carmela Garritano, "Waiting on the Past: African Uranium Futures in *Arlit, deuxième Paris*," *Modern Fiction Studies* 66, no. 1 (2020): 122–40.

135 Adrian J. Ivakhiv, *Ecologies of the Moving Image: Cinema, Affect, Nature* (Waterloo, ON: Wilfrid Laurier University Press, 2013), 64.

136 Martin Heidegger, *What Is a Thing?*, trans. W. B. Barton and Vera Deutsch (Chicago: Henry Regnery, 1967), 7.

137 Bill Brown, *Other Things* (Chicago: University of Chicago Press, 2015), 23–24.

138 Brown, *Other Things*, 23–24.

139 Cubitt, *Finite Media*, 54.

140 Susan Buck-Morss, *Dreamworld and Catastrophe: The Passing of Mass Utopia in East and West* (Cambridge, MA: MIT Press, 2000), x.

141 Anthony J. McMichael, Alistair Woodward, and Cameron Muir, *Climate Change and the Health of Nations: Famines, Fevers, and the Fate of Populations* (Oxford: Oxford University Press, 2017), 17.

142 Aaron Sayne, *Climate Change Adaptation and Conflict in Nigeria* (Washington, DC: United States Institute of Peace, 2011).

143 Wanuri Kahiu, dir., *Pumzi* (2009), 21 min.

144 Diana Adesola Mafe, *Where No Black Woman Has Gone Before: Subversive Portrayals in Speculative Film and TV* (Austin: University of Texas Press, 2018), 8.

145 For examples of films, see Mostéfa Djadam, dir., *Frontières* (2002), 105 min.; Merzak Allouache, dir., *Harragas* (2009), 95 min.; Leïla Kilani, dir., *Tanger, le rêve de brûleurs* (2002), 54 min.

146 Sontag, *Regarding the Pain of Others*, 102–3.

147 Soper, *What Is Nature?*, 266.

148 Lorenzo Kamel, "To Stop Migration, Stop the Abuse of Africa's Resources," *Al Jazeera*, February 15, 2018, https://www.aljazeera.com/indepth/opinion /stop-migration-stop-abuse-africa-resources-180213114944137.html.

149 Keenan, "Uranium Goes Critical," 455.

150 Priscilla Wald, *Contagious: Cultures, Carriers, and the Outbreak Narrative* (Durham, NC: Duke University Press, 2008), 82–83.

CHAPTER FOUR. Human Meets Animal, Africa Meets Diaspora

1 Describing images as "active rhetorical agents" in environmental activism and politics, Finis Dunaway explains that "media images do not simply illustrate environmental politics, but also shape the bounds of public debate by naturalizing particular meanings of environmentalism." Finis Dunaway, *Seeing Green: The Use and Abuse of American Environmental Images* (Chicago: University of Chicago Press, 2015), 1.

2 Here I follow Jemima Pierre, who has lamented the disconnect between both African studies and African diaspora studies, and the missed opportunities to link the process of racialization underpinning both slavery and colonialism. Pierre, *The Predicament of Blackness*, 1.

3 Saidiya Hartman, *Lose Your Mother: A Journey along the Atlantic Slave Route* (New York: Farrar, Straus, and Giroux, 2007), 172.

4 Shaul Schwarz and Christina Clusiau, dir., *Trophy* (2017), 110 min. On the "problematic of race," see Pierre, *The Predicament of Blackness*, 186.

5 For examples of wildlife film scholarship, see Ingram, *Green Screen*; Gregg Mitman, *Reel Nature: America's Romance with Wildlife on Film* (Cambridge, MA: Harvard University Press, 1999).

6 Saskia Sassen, *Territory, Authority, Rights: From Medieval to Global Assemblages* (Princeton, NJ: Princeton University Press, 2006), 383.

7 Orlando von Einsiedel, dir., *Virunga* (2014), 100 min.

8 Mbembe, *On the Postcolony*, 133.

9 Gilroy, *Postcolonial Melancholia*, xv.

10 Paul Gilroy, *Between Camps: Nations, Cultures, and the Allure of Race* (London: Routledge, 2004), 6.

11 Gilroy, *Between Camps*, 2.

12 Cornel West, *Race Matters* (Boston: Beacon Press, 1993), 38.

13 Achille Mbembe, *Critique of Black Reason*, trans. Laurent Dubois (Durham, NC: Duke University Press, 2017), 180.

14   Chielozona Eze, *Race, Decolonization, and Global Citizenship in South Africa* (Rochester, NY: University of Rochester Press, 2018), 18.

15   Huggan and Tiffin, *Postcolonial Ecocriticism*, 135.

16   Bénédicte Boisseron, *Afro-Dog: Blackness and the Animal Question* (New York: Columbia University Press, 2018), ix.

17   Michael Omi and Howard Winant, *Racial Formation in the United States from the 1960s to the 1990s* (New York: Routledge, 1994).

18   Jack Taylor writes that "the animalization of black bodies . . . allows the State and the general public to transform this ideology into the practice of lynching allowing for the destruction of black bodies with impunity." Jack Taylor, "Archives of Death: Lynching Photography, Animalization, Biopolitics, and the Lynching of William James," in *Economies of Death: Economic Logics of Killable Life and Grievable Death*, ed. Patricia J. Lopez and Kathryn A. Gillespie (London: Routledge, 2015), 124.

19   Stuart Hall, "The Spectacle of the Other," in *Representation: Cultural Representations and Signifying Practices*, ed. Stuart Hall (London: SAGE, 1997), 277.

20   Mirzoeff, *The Appearance of Black Lives Matter*, 91.

21   Salma Monani and Matthew Beehr, "John Sayles's *Honeydripper*: African Americans and the Environment," *ISLE: Interdisciplinary Studies in Literature and Environment* 18, no. 1 (2011): 5–25; Christine Gerhardt, "The Greening of African-American Landscapes: Where Ecocriticism Meets Post-Colonial Theory," *Mississippi Quarterly* 55, no. 4 (2002): 515–33.

22   See Sule Egya, "Nature, Animism and Humanity in Anglophone Nigerian Poetry," in *Natures of Africa: Ecocriticism and Animal Studies in Contemporary Cultural Forms*, ed. F. Fiona Moolla (Johannesburg: Wits University Press, 2016), 257–75; Mickias Musiyiwa, "Shona as a Land-Based Nature-Culture: A Study of the (Re)Construction of Shona Land Mythology in Popular Songs," in *Natures of Africa: Ecocriticism and Animal Studies in Contemporary Cultural Forms*, ed. F. Fiona Moolla (Johannesburg: Wits University Press, 2016), 49–76.

23   Allen F. Roberts, *Animals in African Art: From the Familiar to the Marvelous* (New York/Munich: Museum of African Art/Prestel, 1995), 17.

24   Marisol de la Cadena, "Indigenous Cosmopolitics in the Andes: Conceptual Reflections beyond 'Politics,'" *Cultural Anthropology* 25, no. 2 (2010): 334–70.

25   Donna Haraway, *Staying with the Trouble: Making Kin in the Chthulucene* (Durham, NC: Duke University Press, 2016); Wolfe, *Before the Law*; Derrida, "The Animal That Therefore I Am."

26   My intention is not to romanticize these cultural traditions; interaction with the Other is always fraught and theirs is no exception. However, the highlighted cultural practices offer a decolonial possibility for recalibrating human-animal interrelationship in African and African diasporic studies.

27   Gilroy, *Postcolonial Melancholia*, 5.

28   William J. T. Mitchell, *Image Science: Iconology, Visual Culture, and Media Aesthetics* (Chicago: University of Chicago Press, 2015), 55.

29   Frank C. Potts, Harold Goodwin, and Matt J. Walpole, "People, Wildlife and Tourism in and around Hwange National Park, Zimbabwe," in *People and Tourism in Fragile Environments*, ed. Martin F. Price (Chichester, UK: Wiley, 1996), 199.

30   Potts, Goodwin, and Walpole, "People, Wildlife, and Tourism," 202.

31   Potts, Goodwin, and Walpole, "People, Wildlife, and Tourism," 200.

32   Andrew Loveridge, *Lion Hearted: The Life and Death of Cecil and the Future of Africa's Iconic Cats* (New York: Regan Arts, 2018), 214.

33   This is the position of Safari Club International, an organization that touts "protecting hunters' rights and promoting wildlife conservation" as areas of focus (https://www.safariclub.org/who-we-are). Alexander N. Songorwa, the director of wildlife in Tanzania's Ministry of Natural Resources and Tourism, also shared this view in a 2013 *New York Times* editorial where he urged against listing the African lion as endangered, which would make trophy hunting illegal in the United States. The first sentence of the piece reads: "Odd as it may sound, American trophy hunters play a critical role in protecting wildlife in Tanzania." Alexander M. Songorwa, "Saving Lions by Killing Them," *New York Times*, March 17, 2013, https://www.nytimes.com/2013/03/18/opinion/saving -lions-by-killing-them.html.

34   Sontag, *On Photography*, 15.

35   Landau, "Empires of the Visual," 147.

36   Cubitt, *EcoMedia*, 31.

37   Mitchell, *Image Science*, 69.

38   Benjamin, *On Photography*, 68.

39   Njabulo Ndebele, "Game Lodges and Leisure Colonialists," in *Blank—: Architecture, Apartheid and After*, ed. Hilton Judin and Ivan Vladislavić (Cape Town: David Phillips, 1998), 10.

40   Fried, *Why Photography Matters*, 14.

41   Fried, *Why Photography Matters*, 17.

42   Michael Fried, "Art and Objecthood," *Artforum* 5, no. 10 (1967): 12–23; Fried, *Why Photography Matters*, 26.

43   Fried, *Why Photography Matters*, 35.

44   Umberto Eco, *Travels in Hyperreality*, trans. William Weaver (San Diego, CA: Harcourt Brace Jovanovich, 1986), 138.

45   Guy Debord, *The Society of the Spectacle*, trans. Ken Knabb (Berkeley, CA: Bureau of Public Secrets, 2014), 7, 111.

46   Kevin Michael DeLuca, *Image Politics: The New Rhetoric of Environmental Activism* (New York: Guilford Press, 1999).

47   Henry Jenkins, *Convergence Culture: Where Old and New Media Collide* (New York: New York University Press, 2006), 2.

48   Mirzoeff, *The Right to Look*, 291.

49   David W. Macdonald et al., "Cecil: A Moment or a Movement? Analysis of Media Coverage of the Death of a Lion, *Panthera leo*," *Animals* 6, no. 26 (2016): 1–13.

50 Mitchell, *Image Science*, 65–78.

51 Henry Jenkins, Sam Ford, and Joshua Green, *Spreadable Media: Creating Value and Meaning in a Networked Culture* (New York: New York University Press, 2013), 3.

52 Jenkins, Ford, and Green, *Spreadable Media*, 3.

53 Macdonald et al., "Cecil," 8.

54 Derrida, "The Animal That Therefore I Am."

55 Wendy Hui Kyong Chun, "Introduction: Race and/as Technology; or, How to Do Things to Race," *Camera Obscura* 24, no. 1 (2009): 7–35; Lisa Nakamura, *Digitizing Race: Visual Cultures of the Internet* (Minneapolis: University of Minnesota Press, 2008); Lewis R. Gordon, *Her Majesty's Other Children: Sketches of Racism from a Neocolonial Age* (Lanham, MD: Rowman and Littlefield, 1997), 76.

56 Sassen, *Territory, Authority, Rights*, 405–6.

57 Heise, *Imagining Extinction*, 23.

58 Sassen, *Territory, Authority, Rights*, 404.

59 Hartman, *Lose Your Mother*, 6.

60 Hartman, *Lose Your Mother*, 6.

61 Black Lives Matter, "About," accessed December 6, 2018, https://blacklives matter.com/about/.

62 Christopher J. Lebron, *The Making of Black Lives Matter: A Brief History of an Idea* (New York: Oxford University Press, 2017), xii.

63 Mirzoeff, *The Appearance of Black Lives Matter*, 18.

64 Lebron, *The Making of Black Lives Matter*, x.

65 Lebron, *The Making of Black Lives Matter*, x.

66 Spillers, "Mama's Baby," 67.

67 Omi and Winant, *Racial Formation*.

68 Smith, *At the Edge of Sight*, 195.

69 Hazel Carby, "US/UK's Special Relationship: The Culture of Torture in Abu Ghraib and Lynching Photographs," *Nka: Journal of Contemporary African Art* 20 (2006): 66.

70 Cassandra Jackson, *Violence, Visual Culture, and the Black Male Body* (London: Routledge, 2011), 3.

71 Jackson, *Violence*, 77.

72 Theodore Roosevelt, *African Game Trails: An Account of the African Wanderings of an American Hunter-Naturalist* (New York: Scribner, 1910).

73 Roderick P. Neumann, "'Through the Pleistocene': Nature and Race in Theodore Roosevelt's *African Game Trails*," in *Environment at the Margins: Literary and Environmental Studies in Africa*, ed. Byron Caminero-Santangelo and Garth Andrew Myers (Athens: Ohio University Press, 2011), 44.

74 Neumann, "Through the Pleistocene," 44.

75 Mitman, *Reel Nature*, 5.

76 Neumann, "Through the Pleistocene," 47.

77 Mitman, *Reel Nature*, 15.

78 Yuka Suzuki, *The Nature of Whiteness: Race, Animals, and Nation in Zimbabwe* (Seattle: University of Washington Press, 2017), 25.

79 Linda Kalof and Amy Fitzgerald, "Reading the Trophy: Exploring the Display of Dead Animals in Hunting Magazines," *Visual Studies* 18, no. 2 (2003): 117.

80 Grace A. Musila, *A Death Retold in Truth and Rumour: Kenya, Britain and the Julie Ward Murder* (Martlesham, UK: James Currey, 2015), 166.

81 Judith Butler, *Precarious Life: The Powers of Mourning and Violence* (London: Verso, 2006), 20.

82 Calvin L. Warren, *Ontological Terror: Blackness, Nihilism, and Emancipation* (Durham, NC: Duke University Press, 2018), 48.

83 Abdul R. JanMohamed, *The Death-Bound-Subject: Richard Wright's Archaeology of Death* (Durham, NC: Duke University Press, 2005), 2.

84 Lester Spence, "Why Baltimore Doesn't Heat Its Schools," *Jacobin*, January 12, 2018, https://www.jacobinmag.com/2018/01/baltimore-freezing-schools -children-racism-austerity.

85 Robert Hariman and John Louis Lucaites, *No Caption Needed: Iconic Photographs, Public Culture, and Liberal Democracy* (Chicago: University of Chicago Press, 2007), 12.

86 Laurie E. Gries, *Still Life with Rhetoric: A New Materialist Approach for Visual Rhetorics* (Logan: Utah State University Press, 2015), 71.

87 Stefan Carpenter and David M. Konisky, "The Killing of Cecil the Lion as an Impetus for Policy Change," *Oryx* 53, no. 4 (2019): 698.

88 Caminero-Santangelo, *Different Shades of Green*, 13.

89 Huggan and Tiffin, *Postcolonial Ecocriticism*, 18.

90 Julia Martin, "New, with Added Ecology? Hippos, Forest and Environmental Literacy," *ISLE: Interdisciplinary Studies in Literature and Environment* 2, no. 1 (1994): 2; Jane Carruthers, *The Kruger National Park: A Social and Political History* (Pietermaritzburg: University of Natal Press, 1995).

91 Goodwell Nzou, "In Zimbabwe, We Don't Cry for Lions," *New York Times*, August 4, 2015, https://www.nytimes.com/2015/08/05/opinion/in-zimbabwe -we-dont-cry-for-lions.html.

92 For a comprehensive discussion of the crisis of postcoloniality in Zimbabwe and its colonial antecedents, see Sabelo J. Ndlovu-Gatsheni, *Do 'Zimbabweans' Exist? Trajectories of Nationalism, National Identity Formation and Crisis in a Postcolonial State* (Bern: Peter Lang, 2009).

93 Suzuki, *The Nature of Whiteness*, 152.

94 Suzuki, *The Nature of Whiteness*, 30–31.

95 Sabelo J. Ndlovu-Gatsheni, "Rethinking Chimurenga and Gukurahundi in Zimbabwe: A Critique of Partisan National History," *African Studies Review* 55, no. 3 (2012): 8.

96 Akosua Adomako Ampofo, "Re-viewing Studies on Africa, #Black Lives Matter, and Envisioning the Future of African Studies," *African Studies Review* 59, no. 2 (2016): 21.

97 Sassen, *Territory, Authority, Rights*, 405.

98 Sylvia Wynter, "Unsettling the Coloniality of Being/Power/Truth/Freedom: Towards the Human, after Man, Its Overrepresentation—An Argument," *CR: The New Centennial Review* 3, no. 3 (2003): 257–337.

99 Jared Sexton, "People-of-Color-Blindness: Notes on the Afterlife of Slavery," *Social Text* 28, no. 2 (2010): 31–56; Warren, *Ontological Terror*.

100 Fred Moten, "Blackness and Nothingness (Mysticism in the Flesh)," *South Atlantic Quarterly* 112, no. 4 (2013): 774.

101 Alexander G. Weheliye, *Habeas Viscus: Racializing Assemblages, Biopolitics, and Black Feminist Theories of the Human* (Durham, NC: Duke University Press, 2014), 125.

102 Weheliye, *Habeas Viscus*, 92.

103 Moten, "Blackness and Nothingness," 778–79.

104 Weheliye, *Habeas Viscus*, 10.

105 Nzou, "Don't Cry for Lions."

106 Dereck Joubert, dir., *The Last Lions* (2011), 88 min; Bruce Young and Nick Chevallier, dir., *Blood Lions* (2015), 84 min.

107 Simon Cottle, "Producing Nature(s): On the Changing Production Ecology of Natural History TV," *Media, Culture and Society* 26, no. 1 (2004): 82.

108 Claire Molloy, "'Nature Writes the Screenplays': Commercial Wildlife Films and Ecological Entertainment," in *Ecocinema Theory and Practice*, ed. Stephen Rust, Salma Monani, and Sean Cubitt (New York: Routledge, 2012), 170.

109 Shaul Schwarz, dir., *Narco Cultura* (2013), 103 min.

110 Jean Bentley, "'Trophy' Filmmakers Explain How the Film Became More Than an Anti-Trophy-Hunting Exposé," *Indiewire*, September 20, 2017, https://www.indiewire.com/2017/09/trophy-big-game-hunting-documentary-interview-1201877123/.

111 Michele Pickover, *Animal Rights in South Africa* (Cape Town: Double Storey Books, 2005), 18.

112 John Berger, *About Looking* (New York: Pantheon Books, 1980), 13.

113 Reinier J. M. Vriend, "The Paradoxes of Voluntourism: Strategic Visual Tropes of the Natural on South African Voluntourism Websites," in *Natures of Africa: Ecocriticism and Animal Studies in Contemporary Cultural Forms*, ed. F. Fiona Moolla (Johannesburg: Wits University Press, 2016), 133.

114 Musila, *A Death Retold*, 165.

115 Mitman, *Reel Nature*, 107.

116 James Murombedzi, "Devolving the Expropriation of Nature: The 'Devolution' of Wildlife Management in Southern Africa," in *Decolonizing Nature: Strategies for Conservation in a Post-Colonial Era*, ed. William M. Adams and Martin Mulligan (London: Earthscan, 2003), 146.

117 Murombedzi, "Devolving the Expropriation of Nature," 146.

118 Mitman, *Reel Nature*, 72.

119 Carruthers, *The Kruger National Park*, 2.

120 Mark Dowie, *Conservation Refugees: The Hundred-Year Conflict between Global Conservation and Native Peoples* (Cambridge, MA: MIT Press, 2009), xxii.

121 Dowie, *Conservation Refugees*, xxii.

122 For a discussion of recent Maasai conflicts with conservation actors, see

Graham R. Fox, "The 2017 Shooting of Kuki Gallmann and the Politics of Conservation in Northern Kenya," *African Studies Review* 61, no. 2 (2018): 210–36; Jennifer Bond and Kennedy Mkutu, "Exploring the Hidden Costs of Human-Wildlife Conflict in Northern Kenya," *African Studies Review* 61, no. 1 (2018): 33–54.

123 Nixon, *Slow Violence and the Environmentalism of the Poor* (Cambridge, MA: Harvard University Press, 2011), 184.

124 William Beinart, *The Rise of Conservation in South Africa: Settlers, Livestock, and the Environment, 1770–1950* (Oxford: Oxford University Press, 2003), xiii.

125 For further discussion of the link between colonialism and displacement, see Martin, "New, with Added Ecology?"

126 Carruthers, *The Kruger National Park*, 12.

127 Bond and Mkutu, "Exploring the Hidden Costs," 36.

128 See Nancy Lee Peluso, "Coercing Conservation? The Politics of State Resource Control," *Global Environmental Change* 3, no. 2 (1993): 199–217; Rosaleen Duffy, "Waging a War to Save Biodiversity: The Rise of Militarized Conservation," *International Affairs* 90, no. 4 (2014): 819–34; Roderick P. Neumann, "Moral and Discursive Geographies in the War for Biodiversity in Africa," *Political Geography* 23, no. 7 (2004): 813–37.

129 Duffy, "Waging a War," 834.

130 Murombedzi, "Devolving the Expropriation of Nature," 142.

131 Murombedzi, "Devolving the Expropriation of Nature."

132 Deane Curtin, *Environmental Ethics for a Postcolonial World* (Lanham, MD: Rowman and Littlefield, 2005), 143.

133 Pickover, *Animal Rights in South Africa*, 167.

134 Other scholars consider meat-eating as a gendered practice of masculinity, which would link it to the discussion of trophy hunting earlier in the chapter. For examples of scholarship exploring the gendered nature of meat-eating, see Carol J. Adams, *The Sexual Politics of Meat: A Feminist-Vegetarian Critical Theory* (New York: Continuum, 1990); Laura Wright, *The Vegan Studies Project: Food, Animals, and Gender in the Age of Terror* (Athens: University of Georgia Press, 2015).

135 Anat Pick, "Turning to Animals between Love and Law," *New Formations* 76 (2012): 82.

136 S. Eben Kirksey and Stefan Helmreich, "The Emergence of Multispecies Ethnography," *Cultural Anthropology* 25, no. 4 (2010): 545–76.

137 Heise, *Imagining Extinction*, 165.

138 Val Plumwood, "Decolonizing Relationships with Nature," in *Decolonizing Nature: Strategies for Conservation in a Post-Colonial Era*, ed. William M. Adams and Martin Mulligan (London: Earthscan, 2003), 54.

139 Akira Mizuta Lippit, *Electric Animal: Toward a Rhetoric of Wildlife* (Minneapolis: University of Minnesota Press, 2000), 8.

140 See Dan Brockington, *Celebrity and the Environment: Fame, Wealth and Power in Conservation* (London: Zed, 2009).

141 Orlando von Einsiedel, dir., *The White Helmets* (2016), 41 min.; Orlando von Einsiedel, dir., *Lost and Found* (2019), 22 min.

142 Esther Marijnen and Judith Verweijen, "Selling Green Militarization: The Discursive (Re)Production of Militarized Conservation in the Virunga National Park, Democratic Republic of the Congo," *Geoforum* 75 (2016): 274, 277.

143 Stephan Hochleithner, "Beyond Contesting Limits: Land, Access, and Resistance at the Virunga National Park," *Conservation and Society* 15, no. 1 (2017): 100–110.

144 Marijnen and Verweijen, "Selling Green Militarization," 277.

145 Judith Verweijen and Esther Marijnen, "The Counterinsurgency/Conservation Nexus: Guerrilla Livelihoods and the Dynamics of Conflict and Violence in the Virunga National Park, Democratic Republic of the Congo," *Journal of Peasant Studies* 45, no. 2 (2018): 307.

146 See Nancy Rose Hunt, "An Acoustic Register: Rape and Repetition in Congo," in *Imperial Debris: On Ruins and Ruination*, ed. Ann Laura Stoler (Durham, NC: Duke University Press, 2013), 58.

147 Nancy Rose Hunt, *A Nervous State: Violence, Remedies, and Reverie in Colonial Congo* (Durham, NC: Duke University Press, 2016), 2.

148 Kevin Bales, *Blood and Earth: Modern Slavery, Ecocide, and the Secret to Saving the World* (New York: Spiegel and Grau, 2016), 16.

149 Bales, *Blood and Earth*, 15–16.

150 See Marijnen and Verweijen, "Selling Green Militarization," 274–75.

151 See Bales, *Blood and Earth*, 12–46; and Marijnen and Verweijen, "Selling Green Militarization," 277.

152 Bales, *Blood and Earth*, 39.

153 Bales, *Blood and Earth*, 39–40.

154 Hochleithner, "Beyond Contesting Limits," 106.

155 Derek Bousé, "False Intimacy: Close-ups and Viewer Involvement in Wildlife Films," *Visual Studies* 18, no. 2 (2003): 123–32.

156 Brian Massumi, *What Animals Teach Us about Politics* (Durham, NC: Duke University Press, 2014), 2.

157 Massumi, *What Animals Teach Us*, 8.

158 Haraway, *Staying with the Trouble*, 4.

159 Haraway, *Staying with the Trouble*, 105, 116.

160 See https://virungamovie.com/.

161 For Arun Agrawal, environmental subjects demonstrate concern for the environment, which "constitutes for them a conceptual category that organizes some of their thinking" and actions. Arun Agrawal, *Environmentality: Technologies of Government and the Making of Subjects* (Durham, NC: Duke University Press, 2005), 165.

162 Bales, *Blood and Earth*, 166.

163 Cubitt, *EcoMedia*, 41.

CHAPTER FIVE. African Urban Ecologies

1   Bill Freund, *The African City: A History* (Cambridge: Cambridge University Press, 2007).

2   AbdouMaliq Simone, *For the City Yet to Come: Changing African Life in Four Cities* (Durham, NC: Duke University Press, 2004).

3   Jennifer Robinson, *Ordinary Cities: Between Modernity and Development* (London: Routledge, 2006); Filip De Boeck, *Kinshasa: Tales of the Invisible City*, photographs by Marie-Françoise Plissart (Leuven: Ludion, 2004).

4   AbdouMaliq Simone, "The Last Shall Be First: African Urbanites and the Larger Urban World," in *Other Cities, Other Worlds: Urban Imaginaries in a Globalizing Age*, ed. Andreas Huyssen (Durham, NC: Duke University Press, 2008), 100.

5   Guy Tillim, *Jo'burg* (Johannesburg: STE, 2005); Wu Jing, dir., *Wolf Warrior 2* (2017), 123 min.; Femi Odugbemi, dir., *Makoko: Futures Afloat* (2016), 30 min.; Olalekan Jeyifous, *Shanty Megastructures*, 2015, series of digital architectural drawings, http://vigilism.com/filter/Drawings/Improvised-Shanty-Mega structures.

6   Achille Mbembe and Sarah Nuttall, "Writing the World from an African Metropolis," *Public Culture* 16, no. 3 (2004): 353.

7   Tejumola Olaniyan, "African Urban Garrison Architecture: Property, Armed Robbery, Para-Capitalism," in *State and Culture in Postcolonial Africa: Enchantings*, ed. Tejumola Olaniyan (Bloomington: Indiana University Press, 2017), 291–308.

8   Charles Piot, *Nostalgia for the Future: West Africa after the Cold War* (Chicago: University of Chicago Press, 2010), 20; Freund, *The African City*, 165. See also Ryan Thomas Skinner, *Bamako Sounds: The Afropolitan Ethics of Malian Music* (Minneapolis: University of Minnesota Press, 2015), 32.

9   Edgar Pieterse, *City Futures: Confronting the Crisis of Urban Development* (London: Zed, 2008), 1.

10 Homi Bhabha, "Looking Back, Moving Forward: Notes on Vernacular Cosmopolitanism," in *The Location of Culture* (London: Routledge, 2012), xiii.

11 Georg Simmel, "The Metropolis and Mental Life," 1903, in *The Blackwell City Reader*, ed. Gary Bridge and Sophie Watson (Oxford: Wiley-Blackwell, 2002).

12 Pierre Bourdieu, *The Field of Cultural Production: Essays on Art and Literature* (New York: Columbia University Press, 1993), 176.

13 Guy Tillim, *Avenue Patrice Lumumba* (Munich/Cambridge, MA: Prestel Verlag/ Peabody Museum of Archaeology and Ethnology, 2009); Guy Tillim, *Museum of the Revolution* (London: Mack, 2019).

14 Antina von Schnitzler, "Infrastructure, Apartheid Technopolitics, and Temporalities of 'Transition,'" in *The Promise of Infrastructure*, ed. Nikhil Anand, Akhil Gupta, and Hannah Appel (Durham, NC: Duke University Press, 2018), 134.

15 Mike Davis, *Planet of Slums* (London: Verso, 2006).

16 Henri Lefebvre, *The Production of Space*, trans. Donald Nicholson-Smith (Oxford: Blackwell, 1991), 165.

17   Andreas Huyssen, "Introduction: World Cultures, World Cities," in *Other Cities, Other Worlds: Urban Imaginaries in a Globalizing Age*, ed. Andreas Huyssen (Durham, NC: Duke University Press, 2008), 5.

18   Garrison architecture is Tejumola Olaniyan's term for "residential homes enclosed by high walls spiked at the top with barbed wires or broken bottles, huge gates, and built-in iron bars on windows and room doors." Olaniyan, "African Urban Garrison Architecture," 291.

19   Peter J. Taylor, *World City Network: A Global Urban Analysis* (London: Routledge, 2004).

20   Mbembe, "Aesthetics of Superfluity," 394–99.

21   Stephen Graham and Simon Marvin, *Splintering Urbanism: Networked Infrastructures, Technological Mobilities and the Urban Condition* (London: Routledge, 2001), 33.

22   Loren Kruger, *Imagining the Edgy City: Writing, Performing, and Building Johannesburg* (New York: Oxford University Press, 2013).

23   Mbembe and Nuttall, "Writing the World," 363.

24   John Matshikiza, "Instant City," *Public Culture* 16, no. 3 (2004): 483.

25   David Harvey, "The Right to the City," *New Left Review* 53 (2008): 23–40.

26   Louise Meintjes, "Hi-fi Sociality, Lo-fi Sound: Affect and Precarity in an Independent South African Recording Studio," in *State and Culture in Postcolonial Africa: Enchantings*, ed. Tejumola Olaniyan (Bloomington: Indiana University Press, 2017), 208.

27   Daniel Mains, *Hope Is Cut: Youth, Unemployment, and the Future in Urban Ethiopia* (Philadelphia: Temple University Press, 2011), 10.

28   Quayson, *Oxford Street, Accra*, 183–212.

29   Mains, *Hope Is Cut*, 6–7.

30   Alfred J. López, "Dwelling in a Global Age: An Introduction," *Modern Fiction Studies* 63, no. 1 (2017): 7.

31   Tillim, *Avenue Patrice Lumumba*.

32   Tillim, *Avenue Patrice Lumumba*, n.p.

33   Martin Heidegger, "Building Dwelling Thinking," in *Basic Writings*, ed. David Farrell Krell (New York: HarperCollins, 1993), 348.

34   Heidegger, "Building Dwelling Thinking," 349.

35   López, "Dwelling in a Global Age," 3.

36   Heidegger, "Building Dwelling Thinking," 351.

37   Heidegger, "Building Dwelling Thinking," 362.

38   Heidegger, "Building Dwelling Thinking," 360.

39   Wole Soyinka, *Myth, Literature and the African World* (Cambridge: Cambridge University Press, 1976), 2.

40   Soyinka, *Myth*, 1–36.

41   Harriet Sibisi, "The Place of Spirit Possession in Zulu Cosmology," in *Religion and Social Change in Southern Africa: Anthropological Essays in Honour of Monica Wilson*, ed. Michael G. Whisson and Martin West (Cape Town: David Phillip, 1975), 48–49.

42   W. D. Hammond-Tooke, "The Symbolic Structure of Cape Nguni Cosmology," in *Religion and Social Change in Southern Africa: Anthropological Essays in Honour of Monica Wilson*, ed. Michael G. Whisson and Martin West (Cape Town: David Phillip, 1975), 15–33.

43   Kwasi Wiredu, *Cultural Universals and Particulars: An African Perspective* (Bloomington: Indiana University Press, 1996), 165–66.

44   Wendy Woodward, *The Animal Gaze: Animal Subjectivities in Southern African Narratives* (Johannesburg: Wits University Press, 2008).

45   Malindi Neluheni, "Apartheid Urban Development," in *White Papers, Black Marks: Architecture, Race, Culture*, ed. Lesley Naa Norle Lokko (London: Athlone, 2000), 80.

46   Francis Wilson, "A Land out of Balance," in *Restoring the Land: Environment and Change in Post-Apartheid South Africa*, ed. Mamphela Ramphele and Chris McDowell (London: Panos, 1991), 32.

47   Mamphela Ramphele, "New Day Rising," in *Restoring the Land: Environment and Change in Post-Apartheid South Africa*, ed. Mamphela Ramphele and Chris McDowell (London: Panos, 1991), 3.

48   Heidegger, "Building Dwelling Thinking," 363.

49   Adrienne Brown, *The Black Skyscraper: Architecture and the Perception of Race* (Baltimore: Johns Hopkins University Press, 2017), 3.

50   Lesley Naa Norle Lokko, ed., *White Papers, Black Marks: Architecture, Race, Culture* (London: Athlone, 2000).

51   De Boeck, *Kinshasa*, 8.

52   Michel de Certeau, *The Practice of Everyday Life*, trans. Steven F. Rendall (Berkeley: University of California Press, 1984), 108.

53   Edward W. Soja, *Seeking Spatial Justice* (Minneapolis: University of Minnesota Press, 2010), 37.

54   According to Makhulu, "squatter camps, however ill conceived, however unplanned, affixed African people in urban space. In so doing, migrants directly confronted the brute logic of racial biopolitics that stipulated that black life should be reproduced beyond metropolitan South Africa." Anne-Maria Makhulu, *Making Freedom: Apartheid, Squatter Politics, and the Struggle for Home* (Durham, NC: Duke University Press, 2015), 28.

55   Hilton Judin, "Unsettling Johannesburg: The Country in the City," in *Other Cities, Other Worlds: Urban Imaginaries in a Globalizing Age*, ed. Andreas Huyssen (Durham, NC: Duke University Press, 2008), 141.

56   Ann Laura Stoler, "'The Rot Remains': From Ruins to Ruination," in *Imperial Debris: On Ruins and Ruination*, ed. Ann Laura Stoler (Durham, NC: Duke University Press, 2013), 2.

57   Stoler, "'The Rot Remains,'" 8–9.

58   Von Schnitzler, "Infrastructure," 142.

59   Soja, *Seeking Spatial Justice*, 40.

60   Ama Ata Aidoo, "For Whom Things Did Not Change," in *No Sweetness Here and Other Stories* (New York: Feminist Press, 1970), 8–29.

61 James C. Scott, "Everyday Forms of Resistance," *Copenhagen Journal of Asian Studies* 4, no. 1 (1989): 33–62.

62 Okwui Enwezor, "Modernity and Postcolonial Ambivalence," *South Atlantic Quarterly* 109, no. 3 (2010): 616.

63 Howard W. French, *China's Second Continent: How a Million Migrants Are Building a New Empire in Africa* (New York: Knopf, 2014).

64 French, *China's Second Continent*, 13.

65 On Chinese racism and discrimination, see Joseph Goldstein, "Kenyans Say Chinese Investment Brings Racism and Discrimination," *New York Times*, October 15, 2018, https://www.nytimes.com/2018/10/15/world/africa/kenya-china-racism.html. On the ecological dimensions of Chinese involvement, see Jeffrey D. Sachs, *Common Wealth: Economics for a Crowded Planet* (New York: Penguin, 2008), 75–77; French, *China's Second Continent*, 13.

66 Ching Kwan Lee, *The Specter of Global China: Politics, Labor, and Foreign Investment in Africa* (Chicago: University of Chicago Press, 2018), 28–29; Deborah Brautigam, *The Dragon's Gift: The Real Story of China in Africa* (Oxford: Oxford University Press, 2009), 78; Ian Taylor, "Beyond the Drama: Sino-African Ties in Perspective," in *China-Africa Relations: Building Images through Cultural Cooperation, Media Representation and Communication*, ed. Kathryn Batchelor and Xiaoling Zhang (London: Routledge, 2017), 16–26.

67 Lee, *The Specter of Global China*, 9.

68 Lee, *The Specter of Global China*, 28–29.

69 Marc Francis and Nick Francis, dir., *When China Met Africa* (2010), 75 min.

70 Brautigam, *The Dragon's Gift*, 30; Qing Cao, "Chinese Developmentalism and Television Representation of South Africa," in *China-Africa Relations: Building Images through Cultural Cooperation, Media Representation and Communication*, ed. Kathryn Batchelor and Xiaoling Zhang (London: Routledge, 2017), 199–217.

71 Drew Thompson, "China's Soft Power in Africa: From the 'Beijing Consensus' to Health Diplomacy," *China Brief* 5, no. 21 (2005): 1.

72 For a comprehensive study of the TAZARA Railway, see Jamie Monson, *Africa's Freedom Railway: How a Chinese Development Project Changed Lives and Livelihoods in Tanzania* (Bloomington: Indiana University Press, 2009).

73 Brautigam, *The Dragon's Gift*, 301.

74 Brautigam, *The Dragon's Gift*, 309.

75 French, *China's Second Continent*, 252–54.

76 See the essays in Kathryn Batchelor and Xiaoling Zhang, eds., *China-Africa Relations: Building Images through Cultural Cooperation, Media Representation and Communication* (London: Routledge, 2017).

77 Alessandro Jedlowski, "Studying Media 'from' the South: African Media Studies and Global Perspectives," *Black Camera* 7, no. 2 (2016): 184.

78 Wu Jing, dir., *Wolf Warrior* (2015), 90 min.

79 Lefebvre, *The Production of Space*, 11.

80 Paul Greengrass, dir., *Captain Phillips* (2013), 134 min.

81 Davis, *Planet of Slums*, 205.

82   Nixon, *Slow Violence*, 2.

83   Brian R. Jacobson, "Fire and Failure: Studio Technology, Environmental Control, and the Politics of Progress," *Cinema Journal* 57, no. 2 (2018): 24.

84   Cubitt, *Finite Media*, 1–2.

85   Maxwell and Miller, *Greening the Media*, 68.

86   Nadia Bozak, *The Cinematic Footprint: Lights, Camera, Natural Resources* (New Brunswick, NJ: Rutgers University Press, 2012), 62.

87   Adams Bodomo, *Africans in China: A Sociocultural Study and Its Implications on Africa-China Relations* (Amherst, NY: Cambria Press, 2012), 10.

88   Bodomo, *Africans in China*, 13.

89   Kathryn Batchelor and Xiaoling Zhang, "Introduction: Images, Nation Branding, and News Framing," in *China-Africa Relations: Building Images through Cultural Cooperation, Media Representation and Communication*, ed. Kathryn Batchelor and Xiaoling Zhang (London: Routledge, 2017), 4.

90   French, *China's Second Continent*, 221.

91   Garth Myers, *African Cities: Alternative Visions of Urban Theory and Practice* (London: Zed, 2011), 137.

92   Myers, *African Cities*, 138–61.

93   Myers, *African Cities*, 145.

94   Femi Odugbemi, dir., *Bariga Boy* (2010), 28 min.; Tope Ogun et al., dir., *Tinsel* (2008), TV series, 2992 episodes; George Kura et al., dir., *Battleground* (2016), TV series, 260 episodes.

95   For an overview of the Eko Atlantic project and the analysis of its social and ecological costs, see Ben Mendelsohn, "Making the Urban Coast: A Geosocial Reading of Land, Sand, and Water in Lagos, Nigeria," *Comparative Studies of South Asia, Africa and the Middle East* 38, no. 3 (2018): 455–72.

96   Anthony D. King, *Spaces of Global Cultures: Architecture, Urbanism, Identity* (London: Routledge, 2004), xiv.

97   Asef Bayat, "Un-Civil Society: The Politics of the 'Informal People,'" *Third World Quarterly* 18, no. 1 (1997): 57.

98   Bayat, "Un-Civil Society," 58–59.

99   Pieterse, *City Futures*.

100   The quotations are taken respectively from Hern, *What a City Is For*, 98; Rem Koolhaas, "Fragments of a Lecture on Lagos," in *Under Siege: Four African Cities, Freetown, Johannesburg, Kinshasa, Lagos*, ed. Okwui Enwezor et al. (Ostfildern-Ruit: Hatje Cantz, 2002), 183.

101   Karen C. Seto and Meredith Reba, *City Unseen: New Visions of an Urban Planet* (New Haven, CT: Yale University Press, 2018), 243.

102   Raymond Williams, *The Country and the City* (London: Chatto and Windus, 1973), 277.

103   Ashley Dawson, *Extreme Cities: The Peril and Promise of Urban Life in the Age of Climate Change* (New York: Verso, 2017).

104   Ash Amin and Nigel Thrift, *Cities: Reimagining the Urban* (Cambridge: Polity Press, 2002), 5.

105 Melissa Checker, Gary McDonogh, and Cindy Isenhour, "Introduction: Urban Sustainability as Myth and Practice," in *Sustainability in the Global City: Myth and Practice*, ed. Cindy Isenhour, Gary McDonogh, and Melissa Checker (New York: Cambridge University Press, 2015), 10.

106 Dominic Boyer, "Infrastructure, Potential Energy, Revolution," in *The Promise of Infrastructure*, ed. Nikhil Anand, Akhil Gupta, and Hannah Appel (Durham, NC: Duke University Press, 2018), 231.

107 Varun Sivaram, *Taming the Sun: Innovations to Harness Solar Energy and Power the Planet* (Cambridge, MA: MIT Press, 2018).

108 Sivaram, *Taming the Sun*, 8.

109 Sivaram, *Taming the Sun*, 11.

110 Sivaram, *Taming the Sun*, xvii, 63.

111 Harvey, "The Right to the City," 23; Soja, *Seeking Spatial Justice*.

112 Jenny Price, "Remaking American Environmentalism: On the Banks of the LA River," *Environmental History* 13, no. 3 (2008): 552–53.

EPILOGUE. Toward Imperfect Media

1 Zielinski, *Deep Time of the Media*, 2.

2 Bozak, *The Cinematic Footprint*.

3 Ryan Coogler, dir., *Black Panther* (2018), 134 min.

4 The two quotes come respectively from Christopher Lebron, "'Black Panther' Is Not the Movie We Deserve," *Boston Review*, February 17, 2018, http://bostonreview.net/race/christopher-lebron-black-panther; Tim McDonnell, "Ghanaian Fans Have One Nit to Pick but Otherwise Adore 'Black Panther,'" *NPR*, February 20, 2018, https://www.npr.org/sections/goatsandsoda/2018/02/20/587224592/ghanaian-fans-have-one-nit-to-pick-but-otherwise-adore-black-panther.

5 Lebron, "'Black Panther' Is Not the Movie We Deserve."

6 Coronil, *The Magical State*.

7 Robert Pollin, *Greening the Global Economy* (Cambridge, MA: MIT Press, 2015), 30.

8 Marc Malkin captures this tension in an essay on *Black Panther*'s significance for an alternative urban configuration. In his words, "Wakanda also happens to be the wealthiest country in the world; therefore, its ruler, T'Challa, doesn't have to worry about the cost to develop and operate maglev technology, something many actual cities interested in the idea face when considering the feasibility of the transportation." Marc Malkin, "The Real-Life Possibilities of Black Panther's Wakanda, According to Urbanists and City Planners," *Architectural Digest*, February 28, 2018, https://www.architecturaldigest.com/story/the-real-life-possibilities-of-black-panthers-wakanda-according-to-urbanists-and-city-planners.

9 Ngũgĩ wa Thiong'o, *Globalectics: Theory and the Politics of Knowing* (New York: Columbia University Press, 2012), 2.

10 Ngũgĩ, *Globalectics*, 3.

11 Ngũgĩ, *Globalectics*, 6.

12 Samuel Shearer, "Producing Sustainable Futures in Post-Genocide Kigali, Rwanda," in *Sustainability in the Global City: Myth and Practice*, eds. Cindy Isenhour, Gary McDonogh, and Melissa Checker (New York: Cambridge University Press, 2015), 181.

13 Charles Sugnet, "Ousmane Sembene: A Silenced Continent Speaks," *Walker Reader*, October 6, 2010, https://walkerart.org/magazine/ousmane-sembene -a-silenced-continent-speaks.

14 Ousmane Sembene, dir., *Xala* (1975), 123 min; Ousmane Sembene, dir., *Mandabi* (1968), 90 min.

15 Jonathan Haynes and Onookome Okome, "Evolving Popular Media: Nigerian Video Films," in *Nigerian Video Films*, ed. Jonathan Haynes (Athens: Ohio University Press, 2000), 51–88.

16 For example, see Prabhu, *Contemporary Cinema of Africa and the Diaspora*.

17 Carmen McCain, "An Evolution in Nollywood, Nigeria's New Wave: A Conversation with Chris Eneaji," *Black Camera* 7, no. 2 (2016): 208.

18 Julio García Espinosa, "For an Imperfect Cinema," trans. Julianne Burton, *Jump Cut* 20 (1979): 24–26.

19 Julio García Espinosa, "Meditations on Imperfect Cinema . . . Fifteen Years Later," *Screen* 26, nos. 3/4 (1985): 93–94.

20 García Espinosa, "For an Imperfect Cinema."

21 In recent years, some Nollywood filmmakers have sought to improve the quality of their works in response to critiques of the industry's low production standards. These films, brought together under the rubric of "New Nollywood," are characterized by improved quality, transnational themes and characters, as well as theatrical release before DVD release. For a discussion of New Nollywood, see Connor Ryan, "New Nollywood: A Sketch of Nollywood's Metropolitan New Style," *African Studies Review* 58, no. 3 (2015): 59; Haynes, *Nollywood*, 285.

22 Jacob Smith, *Eco-Sonic Media* (Berkeley: University of California Press, 2015), 6.

23 Meintjes, "Hi-fi Sociality."

24 Tsitsi Ella Jaji, *Africa in Stereo: Modernism, Music, and Pan-African Solidarity* (Oxford: Oxford University Press, 2014), 18.

25 Harold Wilhite, "Energy Consumption as Cultural Practice: Implications for the Theory and Policy of Sustainable Energy Use," in *Cultures of Energy: Power, Practices, Technologies*, ed. Sarah Strauss, Stephanie Rupp, and Thomas Love (Walnut Creek, CA: Left Coast Press, 2013), 62.

26 For a discussion of social commitment in African film practice, see Aboubakar Sanogo, "Certain Tendencies in Contemporary Auteurist Film Practice in Africa," *Cinema Journal* 54, no. 2 (2015): 140–49. Akin Adesokan argues that this commitment, which often veers into didacticism, qualifies African films as instances of an "aesthetics of exhortation," characterized by a politics and pedagogy of morality. Akin Adesokan, *Postcolonial Artists and Global Aesthetics* (Bloomington: Indiana University Press, 2011), 81.

27 For an excellent exception, which also shares this book's engagement with African texts for a sophisticated, local articulation of universal ideas, see Jeanne-Marie Jackson, *The African Novel of Ideas: Philosophy and Individualism in the Age of Global Writing* (Princeton, NJ: Princeton University Press, 2021).

28 Wiredu, *Cultural Universals and Particulars*, 29.

bibliography

Filmography

Allouache, Merzak. *Harragas* (Algeria and France: Librisfilms/Baya Films, and France 2 Cinema, 2009), DVD, French and Arabic, 95 min.

Amata, Jeta. *Black Gold* (Nigeria: Jeta Amata Concepts, 2011), DVD, English, 120 min.

Bieleu, Franck. *What Hope for the African Youth* (France and Cameroon: Radio-Television de France Outre-Mer, 2008), TV, French and English, 71 min.

Bieleu, Franck. *The Big Banana* (United States: ArtMattan, 2011), DVD, French, 85 min.

Bieleu, Franck. *Herakles Debacle* (United States: Oakland Institute, 2012), You-Tube, English, 21 min.

Blomkamp, Neill. *District 9* (New Zealand, United States, and South Africa: QED International, WingNut Films, and TriStar Pictures, 2009), DVD, English, 112 min.

Brooks, Kate. *The Last Animals* (United States and the United Kingdom: Atlas Films, 2017), DVD, English, 92 min.

Coogler, Ryan. *Black Panther* (United States: Marvel Studios, 2018), DVD, English, 134 min.

Dahr, Julia. *Thank You for the Rain* (Norway: Differ Media, 2017), DVD, English, 87 min.

Djadam, Mostéfa. *Frontières* [Borders] (Algeria and France: Centre National du Cinéma et de l'Image Animée, 2002), DVD, French, 105 min.

Djebar, Assia. *La nouba des femmes du Mont-Chenoua* (United States: Women Make Movies, 1977), VHS, Arabic, 115 min.

Faye, Safi. *Kaddu Beykat* (Senegal: Safi, 1975), VHS, Serer and French, 98 min.

Francis, Marc, and Nick Francis. *When China Met Africa* (United Kingdom and France: Speakit Films, 2010), DVD, English, 75 min.

Greengrass, Paul. *Captain Phillips* (USA: Columbia Pictures, 2013), DVD, English and Somali, 134 min.

Jing, Wu. *Wolf Warrior* (China: Beijing Dengfeng International Culture Communications Company, and Spring Era Films Company, 2015), DVD, English and Mandarin, 90 min.

Jing, Wu. *Wolf Warrior 2* (China: Beijing Dengfeng International Culture Communications Company, and Spring Era Films Company, 2017), DVD, Mandarin, English, and French, 123 min.

Joubert, Dereck. *The Last Lions* (United States: National Geographic Films, 2011), DVD, English, 88 min.

Kahiu, Wanuri. *For Our Land* (South Africa: M-Net, 2009), DVD, English, 49 min.

Kahiu, Wanuri. *From a Whisper* (Kenya: Dada Productions, 2009), DVD, English, 79 min.

Kahiu, Wanuri. *Pumzi* (South Africa: Inspired Minority Productions, 2009), DVD, English, 21 min.

Kahiu, Wanuri. *Rafiki* (Kenya, South Africa, France, Netherlands, and Germany: Big World Cinema, Afrobubblegum Production, MPM Film, and Schortcut Films, 2018), DVD, English and Swahili, 83 min.

Kilani, Leïla. *Tanger, le rêve de brûleurs* [Tangiers, The Burners' Dream] (France: Institut National de l'Audiovisuel, 2002), DVD, French, 54 min.

Kura, George, et al. *Battleground* (Nigeria: Zuri 24 Media, 2016), TV, English, 260 episodes.

Llansó, Miguel. *Crumbs* (Spain, Ethiopia, and Finland: Lanzadera Films and Bira-Biro Films, 2015), DVD, Amharic, 68 min.

Mora-Kpai, Idrissou. *America Street* (United States: Wave Farm, 2019), www.cinemapolis.org, English, 74 min.

Mora-Kpai, Idrissou. *Arlit: deuxième Paris* (United States: California Newsreel, 2004), DVD, French, Bariba, Hausa, and Tamashek, 75 min.

Mora-Kpai, Idrissou. *Indochina: Traces of a Mother* (France and Benin: MKJ Films and Noble Films, 2011), DVD, French, 71 min.

Odugbemi, Femi. *Bariga Boy* (Nigeria: Dvworx Studios, 2010), DVD, English, 28 min.

Odugbemi, Femi. *Makoko: Futures Afloat* (Nigeria: Zuri 24 Media, 2016), DVD, English, 30 min.

Ogun, Tope, et al. *Tinsel* (Nigeria: DSTV, 2008), TV, English, 2992 episodes.

Saro-Wiwa, Zina. "*Sarogua Mourning.*" Video installation. 2011.

Schwarz, Shaul. *Narco Cultura* (United States: Cinedigm, 2013), DVD, English and Spanish, 103 min.

Schwarz, Shaul, and Christina Clusiau. *Trophy* (United States: CNN Film, 2017), TV, English, 110 min.

Scott, Susan. *Stroop: Journey into the Rhino Horn War* (South Africa: SDB Films, 2018), DVD, English, 134 min.

Sembene, Ousmane. *Mandabi* (France and Senegal: Comptoir Français du Film Production (CFFP) and Filmi Domirev, 1968), VHS, French and Wolof, 90 min.

Sembene, Ousmane. *Xala* (Senegal: Filmi Domirev and Société Nationale Cinématographique, 1975), VHS, French and Wolof, 123 min.

Von Einsiedel, Orlando. *Lost and Found* (UK: Grain Media, 2019), TV, Bengali and Burmese, 22 min.

Von Einsiedel, Orlando. *The White Helmets* (UK: Grain Media, 2016), Netflix, Arabic and English, 41 min.

Von Einsiedel, Orlando. *Virunga* (UK: Grain Media, 2014), Netflix, English, French, and Swahili, 100 min.

Young, Bruce, and Nick Chevallier. *Blood Lions* (South Africa: Regulus Vision and Wildlands, 2015), DVD, English, 84 min.

Other Works

Abiodun, Rowland. "Ako-graphy: Owo Portraits." In *Portraiture and Photography in Africa*, edited by John Peffer and Elisabeth L. Cameron, 341–62. Bloomington: Indiana University Press, 2013.

Acheampong, Emmanuel. *Drink, Power, and Cultural Change: A Social History of Alcohol in Ghana, c. 1800 to Recent Times*. Portsmouth, NH: Heinemann, 1996.

Adams, Carol J. *The Sexual Politics of Meat: A Feminist-Vegetarian Critical Theory*. New York: Continuum, 1990.

Adamson, Joni. "We Have Never Been Anthropos: From Environmental Justice to Cosmopolitics." In *Environmental Humanities: Voices from the Anthropocene*, edited by Serpil Oppermann and Serenella Iovino, 155–73. Lanham, MD: Rowman and Littlefield, 2017.

Adéèkó, Adélékè. *Arts of Being Yoruba: Divination, Allegory, Tragedy, Proverb, Panegyric*. Bloomington: Indiana University Press, 2017.

Adejunmobi, Moradewun. "African Media Studies and Marginality at the Center." *Black Camera* 7, no. 2 (2016): 125–39.

Adejunmobi, Moradewun. "Introduction: African Science Fiction." *Cambridge Journal of Postcolonial Literary Inquiry* 3, no. 3 (2016): 265–72.

Adesokan, Akin. *Postcolonial Artists and Global Aesthetics*. Bloomington: Indiana University Press, 2011.

Adomako Ampofo, Akosua. "Re-Viewing Studies on Africa, #Black Lives Matter, and Envisioning the Future of African Studies." *African Studies Review* 59, no. 2 (2016): 7–29.

Adunbi, Omolade. *Oil Wealth and Insurgency in Nigeria*. Bloomington: Indiana University Press, 2015.

Aghoghovwia, Philip. "Nigeria." In *Fueling Culture: 101 Words for Energy and Environment*, edited by Imre Szeman, Jennifer Wenzel, and Patricia Yaeger, 238–41. New York: Fordham University Press, 2017.

Agrawal, Arun. *Environmentality: Technologies of Government and the Making of Subjects*. Durham, NC: Duke University Press, 2005.

Ahmed, Sara. "Happy Objects." In *The Affect Theory Reader*, edited by Melissa Gregg and Gregory J. Seigworth, 29–51. Durham, NC: Duke University Press, 2010.

Aidoo, Ama Ata. "For Whom Things Did Not Change." In *No Sweetness Here and Other Stories*, 8–29. New York: Feminist Press, 1970.

Alaimo, Stacy. *Bodily Natures: Science, Environment, and the Material Self*. Bloomington: Indiana University Press, 2010.

Alexander, Jeffrey C. *Trauma: A Social Theory*. Cambridge: Polity Press, 2012.

Allara, Pamela. "Zwelethu Mthethwa's 'Postdocumentary' Portraiture: Views from South Africa and Abroad." In *A Companion to Modern African Art*, edited by Gitti Salami and Monica Blackmun Visoná, 469–88. Chichester, UK: Wiley-Blackwell, 2013.

Amin, Ash, and Nigel Thrift. *Arts of the Political: New Openings for the Left*. Durham, NC: Duke University Press, 2013.

Amin, Ash, and Nigel Thrift. *Cities: Reimagining the Urban*. Cambridge: Polity Press, 2002.

Anand, Nikhil, Akhil Gupta, and Hannah Appel, eds. *The Promise of Infrastructure*. Durham, NC: Duke University Press, 2018.

Andrejevic, Mark. "Estranged Free Labor." In *Digital Labor: The Internet as Playground and Factory*, edited by Trebor Scholz, 149–64. New York: Routledge, 2013.

Angelucci, Federica. "Foreword." In *Permanent Error*, by Pieter Hugo, 9–10. Munich: Prestel Verlag, 2011.

Appadurai, Arjun. *Modernity at Large: Cultural Dimensions of Globalization*. Minneapolis: University of Minnesota Press, 1996.

Appiah, Kwame Anthony. *Cosmopolitanism: Ethics in a World of Strangers*. New York: Norton, 2006.

Apter, Andrew. *The Pan-African Nation: Oil and the Spectacle of Culture in Nigeria*. Chicago: University of Chicago Press, 2005.

Aravamudan, Srinivas. "The Catachronism of Climate Change." *Diacritics* 41, no. 3 (2013): 6–30.

Armes, Roy. *African Filmmaking: North and South of the Sahara*. Bloomington: Indiana University Press, 2006.

Armillas-Tiseyra, Magalí. "Afronauts: On Science Fiction and the Crisis of Possibility." *Cambridge Journal of Postcolonial Literary Inquiry* 3, no. 3 (2016): 273–90.

Azoulay, Ariella. *The Civil Contract of Photography*. New York: Zone Books, 2008.

Bal, Mieke. "Introduction." In *Acts of Memory: Cultural Recall in the Present*, edited by Mieke Bal, Jonathan V. Crewe, and Leo Spitzer, vii–xvii. Hanover, NH: University Press of New England, 1999.

Bales, Kevin. *Blood and Earth: Modern Slavery, Ecocide, and the Secret to Saving the World*. New York: Spiegel and Grau, 2016.

Barlet, Olivier. *Decolonizing the Gaze*. London: Zed Books, 2000.

Barrett, Ross, and Daniel Worden. "Introduction." In *Oil Culture*, edited by Ross Barrett and Daniel Worden, xvii–xxxiv. Minneapolis: University of Minnesota Press, 2014.

Barthes, Roland. *Camera Lucida: Reflections on Photography*. Translated by Richard Howard. New York: Hill and Wang, 1981.

Bassey, Nnimmo. "Oil Fever." In *Curse of the Black Gold*, edited by Michael Watts, 90–91. Brooklyn, NY: powerHouse, 2008.

Batchelor, Kathryn, and Xiaoling Zhang, eds. *China-Africa Relations: Building Images through Cultural Cooperation, Media Representation and Communication*. London: Routledge, 2017.

Batchelor, Kathryn, and Xiaoling Zhang. "Introduction: Images, Nation Branding, and News Framing." In *China-Africa Relations: Building Images through Cultural Cooperation, Media Representation and Communication*, edited by Kathryn Batchelor and Xiaoling Zhang, 3–15. London: Routledge, 2017.

Baucom, Ian. "History 4°: Postcolonial Method and Anthropocene Time." *Cambridge Journal of Postcolonial Literary Inquiry* 1, no. 1 (2014): 123–42.

Bayart, Jean-François. *The State in Africa: The Politics of the Belly*. Cambridge: Polity Press, 2009.

Bayat, Asef. "Un-Civil Society: The Politics of the 'Informal People.'" *Third World Quarterly* 18, no. 1 (1997): 53–72.

Beinart, William. *The Rise of Conservation in South Africa: Settlers, Livestock, and the Environment, 1770–1950*. Oxford: Oxford University Press, 2003.

Bell, Clare. "Introduction." In *In/Sight: African Photographers, 1940 to the Present*, edited by Clare Bell, Okwui Enwezor, Olu Oguibe, and Octavio Zaya, 9–16. New York: Guggenheim Museum, 1996.

Benjamin, Walter. *On Photography*. Translated by Esther Leslie. London: Reaktion Books, 2015.

Benkler, Yochai. *The Wealth of Networks: How Social Production Transforms Markets and Freedom*. New Haven, CT: Yale University Press, 2006.

Bennett, Jane. *Vibrant Matter: A Political Ecology of Things*. Durham, NC: Duke University Press, 2010.

Berger, John. *About Looking*. New York: Pantheon Books, 1980.

Berger, John. *Ways of Seeing*. London: British Broadcasting Corporation and Penguin Books, 1972.

Berlant, Lauren. "Cruel Optimism." In *The Affect Theory Reader*, edited by Melissa Gregg and Gregory J. Seigworth, 93–117. Durham, NC: Duke University Press, 2010.

Best, Stephen, and Sharon Marcus. "Surface Reading: An Introduction." *Representations* 108, no. 1 (2009): 1–21.

Beus, Yifen. "Authorship and Criticism in Self-Reflexive African Cinema." *Journal of African Cultural Studies* 23, no. 2 (2011): 133–52.

Beverungen, Armin, Steffen Böhm, and Chris Land, "Free Labour, Social Media, Management: Challenging Marxist Organization Studies." *Organization Studies* 36, no. 4 (2015): 473–89.

Bhabha, Homi. "Looking Back, Moving Forward: Notes on Vernacular Cosmo-politanism." In *The Location of Culture*, ix–xxv. London: Routledge, 2012.

Binder, Lisa, ed. *El Anatsui: When I Last Wrote to You About Africa*. New York: Museum for African Art, 2010.

Bisschoff, Lizelle, and Stefanie Van de Peer. "Representing the Unrepresentable." In *Art and Trauma in Africa: Representations of Reconciliation in Music, Visual Arts, Literature and Film*, edited by Lizelle Bisschoff and Stefanie Van de Peer, 3–25. London: I. B. Taurus, 2013.

Bloch, Ernst. *The Principle of Hope*, vol. 1. Translated by Neville Plaice, Stephen Plaice, and Paul Knight. Cambridge, MA: MIT Press, 1986.

Blum, Hester. *The News at the Ends of the Earth: The Print Culture of Polar Exploration*. Durham, NC: Duke University Press, 2019.

Bodomo, Adams. *Africans in China: A Sociocultural Study and its Implications on Africa-China Relations*. Amherst, NY: Cambria Press, 2012.

Boisseron, Bénédicte. *Afro-Dog: Blackness and the Animal Question*. New York: Columbia University Press, 2018.

Bolter, Jay David, and Richard Grusin. *Remediation: Understanding New Media*. Cambridge, MA: MIT Press, 1999.

Bond, Jennifer, and Kennedy Mkutu. "Exploring the Hidden Costs of Human-Wildlife Conflict in Northern Kenya." *African Studies Review* 61, no. 1 (2018): 33–54.

Bould, Mark. *Science Fiction*. New York: Routledge, 2012.

Bourdieu, Pierre. *The Field of Cultural Production: Essays on Art and Literature*. New York: Columbia University Press, 1993.

Bousé, Derek. "False Intimacy: Close-Ups and Viewer Involvement in Wildlife Films." *Visual Studies* 18, no. 2 (2003): 123–32.

Boyer, Dominic. "Infrastructure, Potential Energy, Revolution." In *The Promise of Infrastructure*, edited by Nikhil Anand, Akhil Gupta, and Hannah Appel, 233–44. Durham, NC: Duke University Press, 2018.

Bozak, Nadia. *The Cinematic Footprint: Lights, Camera, Natural Resources*. New Brunswick, NJ: Rutgers University Press, 2012.

Brautigam, Deborah. *The Dragon's Gift: The Real Story of China in Africa*. Oxford: Oxford University Press, 2009.

Brereton, Pat. *Environmental Ethics and Film*. Oxford: Routledge, 2016.

Brereton, Pat. *Hollywood Utopia: Ecology in Contemporary American Cinema*. Bristol, UK: Intellect Books, 2005.

Brockington, Dan. *Celebrity and the Environment: Fame, Wealth and Power in Conservation*. London: Zed Books, 2009.

Brown, Adrienne. *The Black Skyscraper: Architecture and the Perception of Race*. Baltimore: Johns Hopkins University Press, 2017.

Brown, Bill. *Other Things*. Chicago: University of Chicago Press, 2015.

Bryant, Levi R. "Black." In *Prismatic Ecology: Ecotheory beyond Green*, edited by Jeffrey Jerome Cohen, 290–310. Minneapolis: University of Minnesota Press, 2013.

Buck-Morss, Susan. *Dreamworld and Catastrophe: The Passing of Mass Utopia in East and West*. Cambridge, MA: MIT Press, 2000.

Budolfson, Mark. "Food, the Environment, and Global Justice." In *The Oxford Handbook of Food Ethics*, edited by Anne Barnhill, Mark Budolfson, and Tyler Doggett, 67–94. Oxford: Oxford University Press, 2018.

Buell, Lawrence. "Toxic Discourse." *Critical Inquiry* 24, no. 3 (1998): 639–65.

Burrell, Jenna. *Invisible Users: Youth in the Internet Cafes of Urban Ghana*. Cambridge, MA: MIT Press, 2012.

Busia, Abena P. A. "Silencing Sycorax: On African Colonial Discourse and the Unvoiced Female." *Cultural Critique* 14 (1989/1990): 81–104.

Butler, Judith. *Precarious Life: The Powers of Mourning and Violence*. London: Verso Books, 2006.

Bystrom, Kerry, and Isabel Hofmeyr. "Oceanic Routes: (Post-It) Notes on Hydro-Colonialism." *Comparative Literature* 69, no. 1 (2017): 1–6.

Cabral, M., D. Dieme, A. Verdin, G. Garçon, M. Fall, S. Boushina, D. Dewalee, et al. "Low-level Environmental Exposure to Lead and Renal Adverse Effects: A Cross-Sectional Study in the Population of Children Bordering the Mbeubeuss Landfill near Dakar, Senegal." *Human and Experimental Toxicology* 31, no. 12 (2012): 1280–91.

Calarco, Matthew. *Zoographies: The Question of the Animal from Heidegger to Derrida*. New York: Columbia University Press, 2008.

Caminero-Santangelo, Byron. *Different Shades of Green: African Literature, Environmental Justice, and Political Ecology*. Charlottesville: University of Virginia Press, 2014.

Campt, Tina. *Listening to Images*. Durham, NC: Duke University Press, 2017.

Cao, Qing. "Chinese Developmentalism and Television Representation of South Africa." In *China-Africa Relations: Building Images through Cultural Cooperation, Media Representation and Communication*, edited by Kathryn Batchelor and Xiaoling Zhang, 199–217. London: Routledge, 2017.

Carby, Hazel. "US/UK's Special Relationship: The Culture of Torture in Abu Ghraib and Lynching Photographs." *Nka: Journal of Contemporary African Art* 20 (2006): 60–71.

Carpenter, Stefan, and David M. Konisky. "The Killing of Cecil the Lion as an Impetus for Policy Change." *Oryx* 53, no. 4 (2019): 698–706.

Carruthers, Jane. *The Kruger National Park: A Social and Political History*. Pietermaritzburg: University of Natal Press, 1995.

Caruth, Cathy. *Unclaimed Experience: Trauma, Narrative, History*. Baltimore: Johns Hopkins University Press, 1996.

Castells, Manuel. *The Rise of the Network Society*. Malden, MA: Wiley-Blackwell, 2010.

Césaire, Aimé. *Discourse on Colonialism*. Translated by Joan Pinkham. New York: Monthly Review Press, 1972.

Chakrabarty, Dipesh. "The Climate of History: Four Theses." *Critical Inquiry* 35, no. 2 (2009): 197–222.

Chalfin, Brenda. "Public Things, Excremental Politics, and the Infrastructure of Bare Life in Ghana's City of Tema." *American Ethnologist* 41, no. 1 (2014): 92–109.

Checker, Melissa, Gary McDonogh, and Cindy Isenhour. "Introduction: Urban Sustainability as Myth and Practice." In *Sustainability in the Global City: Myth and Practice*, edited by Cindy Isenhour, Gary McDonogh, and Melissa Checker, 1–25. New York: Cambridge University Press, 2015.

Cheney-Lippold, John. *We Are Data: Algorithms and the Making of Our Digital Selves*. New York: New York University Press, 2017.

Chun, Wendy Hui Kyong. "Introduction: Race and/as Technology; or, How to Do Things to Race." *Camera Obscura* 24, no. 1 (2009): 7–35.

Cohen, Jeffrey Jerome, and Julian Yates. "Ark Thinking." In *Ecologies, Agents, Terrains*, edited by Christopher P. Heuer and Rebecca Zorach, 243–65. Williamstown, MA: Clark Arts Institute, 2018.

Cole, Teju. *Blind Spot*. New York: Random House, 2016.

Cole, Teju. *Known and Strange Things*. New York: Random House, 2016.

Comaroff, Jean, and John L. Comaroff. *Theory from the South: Or, How Euro-America is Evolving toward Africa*. London: Routledge, 2012.

Cooper, Frederick. "What Is the Concept of Globalization Good For? An African Historian's Perspective." *African Affairs* 100, no. 399 (2001): 189–213.

Cooper, Melinda. *Family Values: Between Neoliberalism and the New Social Conservatism*. New York: Zone Books, 2017.

Coronil, Fernando. *The Magical State: Nature, Money, and Modernity in Venezuela*. Chicago: University of Chicago Press, 1997.

Cottle, Simon. "Producing Nature(s): On the Changing Production Ecology of Natural History TV," *Media, Culture and Society* 26, no. 1 (2004): 81–101.

Craps, Stef. *Postcolonial Witnessing: Trauma Out of Bounds*. New York: Palgrave Macmillan, 2013.

Crary, Jonathan. *Suspensions of Perception: Attention, Spectacle, and Modern Culture*. Cambridge, MA: MIT Press, 1999.

Cubitt, Sean. *EcoMedia*. Amsterdam: Rodopi, 2005.

Cubitt, Sean. *Finite Media: Environmental Implications of Digital Technologies*. Durham, NC: Duke University Press, 2017.

Curtin, Deane. *Environmental Ethics for a Postcolonial World*. Lanham, MD: Rowman and Littlefield, 2005.

Davis, Mike. *Planet of Slums*. London: Verso Books, 2006.

Dawson, Ashley. *Extreme Cities: The Peril and Promise of Urban Life in the Age of Climate Change*. New York: Verso Books, 2017.

De Boeck, Filip. *Kinshasa: Tales of the Invisible City*. Photographs by Marie-Françoise Plissart. Leuven, Belgium: Ludion, 2004.

Debord, Guy. *The Society of the Spectacle*. Translated by Ken Knabb. Berkeley, CA: Bureau of Public Secrets, 2014.

De Certeau, Michel. *The Practice of Everyday Life*. Translated by Steven F. Rendall. Berkeley: University of California Press, 1984.

De la Cadena, Marisol. "Indigenous Cosmopolitics in the Andes: Conceptual Reflections Beyond 'Politics.'" *Cultural Anthropology* 25, no. 2 (2010): 334–70.

Deleuze, Gilles, and Félix Guattari. *A Thousand Plateaus: Capitalism and Schizophrenia*. Translated by Brian Massumi. Minneapolis: University of Minnesota Press, 1987.

DeLoughrey, Elizabeth. *Allegories of the Anthropocene*. Durham, NC: Duke University Press, 2019.

DeLoughrey, Elizabeth. "Submarine Futures of the Anthropocene." *Comparative Literature* 69, no. 1 (2017): 32–44.

DeLoughrey, Elizabeth, and George Handley, eds. *Postcolonial Ecologies: Literatures of the Environment*. New York: Oxford University Press, 2011.

DeLuca, Kevin Michael. *Image Politics: The New Rhetoric of Environmental Activism*. New York: Guilford Press, 1999.

Demos, T. J. *Return to the Postcolony: Specters of Colonialism in Contemporary Art*. Berlin: Sternberg Press, 2013.

Derrida, Jacques. "The Animal That Therefore I Am (More to Follow)." Translated by David Wills. *Critical Inquiry* 28, no. 2 (2002): 369–418.

Derrida, Jacques, and Giovanna Borradori. "Autoimmunity: Real and Symbolic Suicides—A Dialogue with Jacques Derrida." In *Philosophy in a Time of Terror: Dialogues with Jurgen Habermas and Jacques Derrida*, edited by Giovanna Borradori, 85–136. Chicago: University of Chicago Press, 2003.

Dery, Mark. "Black to the Future: Interviews with Samuel R. Delany, Greg Tate, and Tricia Rose." *South Atlantic Quarterly* 92, no. 4 (1993): 735–78.

Diagne, Souleymane Bachir. *African Art as Philosophy: Senghor, Bergson and the Idea of Négritude*. Translated by Chike Jeffers. Calcutta: Seagull Books, 2011.

Diala, Isidore. "Nigeria and the Poetry of Travails: The Niger Delta in the Poetry of Uche Umez." *Matatu* 33 (2006): 317–25.

Diawara, Manthia. *African Cinema: Politics and Culture*. Bloomington: Indiana University Press, 1992.

Diawara, Manthia. *African Film: New Forms of Aesthetics and Politics*. Munich: Prestel, 2010.

Didi-Huberman, Georges. *Images in Spite of All: Four Photographs from Auschwitz*. Chicago: University of Chicago Press, 2008.

Diouf, Mamadou. "Wall Paintings and the Writing of History: Set/Setal in Dakar." *Gefame: Journal of African Studies* 2, no. 1 (2005).

Dowie, Mark. *Conservation Refugees: The Hundred-Year Conflict between Global Conservation and Native Peoples*. Cambridge, MA: MIT Press, 2009.

Drewal, Henry John. "Local Transformations, Global Inspirations: The Visual Histories and Cultures of Mami Wata Arts in Africa." In *A Companion to Modern African Art*, edited by Gitti Salami and Monica Blackmun Visonà, 23–49. Malden, MA: Wiley, 2013.

Duffy, Rosaleen. "Waging a War to Save Biodiversity: The Rise of Militarized Conservation." *International Affairs* 90, no. 4 (2014): 819–34.

Dunaway, Finis. *Seeing Green: The Use and Abuse of American Environmental Images*. Chicago: University of Chicago Press, 2015.

Eco, Umberto. *Travels in Hyperreality*. Translated by William Weaver. San Diego: Harcourt Brace Jovanovich, 1986.

Egya, Sule. "Nature, Animism and Humanity in Anglophone Nigerian Poetry." In *Natures of Africa: Ecocriticism and Animal Studies in Contemporary Cultural Forms*, edited by F. Fiona Moolla, 257–75. Johannesburg: Wits University Press, 2016.

Elkins, James. *What Photography Is*. New York: Routledge, 2011.

Enwezor, Okwui. "Modernity and Postcolonial Ambivalence." *South Atlantic Quarterly* 109, no. 3 (2010): 595–620.

Enwezor, Okwui, and Octavio Zaya. "Colonial Imaginary, Tropes of Disruption: History, Culture, and Representation in the Works of African Photographers." In *In/Sight: African Photographers, 1940 to the Present*, edited by Clare Bell, Okwui Enwezor, Olu Oguibe, and Octavio Zaya, 17–47. New York: Guggenheim Museum, 1996.

Eshun, Kodwo. "Further Considerations on Afrofuturism." *CR: The New Centennial Review* 3, no. 2 (2003): 287–302.

Eze, Chielozona. *Race, Decolonization, and Global Citizenship in South Africa*. Rochester, NY: University of Rochester Press, 2018.

Fanon, Frantz. *The Wretched of the Earth*. Translated by Richard Philcox. New York: Grove Press, 1963.

Fast, Karin, Henrik Örnebring, and Michael Karlsson. "Metaphors of Free Labor: A Typology of Unpaid Work in the Media Sector." *Media, Culture and Society* 38, no. 7 (2016): 963–78.

Fay, Jennifer. *Inhospitable World: Cinema in the Time of the Anthropocene*. Oxford: Oxford University Press, 2018.

Feld, Steven. *Sound and Sentiment: Birds, Weeping, Poetics, and Song in Kaluli Expression*, 3rd ed. Durham, NC: Duke University Press, 2012.

Felman, Shoshana, and Dori Laub. *Testimony: Crises of Witnessing in Literature, Psychoanalysis, and History*. New York: Routledge, 1992.

Ferguson, James. *Global Shadows: Africa in the Neoliberal World Order*. Durham, NC: Duke University Press, 2006.

Ferguson, Niall. *The Square and the Tower: Networks and Power, from the Freemasons to Facebook*. New York: Penguin, 2017.

Forns-Broggi, Roberto. "Ecocinema and 'Good Life' in Latin America." In *Transnational Ecocinema: Film Culture in an Era of Ecological Transformation*, edited by Pietari Kääpä and Tommy Gustafsson, 85–100. Bristol, UK: Intellect, 2013.

Fox, Graham R. "The 2017 Shooting of Kuki Gallmann and the Politics of Conservation in Northern Kenya." *African Studies Review* 61, no. 2 (2018): 210–36.

Frazier, Chelsea Mikael. "Thinking Red, Wounds, and Fungi in Wangechi Mutu's Eco-Art." In *Ecologies, Agents, Terrains*, edited by Christopher P. Heuer and Rebecca Zorach, 167–94. Williamstown, MA: Clark Arts Institute, 2018.

Fredericks, Rosalind. *Garbage Citizenship: Vital Infrastructures of Labor in Dakar, Senegal*. Durham, NC: Duke University Press, 2018.

French, Howard W. *China's Second Continent: How a Million Migrants Are Building a New Empire in Africa*. New York: Knopf, 2014.

Freud, Sigmund. *Moses and Monotheism*. Translated by Katherine Jones. New York: Vintage Books, 1939.

Freund, Bill. *The African City: A History*. Cambridge: Cambridge University Press, 2007.

Fried, Michael. "Art and Objecthood." *Artforum* 5, no. 10 (1967). https://www.art forum.com/print/196706/art-and-objecthood-36708.

Fried, Michael. *Why Photography Matters as Art as Never Before*. New Haven, CT: Yale University Press, 2008.

Gabara, Rachel. "War by Documentary." *Romance Notes* 55, no. 3 (2015): 409–23.

Galloway, Alexander R., and Eugene Thacker. *The Exploit: A Theory of Networks*. Minneapolis: University of Minnesota Press, 2007.

García Espinosa, Julio. "For an Imperfect Cinema." Translated by Julianne Burton. *Jump Cut* 20 (1979): 24–26.

García Espinosa, Julio. "Meditations on Imperfect Cinema . . . Fifteen Years Later." *Screen* 26, nos. 3/4 (1985): 93–94.

Garritano, Carmela. *African Video Movies and Global Desires: A Ghanaian History*. Athens: Ohio University Press, 2013.

Garritano, Carmela. "Waiting on the Past: African Uranium Futures in *Arlit, Deuxième Paris*." *Modern Fiction Studies* 66, no. 1 (2020): 122–40.

Garuba, Harry. "Explorations in Animist Materialism: Notes on Reading/Writing African Literature, Culture, and Society." *Public Culture* 15, no. 2 (2003): 261–85.

Gatlin, Jill. "Toxic Sublimity and the Crisis of Human Perception: Rethinking Aesthetic, Documentary, and Political Appeals in Contemporary Wasteland Photography." *Interdisciplinary Studies in Literature and Environment* 22, no. 4 (2015): 717–41.

Geary, Christraud M. "Roots and Routes of African Photographic Practices from Modern to Vernacular Photography in West and Central Africa (1850–1980)." In *A Companion to Modern African Art*, edited by Gitti Salami and Monica Blackmun Visonà, 74–95. Malden, MA: Wiley, 2013.

Gerhardt, Christine. "The Greening of African-American Landscapes: Where Ecocriticism Meets Post-Colonial Theory." *Mississippi Quarterly* 55, no. 4 (2002): 515–33.

Gikandi, Simon. "Globalization and the Claims of Postcoloniality." *South Atlantic Quarterly* 100, no. 3 (2001): 627–58.

Gilroy, Paul. *Between Camps: Nations, Cultures, and the Allure of Race*. London: Routledge, 2004.

Gilroy, Paul. *Postcolonial Melancholia*. New York: Columbia University Press, 2005.

Gitelman, Lisa. *Always Already New: Media, History, and the Data of Culture*. Cambridge, MA: MIT Press, 2006.

Gómez-Barris, Macarena, *The Extractive Zone: Social Ecologies and Decolonial Perspectives*. Durham, NC: Duke University Press, 2017.

Goodman, Nelson. *Ways of Worldmaking*. Indianapolis: Hackett, 1978.

Gordon, Lewis R. *Her Majesty's Other Children: Sketches of Racism from a Neocolonial Age*. Lanham, MD: Rowman and Littlefield, 1997.

Grabski, Joanna. *Art World City: The Creative Economy of Artists and Urban Life in Dakar*. Bloomington: Indiana University Press, 2017.

Grabski, Joanna. "The Ecole des Arts and Exhibitionary Platforms in Postindependence Senegal." In *A Companion to Modern African Art*, edited by Gitti Salami and Monica Blackmun Visonà, 276–93. Malden, MA: Wiley, 2013.

Graham, Stephen, and Simon Marvin. *Splintering Urbanism: Networked Infrastructures, Technological Mobilities and the Urban Condition*. London: Routledge, 2001.

Greenpeace. *Left in the Dust: AREVA's Radioactive Legacy in the Desert Towns of Niger*. Amsterdam: Greenpeace, 2010. https://www.greenpeace.org/archive -international/Global/international/publications/nuclear/2010/AREVA _Niger_report.pdf.

Green-Simms, Lindsey B. *Postcolonial Automobility: Car Culture in West Africa*. Minneapolis: University of Minnesota Press, 2017.

Grierson, John. "First Principles of Documentary." In *The Documentary Film Reader: History, Theory, Criticism*, edited by Jonathan Kahana, 217–25. Oxford: Oxford University Press, 2016.

Gries, Laurie E. *Still Life with Rhetoric: A New Materialist Approach for Visual Rhetorics*. Logan: Utah State University Press, 2015.

Gunning, Tom. "The Long and Short of It: Centuries of Projecting Shadows, from Natural Magic to the Avant-Garde." In *Art of Projection*, edited by Stan Douglas and Christopher Eamon, 23–35. Ostfildern: Hatje Cantz, 2009.

Gunning, Tom. "To Scan a Ghost: The Ontology of Mediated Vision." *Grey Room* 26 (2007): 94–127.

Hall, Stuart. "Introduction to Part 3." In *Visual Culture: The Reader*, edited by Jessica Evans and Stuart Hall, 309–14. London: SAGE, 1999.

Hall, Stuart. "The Spectacle of the Other." In *Representation: Cultural Representations and Signifying Practices*, edited by Stuart Hall, 223–90. London: SAGE, 1997.

Hammond-Tooke, W. D. "The Symbolic Structure of Cape Nguni Cosmology." In *Religion and Social Change in Southern Africa: Anthropological Essays in Honour of Monica Wilson*, edited by Michael G. Whisson and Martin West, 15–33. Cape Town: David Phillip, 1975.

Haney, Erin. "Lutterodt Family Studios and the Changing Face of Early Portrait Photographs from the Gold Coast." In *Portraiture and Photography in Africa*, edited by John Peffer and Elisabeth L. Cameron, 67–101. Bloomington: Indiana University Press, 2013.

Haney, Erin. *Photography and Africa*. London: Reaktion Books, 2010.

Haraway, Donna. *Staying with the Trouble: Making Kin in the Chthulucene*. Durham, NC: Duke University Press, 2016.

Hariman, Robert, and John Louis Lucaites. *No Caption Needed: Iconic Photographs, Public Culture, and Liberal Democracy*. Chicago: University of Chicago Press, 2007.

Harris, Anne. "Pyromena Fire's Doing." In *Elemental Ecocriticism: Thinking with Earth, Air, Water, and Fire*, edited by Jeffrey Jerome Cohen and Lowell Duckert, 27–54. Minneapolis: University of Minnesota Press, 2015.

Harrow, Kenneth W. *Trash: African Cinema from Below*. Bloomington: Indiana University Press, 2013.

Hartman, Saidiya V. *Lose Your Mother: A Journey along the Atlantic Slave Route*. New York: Farrar, Straus, and Giroux, 2007.

Hartman, Saidiya V. *Scenes of Subjection: Terror, Slavery, and Self-Making in Nineteenth-Century America*. Oxford: Oxford University Press, 1997.

Harvey, David. *The Condition of Postmodernity*. Cambridge, MA: Blackwell, 2000.

Harvey, David. "The Right to the City." *New Left Review* 53 (2008): 23–40.

Haynes, Jonathan. *Nollywood: The Creation of Nigerian Film Genres*. Chicago: University of Chicago Press, 2016.

Haynes, Jonathan, and Onookome Okome. "Evolving Popular Media: Nigerian Video Films." In *Nigerian Video Films*, edited by Jonathan Haynes, 51–88. Athens: Ohio University Press, 2000.

Hecht, Gabrielle. *Being Nuclear: Africans and the Global Uranium Trade*. Cambridge, MA: MIT Press, 2012.

Heidegger, Martin. "Building Dwelling Thinking." In *Basic Writings*, edited by David Farrell Krell, 347–63. New York: HarperCollins, 1993.

Heidegger, Martin. *What Is a Thing?* Translated by W. B. Barton Jr. and Vera Deutsch. Chicago: Henry Regnery, 1967.

Heise, Ursula. *Imagining Extinction: The Cultural Meanings of Endangered Species*. Chicago: University of Chicago Press, 2016.

Heise, Ursula. *Sense of Place and Sense of Planet: The Environmental Imagination of the Global*. Oxford: Oxford University Press, 2008.

Helmreich, Stefan. "Nature/Culture/Seawater: Theory Machines, Anthropology, Oceanization." In *Environmental Humanities: Voices from the Anthropocene*, edited by Serpil Oppermann and Serenella Iovino, 217–36. London: Rowman and Littlefield, 2017.

Hern, Matt. *What a City Is For: Remaking the Politics of Displacement*. Cambridge, MA: MIT Press, 2016.

Higgins, MaryEllen. "The Winds of African Cinema." *African Studies Review* 58, no. 3 (2015): 77–92.

Hitchcock, Peter. "Risking the Griot's Eye: Decolonisation and Contemporary African Cinema." *Social Identities* 6, no. 3 (2000): 263–84.

Hochleithner, Stephan. "Beyond Contesting Limits: Land, Access, and Resistance at the Virunga National Park." *Conservation and Society* 15, no. 1 (2017): 100–110.

Huggan, Graham. *The Postcolonial Exotic: Marketing the Margins*. London: Routledge, 2001.

Huggan, Graham, and Helen Tiffin. *Postcolonial Ecocriticism: Literature, Animals, Environment*. London: Routledge, 2010.

Hugo, Pieter. *La cucaracha*. Barcelona: RM, 2019.

Hugo, Pieter. *Nollywood*. Munich: Prestel Verlag, 2009.

Hugo, Pieter. *Permanent Error*. Munich: Prestel Verlag, 2011.

Hunt, Nancy Rose. "An Acoustic Register: Rape and Repetition in Congo." In *Imperial Debris: On Ruins and Ruination*, edited by Ann Laura Stoler, 39–66. Durham, NC: Duke University Press, 2013.

Hunt, Nancy Rose. *A Nervous State: Violence, Remedies, and Reverie in Colonial Congo*. Durham, NC: Duke University Press, 2016.

Huyssen, Andreas. "Introduction: World Cultures, World Cities." In *Other Cities, Other Worlds: Urban Imaginaries in a Globalizing Age*, edited by Andreas Huyssen, 1–23. Durham, NC: Duke University Press, 2008.

Iheka, Cajetan. *Naturalizing Africa: Ecological Violence, Agency, and Postcolonial Resistance in African Literature*. Cambridge: Cambridge University Press, 2018.

Ingram, David. "The Aesthetics and Ethics of Eco-Film Criticism." In *Ecocinema Theory and Practice*, edited by Stephen Rust, Salma Monani, and Sean Cubitt, 43–62. New York: Routledge, 2012.

Ingram, David. *Green Screen: Environmentalism and Hollywood Cinema*. Exeter, UK: University of Exeter Press, 2000.

Iqani, Mehita. *Consumption, Media and the Global South: Aspiration Contested*. London: Palgrave Macmillan, 2016.

Irele, Abiola. "A Defence of Negritude." *Transition* 13 (1964): 9–11.

Ivakhiv, Adrian J. *Ecologies of the Moving Image: Cinema, Affect, Nature*. Waterloo, ON: Wilfrid Laurier University Press, 2013.

Jackson, Cassandra. *Violence, Visual Culture, and the Black Male Body*. London: Routledge, 2011.

Jackson, Jeanne-Marie. *The African Novel of Ideas: Philosophy and Individualism in the Age of Global Writing*. Princeton, NJ: Princeton University Press, 2021.

Jacobs, Lynn F. "Rubens and the Northern Past: The Michielsen Triptych and the Thresholds of Modernity." *Art Bulletin* 91, no. 3 (2009): 302–24.

Jacobson, Brian R. "Fire and Failure: Studio Technology, Environmental Control, and the Politics of Progress." *Cinema Journal* 57, no. 2 (2018): 22–43.

Jagoda, Patrick. *Network Aesthetics*. Chicago: University of Chicago Press, 2016.

Jaji, Tsitsi Ella. *Africa in Stereo: Modernism, Music, and Pan-African Solidarity*. Oxford: Oxford University Press, 2014.

Jameson, Frederic. *Archaeologies of the Future*. London: Verso Books, 2005.

JanMohamed, Abdul R. *The Death-Bound-Subject: Richard Wright's Archaeology of Death*. Durham, NC: Duke University Press, 2005.

Jedlowski, Alessandro. "Studying Media 'from' the South: African Media Studies and Global Perspectives." *Black Camera* 7, no. 2 (2016): 174–93.

Jenkins, Henry. *Convergence Culture: Where Old and New Media Collide*. New York: New York University Press, 2006.

Jenkins, Henry, Sam Ford, and Joshua Green. *Spreadable Media: Creating Value and Meaning in a Networked Culture*. New York: New York University Press, 2013.

Johnson, Bob. *Mineral Rites: An Archaeology of the Fossil Economy*. Baltimore: Johns Hopkins University Press, 2019.

Judin, Hilton. "Unsettling Johannesburg: The Country in the City." In *Other*

Cities, Other Worlds: Urban Imaginaries in a Globalizing Age, edited by Andreas Huyssen, 121–46. Durham, NC: Duke University Press, 2008.

Jue, Melody. *Wild Blue Media: Thinking through Seawater*. Durham, NC: Duke University Press, 2020.

Julien, Eileen. "The Extroverted African Novel." In *The Novel: History, Geography, and Culture*, edited by Franco Moretti, 667–700. Princeton, NJ: Princeton University Press, 2006.

Kääpä, Pietari, and Tommy Gustafsson. "Introduction: Transnational Ecocinema in an Age of Ecological Transformation." In *Transnational Ecocinema: Film Culture in an Era of Ecological Transformation*, edited by Pietari Kääpä and Tommy Gustafsson, 3–20. Bristol, UK: Intellect, 2013.

Kabir, Ananya Jahanara. "Affect, Body, Place: Trauma Theory in the World." In *The Future of Trauma Theory: Contemporary Literary and Cultural Criticism*, edited by Gert Buelens, Sam Durrant, and Robert Eaglestone, 63–76. New York: Routledge, 2014.

Kalof, Linda, and Amy Fitzgerald. "Reading the Trophy: Exploring the Display of Dead Animals in Hunting Magazines." *Visual Studies* 18, no. 2 (2003): 112–22.

Kant, Immanuel. "Critique of Judgment." Translated by James C. Meredith. In *Basic Writings of Kant*, 273–366. Edited by Allen W. Wood. New York: Modern Library, 2001.

Kaplan, E. Ann. *Climate Trauma: Foreseeing the Future in Dystopian Film and Fiction*. New Brunswick, NJ: Rutgers University Press, 2016.

Kaplan, E. Ann. "Theories and Strategies of the Feminist Documentary." In *The Documentary Film Reader: History, Theory, Criticism*, edited by Jonathan Kahana, 680–92. Oxford: Oxford University Press, 2016.

Kashi, Ed. "Shadows and Light in the Niger Delta." In *Curse of the Black Gold*, edited by Michael Watts, 25–27. Brooklyn, NY: powerHouse, 2008.

Keenan, Jeremy. "Uranium Goes Critical in Niger: Tuareg Rebellions Threaten Sahelian Conflagration." *Review of African Political Economy* 35, no. 117 (2008): 449–66.

Keller, Candace. "Framed and Hidden Histories: West African Photography from Local to Global Contexts." *African Arts* 47, no. 4 (2014): 36–47.

Kerridge, Richard. "Foreword." In *Environmental Humanities: Voices from the Anthropocene*, edited by Serpil Oppermann and Serenella Iovino, xiii–xvii. Lanham, MD: Rowman and Littlefield, 2017.

King, Anthony D. *Spaces of Global Cultures: Architecture, Urbanism, Identity*. London: Routledge, 2004.

Kirksey, S. Eben, and Stefan Helmreich. "The Emergence of Multispecies Ethnography." *Cultural Anthropology* 25, no. 4 (2010): 545–76.

Kittler, Friedrich A. *Discourse Networks 1800/1900*. Translated by Michael Metteer with Chris Cullens. Stanford, CA: Stanford University Press, 1990.

Klein, Naomi. *This Changes Everything: Capitalism vs. the Climate*. New York: Simon and Schuster, 2014.

Koolhaas, Rem. "Fragments of a Lecture on Lagos." In *Under Siege: Four African*

Cities, Freetown, Johannesburg, Kinshasa, Lagos, edited by Okwui Enwezor et al., 173–84. Ostfildern-Ruit, Germany: Hatje Cantz, 2002.

Korieh, Chima J. "Alcohol and Empire: 'Illicit' Gin Prohibition and Control in Colonial Eastern Nigeria." *African Economic History* 31 (2003): 111–34.

Kracauer, Siegfried. *Theory of Film: The Redemption of Physical Reality.* Princeton, NJ: Princeton University Press, 1997.

Krauss, Rosalind. "Notes on the Index: Seventies Art in America." *October* 3 (1977): 68–81.

Kristeva, Julia. *Powers of Horror: An Essay on Abjection.* Translated by Leon S. Roudiez. New York: Columbia University Press, 1982.

Kruger, Loren. *Imagining the Edgy City: Writing, Performing, and Building Johannesburg.* New York: Oxford University Press, 2013.

LaCapra, Dominick. *Writing History, Writing Trauma.* Baltimore: Johns Hopkins University Press, 2001.

Landau, Paul S. "Empires of the Visual: Photography and Colonial Administration in Africa." In *Images and Empires: Visuality in Colonial and Postcolonial Africa,* edited by Paul S. Landau and Deborah D. Kaspin, 141–71. Berkeley: University of California Press, 2002.

Laporte, Dominique. *History of Shit.* Translated by Rodolphe el-Khoury. Cambridge, MA: MIT Press 2000.

Larkin, Brian. *Signal and Noise: Media, Infrastructure, and Urban Culture in Nigeria.* Durham, NC: Duke University Press, 2008.

Lazzarato, Maurizio. "Immaterial Labor." In *Radical Thought in Italy: A Potential Politics,* edited by Paolo Virno and Michael Hardt, 133–48. Minneapolis: University of Minnesota Press, 1996.

Lebron, Christopher J. "'Black Panther' Is Not the Movie We Deserve." *Boston Review,* February 17, 2018. http://bostonreview.net/race/christopher-lebron -black-panther.

Lebron, Christopher J. *The Making of Black Lives Matter: A Brief History of an Idea.* New York: Oxford University Press, 2017.

Lee, Ching Kwan. *The Specter of Global China: Politics, Labor, and Foreign Investment in Africa.* Chicago: University of Chicago Press, 2018.

Lefebvre, Henri. *The Production of Space.* Translated by Donald Nicholson-Smith. Oxford: Blackwell, 1991.

Lefebvre, Martin. "Between Setting and Landscape in the Cinema." In *Landscape and Film,* edited by Martin Lefebvre, 19–60. New York: Routledge, 2006.

LeMenager, Stephanie. *Living Oil: Petroleum Culture in the American Century.* New York: Oxford University Press, 2014.

Lesage, Julia. "The Political Aesthetics of the Feminist Documentary Film." In *The Documentary Film Reader: History, Theory, Criticism,* edited by Jonathan Kahana, 668–79. Oxford: Oxford University Press, 2016.

Levinas, Emmanuel. *Ethics and Infinity: Conversations with Philippe Nemo.* Translated by Richard A. Cohen. Pittsburgh: Duquesne University Press, 1985.

Levine, Caroline. *Forms: Whole, Rhythm, Hierarchy, Network.* Princeton, NJ: Princeton University Press, 2015.

Leys, Ruth. *Trauma: A Genealogy*. Chicago: University of Chicago Press, 2000.

Lippit, Akira Mizuta. *Electric Animal: Toward a Rhetoric of Wildlife*. Minneapolis: University of Minnesota Press, 2000.

Lokko, Lesley Naa Norle, ed. *White Papers, Black Marks: Architecture, Race, Culture*. London: Athlone Press, 2000.

López, Alfred J. "Dwelling in a Global Age: An Introduction." *Modern Fiction Studies* 63, no. 1 (2017): 2–8.

Love, Heather. "Close Reading and Thin Description." *Public Culture* 25, no. 3 (2013): 401–34.

Loveridge, Andrew. *Lion Hearted: The Life and Death of Cecil and the Future of Africa's Iconic Cats*. New York: Regan Arts, 2018.

Macdonald, David W., Kim S. Jacobsen, Dawn Burnham, Paul J. Johnson, and Andrew J. Loveridge. "Cecil: A Moment or a Movement? Analysis of Media Coverage of the Death of a Lion, *Panthera leo*." *Animals* 6, no. 26 (2016): 1–13.

MacDonald, Ian P. "'Let Us All Mutate Together': Cracking the Code in Laing's *Big Bishop Roko and the Altar Gangsters*." *Cambridge Journal of Postcolonial Literary Inquiry* 3, no. 3 (2016): 313–28.

Mafe, Diana Adesola. *Where No Black Woman Has Gone Before: Subversive Portrayals in Speculative Film and TV*. Austin: University of Texas Press, 2018.

Mains, Daniel. *Hope Is Cut: Youth, Unemployment, and the Future in Urban Ethiopia*. Philadelphia: Temple University Press, 2011.

Makhubu, Nomusa. "Politics of the Strange: Revisiting Pieter Hugo's Nollywood." *African Arts* 46, no. 1 (2013): 50–61.

Makhulu, Anne-Maria. *Making Freedom: Apartheid, Squatter Politics, and the Struggle for Home*. Durham, NC: Duke University Press, 2015.

Mama, Amina. *Beyond the Masks: Race, Gender and Subjectivity*. London: Routledge, 1995.

Manovich, Lev. *The Language of New Media*. Cambridge, MA: MIT Press, 2002.

Marez, Curtis. *Farm Worker Futurism: Speculative Technologies of Resistance*. Minneapolis: University of Minnesota Press, 2016.

Marijnen, Esther, and Judith Verweijen. "Selling Green Militarization: The Discursive (Re)Production of Militarized Conservation in the Virunga National Park, Democratic Republic of the Congo." *Geoforum* 75 (2016): 274–85.

Marks, Laura U. *The Skin of the Film: Intercultural Cinema, Embodiment, and the Senses*. Durham, NC: Duke University Press, 2000.

Marshall, Tim. *Prisoners of Geography: Ten Maps that Explain Everything About the World*. New York: Scribner, 2015.

Martin, Julia. "New, with Added Ecology? Hippos, Forest and Environmental Literacy." *Interdisciplinary Studies in Literature and Environment* 2, no. 1 (1994): 1–12.

Massey, Doreen. *Space, Place, and Gender*. Minneapolis: University of Minnesota Press, 1994.

Massumi, Brian. "The Future Birth of the Affective Fact: The Political Ontology of Threat." In *The Affect Theory Reader*, edited by Melissa Gregg and Gregory J. Seigworth, 52–70. Durham, NC: Duke University Press, 2010.

Massumi, Brian. *What Animals Teach Us about Politics*. Durham, NC: Duke University Press, 2014.

Marx, Karl. *Capital: A Critique of Political Economy*, Vol. 1. Translated by Samuel Moore and Edward Aveling. 1867. Moscow: Progress Publishers, 1887.

Marx, Karl. *Grundisse*. Translated by Martin Nikolaus. 1939. New York: Penguin Books, 1973.

Matshikiza, John. "Instant City." *Public Culture* 16, no. 3 (2004): 481–97.

Maxwell, Richard, and Toby Miller. *Greening the Media*. Oxford: Oxford University Press, 2012.

Mbembe, Achille. "Aesthetics of Superfluity." *Public Culture* 16, no. 3 (2004): 373–405.

Mbembe, Achille. *Critique of Black Reason*. Translated by Laurent Dubois. Durham, NC: Duke University Press, 2017.

Mbembe, Achille. *On the Postcolony*. Berkeley: University of California Press, 2001.

Mbembe, Achille, and Sarah Nuttall. "Writing the World from an African Metropolis." *Public Culture* 16, no. 3 (2004): 347–72.

McCain, Carmen. "An Evolution in Nollywood, Nigeria's New Wave: A Conversation with Chris Eneaji." *Black Camera* 7, no. 2 (2016): 194–216.

McClintock, Anne. "The Angel of Progress: Pitfalls of the Term 'Post-Colonialism.'" *Social Text* 31/32 (1992): 84–98.

McKibben, Bill. *The End of Nature*. New York: Random House, 2006.

McLaughlin, Fiona. "Dakar Wolof and the Configuration of an Urban Identity." *Journal of African Cultural Studies* 14, no. 2 (2001): 153–72.

McMichael, Anthony J., Alistair Woodward, and Cameron Muir. *Climate Change and the Health of Nations: Famines, Fevers, and the Fate of Populations*. Oxford: Oxford University Press, 2017.

Meintjes, Louise. "Hi-Fi Sociality, Lo-Fi Sound: Affect and Precarity in an Independent South African Recording Studio." In *State and Culture in Postcolonial Africa: Enchantings*, edited by Tejumola Olaniyan, 207–223. Bloomington: Indiana University Press, 2017.

Mendelsohn, Ben. "Making the Urban Coast: A Geosocial Reading of Land, Sand, and Water in Lagos, Nigeria." *Comparative Studies of South Asia, Africa and the Middle East* 38, no. 3 (2018): 455–72.

Menely, Tobias, and Margaret Ronda. "Red." In *Prismatic Ecology: Ecotheory beyond Green*, edited by Jeffrey Jerome Cohen, 22–41. Minneapolis: University of Minnesota Press, 2013.

Mentz, Steve. *Break Up the Anthropocene*. Minneapolis: University of Minnesota Press, 2019.

Mercer, Kobena. *Travel and See: Black Diasporic Art Practices since the 1980s*. Durham, NC: Duke University Press, 2016.

Mercer, Kobena, with Isaac Julien. "Black Masculinity and the Sexual Politics of Race: True Confessions." In *Welcome to the Jungle: New Positions in Black Cultural Studies*, 131–70. New York: Routledge, 1994.

Mhando, Martin, and Keyan G. Tomaselli. "Film and Trauma: Africa Speaks to Itself through Truth and Reconciliation Films." *Black Camera* 1, no. 1 (2009): 30–50.

Milbourne, Karen E. "African Photographers and the Look of (Un)Sustainability in the African Landscape." *Africa Today* 61, no. 1 (2014): 114–40.

Mirzoeff, Nicholas. *The Appearance of Black Lives Matter*. Miami: Name Publications, 2017.

Mirzoeff, Nicholas. *Bodyscape: Art, Modernity and the Ideal Figure*. London: Routledge, 1995.

Mirzoeff, Nicholas. *An Introduction to Visual Culture*. London: Routledge, 1999.

Mirzoeff, Nicholas. *The Right to Look: A Counterhistory of Visuality*. Durham, NC: Duke University Press, 2011.

Mirzoeff, Nicholas. "The Sea and the Land: Biopower and Visuality after Katrina." *Culture, Theory and Critique* 50, nos. 2/3 (2009): 289–305.

Mitchell, Timothy. *Carbon Democracy: Political Power in the Age of Oil*. London: Verso Books, 2011.

Mitchell, William J. T. *Image Science: Iconology, Visual Culture, and Media Aesthetics*. Chicago: University of Chicago Press, 2015.

Mitchell, William J. T. *Picture Theory: Essays on Verbal and Visual Representation*. Chicago: University of Chicago Press, 1994.

Mitman, Gregg. *Reel Nature: America's Romance with Wildlife on Film*. Cambridge, MA: Harvard University Press, 1999.

Molloy, Claire. "'Nature Writes the Screenplays': Commercial Wildlife Films and Ecological Entertainment." In *Ecocinema Theory and Practice*, edited by Stephen Rust, Salma Monani, and Sean Cubitt, 169–88. New York: Routledge, 2012.

Monani, Salma, and Matthew Beehr. "John Sayles's *Honeydripper*: African Americans and the Environment." *Interdisciplinary Studies in Literature and Environment* 18, no. 1 (2011): 5–25.

Monson, Jamie. *Africa's Freedom Railway: How a Chinese Development Project Changed Lives and Livelihoods in Tanzania*. Bloomington: Indiana University Press, 2009.

Morgan, David. *The Sacred Gaze: Religious Visual Culture in Theory and Practice*. Berkeley: University of California Press, 2005.

Morton, Timothy. *Hyperobjects: Philosophy and Ecology after the End of the World*. Minneapolis: University of Minnesota Press, 2013.

Moten, Fred. "Blackness and Nothingness (Mysticism in the Flesh)." *South Atlantic Quarterly* 112, no. 4 (2013): 737–80.

Moten, Fred. *In the Break: The Aesthetics of the Black Radical Tradition*. Minneapolis: University of Minnesota Press, 2003.

Mudimbe, Valentin. *The Invention of Africa: Gnosis, Philosophy, and the Order of Knowledge*. Bloomington: Indiana University Press, 1988.

Muhonja, Besi Brillian. *Radical Utu: Critical Ideas and Ideals of Wangari Muta Maathai*. Athens: Ohio University Press, 2020.

Mukherjee, Rahul. *Radiant Infrastructures: Media, Environment, and Cultures of Uncertainty*. Durham, NC: Duke University Press, 2020.

Mulvey, Laura. "Visual Pleasure and Narrative Cinema." *Screen* 16, no. 3 (1975): 6–18.

Murombedzi, James. "Devolving the Expropriation of Nature: The 'Devolution' of Wildlife Management in Southern Africa." In *Decolonizing Nature: Strategies for Conservation in a Post-Colonial Era*, edited by William M. Adams and Martin Mulligan, 135–71. London: Earthscan, 2003.

Murray, Robin L., and Joseph K. Heumann. *Ecology and Popular Film: Cinema on the Edge*. Albany: State University of New York Press, 2009.

Musila, Grace A. *A Death Retold in Truth and Rumour: Kenya, Britain and the Julie Ward Murder*. Martlesham, UK: James Currey, 2015.

Musiyiwa, Mickias. "Shona as a Land-Based Nature-Culture: A Study of the (Re)Construction of Shona Land Mythology in Popular Songs." In *Natures of Africa: Ecocriticism and Animal Studies in Contemporary Cultural Forms*, edited by F. Fiona Moolla, 49–76. Johannesburg: Wits University Press, 2016.

Musser, Charles. "Trauma, Truth and the Environmental Documentary." In *Eco-Trauma Cinema*, edited by Anil Narine, 46–71. New York: Routledge, 2015.

Mwangi, Evan. *The Postcolonial Animal: African Literature and Posthuman Ethics*. Ann Arbor: University of Michigan Press, 2019.

Myers, Garth. *African Cities: Alternative Visions of Urban Theory and Practice*. London: Zed Books, 2011.

Nakamura, Lisa. *Digitizing Race: Visual Cultures of the Internet*. Minneapolis: University of Minnesota Press, 2008.

Narine, Anil. "Introduction: Eco-Trauma Cinema." In *Eco-Trauma Cinema*, edited by Anil Narine, 1–24. New York: Routledge, 2015.

Ndebele, Njabulo. "Game Lodges and Leisure Colonialists." In *Blank—: Architecture, Apartheid and After*, edited by Hilton Judin and Ivan Vladislavić, 10–14. Cape Town: David Phillips, 1998.

Ndlovu-Gatsheni, Sabelo J. *Do 'Zimbabweans' Exist?: Trajectories of Nationalism, National Identity Formation and Crisis in a Postcolonial State*. Bern: Peter Lang, 2009.

Ndlovu-Gatsheni, Sabelo J. "Rethinking Chimurenga and Gukurahundi in Zimbabwe: A Critique of Partisan National History." *African Studies Review* 55, no. 3 (2012): 1–26.

Nelson, Alondra. "Introduction: Future Texts." *Social Text* 20, no. 2 (2002): 1–15.

Neluheni, Malindi. "Apartheid Urban Development." In *White Papers, Black Marks: Architecture, Race, Culture*, edited by Lesley Naa Norle Lokko, 67–90. London: Athlone Press, 2000.

Neumann, Roderick P. "Moral and Discursive Geographies in the War for Biodiversity in Africa." *Political Geography* 23, no. 7 (2004): 813–37.

Neumann, Roderick P. "'Through the Pleistocene': Nature and Race in Theodore Roosevelt's *African Game Trails*." In *Environment at the Margins: Literary and Environmental Studies in Africa*, edited by Byron Caminero-Santangelo and Garth Andrew Myers, 43–72. Athens: Ohio University Press, 2011.

Neville, Bryan, and Johanne Villeneuve. "Introduction: In Lieu of Waste." In *Waste-Site Stories: The Recycling of Memory*, edited by Bryan Neville and Johanne Villeneuve, 1–25. Albany: State University of New York Press, 2002.

Newell, Stephanie. "Dirty Familiars: Colonial Encounters in African Cities." In *Global Garbage: Urban Imaginaries of Waste, Excess, and Abandonment*, edited by Christoph Lindner and Miriam Meissner, 35–51. London: Routledge, 2016.

Newell, Stephanie, and Onookome Okome. "Introduction." In *Popular Culture in Africa: The Episteme of the Everyday*, edited by Stephanie Newell and Onookome Okome, 1–23. London: Routledge, 2013.

Nfah-Abbenyi, Juliana Makuchi. *Gender in African Women's Writing: Identity, Sexuality, and Difference*. Bloomington: Indiana University Press, 1997.

Ngũgĩ wa Thiong'o. *Globalectics: Theory and the Politics of Knowing*. New York: Columbia University Press, 2012.

Nichols, Bill. *Representing Reality: Issues and Concepts in Documentary*. Bloomington: Indiana University Press, 1991.

Nichols, Bill. "The Voice of Documentary." In *The Documentary Film Reader: History, Theory, Criticism*, edited by Jonathan Kahana, 639–51. Oxford: Oxford University Press, 2016.

Nixon, Rob. *Slow Violence and the Environmentalism of the Poor*. Cambridge, MA: Harvard University Press, 2011.

Nwokeji, G. Ugo. "Slave Ships to Oil Tankers." In *Curse of the Black Gold*, edited by Michael Watts, 62–65. Brooklyn, NY: powerHouse, 2008.

Nyamnjoh, Francis B. "De-Westernizing Media Theory to Make Room for African Experience." In *Popular Media, Democracy and Development in Africa*, edited by Herman Wasserman, 19–31. London: Routledge, 2011.

Obi, Cyril, and Siri Aas Rustad, "Introduction: Petro-Violence in the Niger Delta—the Complex Politics of an Insurgency." In *Oil and Insurgency in the Niger Delta: Managing the Complex Politics of Petro-Violence*, edited by Cyril Obi and Siri Aas Rustad, 1–14. London: Zed Books, 2011.

Obi, Cyril, and Siri Aas Rustad, eds. *Oil and Insurgency in the Niger Delta: Managing the Complex Politics of Petro-Violence*. London: Zed Books, 2011.

O'Brien, Adam. *Film and the Natural Environment: Elements and Atmospheres*. New York: Columbia University Press, 2018.

O'Connell, Hugh Charles. "'We are Change': The Novum as Event in Nnedi Okorafor's *Lagoon*." *Cambridge Journal of Postcolonial Literary Inquiry* 3, no. 3 (2016): 291–312.

Ogola, George. *Popular Media in Kenyan History: Fiction and Newspapers as Political Actors*. London: Palgrave Macmillan, 2017.

Oguibe, Olu. "Photography and the Substance of the Image." In *In/Sight: African Photographers, 1940 to the Present*, edited by Clare Bell, Okwui Enwezor, Olu Oguibe, and Octavio Zaya, 231–50. New York: Guggenheim Museum, 1996.

Ogundipe-Leslie, Molara. *Re-Creating Ourselves: African Women and Critical Transformations*. Trenton, NJ: Africa World Press, 1994.

Ojaide, Tanure. "Migration, Globalization, and Recent African Literature." *World Literature Today* 82, no. 2 (2008): 43–46.

Okeke-Agulu, Chika. *Postcolonial Modernism: Art and Decolonization in Twentieth-Century Nigeria*. Durham, NC: Duke University Press, 2015.

Okonta, Ike, and Oronto Douglas. *Where Vultures Feast: Shell, Human Rights and Oil*. London: Verso Books, 2003.

Okuyade, Ogaga. "Negotiating Identity in a Vanishing Geography: Home, Environment and Displacement in Helon Habila's *Oil on Water*." In *Natures of Africa: Ecocriticism and Animal Studies in Contemporary Cultural Forms*, edited by F. Fiona Moolla, 212–34. Johannesburg: Wits University Press, 2016.

Olaniyan, Tejumola. "Africa, Post-Global: A Reaffirmation." *Cambridge Journal of Postcolonial Literary Inquiry* 4, no. 2 (2017): 323–31.

Olaniyan, Tejumola. "African Urban Garrison Architecture: Property, Armed Robbery, Para-Capitalism." In *State and Culture in Postcolonial Africa: Enchantings*, edited by Tejumola Olaniyan, 291–308. Bloomington: Indiana University Press, 2017.

Omelsky, Matthew. "'After the End Times': Postcrisis African Science Fiction." *Cambridge Journal of Postcolonial Literary Inquiry* 1, no. 1 (2014): 33–49.

Omi, Michael, and Howard Winant. *Racial Formation in the United States from the 1960s to the 1990s*. New York: Routledge, 1994.

Oppermann, Serpil, and Serenella Iovino. "Introduction: The Environmental Humanities and the Challenges of the Anthropocene." In *Environmental Humanities: Voices from the Anthropocene*, edited by Serpil Oppermann and Serenella Iovino, 1–22. Lanham, MD: Rowman and Littlefield, 2017.

Oppermann, Serpil, and Serenella Iovino, eds. *Material Ecocriticism*. Bloomington: Indiana University Press, 2014.

Oyewumi, Oyeronke. *The Invention of Women: Making an African Sense of Western Gender Discourses*. Minneapolis: University of Minnesota Press, 1997.

Palumbo-Liu, David. *The Deliverance of Others: Reading Literature in a Global Age*. Durham, NC: Duke University Press, 2012.

Parham, John. *Green Media and Popular Culture: An Introduction*. London: Palgrave Macmillan, 2016.

Parikka, Jussi. *A Geology of Media*. Minneapolis: University of Minnesota Press, 2015.

Parks, Lisa, and Nicole Starosielski. "Introduction." In *Signal Traffic: Critical Studies of Media Infrastructures*, edited by Lisa Parks and Nicole Starosielski, 1–27. Champaign: University of Illinois Press, 2015.

Parks, Lisa, and Nicole Starosielski, eds. *Signal Traffic: Critical Studies of Media Infrastructures*. Champaign: University of Illinois Press, 2015.

Pasquale, Frank. *Black Box Society: The Secret Algorithms that Control Money and Information*. Cambridge, MA: Harvard University Press, 2015.

Patterson, Orlando. *Slavery and Social Death: A Comparative Study*. Cambridge, MA: Harvard University Press, 1982.

Peffer, John. "Introduction: The Study of Photographic Portraiture in Africa." In *Portraiture and Photography in Africa*, edited by John Peffer and Elisabeth L. Cameron, 1–32. Bloomington: Indiana University Press, 2013.

Peluso, Nancy Lee. "Coercing Conservation? The Politics of State Resource Control." *Global Environmental Change* 3, no. 2 (1993): 199–217.

Pérez Alfonzo, Juan Pablo. *Oil: The Juice of the Earth*. Caracas: Editorial Arte, 1961.

Peters, John Durham. *The Marvelous Clouds: Toward a Philosophy of Elemental Media*. Chicago: University of Chicago Press, 2015.

Petty, Sheila. "*Sacred Places* and *Arlit, deuxième Paris*: Reterritorialization in African Documentary Films." *Nka* 32 (2013): 70–79.

Pezzullo, Phaedra. *Toxic Tourism: Rhetorics of Pollution, Travel, and Environmental Justice*. Tuscaloosa: University of Alabama Press, 2007.

Pick, Anat. "Turning to Animals between Love and Law." *New Formations* 76 (2012): 68–85.

Pickover, Michelè. *Animal Rights in South Africa*. Cape Town: Double Storey Books, 2005.

Pierre, Jemima. *The Predicament of Blackness: Postcolonial Ghana and the Politics of Race*. Chicago: University of Chicago Press, 2013.

Pieterse, Edgar. *City Futures: Confronting the Crisis of Urban Development*. London: Zed Books, 2008.

Piot, Charles. *Nostalgia for the Future: West Africa after the Cold War*. Chicago: University of Chicago Press, 2010.

Plate, Liedeke, and Anneke Smelik. "Performing Memory in Art and Popular Culture: An Introduction." In *Performing Memory in Art and Popular Culture*, edited by Liedeke Plate and Anneke Smelik, 1–22. New York: Routledge, 2013.

Plumwood, Val. "Decolonizing Relationships with Nature." In *Decolonizing Nature: Strategies for Conservation in a Post-Colonial Era*, edited by William M. Adams and Martin Mulligan, 51–78. London: Earthscan, 2003.

Pollin, Robert. *Greening the Global Economy*. Cambridge, MA: MIT Press, 2015.

Poole, Deborah. *Vision, Race, and Modernity: A Visual Economy of the Andean Image World*. Princeton, NJ: Princeton University Press, 1997.

Potts, Frank C., Harold Goodwin, and Matt J. Walpole. "People, Wildlife and Tourism in and around Hwange National Park, Zimbabwe." In *People and Tourism in Fragile Environments*, edited by Martin F. Price, 199–220. Chichester, UK: Wiley, 1996.

Prabhu, Anjali. *Contemporary Cinema of Africa and the Diaspora*. Chichester, UK: Wiley-Blackwell, 2014.

Price, Jenny. "Remaking American Environmentalism: On the Banks of the LA River." *Environmental History* 13, no. 3 (2008): 536–55.

Probyn, Elspeth. *Eating the Ocean*. Durham, NC: Duke University Press, 2016.

Puckett, Jim. "A Place Called Away." In *Permanent Error*, by Pieter Hugo, 97–104. Munich: Prestel Verlag, 2011.

Pyne, Stephen J. *World Fire: The Culture of Fire on Earth*. Seattle: University of Washington Press, 1997.

Quayson, Ato. "Anatomizing a Postcolonial Tragedy: Ken Saro-Wiwa and the Ogonis." *Performance Research* 1, no. 2 (1996): 83–92.

Quayson, Ato. *Oxford Street, Accra: City Life and the Itineraries of Transnationalism*. Durham, NC: Duke University Press, 2014.

Radstone, Susannah. "Trauma Theory: Contexts, Politics, Ethics." *Paragraph* 30, no. 1 (2007): 9–29.

Rajiva, Jay. *Postcolonial Parabola: Literature, Tactility, and the Ethics of Representing Trauma*. New York: Bloomsbury Academic, 2017.

Ramphele, Mamphela. "New Day Rising." In *Restoring the Land: Environment and Change in Post-Apartheid South Africa*, edited by Mamphela Ramphele and Chris McDowell, 1–12. London: Panos Publications, 1991.

Rangan, Pooja. *Immediations: The Humanitarian Impulse in Documentary*. Durham, NC: Duke University Press, 2017.

Renov, Michael. *The Subject of Documentary*. Minneapolis: University of Minnesota Press, 2004.

Renov, Michael. "Toward a Poetics of Documentary." In *The Documentary Film Reader: History, Theory, Criticism*, edited by Jonathan Kahana, 742–57. Oxford: Oxford University Press, 2016.

Rieder, John. *Colonialism and the Emergence of Science Fiction*. Middletown, CT: Wesleyan University Press, 2008.

Roberts, Allen F. *Animals in African Art: From the Familiar to the Marvelous*. New York/Munich: Museum of African Art/Prestel, 1995.

Robinson, Cedric. *Black Marxism: The Making of the Black Radical Tradition*, 2nd ed. Chapel Hill: University of North Carolina Press, 2000.

Robinson, Jennifer. *Ordinary Cities: Between Modernity and Development*. London: Routledge, 2006.

Robinson, Pearl T. "Niger: Anatomy of a Neotraditional Corporatist State." *Comparative Politics* 24, no. 1 (1991): 1–20.

Roe, Emma. "Things Becoming Food and the Embodied, Material Practices of an Organic Food Consumer." *Sociologia Ruralis* 46, no. 2 (2006): 104–21.

Roosevelt, Theodore. *African Game Trails: An Account of the African Wanderings of an American Hunter-Naturalist*. New York: Scribner, 1910.

Rosler, Martha. "In, Around, and Afterthoughts (On Documentary Photography)." In *3 Works*, 61–93. Halifax: Press of the Nova Scotia College of Art and Design, 1981.

Ross, Andrew. "The Ecology of Images." In *Visual Culture: Images and Interpretations*, edited by Norman Bryson, Michael Ann Holly, and Keith Moxey, 325–46. Hanover, NH: Wesleyan University Press, 1994.

Ross, Andrew. "In Search of the Lost Paycheck." In *Digital Labor: The Internet as Playground and Factory*, edited by Trebor Scholz, 13–32. New York: Routledge, 2013.

Ross, Andrew. *Nice Work If You Can Get It: Life and Labor in Precarious Times*. New York: New York University Press, 2009.

Rothberg, Michael. "Preface: Beyond Tancred and Clorinda—Trauma Studies for Implicated Subjects." In *The Future of Trauma Theory: Contemporary Literary and Cultural Criticism*, edited by Gert Buelens, Sam Durrant, and Robert Eaglestone, xi–xvii. New York: Routledge, 2014.

Rouvroy, Antoinette. "The End(s) of Critique: Data Behaviourism versus Due Process." In *Privacy, Due Process, and the Computational Turn: The Philosophy of Law Meets the Philosophy of Technology*, edited by Mireille Hildebrandt and Katja de Vries, 143–68. London: Routledge, 2013.

Rust, Stephen. "Overview: Flow—An Ecocritical Perspective on Broadcast Media." In *Ecomedia: Key Issues*, edited by Stephen Rust, Salma Monani, and Sean Cubitt, 87–98. New York: Routledge, 2016.

Rust, Stephen, Salma Monani, and Sean Cubitt, eds. *Ecocinema Theory and Practice*. New York: Routledge, 2012.

Rust, Stephen, Salma Monani, and Sean Cubitt, eds. *Ecomedia: Key Issues*. New York: Routledge, 2016.

Ryan, Connor. "New Nollywood: A Sketch of Nollywood's Metropolitan New Style." *African Studies Review* 58, no. 3 (2015): 55–76.

Sachs, Jeffrey D. *Common Wealth: Economics for a Crowded Planet*. New York: Penguin Press, 2008.

Sanogo, Aboubakar. "Certain Tendencies in Contemporary Auteurist Film Practice in Africa." *Cinema Journal* 54, no. 2 (2015): 140–49.

Saro-Wiwa, Noo. *Looking for Transwonderland: Travels in Nigeria*. London: Granta, 2013.

Sassen, Saskia. *Territory, Authority, Rights: From Medieval to Global Assemblages*. Princeton, NJ: Princeton University Press, 2006.

Sayne, Aaron. *Climate Change Adaptation and Conflict in Nigeria*. Washington, DC: United States Institute of Peace, 2011.

Schneider, Jurg. "Portrait Photography: A Visual Currency in the Atlantic Visualscape." In *Portraiture and Photography in Africa*, edited by John Peffer and Elisabeth L. Cameron, 35–66. Bloomington: Indiana University Press, 2013.

Scholz, Trebor, ed. *Digital Labor: The Internet as Playground and Factory*. New York: Routledge, 2013.

Scholz, Trebor. "Introduction: Why Does Digital Labor Matter Now?" In *Digital Labor: The Internet as Playground and Factory*, edited by Trebor Scholz, 1–9. New York: Routledge, 2013.

Schoonover, Karl. "Documentaries without Documents: Ecocinema and the Toxic." *NECSUS: European Journal of Media Studies* 2, no. 2 (2013): 483–507.

Scott, James C. "Everyday Forms of Resistance." *Copenhagen Journal of Asian Studies* 4, no. 1 (1989): 33–62.

Sekula, Allan. "The Body and the Archive." *October* 39 (1986): 3–64.

Senghor, Léopold Sédar. "Black Woman." In *West African Verse*, edited by Donatus I. Nwoga, 96–97. London: Longman, 1967.

Senghor, Léopold Sédar. "The Function and Meaning of the First World Festival of Negro Arts." *African Forum* 1, no. 4 (1966): 5–10.

Seto, Karen C., and Meredith Reba. *City Unseen: New Visions of an Urban Planet*. New Haven, CT: Yale University Press, 2018.

Sexton, Jared. "People-of-Color-Blindness: Notes on the Afterlife of Slavery." *Social Text* 28, no. 2 (2010): 31–56.

Shaman, Cory. "Testimonial Structures in Environmental Justice Films." In *Fram-*

ing the World: Explorations in Ecocriticism and Film, edited by Paula Willoquet-Mariconch, 83–100. Charlottesville: University of Virginia Press, 2010.

Shearer, Samuel. "Producing Sustainable Futures in Post-Genocide Kigali, Rwanda." In *Sustainability in the Global City: Myth and Practice*, edited by Cindy Isenhour, Gary McDonogh, and Melissa Checker, 180–84. New York: Cambridge University Press, 2015.

Sibisi, Harriet. "The Place of Spirit Possession in Zulu Cosmology." In *Religion and Social Change in Southern Africa: Anthropological Essays in Honour of Monica Wilson*, edited by Michael G. Whisson and Martin West, 48–57. Cape Town: David Phillip, 1975.

Silverman, Kaja. "The Subject." In *Visual Culture: The Reader*, edited by Jessica Evans and Stuart Hall, 340–55. London: SAGE, 1999.

Simmel, Georg. "The Metropolis and Mental Life." 1903. In *The Blackwell City Reader*, edited by Gary Bridge and Sophie Watson, 11–19. Oxford: Wiley-Blackwell, 2002.

Simone, AbdouMaliq. *For the City Yet to Come: Changing African Life in Four Cities*. Durham, NC: Duke University Press, 2004.

Simone, AbdouMaliq. "The Last Shall Be First: African Urbanites and the Larger Urban World." In *Other Cities, Other Worlds: Urban Imaginaries in a Globalizing Age*, edited by Andreas Huyssen, 99–119. Durham, NC: Duke University Press, 2008.

Singh, Julietta. "Disposable Objects: Ethecology, Waste, and Maternal Afterlives." *Studies in Gender and Sexuality* 19, no. 1 (2018): 48–54.

Sivaram, Varun. *Taming the Sun: Innovations to Harness Solar Energy and Power the Planet*. Cambridge, MA: MIT Press, 2018.

Skinner, Ryan Thomas. *Bamako Sounds: The Afropolitan Ethics of Malian Music*. Minneapolis: University of Minnesota Press, 2015.

Slovic, Scott. "Seasick among the Waves of Ecocriticism: An Inquiry into Alternative Historiographic Metaphors." In *Environmental Humanities: Voices from the Anthropocene*, edited by Serpil Oppermann and Serenella Iovino, 99–111. Lanham, MD: Rowman and Littlefield, 2017.

Smaill, Belinda. *Regarding Life: Animals and the Documentary Moving Image*. Albany: State University of New York Press, 2016.

Smith, Brady. "SF, Infrastructure, and the Anthropocene: Reading *Moxyland* and *Zoo City*." *Cambridge Journal of Postcolonial Literary Inquiry* 3, no. 3 (2016): 345–59.

Smith, Jacob. *Eco-Sonic Media*. Berkeley: University of California Press, 2015.

Smith, Shawn Michelle. *At the Edge of Sight: Photography and the Unseen*. Durham, NC: Duke University Press, 2013.

Soja, Edward W. *Seeking Spatial Justice*. Minneapolis: University of Minnesota Press, 2010.

Solomon-Godeau, Abigail. *Photography at the Dock: Essays on Photographic History, Institutions, and Practices*. Minneapolis: University of Minnesota Press, 1991.

Sontag, Susan. *On Photography*. New York: Picador, 2001.

Sontag, Susan. *Regarding the Pain of Others*. New York: Picador, 2003.

Soper, Kate. *What Is Nature? Culture, Politics, and the Nonhuman*. Oxford: Blackwell, 1995.

Soyinka, Wole. *Myth, Literature and the African World*. Cambridge: Cambridge University Press, 1976.

Spillers, Hortense. "Mama's Baby, Papa's Maybe: An American Grammar Book." *Diacritics* 17, no. 2 (1987): 64–81.

Spitzer, Leo. "Back through the Future: Nostalgic Memory and Critical Memory in a Refuge from Nazism." In *Acts of Memory: Cultural Recall in the Present*, edited by Mieke Bal, Jonathan V. Crewe, and Leo Spitzer, 87–104. Hanover, NH: University Press of New England, 1999.

Stam, Robert. *Film Theory: An Introduction*. Malden, MA: Blackwell, 2000.

Stam, Robert. "From Hybridity to the Aesthetics of Garbage." *Social Identities* 3, no. 2 (1997): 275–90.

Starosielski, Nicole. "Beyond Fluidity: A Cultural History of Cinema Under Water." In *Ecocinema Theory and Practice*, edited by Stephen Rust, Salma Monani, and Sean Cubitt, 149–68. New York: Routledge, 2012.

Starosielski, Nicole. "Fixed Flow: Undersea Cables as Media Infrastructure." In *Signal Traffic: Critical Studies of Media Infrastructures*, edited by Lisa Parks and Nicole Starosielski, 53–70. Champaign: University of Illinois Press, 2015.

Starosielski, Nicole. *The Undersea Network*. Durham, NC: Duke University Press, 2015.

Srigboh, Roland Kofi, Niladri Basu, Judith Stephens, Emmanuel Asampong, Marie Perkins, Richard L Neitzel, and Julius Fobil, "Multiple Elemental Exposures amongst Workers at the Agbogbloshie Electronic Waste (E-Waste) Site in Ghana," *Chemosphere* 164 (2016): 68–74.

Stoekl, Allan. *Bataille's Peak: Energy, Religion, and Postsustainability*. Minneapolis: University of Minnesota Press, 2007.

Stoler, Ann Laura. "'The Rot Remains': From Ruins to Ruination." In *Imperial Debris: On Ruins and Ruination*, edited by Ann Laura Stoler, 1–35. Durham, NC: Duke University Press, 2013.

Strother, Z. S. *Humor and Violence: Seeing Europeans in Central African Art*. Bloomington: Indiana University Press, 2016.

Sturken, Marita, and Lisa Cartwright. *Practices of Looking: An Introduction to Visual Culture*. Oxford: Oxford University Press, 2001.

Sunstrum, Pamela Phatsimo. "Afro-Mythology and African Futurism: The Politics of Imagining and Methodologies for Contemporary Creative Research Practices." *Paradoxa* 25 (2013): 113–30.

Suvin, Darko. *Metamorphoses of Science Fiction*. New Haven, CT: Yale University Press, 1979.

Suvin, Darko. "On the Poetics of the Science Fiction Genre." *College English* 34, no. 3 (1972): 372–82.

Suzuki, Yuka. *The Nature of Whiteness: Race, Animals, and Nation in Zimbabwe.* Seattle: University of Washington Press, 2017.

Szeman, Imre. "Crude Aesthetics: The Politics of Oil Documentaries." In *Oil Culture*, edited by Ross Barrett and Daniel Worden, 350–65. Minneapolis: University of Minnesota Press, 2014.

Szeman, Imre, and Dominic Boyer, eds. *Energy Humanities: An Anthology.* Baltimore: Johns Hopkins University Press, 2017.

Tagg, John. *The Burden of Representation: Essays on Photographies and Histories.* Amherst: University of Massachusetts Press, 1988.

Taylor, Diana. *The Archive and the Repertoire: Performing Cultural Memory in the Americas.* Durham, NC: Duke University Press, 2003.

Taylor, Ian. "Beyond the Drama: Sino-African Ties in Perspective." In *China-Africa Relations: Building Images through Cultural Cooperation, Media Representation and Communication*, edited by Kathryn Batchelor and Xiaoling Zhang, 16–26. London: Routledge, 2017.

Taylor, Jack. "Archives of Death: Lynching Photography, Animalization, Biopolitics, and the Lynching of William James." In *Economies of Death: Economic Logics of Killable Life and Grievable Death*, edited by Patricia J. Lopez and Kathryn A. Gillespie, 115–35. London: Routledge, 2015.

Taylor, Peter J. *World City Network: A Global Urban Analysis.* London: Routledge, 2004.

Tcheuyap, Alexie. *Postnationalist African Cinemas.* Manchester, UK: Manchester University Press, 2011.

Terranova, Tiziana. *Network Culture: Politics for the Information Age.* London: Pluto Press, 2004.

Thompson, Drew. "China's Soft Power in Africa: From the 'Beijing Consensus' to Health Diplomacy." *China Brief* 5, no. 21 (2005): 1–4.

Thompson, Krista A. *Shine: The Visual Economy of Light in African Diasporic Aesthetic Practice.* Durham, NC: Duke University Press, 2015.

Tillim, Guy. *Avenue Patrice Lumumba.* Munich/Cambridge, MA: Prestel/Peabody Museum of Archaeology and Ethnology, 2009.

Tillim, Guy. *Jo'burg.* Johannesburg: STE Publishers, 2005.

Tillim, Guy. *Museum of the Revolution.* London: Mack, 2019.

Tompkins, Jane. *West of Everything: The Inner Life of Westerns.* Oxford: Oxford University Press, 1992.

Tousignant, Noémi. *Edges of Exposure: Toxicology and the Problem of Capacity in Postcolonial Senegal.* Durham, NC: Duke University Press, 2018.

Tripp, Aili Mari. "Women and Politics in Africa" In *Holding the World Together: African Women in Changing Perspective*, edited by Nwando Achebe and Claire Robertson, 145–65. Madison: University of Wisconsin Press, 2019.

Tsika, Noah. "Introduction: Teaching African Media in the Global Academy." *Black Camera* 7, no. 2 (2016): 94–124.

Tsika, Noah. "Projected Nigerias: *Kajola* and Its Contexts." *Paradoxa* 25 (2013): 89–112.

Tue, Nguyen Minh, Akitoshi Goto, Shin Takahashi, Takaaki Itai, Kwadwo Ansong Asante, Tatsuya Kunisue, and Shinsuke Tanabe. "Release of Chlorinated, Brominated and Mixed Halogenated Dioxin-Related Compounds to Soils from Open Burning of E-Waste in Agbogbloshie (Accra, Ghana)." *Journal of Hazardous Materials* 302 (2016): 151–57.

Ugor, Paul. "The Niger Delta Wetland, Illegal Oil Bunkering and Youth Identity Politics in Nigeria." *Postcolonial Text* 8, no. 3 (2013): 1–18.

Ukadike, Frank. *Black African Cinema.* Berkeley: University of California Press, 1994.

Ukiwo, Ukoha. "Empire of Commodities." In *Curse of the Black Gold*, edited by Michael Watts, 70–73. Brooklyn, NY: powerHouse, 2008.

Umez, Uche Peter. "Dark Through the Delta." In *Curse of the Black Gold*, edited by Michael Watts, 69. Brooklyn, NY: powerHouse, 2008.

UNDP (United Nations Development Programme). "Niger Delta Human Development Report." 2006. http://hdr.undp.org/sites/default/files/nigeria_hdr_report.pdf.

Vergine, Lea. *When Trash Becomes Art: Trash, Rubbish, Mongo.* Milan: Skira, 2007.

Verweijen, Judith, and Esther Marijnen. "The Counterinsurgency/Conservation Nexus: Guerrilla Livelihoods and the Dynamics of Conflict and Violence in the Virunga National Park, Democratic Republic of the Congo." *Journal of Peasant Studies* 45, no. 2 (2018): 300–320.

Von Schnitzler, Antina. "Infrastructure, Apartheid Technopolitics, and Temporalities of 'Transition.'" In *The Promise of Infrastructure*, edited by Nikhil Anand, Akhil Gupta, and Hannah Appel, 133–54. Durham, NC: Duke University Press, 2018.

Vriend, Reinier J. M. "The Paradoxes of Voluntourism: Strategic Visual Tropes of the Natural on South African Voluntourism Websites." In *Natures of Africa: Ecocriticism and Animal Studies in Contemporary Cultural Forms*, edited by F. Fiona Moolla, 118–40. Johannesburg: Wits University Press, 2016.

Wald, Priscilla. *Contagious: Cultures, Carriers, and the Outbreak Narrative.* Durham, NC: Duke University Press, 2008.

Walker, Janet. "Trauma Cinema: False Memories and True Experience." *Screen* 42, no. 2 (2001): 211–16.

Warner, Michael. *Publics and Counterpublics.* New York: Zone Books, 2002.

Warren, Calvin L. *Ontological Terror: Blackness, Nihilism, and Emancipation.* Durham, NC: Duke University Press, 2018.

Wasserman, Herman. "Introduction: Taking It to the Streets." In *Popular Media, Democracy and Development in Africa*, edited by Herman Wasserman, 1–16. London: Routledge, 2011.

Watts, Michael, ed. *Curse of the Black Gold.* Photographs by Ed Kashi. Brooklyn, NY: powerHouse, 2008.

Watts, Michael. "Oil Frontiers: The Niger Delta and the Gulf of Mexico." In *Oil Culture*, edited by Ross Barrett and Daniel Worden, 189–210. Minneapolis: University of Minnesota Press, 2014.

Watts, Michael. "Sweet and Sour." In *Curse of the Black Gold*, edited by Michael Watts, 36–47. Brooklyn: powerHouse, 2008.

Weheliye, Alexander G. *Habeas Viscus: Racializing Assemblages, Biopolitics, and Black Feminist Theories of the Human*. Durham, NC: Duke University Press, 2014.

Wenzel, Jennifer. *Bulletproof: Afterlives of Anticolonial Prophecy in South Africa and Beyond*. Chicago: University of Chicago Press, 2009.

Wenzel, Jennifer. "Petro-Magic Realism Revisited: Unimagining and Reimagining the Niger Delta." In *Oil Culture*, edited by Ross Barrett and Daniel Worden, 211–25. Minneapolis: University of Minnesota Press, 2014.

West, Cornel. *Race Matters*. Boston: Beacon Press, 1993.

Weston, Kath. *Animate Planet: Making Visceral Sense of Living in a High-Tech Ecologically Damaged World*. Durham, NC: Duke University Press, 2017.

Whiteley, Gillian. *Junk: Art and the Politics of Trash*. London: I. B. Taurus, 2011.

Wilhite, Harold. "Energy Consumption as Cultural Practice: Implications for the Theory and Policy of Sustainable Energy Use." In *Cultures of Energy: Power, Practices, Technologies*, edited by Sarah Strauss, Stephanie Rupp, and Thomas Love, 60–72. Walnut Creek, CA: Left Coast Press, 2013.

Williams, Raymond. *The Country and the City*. London: Chatto and Windus, 1973.

Wilson, Francis. "A Land out of Balance." In *Restoring the Land: Environment and Change in Post-Apartheid South Africa*, edited by Mamphela Ramphele and Chris McDowell, 27–38. London: Panos Publications, 1991.

Wiredu, Kwasi. *Cultural Universals and Particulars: An African Perspective*. Bloomington: Indiana University Press, 1996.

Wiwa, Ken. *In the Shadow of a Saint*. London: Black Swan, 2001.

Wolf, Clark. "Sustainable Agriculture, Environmental Philosophy, and the Ethics of Food." In *The Oxford Handbook of Food Ethics*, edited by Anne Barnhill, Mark Budolfson, and Tyler Doggett, 29–52. Oxford: Oxford University Press, 2018.

Wolfe, Cary. *Before the Law: Humans and Other Animals in a Biopolitical Frame*. Chicago: University of Chicago Press, 2013.

Womack, Ytasha L. *Afrofuturism: The World of Black Sci-Fi and Fantasy Culture*. Chicago: Lawrence Hill Books, 2013.

Woodard, Vincent. *The Delectable Negro: Human Consumption and Homoeroticism within US Slave Culture*. New York: New York University Press, 2014.

Woodward, Wendy. *The Animal Gaze: Animal Subjectivities in Southern African Narratives*. Johannesburg: Wits University Press, 2008.

Wright, Laura. *The Vegan Studies Project: Food, Animals, and Gender in the Age of Terror*. Athens: University of Georgia Press, 2015.

Wynter, Sylvia. "Unsettling the Coloniality of Being/Power/Truth/Freedom: Towards the Human, After Man, Its Overrepresentation—An Argument." *CR: The New Centennial Review* 3, no. 3 (2003): 257–337.

Yaeger, Patricia. "The Death of Nature and the Apotheosis of Trash; or, Rubbish Ecology." *PMLA* 123, no. 2 (2008): 321–39.

Yaszek, Lisa. "Rethinking Apocalypse in African SF." *Paradoxa* 25 (2013): 47–66.

Yusoff, Kathryn. *A Billion Black Anthropocenes or None*. Minneapolis: University of Minnesota Press, 2018.

Zielinski, Siegfried. *Deep Time of the Media: Toward an Archaeology of Hearing and Seeing by Technical Means*. Translated by Gloria Custance. Cambridge, MA: MIT Press, 2006.

index

and ethical focus, 98–103; banned in Cameroon, 68, 98; destination of bananas in, 98–99; doubt, production of, 97–98; European interviewees in, 99; post-national formation in, 93, 99–100; shanty houses of community residents, 95–96; women in, 101–2, 104. *See also* banana production

Bisschoff, Lizelle, 135

Black Anthropocenes, 7

Black Lives Matter, 14, 21, 153, 164, 169

blackness: constructed in opposition to technology, 31; exoticization of, 12, 65; expendability of black life, theme of, 88–90; negative constructions of, 10; as site of humanistic values, 54; and strategic distancing from nature, 155, 168; in zone of nothingness, 170. *See also* racialization

Black Panther (Coogler), 1–2, 12, 27, 222–23, 270n8

"Black Woman" (Senghor), 55

Bland, Sandra, 164, 165

Blind Spot (Cole), 51

Bodomo, Adams, 213

body: datafied, 88–90; as site of healing, 138

body, black: animalization of, 154–55, 170–71, 258n18; commodification of, 125; embodied performance, 135–38; eroticized, 14, 120–24, 122f, 123f; objectification of, 1, 12; racialization of, 26; targeting of, 164–65

book form, 90–91, 139, 190–91, 224, 228

Born Free USA, 173–74

Bousé, Derek, 183

Bozak, Nadia, 212

Brautigam, Deborah, 206–7

Britain, 153–54

British Colonial Film Unit, 16

British South African Company, 168

Brown, Bill, 146

Brown, Michael, 155, 164, 165

Budolfson, Mark, 102–3

"Building Dwelling Thinking" (Heidegger), 201

Burrell, Jenna, 246n34

Butler, Judith, 167

Butler, Octavia, 27, 34

Camera Lucida (Barthes), 125

Cameroon, 21, 67, 93–103; *The Big Banana* (Bieleu) banned in, 68, 98; corruption, 100. *See also* banana production; *The Big Banana* (Bieleu)

Campt, Tina, 127

capabilities, 163–64

Capital (Marx), 87

capitalism: 1980s restructuring, 18; extraction of value from a distance, 87–88; fossil-fuel/petro-capitalism, 5, 112–14, 120; frontier, 109; global, 9–10; hyper-capitalism, 190, 215; market expansionism, 51; poaching as means of surviving under, 178–79; sea as site of expansion, 45. *See also* consumerism

Captain Phillips (film), 209

Caravaggio, 44

Carby, Hazel, 165

care, ethics of, 154

Carruthers, Jane, 176

cars/automobility, 51, 54f

Cartwright, Lisa, 11

Caruth, Cathy, 109

Casset, Salla, 41

Castells, Manuel, 18, 68, 106

Cawthorne Channel, 113

Cecil the Lion, 9, 14–15, 157; affective dimensions of response to, 162–63; black labor involved in hunt of, 160; changes due to outrage over, 167–68, 172; historical antecedents, 165–66; name of, 168; race as problematic in death of, 153, 165; as research subject, 162; viral image of, 152–53. See also *Trophy* (CNN, Schwarz and Clusiau)

Certeau, Michel de, 201–2

Césaire, Aimé, 26, 53–54

Chakrabarty, Dipesh, 10

Cheney-Lippold, John, 89

Chevallier, Nick, 172

chiaroscuro, 42f, 44, 52

humanism, 54, 110, 171; planetary, 153–56, 169–72, 180, 184–85

Hume, John, 173, 176

humor, as posture of defiance, 106

Hunt, Nancy Rose, 181

Hurricane Sandy, 126

Hwange Park, Zimbabwe, 9, 157, 162

hybrid genres, 111

identity politics, 154

images, 3, 40, 243n114; as active rhetorical agents, 153, 257n1; aural qualities of, 127–28; constructedness of, 11, 17, 70, 90–92, 95–96, 159, 240n61; digital, circulation of, 21, 153–54, 156, 160–64, 167, 169. *See also* film; photography; *specific works*

imagined community, 167

immaterial labor, 82–83

immediacy, 91

imperfect cinema, 225–26

imperfect media, 10, 22, 225–28

indigenous African resources, 30, 34–38, 56–57, 156, 239n37; supernatural entities, 40, 47–56

indirection, 161

inequality, 9, 25, 51, 83, 93; among Western consumers, 103; digital divide, 19, 31; geographies of colonialism, 188–89; and trophy hunting, 178

infrastructural disposition, 3, 83

infrastructure: and China, 206–7; of finitude, 10–11; logic of, 6, 8, 83; in Makoko, 216–18; materiality of, 3, 235n81; media, 5–6, 9, 22, 225–26, 228; of oil, 115, 117–18, 125–26, 144; people as, 186; radiant, 21; radioactive, 147; "revolutionary," 218; technological, 162; urban, 186–87; and urban space, 186–88, 198–99, 202, 206–7; of white supremacy, 155

"insight," as term, 12–13

insightful reading, 11–17, 66, 120, 125; of book-based texts, 228–29

interdisciplinary approaches, 11–12

Intergovernmental Panel on Climate Change, 221

invisibilities, 6–7, 142; of black workers

in safari business, 159–60, 174–76; and ocean/sea, 45; and photographic editing, 42, 49–50; of toxins, 59, 69

Iovino, Serenella, 19

Ivory Coast, 68–69

Jagoda, Patrick, 18, 19, 235n81

Jaji, Tsitsi Ella, 227

Jedlowski, Alessandro, 207

Jenkins, Henry, 162

Jeyifous, Olalekan, 22, 187, 214, 217–20, 218f, 219f

Jing, Wu, 15, 22, 187, 207–13

Jo'burg (Tillim), 22, 187, 188–204, 208; architectural decay in, 195–96, 202; bars and barriers as motif in, 194, 195; book form of, 190–91, 204; displacement/eviction in, 196–99, 198f, 199f, 201–2; indoor images, 194–95, 195f; roof images, 191–95, 192f, 193f, 194f; *Photographs*: child and barbed wire at Milton Court, 195, 197f; Members of Wozani Security, 198f, 199f; on the roof of Jeanwell House on Nugget Street, 193–94, 194f; view from the top of Mariston Hotel looking south, 202–3, 203f; view of Hillbrow looking north from Mariston Hotel, 191f, 191–92; young men sleeping on the roof of Sherwood Heights, 192, 193f; young woman on a roof, 192, 192f

Johannesburg (South Africa), 10, 187, 188–204; as African node of global financial circulation, 191–92, 192f; Central Business District, 203; Hillbrow area, 188–204, 191f; homelessness, 192, 193f; mining as foundation of, 190; as palimpsest, 201; racialized spatial organization of, 189; squatter communities, 202; Wozani Security (Red Ants), 196–97, 198f, 199f

Johnson, Bob, 10, 250n3

Julien, Isaac, 121

Kabir, Ananya Jahanara, 135

Kabiru, Cyrus, 61

Kaddu Beykat (Faye), 16–17, 32, 33

Kahiu, Wanuri, 20–21, 27–28, 57, 149–50;

materialist approaches, 45, 75, 129
materiality, 3–5, 7–8, 59, 83, 120, 235n81
Maxwell, Richard, 74
Mbembe, Achille, 88, 130, 153–54, 169, 190
Mbeubeuss landfill (Dakar, Senegal), 42f, 43, 44, 58–59
McBride, Renisha, 165
McCain, Carmen, 225
McClintock, Anne, 62
McKibben, Bill, 7
media: affordances of, 3, 7, 19–20, 57, 66–67, 91; Chinese, 207; ecological footprint of, 2–4, 103–4, 109, 139, 212, 226; imperfect, 10, 22, 225–28; infrastructure, 5–6, 9, 22, 225–26, 228; low-carbon practices, 10, 22, 227; reactionary, 226, 227; representational (film, photography, sculpture, video), 2–3, 5, 8, 65, 109; representations, 5, 77, 186; socioecological costs of, 2–3, 6. See also elemental media (fire, air, water, earth); resource media
media arts, 3, 4, 6, 8–10, 16–17, 22, 54–56, 67
media infrastructures, 5–6, 9, 22, 225–26, 228
media studies, 3–12, 28, 229; African, 9–12; ecomedia subfield, 3, 5, 226
Mediterranean Sea, 51
mégotage, 225
Meintjes, Louise, 192, 226–27
memory, traumatic, 60, 143–44
Mercer, Kobena, 16, 121
Merode, Emmanuel de, 181, 183
migration, 94–95, 152; and digital imagery, 161–62; and ecological trauma, 21; emigration of artists, 18–19; entry visas denied, 37; migrant crisis (2015), 156–57; rejection in host countries, 149–50; through Arlit area, 147–49; and trauma, 108; Zulu, to Johannesburg, 192
Milbourne, Karen E., 246n42
Miller, Toby, 74
"mineral rites," 10, 109, 250n3
mining: blood minerals, 224; gold, 23, 184, 190; hazardous conditions, 65; and Johannesburg, 190; toxic working conditions, 7–8. See also uranium mining

Mirzoeff, Nicholas, 45
Mitchell, W. J. T., 11, 73, 111, 156, 162
Mitman, Gregg, 166, 175
mode of production, control of, 104–5
modernity, 5–6, 10, 16, 143–44, 148; African, 6, 26, 41, 174, 196, 216; conjunction of waste with Africa at heart of, 26, 28, 57–58, 67, 221; oil/petro, 113–14, 116, 118, 132
Monani, Salma, 9
Monteiro, Fabrice, 15, 20, 27–29; indigenous and global sensibilities in work of, 56–57; Internet as site for photographs, 90–91; supernatural entities in work of, 40, 47–56; theatricality in work of, 70. See also *The Prophecy* (Monteiro)
Mora-Kpai, Idrissou, 15, 21, 108; *America Street*, 140; *Indochina: Traces of a Mother*, 140. See also *Arlit* (Mora-Kpai)
Moses and Monotheism (Freud), 144
Moten, Fred, 127
Moungo region (Cameroon), 93
mourning: and trauma, 125, 137–38; in *Virunga*, 182–83
Mouvement des Nigériens pour la Justice, 141
Movement for the Emancipation of the Niger Delta, 138
multiculturalism, in Britain, 153–54
multispecies ethnography, 179–80
Murombedzi, James, 175
Musam, Mohammed, 80f
music production, lo-fi, 226–27
Musila, Grace A., 167
Mutu, Wangechi, 60–61
Myers, Garth, 214

National Geographic, 64
nation-state, 18, 93, 100
Natives Land Act (1913), 176
nature: Africa associated with, 76–77; African distancing from, 155, 168; as cultural formation, 20; culture-to-nature continuum, 156
Ndebele, Njabulo S., 159
Ndebele people, 168–69

Ndour, Youssou, 57

negative portrayals of Africa and Africans, 16, 26

Négritude, 29, 53–55, 242n97

Nelson, Alondra, 31

neoliberalism, 26, 34, 189, 195, 204

network forms, 3, 17–20; "black box society," 88–89; definitions, 19; digital, 66–67, 69, 81–83, 89, 103–4; discourse networks, 27–28; and e-waste recycling, 66–69, 88–89; food networks, 104–6; positive valuations of, 18–20; at production level, 104–5; as product of network society, 68–69; responsibility for ecological problems, 19–20; text as, 67; and toxicity, 7, 67, 77, 106–7; transnational networks, 6, 8, 17–18, 67–68, 93–94, 100, 107, 186; and urban spaces, 186

network imaginary, 19, 235n81

network society, 17, 68; and free labor, 83–84

Neumann, Roderick P., 166

Newell, Stephanie, 15, 58

New World, "discovery" of, 109

Ngũgĩ wa Thiong'o, 224

Ngwenya, Mathews, 193

Niger: entanglement with energy mining, 140–41; independence, 140; mining, effect on communities, 4–5, 21. See also *Arlit* (Mora-Kpai); Arlit (Niger)

Niger Delta, 14; as contested site for resource control, 109; exclusion from benefits of oil, 113–14; labor economy associated with slave trade, 125; material conditions in, 115f, 115–18, 118f; mining, effect on communities, 5, 21; oil extraction, 21, 108; as site of primitive accumulation, 130; toxic dumping into waters, 47. See also *Curse of the Black Gold* (Watts and Kashi)

Nigeria: Bayelsa state discovery of oil, 113; ineptitude of state, 109, 113; Koko, 68; Nollywood phenomenon in, 32; world standing, 5–6. See also Lagos, Nigeria; Makoko (Lagos, Nigeria)

Nigeria-Biafra civil war, 114

Nixon, Rob, 176, 211

Nollywood, 9, 15, 22, 32, 65, 137, 225–27, 271n21

nonhuman, the, 2, 5; at Agbogbloshie dump, 73, 74f; agency of, 47, 54, 59, 75, 129; animals as Other, 154, 155, 159, 170–72, 184; animist sensibility, 52, 54; disanthropocentric alliance, 19; human-nonhuman interactions, 21–22; less exploitative relations with, 155–56; relationality across species, 154; supernatural entities, 40, 47–56; viewer's responsibility toward, 145. *See also* animals

nostalgia, 61, 143–44

novum, 37

Nsonga, Daniel, 97–98

nuclear weapons, 30, 141, 149, 223

Nuttall, Sarah, 190

Nwokeji, G. Ugo, 112, 113

Nzou, Goodwell, 168, 171–72

Obama, Barack, 105, 164

Obama administration, 172

objects, toxic, 146–47

ocean: Atlantic, 46, 51; as dumping ground, 47; flip-flops in, 59–60; and market expansionism, 51; as site of capitalist expansion, 45; underwater cables, 43, 43f, 47

oceanic turn, 45

Ocean Sole, 59–60, 61–62

Odiama (Niger Delta), 128

Odugbemi, Femi, 15, 22, 187, 214

Ogoniland, 134

Ogoni people, 114

Ogundipe-Leslie, Molara, 38

Ogu people, 215

oil, 5–6, 21; attractiveness of challenged, 120–21; and automobile, 51, 54f; emanation from bodies of kin sold into slavery, 112; everyday contaminated by, 114–15, 115f, 117–18, 118f; freedom, modernity, and democracy associated with, 10; as "happy object," 113; as hyperobject, 131–32; infrastructure of, 115, 117–18, 125–26, 144; magical thinking about, 118, 120, 222;

oil (*continued*)

media forms supported by, 3, 139; multi-generational trauma caused by, 110–26; as network, 140; slavery linked with, 112–13, 121–25, 122f, 123f; social ontology of, 129; transnational and transoceanic portability, 107; water, effects on, 47, 119, 125–26. See also *Curse of the Black Gold* (Watts and Kashi)

Ojaide, Tanure, 18

Okeke-Agulu, Chika, 29

Okome, Onookome, 15

Okorafor, Nnedi, 27

Omelsky, Matthew, 34, 38, 39

On Photography (Sontag), 90–91

Oppermann, Serpil, 19

oral storytelling, 36

origins, 34–35

Other, 12–13, 139, 145, 212; animals as, 154, 155, 159, 170–72; consideration of, 184–85; face of, response to, 129; of Man, 170–71; responsibilities to, 184–85, 229. *See also* animals; nonhuman, the

Ouedraogo, Nyaba Leon, 23, 64, 65

Oxford University's Wildlife Conservation Research Unit (WILDCRU), 157, 161–62, 162–63

Oyewumi, Oyeronke, 135

Pagano, Alfonse, 40

Palmer, Walter, 156, 157, 158f, 160–61, 175, 180

Parham, John, 9

Parikka, Jussi, 3, 4

Paris Agreement, 105

Parks, Lisa, 3, 83

participatory culture, 167

Partners for Just Trade, 99, 100–101

Pasquale, Frank, 88–89

past: animist sensibility, 52, 54; apartheid, 189, 195; colonial, 200–202, 209; role in alternative futures, 25–28, 35, 39, 52–53, 62–63; as site of recuperation, 52–56; of slavery, 113, 125; of toxic exposure, 147; traditional photograph as, 53; traumatic, 108, 126, 135, 142–44

Permanent Error (Hugo), 21, 64, 66, 103, 246n42; abbreviations for metals and "actants," 75; afterword, 91–92; book form of, 90–91; as constructed artifact, 90–92; documentary approach of, 70; as ethico-politico-ecological project, 91; fire motif, 69, 71–75, 72f, 74f; free labor and digitality in, 68–81; laborers left out of discussions of, 69; landscape photographs in triptych form, 75f, 75–77, 76f; metal-workers, photographs of, 76, 76f, 78f, 78–81; possibility of transformation or change in, 92–93; title, 92; triptych form, 75f, 75–77, 76f; and world-making, 93; *Photographs:* "Abdulai Yahaya," 65, 78f, 78–80; computer detritus in dirt, 70–71, 71f; cow resting on ground, 73, 74f; "Ibrahim Sulley," 81–82, 82f; "Mohammed Musam," 80f, 80–81; "Zakaria Salifu," 75f, 75–76, 76f. *See also* Agbogbloshie (Ghana); Hugo, Pieter

Peters, John Durham, 3, 4, 5

petro-capitalism, 5, 112

"petro-magic realism," 118, 120

Petty, Sheila, 256n27

photography: absorption *vs.* theatricality, 70, 160; affective, 40; African, 9, 41, 81; bodily reaction to, 53, 72–73, 79; in book form, 90–91; as "certificate of presence," 42, 52; civic duty of viewer, 12; counter-narratives to colonial, 14–16; crime-scene connection, 43–44, 47, 58, 69–71, 71f; death associated with, 125, 158–59; democratic potential of, 15–16, 41; digital, 42; exclusion of humans from, 48, 70–73, 71f, 72f, 77; frontality in, 160; guns, correlated with, 159, 174; history of, 15–16, 40–41; honorific functions of, 79–80; mediated documents, 42–43; naming of subjects, 79; performative role for Africans, 81; photo-essay, 111; and praise poetry, 16; and repression, 79–80; size and wall hanging of, 160; Spirit Photographs, 50; studio portraits, 15–16, 41. See also *Curse of the Black Gold* (Watts

and Kashi); *Jo'burg* (Tillim); *Permanent Error* (Hugo); *The Prophecy* (Monteiro)
Pick, Anat, 179
Pickover, Michele, 174, 179
Picture Theory (Mitchell), 73, 111
Pierre, Jemima, 257n2
planetary crisis, 3, 9–10
planetary humanism, 153–56, 169–72, 180, 184–85
planetary politics, 17–20
planned obsolescence, 4, 7–8, 88, 93, 224; of photographs, 44; and rollout of on-line tools, 83
play, 183–84
police brutality, 167
poor theory, 224
postcolonial contexts, 21, 26, 50, 62–63, 153–54, 168, 171, 228; and African filmmakers, 94; colonial vestiges in, 86, 188–89; and trauma, 62, 108–14, 140; underdevelopment, 86, 113, 132–33, 195
postcolonial exotic, 12
postcolonial studies, 9, 11, 28, 110
postcolony, 62–63
poverty porn, 12
Precarious Life (Butler), 167
precarity: displacement and eviction, 196–98, 198f, 199f; ecological, 3, 10, 73; economic, 8; in Johannesburg, 188–204; and urban spaces, 10, 22, 187
Price, Jenny, 220
primitivism, 57
privatization, rebuke of, 36–37
Probyn, Elspeth, 46–47
progress, teleology of, 62
The Prophecy (Monteiro), 20, 27–28, 29, 40, 62; chiaroscuro, use of, 42f, 44, 52; Set Setal movement coheres with, 56–57; spectacle/terror dichotomy, 48–49; supernatural entities in, 47–54; water, images of, 45–49, 46f, 48f, 51–52, 55; *Photographs*: figure clothed in nets, 46f, 46–47; discomfited winged figure and animal waste, 43f, 44–45, 48–49; female and bare trees, 50–51, 52f; female coming onshore with ship behind her,
51, 55f; female figure, car, and truck, 51, 54f; female figure, trees, and fire, 51, 53f; female underwater, 48, 49f; landfill at Mbeubeuss, 42f, 43, 44, 58
proximity: aesthetics of, 131; facilitated by camera, 72, 72f, 79, 91
Puckett, Jim, 91–92, 93
Pumzi (Kahiu), 27–28, 30–39, 149–50; as apocalyptic fiction, 30, 33, 223; ark image in, 30, 31; blind spots in, 38–39, 62–63; disappearance of protagonist, 20–21, 29, 38–39, 150; dream sequence in, 32–33; ending of, 38–39; Kikuyu cosmology in, 29, 34–36; multispecies ontology in, 38; neoliberal logic in, 34; opening of, 30–31, 39; recycling of waste in, 39, 57, 59. *See also* Kahiu, Wanuri
punctum, 53

Quayson, Ato, 69, 86, 114, 193

racialization, 26, 153–55, 257n2; geographical divisions of urban spaces, 188–90, 201–3. *See also* blackness
racism, 7, 14, 68, 155–56, 169; and China, 205, 207; French, 54; and migrants, 151
radiation hazards, 21, 141–42, 147
Rafiki (Kahiu, director), 30
Ramphele, Mamphela, 201
Rangan, Pooja, 17
reality, illusion of, 70
Reba, Meredith, 217
reconnection, work of, 100
recycling: African repair of media devices, 224; art from waste materials, 56–62; at core of future, 61–62; everyday, 22; e-waste burning, 64; reuse, 224; toxic risk of, 4, 8, 147. *See also* Agbogbloshie (Ghana); *Permanent Error* (Hugo); waste
Regarding the Pain of Others (Sontag), 90
religion, 85–87
RELUFA, 99, 100, 102
representational media (film, photography, sculpture, video), 3, 8, 19, 65, 109. *See also* film; photography; *specific works*

time (*continued*)
171; and trauma, 144–45. *See also* Afrofuturism; future; past
tipping point, 163–64
to-be-seenness, 70, 160–61
toxicity: of banana cultivation, 97–98; disappearance and distancing of realities,
70, 82–83, 87–88, 101, 107; and elemental
media, 6; of e-waste, 74–75; exposure to
at African sites, 4; invisibility of, 59, 69;
as network form, 7, 67, 77, 106–7; of oil,
119; and recycling work, 4, 8; of working conditions, 7–8. See also *Curse of the
Black Gold* (Watts and Kashi); *Permanent
Error* (Hugo); waste
Trafigura incident (Ivory Coast), 68–69
trans-corporeality, 75
transhuman, 186, 217
transnational networks, 6, 8, 17–18, 67–68,
93–94, 100, 107, 186. *See also* network
forms
trauma: and children, 60–61; collective,
110, 114; darkened sites of, 116; decolonized view of, 110, 135; in El Anatsui's art,
60; and embodied performance, 135–38;
ethical concerns, 132; of the future, 21,
108, 126–35; healing through art, 61–62;
incubation period and latency stage,
144–45; literary tragedy applied to, 114;
and migration, 108; multigenerational,
110–26; postcolonial, 62, 108–14, 140; pretrauma, 126–27; repetitiveness of, 111, 112–
13; of slavery, 109; social transformation,
opportunity for, 112–13; survivors, 132–35,
134f; and temporality, 144–45
trauma studies, 21, 108, 126, 140; Western
models, 109–10, 135
trees, as sacred, 36
Trevor, Will, 173–74
Tripp, Aili Mari, 135
triptych form, 75f, 75–77, 76f
Trophy (CNN, Schwarz and Clusiau), 21–
22, 153, 161, 172–80; dispossession not
addressed, 176; naturalistic image of
Africa, 174–75; people of color absent
from, 175–76; poaching in, 173, 177–79;

pro-hunting and anti-hunting perspectives in, 173–74; wildlife loss documented, 173. *See also* Cecil the Lion
trophy hunting: black workers, invisibility
of, 159–60, 166, 175–76; legality, language
of, 157–58, 165; Safari Club system, 159;
"taken" as term, 157
Trump, Donald, 105, 156
Trump administration, 172
Tuareg rebellions, 141

Ukiwo, Ukoha, 112, 113
Umez, Uche Peter, 127, 129–31
unfreedoms, scale of, 90
United Nations Conference on Climate
Change (COP 21), 105
United Nations Development Programme
report (2006), 116–17, 117f
United Nations' e-waste guide, 92
United States: degradation of ecosystem,
14; Endangered Species List, 167–68; gun
violence, 178; and traumas of the future,
126; unilateral interventions by, 207. *See
also* trophy hunting
University of Cape Town, 169
uranium mining, 4–5, 8, 107, 140–51; radiation hazards, 21, 141–42, 144, 146–47
urban spaces, 10, 186–220; China in the
African city, 205–13; everyday in the
African city, 188–204; "failed cities" of
Third World, 210; "garrison architecture," 189, 266n18; geographical divisions, 188–90; precarity, focus on, 22;
spatial practices in, 201–2; "splintering
urbanism," 189–90; sustainability, narratives of, 22, 217–20; times and spaces
intermingled in, 20. *See also* Johannesburg, South Africa; Makoko (Lagos,
Nigeria); space
Urhobo people, 120
utopian spaces, 27

Van de Peer, Stefanie, 135
veganism, 179
viewer: away, orientation to, 98–99; bodily
reaction to photography, 53, 72–73, 79,